SPORT AND PHYSICAL ACTIVITY

Sport and Physical Activity

The Role of Health Promotion

edited by

Jacqueline Merchant,
Barbara L. Griffin and Anne Charnock

palgrave
macmillan

First published 2007 by
PALGRAVE MACMILLAN
Houndmills, Basingstoke, Hampshire RG21 6XS and
175 Fifth Avenue, New York, N.Y. 10010
Companies and representatives throughout the world

PALGRAVE MACMILLAN is the global academic imprint of the Palgrave Macmillan division of St. Martin's Press, LLC and of Palgrave Macmillan Ltd. Macmillan® is a registered trademark in the United States, United Kingdom and other countries. Palgrave is a registered trademark in the European Union and other countries.

ISBN-13: 978–1–4039–3412–3
ISBN-10: 1–4039–3412–6

This book is printed on paper suitable for recycling and made from fully managed and sustained forest sources. Logging, pulping and manufacturing processes are expected to conform to the environmental regulations of the country of origin.

A catalogue record for this book is available from the British Library.

10 9 8 7 6 5 4 3 2 1
16 15 14 13 12 11 10 09 08 07

Printed in China

Contents

Foreword, David F. Seedhouse   viii

Acknowledgements   x

Notes on Contributors   xi

List of Figures   xvii

List of Tables   xviii

List of Boxes   xix

List of Abbreviations   xx

Introduction   1
  Barbara L. Griffin, Jacqueline Merchant and Anne Charnock

PART I

  **INTRODUCTION TO HEALTH PROMOTION,
  AND SPORT AND PHYSICAL ACTIVITY**   9

1 **Definitions, Values, Models and Approaches in Health
  Promotion**   11
  Barbara L. Griffin and David F. Seedhouse

2 **Definitions, Models and Development Issues in Sport**   21
  Zofia Pawlaczek

3 **Planning and Project Management**   35
  Barbara L. Griffin and Alyson Learmonth

4 **Research and Evaluation**   45
  Barbara L. Griffin and Alyson Learmonth

PART II

  HEALTH OF THE INDIVIDUAL   61

5 **Heath Benefits of Physical Activity across the Lifespan**   63
  David Blackwell

6 Drug Use in Sport   83
   Alison McInnes, Ralph Heron and Mark Harrison

7 Culture, Lifestyle and Identity:
   Constructing the Healthy You   95
   Nigel Watson

8 Health Promotion and Healthy Lifestyles: Motivating
   Individuals to Become Physically Active   103
   István Soós, Jarmo Liukkonnen and Rex W. Thomson

9 Psychology and Home Exercise Prescription   118
   Sandra Darkings and Anne Charnock

PART III

   HEALTH OF COMMUNITIES   131

10 Physical Activity across the Lifespan: Establishing
   Community-Based Classes for the Older Person   133
   Lorraine Hughes

11 How Understanding Community Development
   Will Help Your Career   145
   Mark Burns and Barbara L. Griffin

12 From 'Personal Exercise on Prescription' to 'HELP':
   Evolution of an Exercise on Referral System   157
   Sue Collins and George Goodson

13 Ethnicity and Health Promotion   174
   Rex W. Thomson and István Soós

14 Gender and Sport: Promoting/Preventing Health in
   Our Schools   186
   Kate M. Russell

15 Disability, Sport and Exercise   203
   Hayley Fitzgerald and Di Bass

PART IV

   HEALTH OF SOCIETY   221

16 Social Inequalities, Social Exclusion and Health   223
   Jacqueline Merchant

17 Getting Evidence about Physical Activity into Practice:
   Inequalities in Health and their Reduction   248
   Michael P. Kelly and Hugo Crombie

18   Global Health Promotion: Issues, Principles and Practice   262
      Chris Llewellyn

19   Australian Government Policy on Sport and Health
      Promotion: A Look at '*Active Australia*'   282
      Trent D. Brown

Index   297

Foreword

There's no doubt sport is bad for us. Ask the physically awkward child routinely taunted in PE class, the ageing runner with permanent shin splints caused by his refusal to give up marathons, or the young squash player who plunges into anxious depression every time she loses – each will tell you that more sport doesn't necessarily equal more health.

Of course there's no doubt that sport is good for us too. Whenever sport stretches our bodies without injury and eases our minds away from life's troubles we undoubtedly gain in health. But just as there are limits to sporting achievement, there is always a point at which sport ceases to be health promoting.

The great merit of this book is that its contributors are so well aware of the complex relationship between sport and health promotion. One way or another each sees that social and mental issues are at least as important as physical development. And each recognises that we need to be crystal clear about what we mean by success and failure whenever we set out to use a sport to promote health. When, for example, are the medical benefits of sport outweighed by the social deficits of denying a talented young sportsperson a normal adolescence? How can sporting opportunities be offered fairly and equally to all people – regardless of social circumstances? How can we ensure that girls are not discriminated against in school sports? How can we use sport not just to help people become physically fitter, but to help them feel an increased sense of community inclusion?

Sport and Physical Activity: The Role of Health Promotion doesn't shy away from these complicated yet necessary questions. But it is never over-academic or confusing. Indeed, students and practitioners of sport studies and health promotion will find the book both thoughtful and down-to-earth, and will glean much that will help them in their professional practice.

Sport and Physical Activity: The Role of Health Promotion strikes an impressive balance between practical advice and scholarly reflection. It shows us that while sport is not always health promoting, given solid theory, careful thinking and practical commitment, many more people will have the opportunity to enjoy sport both for its own sake and for its numerous health benefits.

David F. Seedhouse
Professor of Health and Social Ethics
Auckland University of Technology
Auckland
New Zealand
April, 2007

Acknowledgements

The editors wish to thank the following Sport Exercise and Development students from the University of Sunderland (2001–2004) who helped shape the book with their pertinent comments and criticisms of chapters: Graeme Armstrong, John Carslake, Wayne McGowan, Adam McLane, Brendan McMillan, Laura Pearce and Alan Rivett. The continued support of Lars Humer (GB Head Coach British Disability Swimming) has also been greatly appreciated.

The authors of chapter 8, Health Promotion and Healthy Lifestyles, István Soós, Jarmo Liukkonen and Rex W. Thomson, would like to thank Professor Stuart Biddle for his invaluable comments on an earlier draft of the chapter.

The authors of chapter 15, Disability, Sport and Exercise, Hayley Fitzgerald and Di Bass Wish to acknowledge and thank Sarah Bailey and Fiona Neale for the contributions they made to this chapter.

Notes on Contributors

Di Bass came to Loughborough University in 1979 as a mature student after a career in personnel management and graduated in 1982 with a degree in PE, Sports Science and Recreation Management. In 1996 she obtained an M.Phil and is currently working on her PhD investigating coach, parent, athlete relationships. Di has had an interest in disability sport since being at Loughborough and worked for BSAD on a voluntary basis for 2 years. She has also been coach to the British Paralympic Swim team and was a member of the squad, in the role of coach, at the Sydney Olympics. She also coaches one of the University swim squads. Other research interests include identity; children in sport; age group swimming.

Dr David Blackwell is Associate Director for quality in the School of Health, Natural and Social Sciences at Sunderland. He teaches Applied Biology/Physiology to undergraduate and postgraduate students on a range of programmes from Pharmacy to Health and Social Care. David has carried out research and published papers on a wide rage of health issues as a member of various multidisciplinary research teams. He has delivered public and community lectures and has appeared on national television and radio programmes. David has over 30 years' experience in education, starting as a secondary school teacher before working in a college of further education and, for the last 11 years, at the University of Sunderland.

Dr Trent D. Brown is Lecturer in Sport and Outdoor Recreation, Faculty of Education, Monash University – Gippsland campus. He currently teaches undergraduate students in the areas of Lifespan Fitness and Wellness; Sport and Movement Education and Methods of Teaching in Physical Education. His research interests include measurement of physical activity and fitness, health-related physical education and factors associated with children/youth physical activity.

Mark Burns is Co-ordinator for Communication, Campaigns and Training, Health Development Unit, Sunderland Teaching Primary Care Trust. He works at the Health Development Unit, Sunderland Teaching Primary Care Trust. His educational background is in Politics at the University of Lancaster followed by studying for a Post-graduate Diploma in Health Education at Bristol Polytechnic.

Dr Anne Charnock is a Senior Lecturer in Health and Psychology at the University of Sunderland. Her doctoral work investigated the psychological needs of women with breast cancer, and her recent research has included areas of public health such as exercise on presciption interventions, obesity and diabetes prevention lifestyle interventions.

Sue Collins has worked for 20 years in the fitness industry in a number of guises from freelance fitness instructor to Club Manager. She has a BSc in Applied Physiology and an MSc in Health Promotion Research. She started working for the health promotion department in Sunderland in 1998 as a community fitness officer, responsible for the day-to-day running of the Personal Exercise on Prescription programme. Later she became the Physical Activity Development Officer responsible for the development, setting up and running of the Healthy Exercise and Lifestyle programme.

Dr Hugo Crombie is Analyst Advisor with the National Institute for Clinical Excellence and was previously Senior Public Health Adviser at the Health Development Agency. He originally graduated in medicine from the London Hospital Medical College. After working in a variety of clinical posts in hospital and primary care, Hugo gained a Masters degree in Public Health from Liverpool University. Prior to joining the Health Development Agency, Hugo worked for a variety of public health organisations, including the Public Health Alliance and the Royal Society of Health. At the HDA, Hugo worked primarily on developing guidance and maintaining the evidence base on interventions to promote physical activity. He also works on obesity.

Sandra Darkings has taught psychology for the past 15 years and is currently working as Senior Lecturer in Sport Science at the University of Sunderland. She has a BSc (Hons) in Psychology and an MSc in Health Psychology. Sandra's specialist academic subject area is sport and exercise psychology. She is a founder member of the British Psychological Society Division of Sports and Exercise Psychology. Her main research interests are issues surrounding motivation and adherence in the context of health related exercise in both clinical and non-clinical samples. She is currently completing her PhD in this area.

Hayley Fitzgerald is a researcher with the Institute of Youth Sport at Leeds Met. Prior to taking this position she worked for a disability sport organisation co-ordinating a self-advocacy project for people experiencing learning difficulties. Hayley currently manages evaluation and research projects focusing on including disabled people in physical education and sport. She is also developing a number of research approaches that will enhance the involvement and participation in research by young people experiencing severe learning difficulties.

George Goodson holds a Post Graduate Diploma in Health and Social Research and an MSc in Health Promotion. He has worked within health promotion for 14 years. He was originally responsible for initiating the Personal Exercise on Prescription programme, overseeing its development and expansion as Senior Health Promotion Officer responsible for the Coronary

Heart Disease prevention programme. He now leads on Accident Prevention and Community Safety for Sunderland Teaching Primary Care Trust.

Dr Barbara L. Griffin is Senior Lecturer of Health Promotion at the University of Sunderland. Her doctoral work focused on the performance of medical power in videotapes for health. She is a member of the University of Sunderland Primary and Community Care research group with an interest in contributing to a videotape for health archive. She has published work in evaluation of health promotion projects.

Mark Harrison is Substance Misuse Service Manager, County Durham and Darlington Priority Services NHS Trust. With Ralph Heron, he established the DISCUS Clinic and they both continue to manage this service.

Ralph Heron is Clinical Co-ordinator for Harm Minimisation Services, County Durham and Darlington Priority Services NHS Trust.

Lorraine Hughes graduated from the University of Hull with an Honours Degree in Sociology and Social Anthropology. She has worked in the area of health promotion for over 7 years, first in the voluntary sector and then within the NHS. Her areas of work have included older people, accident prevention, physical activity and nutrition. Lorraine currently works in the area of health inequalities as a locality manager, employed within the Health Development Unit of Sunderland Teaching Primary Care Trust. Since graduating Lorraine has completed a Certificate in Health Promotion with the Open University, an MSc Health Sciences (Health Promotion) and a Teaching Certificate for post 16 education, which has been complemented by periods working as a visiting lecturer at the University of Sunderland.

Professor Michael P Kelly is Director of the Centre of Public Health Excellence at NICE. He originally graduated in Social Science from the University of York, holds a Masters degree in Sociology from the University of Leicester, and undertook his PhD in the Department of Psychiatry at the University of Dundee. Before joining the new National Institute of Clinical Excellence he was Director of Evidence and Guidance at the Health Development Agency. Professor Kelly has held posts at the Universities of Leicester, Dundee, Glasgow, Greenwich and Abertay. He now has an honorary chair in the Department of Public Health and Policy at the London School of Hygiene and Tropical Medicine, University of London. Professor Kelly is a medical sociologist with research interests in evidence based approaches to health improvement, methodological problems in public health research, coronary heart disease prevention, chronic illness, disability, physical activity, health inequalities, social identity and community involvement in health promotion.

Dr Alyson Learmonth is Director of Public Health and Health Improvement, Sedgefield PCT. She became Director in September 2003, from a post working regionally with the Health Development Agency. It was during this previous role that her interest in action learning as a tool for managing change, implementing evidence-based practice and developing services developed. Alyson's current role involves partnership 'working with local neighbourhoods and communities, leading and driving programmes to improve health and well-being and reduce inequalities'. Increasing levels of physical activity is a crucial aspect of improving the health of the community. Applying an action learning approach to developing physical activity, and contributing to this book, has brought together these two important strands.

Dr Jarmo Liukkonen is Specialist in Sport Sciences at the University of Jyvaskyla, Department of Physical Education, Finland. He has been Docent in Sport and Psychological Wellbeing, and Assistant Professor of Sport Pedagogy and has previously held the roles of Head of the Psychological Training Center, Pohja, Finland and Managing Director of Likes Occupational Wellbeing Services Ltd, Jyvaskyla, Finland. He has also also been a member of the Managing Council of the European Federation of Sport Psychology (FEPSAC) and a Psychological Consultant in several Finnish National Sport Teams.

Dr Chris Llewellyn is currently Research Associate at the University of Sunderland investigating the theory and practice of formative assessment. After several years' management experience in the private, public and voluntary sectors, and completing a PhD on Social Enterprise, his interests are now in the development of Social Policy as an academic discipline to meet the practical needs of a wide range of 'stakeholders'.

Dr Alison McInnes is now Senior Lecturer in Criminology, (specialising in problematic drug and alcohol use) at the University of Teesside. Previously she was Senior Lecturer at the University of Sunderland where she ran the Diploma in Drug and Alcohol Studies and worked as a drugs counsellor. Prior to that she was a mental health social worker with Durham County Council.

Jacqueline Merchant is Senior Lecturer in Health, teaching in the area of sociology of health at Sunderland University, where she has worked for 11 years. Previously she worked in health promotion as a research and evaluation officer after completing her MSc in Health Promotion and Health Education at the University of Edinburgh. Her teaching and research interests include women and mental health, reproductive health and young people and drug use, and currently she runs a Diploma in Drug and Alcohol Studies at Sunderland.

Dr Zofia Pawlaczek is Senior Lecturer in Health and Physical Education at the Faculty of Education, Monash University, Australia; lecturing on the primary and secondary education degrees (and Graduate Diplomas) as well as the Bachelor of Sport and Outdoor Recreation. She has recently completed her PhD in Physical Education Reform in Post-communist Poland and has also worked with Professor Celia Brackenridge on the FA Child Protection research.

Dr Kate M. Russell is Senior Lecturer in Psychology at the University of Coventry. Her PhD, completed in 2002, investigated the development of body satisfaction and identity among women who play rugby, cricket and netball and the role context plays in determining this. She was recently awarded a Fellowship of Social Sciences from the NZ-UK Link Foundation (2003), in association with the Academy of Learned Societies, to spend 6 weeks in New Zealand collecting similar data. More recent research focuses on the development of perceptions of physical attractiveness among young children, and the role PE takes in the development of positive and negative body images. Other recent publications refer to the development and implementation of the FA's Child Protection strategy and the impact of this on players, referees, coaches and parents. Kate is also a BASES accredited Sport and Exercise Scientist (Psychology) and a Chartered Psychologist within the British Psychological Society's Division of Sport and Exercise Psychology.

Professor David F. Seedhouse is Professor of Health Care Analysis, Co-Director of the Centre for Decision Analysis and Risk Management, School of Health and Social Sciences, and Professor of Health and Social Ethics, Auckland University of Technology, Auckland, New Zealand. His studies include: BA. (Hons), 1981 Philosopy, Manchester University; PhD, 1984, Philosophy, Manchester University; Founding Editor (1992–1999), *Health Care Analysis: International Journal of Health Philosophy and Policy*; Professor of Health and Social Ethics, Auckland University of Technology, New Zealand. His research interests are primarily and the application of philosophical thinking and methods to improve health care and specifically the philosophy of health, ethical analysis, the nature of ethics, the relationship between ethical analysis and real world decision-making, and health promotion. Strong interest in values-based decision-making and the development of values-based computer software for use in health care practice. David Seedhouse has published extensively on ethical and health care issues and is an internationally recognised authority on health and social ethics.

Dr István Soós is Senior Lecturer in Sport Sciences in the School of Health, Natural and Social Sciences at the University of Sunderland, teaching Sport Psychology. He obtained BSc (Hons) and MEd at the University of Pecs, Hungary (formerly Janus Pannonius University), MSc at the Semmelweis University, Budapest (formerly Hungarian University of Physical Education), and PhD at the Eötvös Loránd University, Budapest, Hungary. His research interests include cross-cultural studies in sport motivation, lifestyle, health and exercise, and sports for young people. His hobbies are playing squash and other racket games, improving his computer skills and listening to music.

Dr Rex W. Thomson is Associate Professor in the School of Sport at Unitec New Zealand in Auckland, New Zealand. After completing his PhD at the University of Alberta, Canada, he returned to New Zealand and taught for 26 years at the School of Physical Education, University of Otago before moving to Unitec in 2002. He has published in scholarly journals including the *International Review for Sociology of Sport, New Zealand Sociology, International Journal of the History of Sport, Journal of Sport Behavior*, and *International Sports Studies*.

Nigel Watson teaches at the University of Sunderland in the UK and has a particular interest in the cultural factors which affect health and the development methods used to address them. He has worked in a wide range of educational settings including schools and the community. He was employed as a health promotion specialist in the UK National Health Service and helped to run a community based health development project. He is currently researching the use of development theatre and participatory drama in HIV/AIDS education in Lesotho in southern Africa. His project is based in the National University and he is working with the staff and students to develop ways of overcoming the stigma and exclusion associated with the disease. The aim is to produce a short play with the students, which can then be taken around the villages and which will involve the local people.

List of Figures

2.1	A Simple deconstruction of physical activity	24
2.2	Sports continuum	26
2.3	Cooke's (1996) house of sport	27
2.4	Active framework – Sport England (2000)	28
2.5	A diagrammatic explanation of physical culture	31
3.1	Precede/proceed model (Green and Kreuter, 1999)	38
4.1	Reflection: adapted from Kolb (1984) experiential learning theory	53
6.1	DISCUS – care pathway	87
8.1	Precede-proceed model (Green and Kreuter, 1999)	107
8.2	Exercise behaviour model (Noland and Feldman, 1984)	108
8.3	Prochaska and DiClemente's (1985) stages of change model applied to physical activity applied to physical activity (Marcus and Forsyth, 2003)	109
8.4	Theory of planned behaviour (Biddle and Mutrie, 1991)	111
8.5	Sport commitment model (Scanlan and Simons, 1992) modified to exercise	112
10.1	Beattie's model of health promotion (1991)	139
12.1	Data summary of average results comparing physical measures at baseline and follow up (10-weeks)	166
12.2	Revised Exercise on Referral model adopted by the Sunderland programme	168
12.3	Issues that need considering when setting up an Exercise on Referral scheme	170
15.1	Inclusion spectrum (modified from Winnick, 1987)	205
15.2	Organisations supporting sports participation by disabled people	212
17.1	Participation in physical activity by ethnic group	251
17.2	Participation in sport by ethnic group	252
17.3	The 'evidence into practice cycle'	258
19.1	Australia's National Physical Activity Guidelines	286

List of Tables

6.1	Weekly Liver Function Test results	89
12.1	Overview of setting up personal exercise on prescription	160
12.2	Scheme structure	161
12.3	Solutions to issues highlighted from information seminars	162
12.4	Chronological sequence of events in setting up the HELP programme	167
15.1	Coach education and continuing professional development opportunities	209
15.2	Activity programmes	210
15.3	Advocacy and awareness initiatives	211
16.1	Average age of death by social class and area of residence, 1838–41	224
16.2	Examples of occupations in their social class groupings	225
16.3	The National Statistics Socio-economic Classifications (NS-SEC)	225
16.4	SMRs for adult males, England and Wales (all causes of death)	226
16.5	The Black Report: class and health inequalities	229
16.6	Trends in participation in sports, games and physical activities in the four weeks before interview by occupational social class, men and women (aged 16 and over, % participating), Britain (1987–96)	237

List of Boxes

3.1   Action learning tool that promotes questioning and
reflection (Pedler, 1996)   40

3.2   An example written by a sport exercise and development
student to illustrate the use of the action learning tool
(Pedlar, 1996)   40

4.1   Delphi study and Likert scales: an explanation   47

6.1   Positive and negative aspects of drug use: user reflections   92

6.2   Side effects of drug use   93

10.1   Activity identifying main links between health, physical
activity and accident prevention   137

10.2   Activity identifying the issues to consider when planning a
community based programme of physical activity   138

10.3   Activity identifying what needs to be done to ensure the
sustainability of the group   142

11.1   New games   149

11.2   Learn from the Groningen Active Living Model;
an award winning physical activity project   152

11.3   Sports development project manager: equity in communities   155

List of Abbreviations

AAS	Anabolic/Androgenic Steroids
ACMD	Advisory Council on the Misuse of Drugs
ACT	Activity Co-ordinating Team
ALT	Aspartate Transferance
AIS	Australian Institute of Sport
ASC	Australian Sports Commission
AST	Alanine Transferance
BMA	British Medical Association
BMD	Bone Mineral Density
BMI	Body Mass Index
BP	Blood Pressure
DCITA	Department of Communications, Information Technology and the Arts
DCMS	Department of Culture, Media and Sport
DCO	Doping Control Officer
DfES	Department for Education and Schooling
DHAC	Department of Health and Aged Care
DHFS	Commonweath Department of Health and Family Services
DISCUS	Drugs in Sport Clinic and User's Support
DfT	Department for Transport
DoH	Department of Health
ECG	Electro Cardio Gram
EoR	Exercise on Referral
EPO	Erythropoietin

FFM	Fat Free Mass/Lean Body Mass
GALM	Grinongen Active Living Model
GGT	Gamma Glutamyl Transferase
GOARN	Global Outbreak Alert and Response Network
HAPA	Health Action Process Approach
HDA	Health Development Agency
HDL	High Density Lipoprotein
HEA	Health Education Authority
HELP	Healthy Exercise and Lifestyle Programme
HGH	Human Growth Hormone
HIV	Human Immuno-deficiency Virus
IGF-1	Insulin-like Growth Factor
IOC	International Olympic Committee
IU	International Unit
LDL	Low Density Lipoprotein
LEAP	Local Exercise Action Pilots
LFT	Liver Function Test
NGOs	Non-Governmental Organisations
NHS	National Health Service
NHSS	National Healthy Schools Standards
NICE	National Institute for Clinical Excellence
OIHP	Office of International Public Hygiene
ONS	Office for National Statistics
OTC	Over the Counter medication
PA	Physical Activity
PACE	Physician-based Assessment and Counselling for Exercise
PAHO	Pan American Health Organisation
PE	Physical Education
PEDS	Performance Enhancing Drugs

PHC	Primary Health Care
RMO	Responsible Medical Officer
SAZs	Sport Action Zones
SDG	Sport Development Group
SE	Sport England
SES	Socio-Economic Status
SMR	Standardised Mortality Ratio
STAG	School Travel Advisory Group
SUPER	Sports United to promote Education and Recreation
TPB	Theory of Planned Behaviour
UL	Units per Litre
UN	United Nations
UNCTAD	United Nations Conference on Trade and Development
UNDP	United Nations Development Fund
UNEP	United Nations Environment Programme
UNICEF	United Nations Childrens Fund
UNESCO	United Nations Educational, Scientific and Cultural Organisation
UNFPA	United Nations Populations Fund
UNHSP/UN-Habitat	United Nations Human Settlements Programme
US DHHS	United States Department of Health and Human Services
WADA	World Anti-Doping Agency
WFP	World Food Programme
WHO	World Health Organization
WHA	World Health Assembly

Introduction

Barbara L. Griffin, Jacqueline Merchant and Anne Charnock

This book aims to make a positive contribution to students who study sport, exercise and physical activity by helping them to understand elements of health promotion. The editors chose to compile this book to help students engage in subjects that can enhance the application of sport programmes to wider areas of study and future employment. Therefore, we decided to explain why health promotion has a role in sport and physical activity programmes. In the context of this book, health promotion is diverse and comprised of different disciplines (Bunton and MacDonald, 2002). Nevertheless, health promotion as a subject can facilitate action at a practical level particularly in relation to problem solving. With the diversity in mind, we invited a number of different authors to contribute in order to explore how a variety of disciplines related to sport and physical activity can come together.

Background context

One of the aims of the United Kingdom white paper 'Choosing Health' (Department of Health, 2004) is to increase physical activity levels in the population. The government are recommending the appointment of lifestyle practitioners in primary care to improve people's personal skills in changing health damaging behaviours. Since the 1970s, lifestyle issues have been part of government policy (Learmonth and Watson, 1999). Western governments have shifted the responsibility of health onto individuals and have relied on the medical model to shape their policies (Nettleton, 1997). Katz et al. (2000) argues that health promotion utilises elements of a medical model such as evidence based practice and lifestyle management, for example to increase physical activity. The argument in this book is that health promotion is a process that can increase understanding and application by introducing different perspectives and approaches to an issue. Health promotion engages with health issues, such as low levels of physical activity directly at a practice level in order to improve people's health. As Seedhouse (1997) and Bunton and MacDonald (2002) suggest in their books the scope and the diverse composition

1

of disciplines means that philosophically health promotion is problematic because of the different theoretical traditions that it encompasses. Similarly, Watson (1996), states health promotion as a subject is contested and difficult to define as exemplified by the problems of defining health.

A problem management approach

Nevertheless, if students take a problem-based approach (Chapter 4) then perhaps the Gordian knot of theoretical dilemmas and debates ceases to take centre stage. Rather, the management of an issue becomes the focus of attention. This means that if one accepts the medical position that health risks are associated with low levels of physical activity then from a project management approach the issue is how can physical activity levels in the population increase?

The emphasis on a project management approach does not necessarily ignore the theoretical problems and tensions in health promotion. To a certain extent, the opposite takes place whereby health promotion practitioners recognise that in order to improve the health of a population by increasing sport and physical activity it is essential to engage a diverse range of disciplines. Therefore, using the example of the chapters in this book the structure exemplifies one approach to explaining the role of health promotion in sport and physical activity. For instance, the editors extended an invitation to others professionals and academics to make their contribution to this volume. Without over elaborating the detail of the book the contributors' understood their remit because the overall aim was to produce a book that explored sport and physical activity and the role of health promotion. An awareness of broad issues in defining health, community and individual issues helps to identify potential problems and solutions.

Organisation of the book

From the outset sport and physical activity students contributed their views about what they thought should be included in a book such as this and their ideas included:

1. Knowledge and understanding about health promotion.
2. External influencing factors.
3. Individual factors.
4. Skills for practitioners.

Therefore we drew upon the above list and produced a book in four parts; Part I an introduction to sport and physical activity and health promotion. Part II covers the health of the individual and Part III covers the health of communities. Finally, Part IV introduces sociological and policy issues. The mixture of authors and disciplines exemplifies the range of contributions that contribute to the scope of health promotion.

Part I Introduction to health promotion, and sport and physical activity

Chapter 1 raises the issue of having a clear definition of health in order to examine values that underpin practitioners' work and organisations. The chapter introduces issues and tensions between health promotion in general and its relationship to a more focused area of sport and physical activity. The conclusion is that there need to be clear aims and definitions about what a person promotes. Chapter 2 focuses on the meanings of sport and physical activity and the tensions between different practitioners and their areas of expertise. Sport and physical activity are contested areas; however, arguably the disciplines in sport and physical activity draw on a scientific paradigm. This paradigm gives students a background in measuring health and illness from a medical perspective. In relation to health promotion, this approach might be a limiting factor in accepting health promotion because of its cross-disciplinary study. Chapter 3 emphasises the importance of research and evaluation in sport and physical activity in order to establish discussion and debate. Chapter 4 in this section suggests that a planned approach helps to focus attention on the project in order to resolve issues. Project management can help to focus attention on issues; however, practitioners need to pay attention to what is going on in the literature otherwise important developments might be missed.

Part II Health of the individual

To introduce the 'Health of the individual', Dr David Blackwell examines the physiological effects of physical activity across the lifespan in Chapter 5. In Chapter 6, McInnes, Heron and Harrison address the topical area of drug use in sport, from a biopsychosocial perspective. This commences with a historical overview of the development of drug use in sport and discusses important issues in present day practice, for example, anti-doping and testing, and harm reduction/minimisation. Performance enhancing drugs and performance continuation drugs are discussed in relation to health promotion constraints such as social harm, deterioration in interpersonal relationships, together with physiological and psychological consequences. The chapter describes the dynamic and innovative service, Drugs in Sport Clinic and User's Support (DISCUS) in the North East of England, which commenced in 1994. Identified issues discussed in the chapter are applied to some very interesting case studies that have emerged from the DISCUS project.

The author, Nigel Watson takes a social constructionist approach to critique culture, lifestyle and identity: constructing the healthy you in Chapter 7. His introduction is called, 'Can you be what you want to be?' This sets the scene for a chapter that interestingly examines the relationships between capitalist society's consumption of goods and services, the predominance of leisure as a source of meaning and identity; and the domination in visual culture of images of perfect bodies. A presentation of how our engagement with physical activity has change in the last 50 years is given, together, with an assessment of how large changes in social structures and social processes impact upon the individuals' lived experiences. How our physical bodies, identities, both masculine and feminine, together, with our fitness needs are socially constructed. The rest of the chapter explores how these overlapping discourses associated with sport, health and fitness all contribute in a significant way to constructing our lived expectations of normality in the contemporary world.

A change in direction occurs in Chapter 8, whereby a psychological theoretical discussion by Soó's, Liukkonen and Thomson addresses the important area of health promotion and healthy lifestyles in relation to 'Motivating individuals to become physically active'. It introduces the reader to a number of important theoretical approaches that attempt to explain how motivation in relation to physical activity can be influenced with particular reference to the dominance of the cognitive orientation. The chapter continues with the discussion of practical applications of health promotion.

In Chapter 9, the authors, Darkings and Charnock continue with a psychological approach that discusses important issues in relation to 'Psychology and Home Exercise Prescription' in the undertaking of home-based exercise programmes. 'Health promotion has a major role in helping people develop the skills necessary to gain control over their lifestyle and health, in order, to lead a fulfilling social and economically productive life' (Tones, 2001). This chapter explores some of the major issues that influence both the delivery, adoption and maintenance of individual home-based exercise programmes. It commences with a discussion of the rationale for home exercise, and evaluates psychological strategies that have been found to be effective in assisting individuals to adopt physical activity as part of a healthy lifestyle. In order, to facilitate individual adherence to a prescribed home-based exercise programme, it argues that we need to focus on the development of self-regulatory skills that can be called upon when the health professional is not present.

Part III Health of communities

Chapter 10 takes a case study approach to the development of a physical activity intervention with older people. The approach combines sociological insight and encourages participant led activities. The approach in Chapter 11 draws on a training model. The ideas challenge readers to consider what practitioners are promoting in a community, for instance what type of physical activity? Do some activities produce co-operation as opposed to competition?

In contrast Chapter 12 explains the development of an exercise on referral project which incorporates many of the tensions practitioners face such as different definitions of health, the continuing management of the project without losing momentum, and responding to different workplace participants' concerns.

Chapter 13 explores how increasing interest is being paid to differences in the health experience of individual from different ethnic group. Here, Rex Thomson and István Soós provide an understanding of the concepts of ethnicity and ethnic identity, to appreciate ethnic differences, and to determine how these ethnic identities might be used in the cause of health promotion for ethnic minority groups. Thomson takes three ethnic groups: the indigenous Aborigines in Australia, the Roma population in Europe and Pacific Island immigrants in New Zealand, and uses them as examples of how the relationship between ethnicity and health promotion might well be positively influenced through participation in sport and physical activity.

Chapter 14 aims to identify how schools promote and\or prevent health through the medium of physical activity and sport. Kate Russell explores not only the factors that can create barriers to active participation in school-based activities, but also how such experiences can lead to long-term health related problems. The focus here is on the gendered structures of PE lessons, and the author seeks to understand how and why girls, in particular, participate in school activities far less than boys.

In Chapter 15 Fitzgerald and Bass look at a range of issues relating to disability and sport. The issues concern sport for disabled people within a broader equity and inclusion context, considering four key developments that have strengthened the position of disability within sports equity and inclusion agendas. A range of initiatives are reviewed which have recently been developed to enhance the experiences of disabled people in sport, as well as a consideration to particular barriers limiting participation. Organisational structures are examined as well as issues around elite disability sport.

Part IV Health of society ⚘

To introduce the section on health of society, Chapter 16 looks at social inequalities, social exclusion and health. This chapter examines the evidence for health inequalities according to social class by exploring differentials in mortality and morbidity levels between the Britain's social classes. By describing how social class is defined and measured, the chapter traces the continuing evidence of a widening health gap and proposals for change which we have seen in recent years, including work the potential contribution of social capital. Explanations for class differentials in health are explored as well through the work of Wilkinson (1996), and his psychosocial interpretation of illness. Finally the chapter explores the relevance of the above work for physical activity, together with some examples of government strategies and local initiatives which have been created in order to forge links between physical activity and social inclusion.

Continuing in a similar vein, Chapter 17 examines the evidence about effective interventions to promote physical activity, especially as it may relate to reducing inequalities in health. The case for the importance of physical activity in disease prevention and health promotion is well established. The key policy problem is addressed here: that is to ensure that those interventions which encourage and promote physical activity reach all, and are appropriate to all sectors of the population, and do not further steepen the inequalities gradient by appealing to the affluent rather than those most at risk.

The authors, Kelly and Crombie, move on to analyse the evidence about effectiveness of physical activity interventions and then describe the methods developed by the HDA to get effective evidence into practice.

Chapter 18 moves on to look at a far more global perspective of health inequalities. It aims to look further afield and to describe how, in the past few years, the so-called diseases of affluence have been 'exported' to developing countries throughout the world thereby imposing a 'double burden of disease'. The author considers how the World Health Organization as the directing and co-ordinating authority on international health work has responded to the challenges posed by this trend, leading eventually to the adoption by the World Health Assembly of a global strategy for diet, physical activity and health in May 2004.

Finally, Trent Brown presents government policy on sport and health promotion in Chapter 19. The chapter gives special reference to 'Active Australia' and the use of sport as a vehicle for promotion of lifelong physical activity within an 'Active School' concept. This is a critically reflective piece of writing which is aimed at encouraging debate at all levels, especially to students of sports science and related disciplines.

Conclusion

The editors recognising that other disciplines could have been included apologise for the omissions such as the contribution of environmental disciplines that examine the regeneration of urban and city landscapes in order to facilitate safe and pleasant places for people to participate in sport and physical activity. None the less there has been a high level of co-operation in the production of this book and the editors would like to thank all the authors of the chapters. The contribution of health promotion is to bring people together in order to learn from each other's experience.

References

Bunton, R. and MacDonald, G. (2002) 2nd edition *Health Promotion, Disciplines, Diversity and Developments.* London: Routledge.

Department of Health (2004) *Choosing Health, White Paper.* London: HMSO.

Katz, J., Peberdy, A. and Douglas, J. Eds. (2000) 2nd edition *Promoting Health Knowledge and Practice.* Milton Keynes: Open University and Macmillan Press.

Learmonth, A. M. and Watson, N. J. (1999) Constructing evidence-based health promotion perspectives from the field, *Critical Public Health*, 9, 4, 317–333.

Nettleton, S. (1997) Governing the risky self how to become healthy, wealthy and wise in Petersen, A. and Bunton, R. Eds. (1997) *Foucault and Health.* London: Routledge.

Seedhouse, D. (1997) *Health Promotion Philosophy, Prejudice and Practice.* Chichester: Wiley.

Watson, N. (1996) Health promotion and lay beliefs in Cooper, N., Stevenson, C. and Hale, G. (1996) *Integrating Perspectives on Health.* Open University Press: Buckingham.

Wilkinson, R. G. (1996) *Unhealthy Societies.* London: Routledge.

PART I

INTRODUCTION TO HEALTH PROMOTION, AND SPORT AND PHYSICAL ACTIVITY

Definitions, Values, Models and Approaches in Health Promotion

BARBARA L. GRIFFIN AND DAVID F. SEEDHOUSE

Introduction

The aim of the chapter is to encourage a critical approach to the role of health promotion in relation to sport and physical activity. The authors decided to write this chapter as a dialogue and this means that there are comments to follow each part in order to facilitate a critical perspective on the concepts of values, definitions, models and approaches in health promotion.

In this chapter, the proposal offered by Barbara Griffin is that health promotion facilitates the process of engaging individuals or communities in increasing their uptake of sport and physical activity. The argument draws on current scientific evidence that regular engagement in physical activity reduces the risk of coronary heart disease (The European Heart Network, 1999). Nevertheless, this proposal requires further examination because of difficulties in defining the concepts that exist within it such as what is regular engagement in physical activity. Encouragement of physical activity to the general population is part of a lifestyle modification approach whereby the health experts recommend a change in behaviour to an individual's lifestyle.

Learmonth and Watson (1999) argue that lifestyle education is the cornerstone of United Kingdom health policy since the 1970s. In addition, because of the changes in employment, in that work is less physical, the lifestyle changes include how people spend their leisure time. For instance, participating in physical activity might mean spending time walking, jogging or cycling as part of a leisure routine. Nevertheless, the decision to support increasing levels of physical activity in the general population is an evaluative statement that draws on a person's or a society's values. In this context values mean something that a person or persons' believes to be important. Therefore, I intend to explore the underpinning values in the next section.

Before you do that Barbara, let me stop you for a moment, so that I might begin to explain why we have to be so careful about definition. There are many different types of definition, and each of these ultimately has an ethical ramification, dependent on how a definer chooses to use it. For example, there is a very significant difference between defining a tree by pointing at it and saying 'tree', and defining a person by pointing at her and saying 'healthy'. It is easy enough for people to agree about the difference between a tree and vegetable. Once this way of talking about trees and vegetables becomes conventional there is usually little reason to change it, unless technical developments (say in genetics) mean that it makes sense to refine plant taxonomy. Nonetheless, defining people as healthy and unhealthy is much more problematic. People are complex – which parts of them are we pointing at as we define 'healthy'? Why do we think some parts of them are healthy? Is it the way they look? The way they function? The way the person uses the parts as she lives her life? In other words, we always need to be careful about which sort of definition we make, and we always need to examine why we have chosen to use that sort of definition rather than an alternative.

With definitions in mind, health promotion workers, in the area of sport and physical activity such as sport development officers, who in their daily work have a responsibility to promote health, need to analyse their definition of health. Arguably sport, exercise and physical activity students draw on definitions of health operating within a scientific paradigm such as the medical model. The medical model follows a causal pathway of identifying a problem, locating a solution and measuring the outcome.

Yes. Another way of putting this is to point out that the primary reason the nature and meaning of health is contested is because health is not 'out there' to point at like trees are. Presumably a tree looks and feels the same to everyone who notices it, and responds in replicable ways to laboratory tests, but this is not the case with health. You can walk into the woods and find countless trees, and everyone will agree that they are trees. You cannot walk onto a city street and find countless healthy people (or lifestyles, or attitudes, or exercise regimes) that everyone will agree are healthy since health is not an idea you can define ostensively, (i.e. just by pointing).

Many people involved in very practical, physical health promotion do not fully appreciate this point. They believe that the fact they can measure – say – improved respiration and blood pressure levels in an individual following a programme of 'healthy' exercise and nutrition, means that they can measure an objective improvement in that person's health. This is a serious philosophical error – one which has potentially severe ethical and practical consequences.

Health is not an objective idea – it is an evaluative idea. What we think of as healthy and unhealthy depends upon our values and preferences: I may consider a defiant cancer patient as extremely healthy; her doctor may see her as profoundly unhealthy. A physically activity health promoter may see a previously overweight person who now goes to the gym daily as much more healthy than she was, while her husband may be wondering why she is beginning to pay less attention to him and their children as a result of her new-found interest in her physical appearance. Our different assessments of health have very little to do with the bits of people and people's behaviour that we can point at and measure; but they have everything to do with the extent to which we approve of them.

Therefore, it is worth noting that bio-medical explanations of health tend to reduce complex issues to single problems such as reducing coronary heart disease by recommending an increase in physical activity (The European Heart Network, 1999). Following on from the medical link between coronary heart disease and physical activity, the current scientific medical literature, which suggests that the maintenance for adults of 30 minutes physical activity that make the individual warm and slightly out of breath, 3–4 times a week, is beneficial for reducing the risk of coronary heart disease (The European Heart Network, 1999).

This may be statistically true for groups of individuals, though presumably the ⚔ *research evidence is not decisive (it hardly ever is). Nevertheless, it does not necessarily apply to any given single individual, since the causes of coronary heart disease are multifactorial and by no means all to do with exercise (see Wilkinson, below, for example). If people are encouraged to do something (exercise) which they don't like to do on the ground that it is certainly good for them, then there is clearly some cause for ethical concern (for example, if it makes them feel tired and means they can spend less time on activities they like better).*

Given that medical experts argue that physical activity helps reduce the incidence of coronary heart disease, diabetes, and obesity there appears to be a mismatch between the medically defined problem of the consequences of people's low physical activity levels and people's willingness or desire to change their behaviour in ⚔ relation to increasing their physical activity level. One explanation of this mismatch could be that health promoters assume that people can and want to change their behaviour. In addition, Wilkinson (1996) argues that poverty, poor nutrition, inadequate housing and unemployment also contribute to the high levels of coronary heart disease in the United Kingdom.

And genetic predisposition.

Therefore, one can conclude that taking a single medical perspective on a health issue only provides ONE perspective. It is essential to recognize other factors play a part. So why is physical activity given such a high profile?

In my opinion, because:

- *It is relatively easy to promote.*
- *It produces aesthetic changes to the body that are also enthusiastically promoted by a wide range of commercial interests (the diet, fashion and lifestyle industries to name but three).*

- *It is supported by the medical profession who see it as a direct way to reduce the incidence and severity of disease.*
- *It doesn't require much thought.*
- *It doesn't require significant social change, for example, in work patterns, income distribution, equity, living conditions and so on.*
- *It is perceived as helping to keep people 'out of mischief' – if they are exercising then they are not doing something else that might be bad for them.*

Following on from these points the promotion of physical activity tends to oversimplify the issue. For example, to illustrate this point I intend analysing a quotation from the United Kingdom, Ministry of Culture, Sport and Media website (2003) 'Sport is very powerful both in the pursuit of excellence and helping to tackle social and health problems'.

This quotation contains what could be conflicting concepts and requires further examination. First, the notion that sport can embrace excellence and secondly, that sport can combat social and health problems. Sporting excellence can achieve reward, for instance England's success in the rugby World Cup on 22 November 2003. Pursuing the goal of sporting excellence necessitates the exclusion of those people who cannot achieve success. Conceivably, the values that underpin sporting excellence relate to national status, cultural identity and competition. Sport at a national level has the potential for being high risk and means that sportsmen and women are often in sport rehabilitation for periods of their sporting career. Arguably, this quotation expresses a shared value about the role of sporting excellence in society. For instance, in relation to competitive sport, Hendry et al. (1993) argue that young men who are fans of competitive teams are more likely to engage in physical activity than those young men who are not fans of competitive teams.

The second element of the quotation is that sport and physical activity contribute to combating health and social problems. Therefore, I intend illuminating the values that could underpin physical activity that relate to tackling social and health issues. Increasing levels of physical activity in a population requires participation particularly by those people who do not usually engage in physical activity, such as women and ethnic minorities (The European Heart Network, 1999).

Is this true? My everyday observation in New Zealand of aerobics classes, swimming pool use, netball games, tennis play and so on reveals a female representation of at least 50 per cent, probably more.

One conclusion to the above point might be that there are differences between cultures and social class in relation to women's participation in sport. The European Heart Network (1999) and Mulvihill et al. (2000) suggest that women participate less in sport. The value of increasing levels of physical activity in a population means that the emphasis is upon engagement rather than excellence. Nevertheless, the recommendation to engage in physical activity is normative meaning that experts drawing on scientific evidence believe that low levels of activity damage people's health. Engagement here means participating in either a sport or physical activity in order to improve or maintain one's health rather than participating to achieve sporting excellence. The reference to social issues could mean that engaging in purposeful physical activity maybe an alternative to participating in unsocial behaviour. Possibly, in a social sense the goal of engagement connects to aspects of social exclusion.

Therefore, the values that underpin sporting excellence and participation in physical activity are different. For instance, I mean a person who is an international swimming coach has different goals to a person who is a community physical activity officer. In support of sensitivity to a person's role Learmonth and Watson (1999) argue that health promoters need to be aware of the theoretical basis of their work. This means that the task of defining concepts is important otherwise there is an assumption that there are shared definitions in relation to health. Health promotion is a complex area because the core concept of health is difficult to define. What are you trying to promote? Arguably, to be able to establish a working definition it is critical that health promoters examine their values in order to avoid misunderstandings in relation to how different people define health (Seedhouse, 1997; Raphael, 2000).

There can be no argument about this. Unless health is explicitly defined by health promoters the health promoters' values will be at least partially hidden. Given the widespread but mistaken belief that health is an objective notion, many health promotion recipients will experience the effects of those values under the impression that they are objective – but values are never objective.

This point cannot be overstated. At the very least we need to be clear about:

a) *Which health obstacles we should remove – should we remove all and any health obstacles or only some of them?*
b) *If we can't remove them all at once, or can't afford to remove them all at once, which obstacles we should remove first?*
c) *What we do if we as health promoters select different obstacles from those selected by our health promotion clients? Are we always right? Are our values always best?*

Let's flesh this out a little more. In order for me to be healthy (in my view), at this moment (1.41 p.m. NZ time on Friday January 23rd 2004), I feel I need, among other things:

a) *A customer for my software business.*
b) *NZ$100,000 to build the level of product I need.*
c) *A letter from a playwrights' agency telling me they like my latest play.*
d) *More close friends.*
e) *A good night's sleep.*

Should I go to my local health promotion office and ask them to help me with these things? I don't suppose I'd get very far with any of them except e). The trouble is that without these things I definitely do not feel that I am as healthy as I can be, and to some extent the lack of them does provoke anxiety.

Would the health promoter be right to focus on the sleep issue? If so, why? Is it more of a health issue than the others? If so, why? What if the health promoter decided that the chief obstacle is that I'm overworking? What if I took the view that the health promoter didn't have a clue? Which of us would be right? Who would understand health best?

Normative health messages such as 'take more physical activity' focuses on one issue rather than taking into account the problems that people face in their daily lives. For example, if cost was a factor in why people do not participate in more physical activity then there could be collective initiatives in workplaces to encourage people to participate in physical activity, such as reduced fees at sport centres. Conceivably, this argument assumes that physical fitness is of prime importance for health; however, how does one decide how much physical activity is beneficial for health? An elite sportswoman might not consider her health as the prime goal, but rather achieving sporting excellence in a particular sport. It could be the case someone who does achieve sporting excellence might say that they have achieved fulfilment in their lives through their success. Clearly, the concept of health in relation to sport and physical activity is a contested area that requires scrutiny and debate because individuals and groups define health in different ways.

To explain possible definitions of health in relation to sport and physical activity, I plan to introduce quotations about health from the Stockport Certificate in Health Education course (Stockport Health Promotion, 1993). In a preliminary exercise to define health, the participants complete the sentence *'I feel healthy when . . .'* What follows in the exercise are examples of quotations that cover elements of physical health such as having all the parts of your body in working order, being the ideal weight for your height. Additionally there are quotations about social health such as feeling healthy when with family and friends, or mental health such as coping with everyday stresses. Nevertheless, when I have used this exercise in groups of students there is a sense of shared meaning at one level because the concepts of physical, social and mental health appear in the World Health Organization (1946) quotation:

> Health is a state of complete physical, mental and social well-being, not merely the absence of disease and infirmity.
> (WHO, 1946)

In this definition, health appears to be a separate state and Buetow and Kerse (2001) suggest that well-being replaces the word health. Arguably, the definition of well-being is problematic.

Of course it is, and for just the same reasons that defining health is problematic. People disagree about the nature and importance of well-being.

Nevertheless, if the terms remain vague, in health promotion practice there is scope for different practitioners from agencies to misunderstand the problems and the resolution of those problems. For instance, health promoters in Sedgefield District Council have put together a successful proposal (see Chapter 3 of this book) in order to increase the levels of physical activity in adolescent girls in two local schools because from the current evidence (Mulivill et al., 2000) adolescent girls do not participate in levels of physical activity that is beneficial to their long-term health.

Has anybody asked the girls what they think? Has anybody asked the girls what they think health is?

The health promoters will be asking the girls, which physical activity they want to undertake rather than what they think about health? Nevertheless, health promotion practitioners can make assumptions that can easily ignore important ethical issues. For example, the scientific argument that physical activity is good for you therefore you should do it ignores people's thoughts and feelings about physical activity in particular, and generally about what are their priorities. For example, if a young female is more interested in relationships with friends and listening to music then taking daily physical activity may not be her number one priority.

Exactly.

Another assumption is that despite the acknowledgement of different interpretations of health there is still an underlying pull towards health from a positivist perspective, meaning, that health promoters of physical activity measure and observe health. The positivist perspective sees health as 'out there' in the same way as illness and disease are 'out there' rather than interpretation of what one sees. Therefore, explanations about health are an interpretation of evidence. In a physical activity context, for example someone who has battled all their adult lives with an injury from a car accident that occurred in their late teens might be considered to be healthy because of their 'fighting spirit' or considered to be ill because of the complications from their car accident. Therefore, health is an evaluative judgement of evidence not a specific object and health promotion practice requires caution and there needs to be priorities, but who decides on the priorities?

Exactly.

A second issue in accepting that physical activity is beneficial tends to draw on a medically orientated definition of health. In a sport and physical activity context, the definition of health tends to focus on the maintenance of physical health and the prevention of disease. One understanding of the medically orientated definition of health might be that if people do not engage in 30 minutes of physical activity 3–4 times a week they are not healthy. In other words according to this definition very few of us are healthy and interventions that prevent disease become desirable.

Caplan (1964) argues that the prevention of disease takes place at different levels. To illustrate this typography I will use physical activity examples to illustrate each level:

- Primary prevention meaning the interventions that reduce the onset of disease, for example young people (5–18) should aim to take one hour accumulated moderate-intensity activity to promote optimal growth, and development and help to foster appropriate activity patterns into adulthood. The inclusion of physical activity in the school curriculum contributes to encouraging young people to remain active; however, adolescent females do not continue to participate. Therefore, the health promotion intervention needs to take into account the preferences and priorities of the adolescents.
- Secondary prevention means preventing a recurrence of an illness or disease in its early stages and treatment. For instance, the Department of Health (2000) coronary heart disease National Service Framework outlines 12 standards for the reduction of coronary heart disease. In the first two standards, there is reference to the prevention of coronary heart disease in high-risk patients. I understand this to mean that nurses or doctors will screen for patients in a primary care or hospital setting who experts identify as high-risk or who have had a heart attack. One response to identify people who are at high risk might be to recommend information about the benefits of engaging in physical activity.
- Tertiary prevention means restricting the disease in terms of recurrence and complications. Referring back to the United Kingdom, coronary heart disease National Service Framework standards the final standard refers to the rehabilitation of coronary heart disease patients. In a physical activity context this means physical rehabilitation as exemplified by my colleague Zofia Pawlaczek's (Chapter 3 this book) definition:

Physical Rehabilitation is the use of physical movement to support or improve rehabilitation in the human body and or mind (as mental health can be improved through physical movement). The type of activity selected by the professional or individual (self-administering) is normally congruent with the rehabilitation goal. Professionals undergo training that enables them to respond appositely to a disease and or condition in relation to the general medical consensus. A presiding body does not govern the lay-referral system, however certain lay-beliefs will influence choice of activity, for example, for weight-loss the health and fitness industry has overtaken as the body responsible for disseminating advice on such issues (as opposed to GP's in the past). Physical rehabilitation can include sporting activities, physical games, exercise, and any physical movement.

With these levels of prevention in mind, I would argue that defining people as healthy or unhealthy in relation to coronary heart disease reduces the definition of health to one that is medically orientated. Arguably the medical definition of health is dominant and as Katz et al. (2000: 29) argue it is, 'the most powerful and influential discourse about health and, as we have seen, one which defines health quite narrowly'.

Exactly.

So far, I have tried to suggest that in a sport and physical activity context the dominant arguments draw on a medially orientated definition of health. In relation to reducing the incidence of illness and disease, the disciplines that support the promotion of physical activity for health are physiology, medicine, psychology, sociology and education. If we limit health promotion and physical activity to the dominant argument, that is, the medical arguments then we reduce the approaches that are mainly the physical measurements that constitute a healthy person. Arguably, the medical perspective relates to the way people look perhaps in terms of their weight and their participation in physical activity. For example, the recent United Kingdom government targets for reducing obesity as well as increasing levels of activity (Department of Health, 2000). This means ordinary people's lives become the object of scrutiny in relation to how they live their everyday lives (Bercovitz, 2000). As stated earlier, recent United Kingdom government policies promote altering lifestyles such as reducing intake of alcohol, smoking cessation, reducing weight and increasing activity levels. To avoid a dogmatic approach a health promoter needs to consider their own values, the values of their organizations and the values of the people they aim to help. This requires a scrutiny of health promotion practice rather than scrutiny of whether people are physically active or not.

In order to offset the limitations of the medical model, I suggest that sport and physical activity experts adopt a broader definition of health. This would facilitate broader health promoting possibilities such as engaging people in the planning and management of sport and physical activity projects. To explain this point further I want to return to my original aim of the book. I have taught health promotion to sport scientists and sport, exercise and development students for ten years. The students' main criticism of health promotion is that it is not relevant to their course. This is despite the employment of sport, exercise and development graduates in health promotion departments (James and Johnston, 2004). The role of health promotion to sport and physical activity is the way health promotion works or the processes health promotion employs. For instance, using communication strategies to raise awareness on an issue, professional training in project management, health education development in the curriculum in schools, including the hidden curriculum and community development approaches to help people identify their health needs.

Conclusion

A main component of health promotion is values, as all other activities follow on from an understanding of the importance of values in making judgements about what are the definitions of health, the problems and what actions to take. Health promoters need to examine their own values in relation to why they might prefer certain definitions of health, as opposed to others, and why certain interventions are taken in preference to others. The values a health promoter has might be individual value or one that society shares. Nevertheless, it is important to note that not everyone will share the same values and definitions of health. Health is a contested subject and there are different definitions of health. Health promoters need to define what they are doing in order to avoid confusion and misunderstanding.

References

Bercovitz, K. L. (2000) A critical analysis of Canada's Active Living: science or politics?, *Critical Public Health*, 10, 1, 19–39.

Buetow, S. A. and Kerse, N. M. (2001) Does reported health promotion activity neglect people with ill-health?, *Health Promotion International*, 16, 1, 73–78.

Caplan, G. (1964) *Principles of Preventive Psychiatry*. New York: Basic Books.

Department of Health (2000) National Service Framework for Coronary Heart Disease. London: HMSO.

The European Heart Network (1999) Physical Activity and Cardiovascular Disease Prevention in the Euopean Union. www.ehnheart.org/Visited 26-01-04.

Hendry, L. B., Shucksmith, J., Love, J. G. and Glendenning, A. (1993) *Young People's Leisure and Lifestyles*. London: Routledge.

James, A. D. and Johnston, L. H. (2004) The emerging role of the physical activity promoter within health promotion, *Health Education*, 104, 2, 77–89.

Katz, J., Peberdy, A. and Douglas, J. Eds. (2000) 2nd edition *Promoting Health Knowledge and Practice*. Milton Keynes: Open University and Macmillan Press.

Learmonth, A. M. and Watson, N. J. (1999) Constructing evidence-based health promotion perspectives from the field, *Critical Public Health*, 9, 4, 317–333.

Ministry of Culture, Sport and Media (2003) http://www.culture.gov.uk/sport/default.htm Visited 17-07-04.

Mulvihill, C., Rivers, K. and Aggleton, P. (2000) Views of young people towards physical activity: determinants and barriers to involvement, *Health Education*, 100, 5, 190–199.

Raphael, D. (2000) The question of evidence in health promotion, *Health Promotion International*, 15, 4, 355–367.

Seedhouse, D. (1997) *Health Promotion Philosophy, Prejudice and Practice*. Chichester: Wiley.

Stockport Health Promotion (1993) *Certificate in Health Education Course*. Stockport: Stockport Health Promotion.

WHO (World Health Organization) (1946) *Preamble of the Constitution of the World Health Organization*. Geneva: WHO.

Wilkinson, R. G. (1996) *Unhealthy Societies*. London: Routledge.

CHAPTER 2

Definitions, Models and Development Issues in Sport

ZOFIA PAWLACZEK

Introduction

One of the reasons that students of sport find it difficult to link association between health promotion and sport is because the definitional framework for *sport* contains values that are opposed to those within health promotion. Sport in the 21st century has captured the imagination of the masses through its portrayal in the media; presenting itself as *opium for the people* as many sedentary audiences live out lives vicariously through the achievements of footballers and other athletes (Krawczyk, 1995). Sport as a cultural phenomenon, is many things, but its congruence with health promotion is not however obvious. Sport in Great Britain has a complex association with other concepts that are directly related through shared characteristics; such as physical activity, exercise, leisure experience, physical rehabilitation and physical education. Many writers across the globe have attempted to define the term sport often as a way of extricating it from its associates (Demel, 1969; Krawczyk, 1995; Penney, 2000; Tinning et al., 2001; Pawlaczek, 2004; Lee, 2004) This tradition of deliberate separation has been done to try to establish a shared definition amongst those who are supposed to be its advocates, developers, leaders, educationists and managers; particularly as contemporary Britain needs to have a clear working definition for the purpose of applying it to government policies on health. The prominence of sport in society, as a concept transmuting between modern entertainment and a vehicle for enhancing national (or regional) self-esteem exacerbates the confusion. Sports' potential as a cultural activity for the purpose of enhancing the health of groups and individuals is a tricky association as its contemporary function is increasingly aligned with business (Robinson, 2003), hence emphasising its status as a commodity. This chapter, through a critical discussion, will attempt to explain how definitions and models in sport do not explicitly show clear links between sport and health promotion. It is because of this conceptual and theoretical incongruence that some students of sport may have any preconceptions on the values

21

and functions of sport confirmed; particularly as health promotion as a discipline in undergraduate degrees of sport is an adjunct to its curriculum, rather than being embedded within an intellectual rationale of its curriculum outcomes. This reductionistic approach to teaching sport has its roots in the scientific paradigm, which the coeval discipline of sport becomes a part. The teaching of physiology, biomechanics and psychology are often its core disciplines with particular modes of focus such as health, sport and exercise development and management introduced as sub-categories. This presents a number of problems as sport is therefore not clearly seen as an activity that is a part of health and wellness. This view is not entirely inaccurate as there are justifiable reasons for why *sport* should not necessarily be a part of the health rhetoric. This argument will be explored by reviewing some of the definitions and models that currently exist.

Definitions and context

The Modern Olympic Games, which, were established in 1896 are held every four years, and stage sequences of sporting competition at the highest level. The Olympic Games are a tremendous example of human excellence in sport-ing ability, and a coming together of nations across the globe to share in an experience that transcends the human body, and inspires others to celebrate the extraordinary ability of elites. To say that the Olympic Games promote health related physical activity is a muddling of cultural meaning; what this means is that getting off the bus a couple of stops before one's destination for the purpose of increasing levels of physical activity is a completely separate motive from walking as a warm-up before athletic performance. Sport is sup-posed to contain the following features to establish it as such:

- An engagement in physical or psychomotor skills.
- Competitive framework.
- Codification of rules that bound movements and activities within clear and stringent parameters.
- Enacted within a predetermined time-frame.
- Tradition and or history of past practice.

Blanchard (1995: 50) problemetises this definition by asking '. . . *when are sport activities to be viewed as games and when as something else?*' This really is the question that draws out the axis along which the definition of sport can be located. Sports significance as a cultural activity adapts through time and reproduces society and its culture. Krawczyk (1995) explains that as a sub-culture it contains all the main features of its society and its emphasis can be located within political, cultural, environmental, technological and tempo-ral dimensions. So despite its obvious appearance in society as a highly techni-cal and elite expression of human choreography it is also enacted within educational, public health and leisure contexts; thus providing a variety of cultural experience and the arising of conflicting values. Lee (2004) extricates the underlying values in sport by isolating four components; (a) the promotion of elitism and pursuit of excellence; (b) inculcation of regional and national identity; (c) a facet of the entertainment industry; and (d) a context for identifying talent for regional and national performance. It can be argued that sport in the British context is meant to include other physical activities. Haywood et al. (1990) argue that given the specificity for the term of sport it is not unambiguous enough to exclude activities that are diverse, emergent and/or even controversial in practice; base-jumping, fox-hunting, billiards, bush-walking and ice wind-surfing to suggest a few, which are contested in some way as being sports. Sport is subject to interpretation 'the attempt to [define it] is misconceived' (Haywood, et al., 1990: 53). This view however does not help those whose work goal it is to implement sporting activity for a particular objective; for example sports development (amongst many other goals) is about integrating excluded groups in society with the rest of its community (Collins and Kay, 2003). Sports developers use activities that fall outside of this parsimonious definition in order to achieve the objectives of social inclusion, such as adapted sports, fitness programmes and active for life campaigns.

Therefore, any definition of sport is dependent on its context, so if it is contained within a physical education lesson, its primary function is educational; sport as a method of educating pupils or sport education (Penney, 2000; Tinning et al., 2001). Sport education is about employing pedagogical frames whilst delivering the activity of sport, which results in engagement of all pupils. On the other hand, a school-based sports team involved in intra and inter-school competition shifts its context, as it no longer resides in an educational situation, because it now belongs to a competitive frame. For example, despite being organised through the school, its principal role is competition and its alliance with the standard definition of sport is precise.

In 2000, the then Chair of Sport England Trevor Brooking (Sport England, 2000), stated that,

> sport needs to demonstrate tangible benefits to individuals, communities and the nation as a whole, if it is to compete with many other worthy causes for a share of limited public resources
>
> (Brooking, 2000: 1)

In this position statement Brooking was deliberately trying to shift the focus of sport away from elitism towards an all embracing context that responded to social coherence. The reason for this is simple, economic pragmatism leads to higher levels of accountability and limited resources; sport needs to find itself a justifiable context if it has to attract high levels of public funding. Sports' infrastructure is dependent on public funding as sport and leisure facilities have traditionally been funded by the public purse (Torlkidsen, 1986).

The role of funding in sport will be further explored in Trent Brown's chapter (Chapter 19), where he explores the development of health policy and its implications on sport and participation.

Physical activity

Sport as a concept belongs to the much larger category of physical activity, which has always been present in human ritual; such as religious ceremony, warfare, games, dance, occupation, travel and individual chore (Bouchard, 1997; Gaj and Hadzelek, 1997). Physical activity, as a modern concept is multifaceted and includes within its characteristics *any bodily movement*. It is therefore necessary to distinguish the sub-categories of physical activity, particularly for those whose purpose it will be to develop physical activity opportunity in society.

The diagram in Figure 2.1 below provides a simple overview of the sub-categories that make up physical activity:

Humans are constantly physically active; it is a state of existence as we are embodied and thus every human experience is through the body (Kirk, 2002). As long as we breathe, we are physically active. Regardless of context, this is a basic function of the physical being and for physical activity to occur two other conditions are necessary, these are, *purpose* and *intensity*. Spontaneous

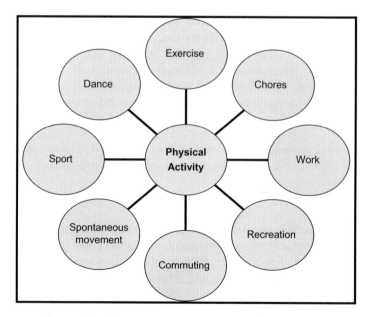

Figure 2.1   A simple deconstruction of physical activity

movement can be purposeful in terms of physical activity, for example running away from one of your playful undergraduate peers who is trying to throw a pint of beer over you at the students' union, is a purposeful engagement in physical activity; it was just brought on spontaneously. Crossing a road is a predetermined movement and if during this a fast moving motor-vehicle appeared at an uncomfortable distance, it may elicit a spontaneous movement for the purpose of survival. When the term physical activity is used it can refer to any of the purposes named in the model, again context determines its exact cultural meaning. This means that in Greece, you may be expected to engage in a ritual wedding dance if you were an invited guest; the cultural context demands that you participate in the symbolic meaning of marriage and the traditional dance – physical activity. In the case of sport, the fact that playing sport is a job for some people means that the physical activity itself holds more than one value to them; it means physical activity in the course of work and profession including being an entertainer; and adherence to the rules of the sport and being defined, therefore, as an athlete as an athlete. Sport can also mean exercise for some individuals as they deliberately select the activity of sport for the purpose of maintaining or enhancing physical fitness.

Exercise however has a clinical component to it, which means that it can be attributed to the practice of prescription by health or medical specialists. For example, physiotherapists use exercise, as controlled movement for the purpose of rehabilitating human bodies. Health and fitness professionals on the other hand do exactly the same, sometimes for rehabilitation and other times as a method of instructing individuals and groups for the purpose of enhancing fitness components. In addition to this, dance, yoga, pilates, etc. have been introduced into exercise environments as techniques for developing fitness; all of which have other cultural symbolism associated with them. All of this means that if a health promotion context was applied to physical activity, its purpose would have to induce positive health outcomes in some way, through actual activity or the education of health. Therefore, the message is that any physical activity engaged in at the appropriate intensity, regardless of context should be the goal of a health promotion initiative for the uptake of physical activity. Sport is a valid physical activity, therefore, given the criteria of increasing its levels for the purpose of improving health; it can be adapted and modified to take into account the target population group. Sports developers have been aware of this for decades as they work at grassroots level across communities from different sectors in society; and have managed to work with the complexity of sport and health promotion. Projects such as the Peckham Pulse in London[1] have integrated several components from the physical activity category, and created separate contexts within its parameters to enhance opportunities for engaging in healthy life-styles. Its basic premise is to provide the local community with space for physical rehabilitation, physical recreation, health education and sport.

Some of the problems arising from using sport as part of a health promotion strategy mean that traditional models of sports development do not assist the

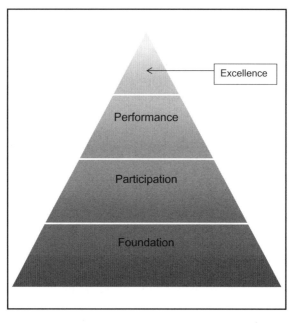

Figure 2.2 Sports continuum

planning of health strategies. The traditional sports continuum model (see Figure 2.2), which has no authorial origin, is taught on degree programmes, included in sports development plans and generally accepted as a coherent explanation of how sports participation should appear. The model does not say anything about context and presumes that all those within the model are participants without any discernible pathways that allow for access and exit.

Foundation is meant to include participants of sport who engage in it as a first point of contact; it would be erroneous to explain that it is the recreational level as all four levels could very well include the recreational participant. It is more than likely meant to describe those who are new to sport through it being introduced as a component of physical education, and/or through local sports club participation at the early stages of acquiring the requisite skills and knowledge.

Participation is meant to describe those who participate on a regular basis, but who are seemingly discerned between the levels of Foundation and Performance on the basis of skill and technicianship; *foundation* being a primary skill development group and *performance* being those who can compete at local and regional levels.

Performance is meant describes those participants who are involved in sport through regular competition at local and regional level. They represent their town or county (and sometimes country) in organised sports competitions. This level is about higher skill ability.

Excellence is supposed to represent the elite level of sports participation and includes playing sport as a profession, such as soccer or tennis, and international competition. This category is now heavily invested in through the media, business finance and sports council strategies for elitism.

Hylton et al. (2001: 3) describe this model as *'simple and powerful'*. Its simplicity, however, has contributed to the misunderstanding that sporting excellence is at the pinnacle of participation, which can alienate the health related participant. It is also not compatible with Sport England's claims that sport can reduce health inequalities; particularly as elite sport carries its own issues of health, such as injury, drug abuse, over-training and life-work balance. In 1996, Cooke attempted to redraw this understanding by devising an alternative model named *the house of sport* (Hylton et al., 2001).

This model can be criticised as being an abstraction without any obvious indication that policy makers, sports developers, educationists or leisure managers have contributed to its mechanisms. It originally was useful as a mechanism for starting a discourse in the area of sports development. Nonetheless, it is an uncertain approach to conceptual and theoretical approaches in sports development; it can also cause some confusion for having many foci but no explanation of context. In addition, elitism surfaces to the top of the agenda, which portrays its central value in sport as elitism being at the pinnacle; *penthouse* conjures up images of money and success, which does not help promote equality and health related physical activity. This of course is the tradition of sport, to win (Blanchard, 1995; Lee, 2004), so it is of no surprise that these

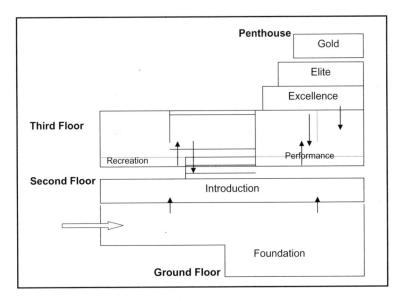

Figure 2.3 Cooke's (1996) house of sport

values often replicate themselves in models and theories on its development. The reality, however, is that organisations charged with the role of providing public services in sport and active recreation, attempt to do so on diminishing funds and are guided by socially responsible government charters (Collins, 2003; Collins and Kay, 2003). Models in sports development do not make allowances for the concept of health or even the diverse contexts that sport operates within, therefore in terms of health promotion these models can provide little assistance in developing initiatives and strategies for increasing active lifestyles. Some would argue that the foundation and introduction levels in the *house of sport* would cater for this, although the arrow depicting access into the model is rife with social issues that create problems for health strategists. Real barriers exist in terms of accessing sport (Haywood et al., 1990; Egger et al., 1999; O'Connor-Fleming, 2001; Brackenridge, 2001; Tinning et al., 2001; Collins and Kay, 2003). Using it as a vehicle for health promotion, therefore, brings with it problems that require 1) identification of issues 2) understanding as to why they have emerged and 3) pragmatic solutions. It is not unreasonable to exploit sport participation as a method of health intervention; it is just that those responsible for devising strategies need to be aware of its problems.

In 2000, Sport England in tandem with the Blair-Labour government produced the *Sporting Future for All* (Sport England, 2000) document, which contained within it an *active framework* for promoting sporting activity. Again, this model takes the approach of sports participation as the context, and the aim of achieving 'active communities' is placed inside the model as if it is unproblematic to do so. This tactic is the reverse approach to what should be a starting point for models of sports development. Development of sport as an expression of a model should aim to highlight the context in which it will operate and show how sport fits into that in a realistic and pragmatic way. This approach would go some way in reasserting the importance of physical

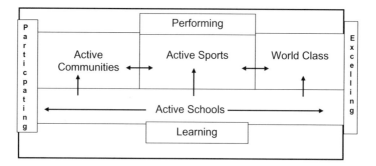

Figure 2.4 Active framework – Sport England (2000) crown copyright mateial in reproduced with the permission of the controller of HMSO and the Queen's Printer for Scotland

activity as a proponent of culture and context. Students of sport will have had sport contextualised, which is necessary for understanding how sport will be enacted; the realisation of sport is underscored by a situational dimension. For example, if health promotion is the goal and raising awareness of the benefits of active living is part of the strategy, then elite sport has no place in that strategy. The use of sports development models, therefore, can be unsupportive in health promotion as they depict progression through a hierarchy with excellence always featuring prominently; and this is a condition of sport, excellence and not health.

Issues arising

Sport England attempts to make a case for sport as a proponent of good health, so it must also include other activities as belonging to this category. Its broad claim that 'sport, in combination with other lifestyle interventions, can prove to be one of the *best buys* in preventative and rehabilitative health care' (Sport England, 2000: 3) is empirically unsubstantiated. In fact, the current figures for physical activity participation in the UK place *active play* (which is not sport or exercise) as the most frequently engaged in form of physical activity for children between the ages of 2–15, with walking being the second most popular activity amongst both boys and girls (Department of Health, Health Survey for England, 1998). Health inequalities are an outcome of many factors, poor-housing, low socio-economic background, inadequate education, environmental stressors and the lack of opportunity to engage with the community (World Health Organization, 2004). Sport as a tradition was devised for men as a way of schooling their bodies for militaristic purpose (Gaj and Hadzelek, 1997; Houlihan, 1997; Kay, 2003). If tradition and practice delineates the boundary of sport then the tradition of male bodies being trained for peak fitness for the purpose of fighting is at odds with diminishing health inequalities. It is true to say that time has changed and expanded the role of sport, however, many barriers still exist for those who would like to participate in sport (Theberge, 1997; Brackenridge, 2001; Humberstone, 2002; Collins, 2003). This means that several issues arise for health educationists when using sport as a vehicle for health promotion. Some of these issues will be covered in greater detail in this book, such as Kate Russell's chapter (Chapter 14) on women in sport and their health, and Chapters 16 and 17 on social issues. The point of this chapter is to establish the barriers that already exist in sport and how this will impact on health promotion.

Gender

Gender and the bias towards masculinity in sport (Penney, 2000; Brackenridge, 2001; Kay, 2003) will create problems for the health promoter as in an instance just over half of the UK population will have an invisible barrier placed between them and the accessibility of sport. In the 1998 Health Survey for England (National Statistics, 1998), 58 per cent of women reported 'housework' as their main physical activity. Issues of expendable leisure time (Torkildsen, 1986; Haywood, 1990) and perceptions of femininity (Cockburn and Clarke, 2003) are real barriers linked to social expectation to actual discrimination (Brackenridge, 2001) that exists both overtly and implicitly as part of male hegemony. Issues centring on financial outlay in sport also become barriers for women's participation in sport as the *gender poverty trap* means that '*women are more likely than men to be poor, at all stages in their lifetimes*' (Trade Unions Congress, 2003: 1). When commitment to sport participation requires car ownership because of out-of-town developments and safety issues for lone-travelling women, on top of participation costs, then the barriers are raised even higher. 'Whether measured in terms of gross, net or disposable income, women have an income in their own right little more than half that of men' (Trade Unions Congress, 2003: 2). Therefore, the accessibility issue is complex, and riddled with socio-political problems that require a serious undertaking in planning if sport is to be used as a vehicle for health promotion.

Structure of sports organisations

The way that sports organisations are structured is also complex. The business model of organisation seems to be being adopted and is occurring across economic sectors. Public, private and voluntary sector organisations are all moving towards the corporate management style of structure (Slack, 2000). This may seem like a responsible model for delivering on investment funding, whether publicly or privately donated; it does, however, introduce issues that create barriers to participation. The business model in sport necessitates accountability, which is a reasonable financial position; however it excludes small and diverse groups who do not have critical mass or large expendable incomes, so when sports activities are provided on the basis of ability to sell units then some social groups will be excluded. Those groups who have the worst health inequalities in their communities, such as low socio-economic background, disability, the aged and those who are powerless in terms of financial standing, such as children and youth, will have problems accessing sports participation. Reducing sports provision to a factor of financial feasibility will also limit the types and frequencies of certain sports, which will in turn reduce the number of keen participants for those sports.

Coaching

For sports participation to be effective as an activity for inducing positive health benefits, reduction of risk to injury would be a requisite consideration.

Coaches for sports would need to be provided, so that in the first instance proficiency of skill was established and secondly, for appropriate levels of instruction such as warming-up, stretching and general health and safety practises be adopted. Leisure and recreation providers would need to provide this facility, in the way that they already do in controlled health and fitness environments. Nevertheless, the problem is that for a health and fitness club to run a facility with an average 800 membership, between 2–4 instructors are necessary at any one time; including exercise classes. Sports participation would require far more coaches than this because of the unpredictability of sporting movement. So regardless of fixed movement parameters, exercise environments exert far greater control over movement than sports play can. The risk to injury, which contraindicates health principles (O'Connor, 2004) is therefore vast.

Pragmatic solutions

Pragmatic solutions are therefore necessary for tackling some of the problems and issues that have been discussed above. As a conceptual framework it would be useful for students of sport and health to view sport as belonging to an overall category of physical culture. Physical culture includes all human movement that has cultural resonance, and this includes health related activity and rehabilitation.

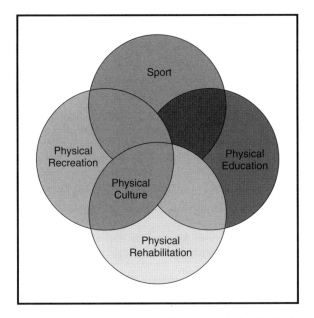

Figure 2.5   A diagrammatic explanation of physical culture

The definitional framework for physical culture presents a clearer vision for health promotion strategists as it provides a multifaceted approach to understanding its operational context. For instance, planning a health campaign for increased levels of physical activity can be aimed at schools, such as a Walking Bus (www.walkingbus.com) campaign, which is currently popular in Australia and is also being used in St. Albans (UK), as it introduces a safe and alternative solution for transportation to school. The idea is that a school, and often the health and physical education teacher, organises a rota and route for picking up children at particular points so that children can be escorted by foot, to school.

It is also necessary that culturally we begin to realise that sport does not necessarily mean physical activity, but is a part of it and further contextualised by cultural practices. Health educationists will know that a sprung-floor in a leisure centre can accommodate only four people at maximum for a game of badminton for 45 minutes; the same space can, however, be used for fitness classes or adapted sports, where the emphasis is on fitness and not sport specific skill development, for numbers of 20–25. It is important that the activity of sport is adapted to fit the context and the aims of those who deliver it.

Conclusion

In conclusion, it is proposed that health promotion strategies consider the definitional accuracy of physical activity and sport so that pragmatic solutions can be applied to the current and future problems that sedentary lifestyles have caused; particularly as sport, in its most precise condition, is not necessarily a method for improving the health status of all individuals, groups and communities.

Note

1 Peckham Pulse is a healthy living centre in Peckham, London. Details of a strategy can be found at http://www.fusion-lifestyle.com/CentreDetails.asp/cat-8

References

Blanchard, K. (1995) *The Anthropology of Sport: An introduction*. United States of America: Bergin and Garvey.

Bouchard, C. Ed. (1997) *Biological Aspects of the Active Living Concept*. Physical activity in human experience: Interdisciplinary perspectives. United States of America: Human Kinetics.

Brackenridge, C. (2001) *Spoilsports: Understanding and Preventing Sexual Exploitation in Sport*. London, UK: Routledge.

Brooking, T. (2000) Sport England in *Positive Futures* http://www.english.sports.gov.uk

Cockburn, C. and Clarke, G. (2003) 'Everybody's looking at you!' Teenage girls negotiating the 'femininity deficit' they incur in physical education, *Womens Studies International Forum*, 25, 6, 651–665.

Collins, M. Ed. (2003) Social exclusion from sport and leisure in Houlihan, A. *Sport and Society*. London: Sage.

Collins, M. F. and Kay, T. (2003) *Sport and Social Exclusion*. London, UK: Routledge.

Cooke, G. (1996) A strategic approach to performance and excellence, supercoach, national coaching foundation *National Coaching Federation*, 8, 1, 10.

Demel, M. (1969) *Otrech Wersjach Teorii Wychowania Fizycznego: Proba Ujecia Komplementarnego*. Krakow, Poland: Akademia Wychowania Fizycznego w Warszawie.

Department of Health (1998) Health Survey for England. London: HMSO.

Egger, G., Spark, R., Lawson, J. and Donovan, R. (1999) *Health Promotion Strategies and Methods*. Sydney, Australia: McGraw Hill.

Gaj, J. and Hadzelek, K. (1997) *Dzieje Kultury Fizycznej w Polsce*. Poznan, Poland: Akademis Wychowania Fizycznego im.Piaseckiego w Poznaniu.

Haywood, L., Kew, F., Bramham, P., Spink, J., Capenerhurst, J. and Henry, I. (1990) *Understanding Leisure*. London, UK: Stanley Thornes .

Houlihan, B. (1997) *Sport, Policy and Politics: A Comparative Analysis*. London and New York: Routledge.

Humberstone, B. Ed. (2002) Femininity, masculinity and difference: What's wrong with a sarong? Chapter 4 in Laker, A. *The Sociology of Sport and Physical Education: An Introductory Reader*. London and New York: Routledge-Falmer.

Hylton, K., Bramham, P., Jackson, D. and Nesti, M. (2001) *Sports Development: Policy, Process and Practice*. London and New York: Routledge.

Kay, T. Ed. (2003) *Sport and Gender. Social Exclusion from Sport and Leisure*. Sage, London: Sport and Society.

Kirk, D. Ed. (2002) The social construction of the body in physical education and sport in *The Sociology of Sport and Physical Education: An Introductory Reader*, London and New York: Routledge-Falmer.

Krawczyk, Z. (1995) *Socjologia Kultury Fizycznej*. Warsaw, Poland: Akademi a Wychowania Fizycznego Jòzefa Pitsudskiego w Warszawie.

Lee, M. (2004) Values in physical education and sport: A conflict of interests? *The British Journal of Teaching Physical Education*, 35, 1.

National Statistics (1998) *Health Survey for England* at www.statistics.gov.uk

O'Connor, J. (2004) Monash University, *Personal Communication*, Faculty of Education, Gippsland Campus, VIC, Australia.

O'Connor-Fleming, M. L. and Parker, E. (2001) *Health Promotion: Principles and Practice in the Australian Context*. Sydney, Australia: Allen and Unwin.

Pawlaczek. Z. (2004) Australia's obesity crisis points to a question of how PE is taught. *The Age*. Melbourne, VIC, Australia: 4 Education.

Penney, D. Ed. (2000) Physical education . . . In what and whose interest? Chapter 5 in Jones, R. and Armour, K. M. *Sociology of Sport; Theory and Practice*. Harlow UK: Longman.

Robinson, L. Ed. (2003) The Business of Sport. Chapter 9 in *Sport and Society*, London: Sage.

Slack, T. Ed. (2000) Managing voluntary sports organisations: A critique of popular trends. Chapter 4 in Jones, R. and Armour, K. M. *Sociology of Sport; Theory and Practice*. Champaign: Sage.

Sport England (2000) *A Sporting Future For All*. Harlow, London: Department for Culture, Media and Sport.

Therberge, N. Ed. (1997) Sociological perspectives on physical activity in *Physical Activity in Human Experience: Interdisciplinary Perspectives.* New York: Human Kinetics.

Tinning, R., Macdonald, D., Wright, J. and Hickey, C. (2001) *Becoming a Physical Education Teacher: Contemporary and Enduring Issues.* Sydney, Australia: Prentice Hall, Pearson Education.

Torkildsen, G. (1986) *Leisure and Recreation Management.* Cambridge, UK: E. and F. N. SPON, Cambridge University Press.

Trade Unions Congress (2003) Beating the gender poverty gap. *Report to TUC Women's Conference 2003.* London: Trades Union Congress.

World Health Organization (2004) www.who.com Accessed 4th August 2004.

www.walkingbus.com or www.walkingbus.org/ Accessed 18th September 2004.

CHAPTER 3

Planning and Project Management

BARBARA L. GRIFFIN AND ALYSON LEARMONTH

As with the first chapter, the authors have written this chapter as a dialogue between two colleagues. The aim is to capture some of the issues in the planning and project management of sport and physical activity in relation to health promotion. The first part is an introduction to the authors and the format of the chapter. The second part outlines the planning element and explains the use of the 'action learning problem' as a planning tool. Finally, we conclude the chapter by reflecting on the process of planning and project management.

Introduction

In this chapter we aim to present the role of health promotion from an academic perspective and from the perspective of a public health practitioner. We, connect the dialogue by a question in order for you, the reader to understand different perspectives on issues we raise in each part. The relationship between theory and practice in health promotion is problematic because as Kelly (1989) suggests health promotion is essentially practice driven, meaning a greater emphasis is on practice rather than theory in health promotion. So the first question aims to address the question of theory in practice.

Alyson, how does theory and practices operate in your work?

Two weeks before agreeing to co-author this chapter, I started my post as Director of Public Health with Sedgefield Primary Care Trust. This Primary Care Trust has 52 GPs in 11 practices, and is coterminous with Sedgefield Borough Council with an ageing population of just under 90,000 in a deprived part of the North East. Health experience in Sedgefield is poor, for example, life expectancy for both men and women ranks amongst the worst 50 local authorities in England that is the bottom 20 per cent. The health domain of the Index of Multiple Deprivation shows that health experience is worse than would be predicted from other aspects of deprivation such as education, employment and access to services (Reilly and Eynon, 2003).

While on one hand knowing that, a significant part of my role would be to assist the Primary Care Trust in developing effective secondary prevention measures to address the burden of long standing conditions I was keen to find ways to maintain a pro-active approach to primary prevention. I have always had a conviction that physical activity is an important element of a health enhancing lifestyle, and both evidence and policy to support this view has been increasingly available over the last few years (WHO, 2002; Blair and Connelly, 1996). I have also used an action learning approach previously to help maintain focus and develop partnerships around a developmental area that might otherwise get squeezed out of a hectic schedule (Learmonth and Pedler, 2004). Contributing to this chapter, therefore, seemed an opportunity to help create motivation and external stimulation for myself in leading and supporting work to increase physical activity. This then would enable me to draw on more traditional planning tools and theory about the factors that actually lead to behaviour change in this area. In achieving this goal; however, it was vital that I did not lose sight of the intended readers, students of sports science. A breakthrough point for me was therefore when, Barbara asked a group of her students to carry out a quick brainstorm of what they find difficult about health pro- motion. I would like to use the clusters of issues they generated as a reference point for this chapter, because an important part of public health theory is that activ- ity must relate to a needs assessment of the population we are concerned with: so this chapter is written for you the student drawing on my experiences in 'planning for real'. In summary Barbara, theory is important in my practice in defining needs in the population, determining how public health might address these issues, ensur- ing that the motivation and leadership that are essential for an integrated approach across agencies are in place, and helping to review and evaluate.

What is your perspective Barbara on what sports students interested in health related issues and applications need to know about both theoretical health promo- tion planning tools and their use, and action learning as an approach?

In response to your question, I intend explaining my general perspective on plan- ning. Secondly, I will explain one traditional planning tool that is relevant to physical activity and health promotion. Finally, I will explain the use of action learning in planning this chapter.

My general perspective on planning is that the construction of a plan helps to achieve a particular venture. In terms of health promotion practice, planning is a key concept as exemplified by references to planning in health promotion texts such as Katz and Peberdy (1997), Naidoo and Wills (2000) and Ewles and Simnett (2003). The models include rational planning models such as McCarthy's (1982) rational health planning, Tannahill's (1990) integrated planning model and Green and Kreuter's (1999) Precede/Proceed model of planning.

The previous models of planning share one feature, that is each model illustrates a series of steps or stages of planning and to illustrate this point further I intend explaining Green and Kreuter's (1999) Precede/Proceed model of planning. The Precede/Proceed model fits into a flexible approach to the physical activity strategy because it is sufficiently broad based to encompass environmental, community and individual issues; because the process is sensitive to values and beliefs; because it explicitly encompasses process and outcome evaluation. Therefore, this model forms a good foundation for planning. The key terms are as follows;

Precede = Predisposing, Reinforcing, Enabling, Causes in, Educational Diagnosis and Educational

Proceed = Policy, Regulatory, Organisational, Constructs in Educational and Environmental Development

To achieve results in health promotion the authors have two basic principles, firstly, participation of the target audience for successful change and secondly, community development. Community development draws on empowerment and educational models. The aim is for health behaviour to become voluntary behaviour by removing obstacles; however, health means different things to different people therefore the process cannot be rigid. Rather the process needs to take into account the multi-dimensional nature of health projects that take place in a variety of settings such as schools or workplaces.

Next, I want to explain the Green and Krueter (1999) model. The focus of the Precede/Proceed model (also discussed in Chapter 8) is on outcomes and therefore links to evaluation at the outset. The planning process takes place backwards, that is, starting at the end of the project. This means that the health programme planners have to have a clear idea about what they intend implementing. To assist in this process Green and Krueter (1999) identify six phases in the Precede/Proceed model (see Figure 3.1).

First, a social diagnosis that explores the social problems that impact on a community and establishing a link as to how this influences health; the second phase is the epidemiological diagnosis that, for instance, draws on statistical data to establish priorities; thirdly the behavioural and environmental diagnosis systematically explores health practices and environmental factors that link to quality of life. Another element of this phase is to identify the extent to which change can be achieved either at an individual or community level. This assessment of potential change helps to establish meaningful strategic policies such as specific educational interventions.

This links to the fourth phase that comprises of an educational and organisational diagnosis examining the causes of the health behaviours identified in phase three. This part examines the feasibility of the educational strategies in achieving change. For instance, returning to the notion that health promotion is about removing obstacles, this fourth phase explores areas that support or hinder health behaviours. The relevant areas include; predisposing factors in individuals or communities such as values, beliefs, attitudes and knowledge. An area that supports change includes accessibility, availability and skills. An example of combining health behaviours and the environment is Pikora et al. (2003) who locate the concept of moderate activity

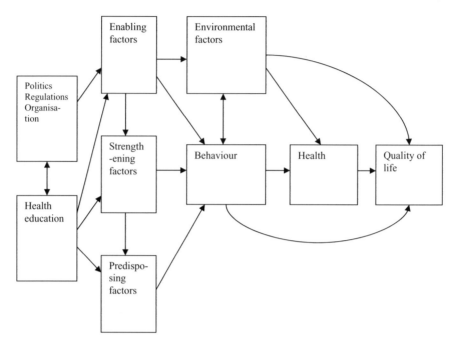

Figure 3.1 Precede/proceed model from: Green and Kreuter Health promotion planning 3/e, 1999, McGraw-Hill companies. Reproduced with permission of the McGraw-Hill Companies

into a social ecological framework, in order to identify the environmental features that hinder or promote moderate activity. The physical environmental features that influence walking and cycling include functional elements such as the physical features of a pathway, safety such as crossing aids, aesthetic qualities such as cleanliness and the destination such as a park or shops. These features support walking or cycling in a local setting. With these features in mind the model links to the individual who has different levels of motivation, support and interest. In addition, Pikora et al. (2003) identify inhibiting factors to physical activity including; air pollution, litter, dangerous traffic and poor lighting. With Pikora et al.'s (2003) work in mind the final part of the precede educational diagnosis is the factors that reinforce health behaviours including rewards or punishments from family, friends and teachers.

The fifth phase of the Precede model is the administrative and policy diagnosis that includes an assessment of the resources, budget constraints, time factors and personnel on the programme. The administration elements focus on the organisational situation including noticing the features in an organisation that will prevent or promote progress in the programme.

Finally, the sixth phase of the Precede/Proceed model has four phases; implementation, process evaluation, impact evaluation and outcome evaluation.

After the precede elements there is the implementation of the programme. The first part of the evaluation phase examines the process, meaning how the programme developers implement the programme such as the number of venues in operation, the number of participants and the amount of dedicated resources.

Secondly, impact evaluation considers intermediate objectives. For instance, how many people remain on a particular programme and the changes in predisposing, enabling and reinforcing factors. Finally, the outcome evaluation measures change in relation to individuals' health behaviours, changes in social factors and quality of life. Nevertheless, outcome evaluation is difficult to measure and may take years to manifest.

The Precede/Proceed model is one of many planning models; however, French and Milner (1993) argue that planning models are illusory and in 'real life' the stages are not clear and the processes to implement a plan do not necessarily follow a pattern. I will comment on planning and 'real life' drawing on my experiences of the use of the action learning tool at the end of this part of the chapter. Nevertheless, French and Milner (1993) raise an important point because theoretical models of planning can appear separate from other elements of everyday life and work activity.

One way of explaining the differences between the models of planning and what we experience in everyday life is to think of the models as being firstly, formal such as Green and Kreuter's (1999) Precede/Proceed model and secondly, as informal. Informal planning might include informal conversations and serendipity. In this context, serendipity means an unplanned event such as a coincidental meeting with a person who is able to assist in the implementation of a health promotion project. When a health promoter is working in the area of the promotion of physical activity, she/he needs to draw on a formal model of planning and be alert to the contribution informal processes make to completion of the task.

To summarise this part of the chapter, the Precede/Proceed model provides a comprehensive framework for planning, implementing and evaluating physical activity and health programmes, because it includes elements that influence individuals' and communities' health by taking into account, social and environmental factors. This model draws on social and behavioural sciences using a systematic approach to planning. The three feeder disciplines are epidemiology, administration and education. Nevertheless, I would argue that any systematic planning tool assists in organising health promotion projects; however, the appeal of the Precede/Proceed model is the inclusion of the three disciplines, epidemiology, administration and education. In the next paragraph, I will explain how the action learning tool (Pedler, 1996) helps in managing the planning process. This explanation draws on my experiences of using the action learning tool during the production of this chapter.

The action learning tool provides a framework that focuses on a specific issue, because as Revans states 'There can be no learning without action and no (sober and deliberate) action without learning.' (Revans in Pedler, 1996: 8). The action learning tool (Box 3.2) has two parts, programmed knowledge and questioning insight. This means to make progress we need knowledge about an issue and then we need to be prepared to question or reflect on that issue. According to Pedler

(1996) the person using the action learning tool Box 3.1. needs to engage voluntarily in relation to problems that have no right answers but rather the solutions require knowledge, questioning and insight.

Box 3.1   Action learning tool that promotes questioning and reflection Pedler (1996)

Action Learning Tool:
What are my current questions about this work?
Main learning points since (time when commenced)
Describe your problem situation in one sentence:
Why is this important?
    (i) To you?
    (ii) To the others?
    (iii) To the wider group?
How will you recognise progress on this problem?
Who else would like to see progress on this problem?
What difficulties do you anticipate?
What are the benefits if this problem is reduced or resolved?
    (i) To me?
    (ii) To others that are close?
    (iii) To the wider group?
Immediate next steps:

The action learning tool helps to focus attention on the issues in this example that hinder progress in writing. For instance, the headings prompt clear thinking about a problem. By identifying specific questions, it is possible to consider possible solutions. One example could be a person deciding to start taking regular physical exercise.

Box 3.2   An example written by a sport exercise and development student to illustrate the use of the action learning tool (Pedler, 1996)

Describe your problem situation in one sentence:
I want to set up sports activities in my local community during the summer holidays.
Why is this important?
    (i) To you?
  I want to make a contribution to children and sport in my community.

(ii) To others?
A community sport scheme gives children the chance to have fun and take part in sport.
(iii) To wider group?
Community sports in summer holidays helps parents to keep working knowing that their children have somewhere positive to go.

How will you recognise progress on this problem?
I need to complete a check list as a way of making progress, for instance, what already happens in the area. I can check what courses children like to attend. Then I can plan in conjunction with local facilities the type of summer courses that children and parents want.

Who else would like to see progress on this problem?
The government and local authority want children to take part in sport.

What difficulties do you anticipate?
Lack of money, suitable facilities and lack of interest from children.

What are the benefits if this problem is reduced or resolved?
(i) To you?
Provides employment for myself as I am a football coach.
(ii) To others?
Creates an opportunity for children for improved health and fitness.
(iii) To wider group?
Keeps children off the streets and gives them new experiences.

Immediate next steps:
Check my qualifications are up to date and to hand.
Check what is on offer in the community already.
Contact local authority about funding opportunities.

The example in Box 3.2 illustrates specific details about a problem in terms of planning and management. The problem solving tool helps to focus on a particular issue and prompts the immediate next steps in order to make progress on a particular issue.

Alyson, because you have used the action learning tool can you add further information.

I think the main thing I have learnt about action learning is that it helps motivate me because of the focus on why the issue is important . . . to me and to others. As you have already explained there is a tension between the logic of step-wise planning models and 'real life'. Action learning I have found to be useful for continuing to engage in 'real life', despite the fact that it rarely follows the sequence you would logically choose. This does not mean that the models are a waste of time, because thorough and logical preparation means that the different elements you need are ready when the opportunity arises. For example in the case study of developments in Sedgefield, many of the components listed below under the headings of the Precede/Proceed model are there as a result of a rational planning approach to assessing need, identifying what works, and planning to fill gaps using available or freshly bid for resources.

Social/economic/cultural issues *in the ex-mining communities that form some of the most deprived villages have been delineated by Bennett et al. (2003).*

Epidemiologically, *the Standardised Mortality Ratio for circulatory disease in Sedgefield is 121 (1999–2001, Ball et al., 2002 Compendium of Health Indicators), where the standard mortality rate for a population is 100 deaths is the average for England and Wales, adjusted to allow for the age and sex structure of the population.*

Behavioural/environmental diagnosis: *there is recent statistical information that 9.3 per cent of the population take no physically activity (North East Public Health Observatory, 2006). This problem is particularly difficult in environments where traditionally jobs have involved heavy labour, when those forms of employment disappear. In addition an initial mapping exercise of facilities for people to take physical activity in the form of sport or classes had recently been undertaken by the Countywide Physical Activity Strategy Coordinator, working with some local key activists. Gaps appeared in relation to community based work, work with young women and work with older people as three major target groups.*

Assessment of change potential: *this work was carried out at the time of rising national concern about the obesity epidemic and the launch of the latest Sport England 'Get Active' programme. The readiness to change in both individuals and communities forms the first part of any successful change programme, building on the enthusiasm of key activists and young people. The literature review you undertook Barbara, helped to throw some light on factors likely to create the right circumstances for successful change to take place.*

Educational and organisational diagnosis: *there are some key activists in important and influential positions keen to create change. There is a protocol for exercise referral schemes that use the GP as an entry point; following assessment of readiness to change, the offer of subsidised access to exercise facilities for a limited period (after which it is hoped the individual will take on the changed behaviour themselves) and it has been evaluated recently as a scheme through the Scrutiny function of the Local Authority. There is unmet need in the community and a pressing rationale in terms of the burden of mortality. There are some environmental features that help people to become physically active such as good access to health clubs and leisure centres, but others such as lack of cycleways that do not. However co-ordination mechanisms are weak and the gulf between 'sport' and 'health' threatens our ability to work smoothly together.*

Administrative and policy diagnosis: *during the final stages of the case study the key activists have worked to put together a bid for the Active England programme. This has again highlighted the lack of clear mechanisms and administrative support, which is offset by the enthusiasm of some keen individuals. During the period of the case study a Healthy Lifestyles Steering group was established, with the purpose of improving the co-ordination of effort at a strategic level*

(Professional Executive Committee, 28th January, Health and Social Care Policy Group, 8th January).
Implementation, process evaluation, impact of evaluation and outcome evaluation: *it is too early to say whether this bid will be successful. Current discussions are under way to ensure that it draws on the literature in terms of what is known to work so far, and specifies appropriate outcomes based on individual and community readiness to change.*

Nevertheless, the process of sustaining a proactive approach to the issue through an action learning approach, drew on a constant re-focusing on the issue in such a way as to avoid the problems of inertia and lack of co-ordination that seem endemic.

Conclusion

In this chapter we have explored elements of health promotion practice in relation to planning and management drawing on Green and Kreuter's (1999) Precede/Proceed model. The general planning principles of this model include tackling health promotion interventions through a series of steps in order to try to accommodate different factors such as epidemiological material and policy developments. If an individual is involved in health promotion work then the action problem learning tool (Pedler, 1996) helps to focus on personal and localised issues.

References

Bennett, K., Beynon, H., Hudson, R. and Pike, A. (Rev.) (2003) Coalfields regeneration: dealing with the consequences of industrial decline. Review. *Regional Studies*, Jun, 35, 4, 372–373.

Ball, C., Leahy, G., Mole, G., Neave, P. and Wright, B. (2002) 1999–2001, *Compendium of Health Indicators*. Tower Hamlets: NHS. http://www.lifestylesurevey.org.uk/pdfs/rbank/Towerhamletshealthprofile.pdf

Blair, S. N. and Connelly, J. C. (1996) How much physical activity should we do? The case for moderate amounts and intensities of physical activity. *Research Quarterly for Exercise and Sport*, 67(2), 193–205.

Ewles, L. and Simnett, I. (2003). 4th edition. *Promoting Health: A Practical Guide to Health Education*. London: Wiley.

French, J. and Milner, S. (1993) Should we accept the status quo? *Health Education Journal*, 52, 98–101.

Green, L. W. and Kreuter, M. (1999) 3rd edition. *Health Promotion Planning: An Educational and Ecological Approach*, Mountain View: Mayfield Publishing Co.

Katz, J. and Peberdy, A. Eds. (1997) *Promoting Health Knowledge and Practice*. Milton Keynes: Open University and Macmillan Press.

Kelly, M. P. (1989) Some problems in health promotion research, *Health Promotion*, 4, 4, 317–330.

Learmonth, A. and Pedler, M. (2004) Auto action learning: a tool for policy change: Building capacity across the developing regional system to improve health in the North East of England, *Health Policy*, 68, 2, May, 169–181.

McCarthy, M. (1982) *Epidemiology and Policies for Health Planning*. London, King Edward's Hospital Fund for London.

Naidoo, J. and Wills, J. (2000) *Health Promotion Foundations for Practice*. London: Bailliere and Tindall.

North East Public Health Observatory (2006) *Mapping Physical Activity in the North East Region* http://www.nepho.org.uk/index.php?c=1510

Pedler, M. (1996) *Action Learning for Managers*. Sheffield: Learning Company Project.

Pikora, T., Giles-Corti, B., Bull, F., Jamrozik, K. and Donovan, R. (2003) Developing a framework for assessment of the environmental determinants of walking and cycling, *Social Science and Medicine*, 56, 1693–1703.

Reilly, M. and Eynon, C. (May 2003) *Miserable measures: The range and severity of deprivation for the County Durham and Tees Valley area*. NHS Public Health Intelligence Service, County Durham and Tees Valley Public Health Network, Poole House, Stokesley Road, Nunthorpe, Middlesbrough TS7 0NJ, tel 01642 320000.

Tannahill, A. (1990) Health education and health promotion planning for the 1990s. *Health Education Journal*, 49, 4, 194–198.

WHO (2002) Committee on physical activity for health move for health, Bulletin of the World Health Organisation. http://www.who.int/moveforhealth/en/

CHAPTER 4

Research and Evaluation

BARBARA L. GRIFFIN AND ALYSON LEARMONTH

Introduction

In this Chapter we plan to explain features of research and evaluation by providing examples from current literature in the area of sport, physical activity and health promotion. Firstly, there is an outline of the aim of research in health promotion, including examples to illustrate the body of knowledge that health promotion draws on such as the typography suggested by Park (1993, in Raphael, 2000) including instrumental knowledge, interactive knowledge and critical knowledge. These examples include an analysis of the methods and an analysis of the contribution to knowledge about physical activity and health promotion. In the final part, there is an example of evaluation in health promotion to demonstrate how health promoters evaluate specific projects, employing a variety of quantitative and qualitative methods. This example informs the proposed bid to Active England from the Sedgefield Primary Care Trust. In the summary about research and evaluation there is a dialogue between Barbara Griffin and Alyson Learmonth.

Arguably, research in health promotion examines three questions; first, is there a health issue? Secondly, what are the reasons for this health issue? Thirdly, which health promotion intervention can alleviate the issue? (Raphael, 2000). Nevertheless, the interpretation of the evidence to answer these questions depends upon the values of the health promoter (Seedhouse, 1997 and Raphael, 2000). The argument here is that questions about evidence in research represent a value judgement about reality and what is believed to be the truth. Research aims to provide explanations about truth; however, there is more than one type of explanation about knowledge that contributes to our understanding of reality.

With types of evidence and knowledge in mind, this chapter begins with explaining types of knowledge. Raphael (2000: 7) drawing on the work of Park (1993 in Raphael, 2000) outlines three types of knowledge, instrumental, interactive and critical knowledge and an explanation of each follows.

Instrumental knowledge includes concepts such as traditional, scientific, positivist and quantitative knowledge. In the context of sport, physical activity and health promotion instrumental knowledge develops through scientific processes such as the systematic collection of epidemiological data which is the study of the mass incidence of mortality (deaths) and morbidity (illness and disease). In the European document *Physical Activity and Cardiovascular Disease Prevention* in the European Union (Williams, 1999), for example, the researchers draw on traditional research and data collection including theories about quantitative research methods, sampling, reliability and validity. One of the concerns of instrumental knowledge is controlling physical and social environments.

In order to explain elements of the physical and social environments I plan to analyse an example of research that develops a framework for assessing the environmental determinants for walking and cycling (Pikora et al., 2003). The aim is to illustrate how underpinning definitions influence the development of research. Essentially the following example is first about whether people walk or cycle for pleasure or transport. If the answer to this question is 'yes', then is the physical activity they take sufficient to improve health? What is the local environment like? Are there features in the environment that help or hinder walking or cycling? These questions underpin the development of strategies to increase levels of physical activity. Pikora's (2003) research locates individuals in their socio-environment in order to ascertain how the quality of the environment influences walking and cycling. Therefore, in this research the measurement is of individual factors including personal skills, behaviour and attitudes, and social factors such as membership to a club, social environmental factors including dog ownership and exercise partners. Physical environment factors include access to public space, destinations such as parks or shops, appealing neighbourhoods and natural facilities. The theory is that people will engage in physical activity if the surroundings are acceptable.

Nevertheless, the measurement of these factors is complex because the research combines individual psychological factors with social factors and environmental features. To overcome this complexity the researchers developed a theoretical framework to assess the physical socio-environmental factors. The framework includes functional elements such as the physical features of a pathway, safety features such as crossing aids, aesthetic qualities such as cleanliness and the destination such as shops. Pikora (2003) suggest that these features support walking or cycling in a local setting.

Secondly, the researchers identify inhibiting factors to physical activity such as air pollution, litter, dangerous traffic and poor lighting. With these features in mind, the theoretical model links the individual who has different levels of motivation, support and interest to their local environment. Therefore, there is research into individual levels of physical activity in relation to four behaviours; walking for transport, walking for pleasure, cycling for transport and cycling for pleasure. The first phase of the research was with key local experts using semi-structured interviews. The second phase was with national and international experts to rank and identify environmental variables using a Delphi study (Box 4.1) with three rounds of systematic enquiry to find out information by a series of questions that measure the validity of the extensive list of environmental features.

> **Box 4.1   Delphi study and Likert scales: an explanation**
>
> Linstone and Turoff (1975: 3) describe a Delphi study as 'a method for structuring a group communication process so that the process is effective in allowing a group of individuals, as a whole, to deal with a complex problem.' Delphi studies adopt a range of techniques such as Likert scales. A Likert scale includes a series of responses on a continuum such as 'strongly agree', 'agree', 'disagree' and 'strongly disagree'. Nevertheless, a typical study involves an expert panel who analyse information, which provides the basis for the next round of analysis. The panelists have an opportunity to revise their opinions within a process that offers a degree of anonymity of individual contributions.

The aim of the Delphi study is to achieve a consensus on information that previously is not available. The researchers used Likert scales to identify key issues from respondents. After the first Delphi round of questions, the panel received a revised list of features and they were asked to measure the relative importance by allocating a total of 100 points between the factors. Pikora et al. (2003) collated and estimated a median score from the numerical data. Finally, the panel members compared the first and second lists and asked if they wished to make any changes in the light of the median scores.

The findings included issues about personal safety, attractive surroundings and destinations. In addition, the transport journeys for cycling identified the consistency of the cycle way surface was relevant and the demarcation between heavy traffic and cycle-ways. In terms of the evidence, the researchers noted that the subjective nature of the assessment of obstacles is difficult to provide consistent weightings to strong personal opinions. Another limitation is that the selection of the panel relied on the literature and knowledge of the selection team. Nevertheless, this research drawing on quantitative methods provides an example of a framework to identify features in the environment that hinder or promote walking or cycling for pleasure or transport.

The second type of knowledge in Park's (1993 in Raphael, 2000) typography is interactive knowledge meaning that the knowledge draws on lived experience and includes concepts such as constructionist, naturalistic, ethnographic or qualitative knowledge. The central aim is to understand people's experiences, the meanings and interpretations of individuals' lived experience. An example of this in relation to physical activity and health promotion is Swain's (2000) account of how playground football facilitates the construction of a young boy's masculinity.

The relevance of this article is that it explains issues of self-image, gender, and participation in sport. Arguably, these issues are relevant in promoting physical activity with young people.

Swain (2000) undertook the observational fieldwork over a period of 8 weeks in winter and 25 semi-structured interviews with staff, lower and upper school pupils in one school in England. The non-participant observation was with one class of 10–11 year old boys. Swain (2000) is careful to explain the basis of the research process, namely that the interview process shapes the responses, meaning that the children are not just reflecting on the outside world. Nevertheless, the interview transcripts and non-participant observation forms the basis of the research. Swain's (2000) research is similar to Pikora et al.'s (2003) in that there is material about individuals' skills, attitudes and behaviours in relation to the socio-environment which in Swain's work is specifically the school playground and in a general sense the school and its policies. The data contains boys' explanations of events on the playground. The difference between the two papers is that Swain's (2000) work explores the boys' experiences of football on the playground at break time whereas Pikora et al. (2003) draw data from experts about potential barriers to walking and cycling in environments. Another difference between the papers is that Swain (2000) sets the specific location of the school into a broader context of football's commercialisation and symbolism in society with specific refer-ence to cultural images of masculinity.

The third type of knowledge is critical or reflective knowledge. Critical knowledge explores what is right and just. The issues are about societal struc-tures and power. Therefore, to illustrate critical knowledge the examples in this part draw on feminist theories about decision – making in society and the social construction of policy making. Before explaining Park's critical knowledge I want to digress for a moment to make an observation. There appears to be a sort of blindness in relation to physical activity research in relation to gender. The European Heart Network (1999) comment that the majority of studies into physical activity use male subjects. Nevertheless, to return to critical knowledge current research illustrates that females are less likely to participate in physical activity (Mulvihill et al., 2000). There is therefore a mismatch in that women participate less, but there is more research into what men do.

The aim of Mulvihill et al.'s (2000) research was to determine the drivers and barriers for young people in relation to physical activity. Over a five-month period 100 young people aged between 11–15 and their parents were inter-viewed in their school or outside school settings. The definition of sufficient physical activity for a young person aged between 11–15 years was one hour a day of moderate activity. Moderate activity included brisk walking that would leave the young person warm and slightly out of breath. Generally, Mulvihill et al. (2000) stated that favourable psychosocial environmental factors such as being part of a group and being with friends encouraged physical activity. Nevertheless, there are clear gender differences such as young women being less likely to participate in physical activities and being more critical of physical activity.

The researchers concluded from the semi-structured interviews that the young people were aware of the benefits of physical activity mentioning people live longer, maintain their weight (this was particularly important for females) and avoid becoming a 'blob'. The motivation was that young people experienced an improvement in their well-being, pleasure and prevented boredom when they engaged in physical activity. When asked if the person considered themselves active or inactive out of 61 participants, 23 males out of 33 males (66 per cent of males) regularly took part in physical education at school and out of 28 females 14 (50 per cent of females) stated they took part in physical education at school.

At a general level in relation to out of school time females preferred sedentary home-based activities at their own home or a friend's home. Outside of school, females enjoyed dancing. Young men preferred to engage in outside activities such as football or rugby in and out of school.

More specifically the young people differed in their opinion about school physical education. Females thought physical education was boring and that teachers paid more attention to males. The females disliked the teachers making them take part in physical education and disliked the teachers watching them when they were changing. In conclusion, the young women did not like school physical education because of a lack of privacy, sharing activities with boys and a loss of autonomy. The barriers include the inertia of the older females, embarrassment about their bodies, a lack of time in relation to the demands of homework and preference for non-physical activities. Nevertheless, they stated they would like less structured activities such as trampolining and dancing at non-school sites.

The young men enjoyed competitive team sports because they experienced less pressure in a team as opposed to performing in an individual sport. This applied to young men who were good at sport, while less able young men found team sports less enjoyable. Nevertheless, barriers for the young men include a lack of transport in rural areas to access facilities and a lack of money to go to facilities. Therefore, they thought that free facilities would be beneficial. Out of school, the young men preferred to take up sports such as basketball without the element of compulsion they experienced at school.

The parents considered their attitude towards physical education influenced their children, for instance whether a parent had enjoyed physical education or not. Although the role of parents became less influential as the young people grew older, because they recognised that the young people tended to engage in more formal activities rather than informal playing at home. The parents did not consider finance as a potential barrier to participating in physical activity. Nevertheless, they understood that engaging in physical activity had benefits such as weight control and increased concentration.

Finally, Mulvihill et al. (2000) recommends a flexible approach to the provision of physical activities for young people that takes into account sex differences and encourages more of what young people do already. Nevertheless, what young people do is a bit of a moving target because of changing fashions and interests of young people.

One explanation to female adolescents participating less in organised sport comes from an Icelandic study by Vilhjalmsson and Kristjandottir (2003) who argue that older female children and female adolescents do not engage in organised sport because of the bias towards masculine perceptions of sport and physical activity in leisure and sport centres. Vilhjalmsson and Kristjandottir (2003) suggest that the majority of senior decision – makers in sport in Iceland are male and that increasing the numbers of women into senior managerial and coaching positions will help to reflect the interests of women. Vilhjalmsson and Kristjandottir (2003) undertook quantitative research with a random sample of 3600 students using questionnaires with a response rate of 90.8 per cent. The respondents were 49.5 per cent female, 38.1 per cent were from working class families and 61.9 per cent from middle class families. This example illustrates how large-scale studies can draw on a wide variety of the population. In Iceland, the sporting organization is mainly private and schools offer physical education classes rather than organised sport. Therefore, sports clubs play a large part in leisure time activities with young people. Although the research takes place in Iceland conceivably, the argument that the organisation of sport clubs contributes to a higher proportion of males taking part than females deserves further investigation. In conclusion, to this part Vilhjalmsson and Kristjandottir (2003) provide an example of critical knowledge in relation to the organisation and planning of organised sport in relation to young women.

To continue with another example of critical knowledge, I intend using Bercovitz (2000) who argues that the health promotion interventions in Canadian Active Living are socially constructed. The first key point is that research into health promotion requires an open approach in order to clarify the value position that underpins the initial definitions of health. Secondly, Bercovitz (2000) is not opposed to interventions concerning physical activity rather the aim is to highlight the constructed nature of current policies. The Canadian Active Living example illustrates the point that health promotion researchers need to justify their definitions about health prior to the research and explain their position in relation to the recommendation of health promotion interventions.

Bercovitz (2000) argues Canadian Active Living represents a shift away from the more elitist sport's programmes to the concept of sport for all that moves towards interventions that generally increase people's participation in physical activity. This shift from elitist sport to sport for all embodies other political arguments. For instance, Bercovitz (2000) argues that during the 1970s and 1980s the Canadian government fostered elite sport because of its association with cultural identity. The furtherance of elite sport combines an emphasis on a scientific approach to sport, meaning an emphasis on individualistic interventions and physiological changes. This engenders a dependency on experts to manage sporting achievement with individuals. If health promoters use individualistic approaches there is low adherence (Hunt et al., 2001). Simultaneously, Bercovitz (2000) argues that the notion of elitist sport excludes groups such as the elderly, the disabled, people living in socially deprived areas and women. In summary, the elite sport approach excludes the majority of the population favouring individualistic methods that do not produce high levels of adherence.

Given the above limitations of the interventions promoted by Sport Canada, an allied organisation Fitness Canada, promoted the benefits of Active Living as an opportunity to engage larger segments of the population including the elderly, ethnic minorities and women. Nevertheless, Burcovitz (2000) suggests that the move towards more inclusive strategies provides a broader base for sport and increases elements for social control. For instance, those in power define what is beneficial concerning physical activity and promoting active living defines how people spend their leisure time.

With the political agenda in mind, Canadian Active Living provides a cost effective method of increasing physical activity levels and shifts the responsibility of health and leisure provision away from Governments to individuals. The distinction between health, social care and leisure becomes blurred in relation to increasing physical activity levels because arguably leisure facilities are only provided for when health and social care needs are met in a population. Arguably, in the sense of a reduction in the Government's role in provision Canadian Active Living represents a cut in the welfare state. In relation to research, Bercovitz's (2000) article is an important critique of approaches to evidence in health promotion and the subsequent action taken in terms of an intervention. For example, media campaigns recommending the use of stairs instead of escalators are part of health interventions that encourage increasing physical activity in people's daily lives as opposed to participation in a sporting activity (Kerr et al., 2001).

In conclusion, the problematisation of inactive populations has received two solutions, first, an individualistic approach to maximise physiological benefits, although this approach has low adherence rates and excludes ethnic minorities, women and the elderly. Secondly, the more inclusive Canadian Active Living is in keeping with cuts in the welfare state whilst simultaneously arguing for higher levels of activity on a daily basis such as using stairs, and briskly walking short distances. Therefore, with Bercovitz's (2000) research in mind my argument is that research into health promotion needs to be taken 'cautiously', meaning there is a critical approach to concepts, definitions, findings and conclusions. Inevitably most health promoters while seeking to utilise evidence-based practice, will also be involved with their own evaluation of programmes and activities.

Evaluation

I plan to illustrate elements of evaluation in relation to sport, physical activity and health promotion by providing an example that informs a bid to Active England (2003) from the Primary Care Trust in Sedgefield district. First,

I will provide a general background as to why health promoters evaluate their work and elements for consideration prior to evaluating health promotion projects.

The demand for value for money in health care requires health practitioners in different locations to evaluate their work. This might be to justify an increase in staff, to secure a source of funding or produce a report to managers on a special initiative. The process of evaluating health promotion projects is an important area to understand as it contributes to evidence based practice: from evaluation comes the ideas and justification for more resource intensive research (Learmonth, 2000a).

There are a range of reasons to evaluate a health promotion intervention including:

- Accounting for the initiative achievements for funders.
- Exploring what worked and what did not work.
- Contributing to a body of knowledge on evaluation.
- Higher quality initiatives to secure future funding.
- Improved project management.
- Future policy development.

(Adapted from Health Canada, 1996)

In addition, Health Canada (1996) suggest evaluators manage three types of activity.

1. Carrying out a health needs assessment, for instance the preliminary investigation before commencing a physical activity programme.
2. Developing an innovative model, for example the introduction of a new physical activity programme into a community.
3. Increasing evaluation skills, such as keeping accurate records that contribute to the processes and activities that constitute a programme.

The following overview includes elements that impact on evaluation such as values, ethics and educational issues. Evaluation is not a value free activity, as the word suggests. Drawing on Øvretveit (1998) there are issues that an evaluator needs to consider such as, first, ethical considerations meaning, a duty to demonstrate that an intervention is worthwhile and as mentioned earlier a duty to demonstrate appropriate use of public funds. Secondly, there are educational issues for health promotion workers that evaluation can highlight such as highlighting areas of future action and disseminating findings. Thirdly, strategic planning elements can improve the initiative and this can help to compete effectively with other priorities. The strategic planning can encourage a clarification of objectives and promote conscious raising and continued action. Arguably, these issues help to develop health. Fourthly, to encourage the allocation of resources evaluation can identify savings in programmes of work.

In many ways, the process of evaluation is a time for reflection. Next, I want to introduce the concept of reflection using Kolb's (1984) learning theory because this I think it illuminates the evaluation process as in Figure 4.1.

In Kolb's (1984) learning theory, there are four elements, a concrete experience, observations, formation of abstract concepts and testing the concepts in new situations. This theory is considered to be a sequential model, that is a person moves from one stage to another. Nevertheless, Cowan (1998) usefully develops Kolb's (1984) concepts describing the learning theory as reflection-for-action. Reflection-for-action describes a process whereby a practitioner looks back on a process and forward to future practice. This is not a smooth analytical journey. Rather, the practitioner needs to be constantly reflecting on a process in order to improve their practice.

The challenge for health promoters is to secure elements of health promotion in contemporary health care services because often health promotion has to compete for funds in health care settings where fund holders value random control trials. In the context of the medical model, random control trials are the 'gold standard' for research and evaluation (Learmonth, 1999). Nevertheless, there are three problems facing health promotion practitioners (Raphael, 2000) if they want to remain close to the principles of a random control trial:

- Problem of a control group.
- Controlling variables.
- Measuring outcomes.

The argument for trying to tackle these problems is that a weakness in health promotion practice is that lack of comparison. A control group is a device to introduce the element of comparison. It is unlikely there will be sufficient resources to find matched pairs and control variables such as social class or

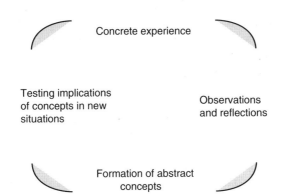

Figure 4.1   Reflection: adapted from Kolb (1984) experiential learning theory

age of participants. Nevertheless, addressing the problem of a control group strengthens the evaluation despite the problems.

According to Øvretveit (1998: 184) there are common problems facing health promoters in evaluation including;

- Fuzzy boundaries (meaning unclear edges to the intervention).
- Wobbly interventions (unclear interventions).
- Ghostly goals (uncertain outcomes).
- Gate-crashing confounding variables (unexpected variables).
- Prior information (information that might bias evaluation).
- Chalk and cheese (not comparing like with like).
- Police car effect (the initiative changes because of the evaluation).
- Distant outcomes (problem of long – term measures).

The quality of the evaluation depends on clear links with the aims and objectives of the initiative. The complex nature of health interventions should not hinder the creativity required to manage successful evaluations. You need to be clear about process or health measurement outcomes and long or short-term outcomes. With this background in mind, I intend to present an example of a health intervention that informs the Active England bid and consider the evaluation issues in the example.

Dzewaltowski et al.'s (2002) evaluation aims to test whether an intervention strategy changes a school environment in relation to pupils' nutrition and participation in physical activity. At this point is should be noted that this is an American study and the meaning of environment in this context is the immediate setting including the school climate, school culture, cost of the intervention and the person's capacity for physical activity. This approach concurs with Estabrooks and Gyurcsik (2003) and Spence and Lee (2003) who acknowledge that concentrating on the individual is unsuccessful. Therefore, the conclusion is a model that incorporates a person's social environment is critical to the success of the intervention.

Dzewaltowski et al.'s (2002) evaluation comprises of eight places that implemented the intervention and eight controls for comparison. The aim of the health intervention is to manage elements of the environment, to develop behaviour change in individuals based on Bandura's (1971) theory of social learning theory and at an organisational level the intervention develops a strategy to improve the process of the implementation of health initiatives in young people's settings. Within the social environment, there are four elements; first, the extent to, which, young people feel they belong and secondly, the level of autonomy or control a young person has in relation to the intervention. Thirdly, skill-building, meaning how much a young person has to learn to develop their skills and finally developing healthy norms within a group. Dzewaltowski et al. (2002) aimed to use time within the classroom, lunchtime and after school as opportunities for implementing the programme. The intervention included setting leaders who were responsible for implementing the intervention in their particular location. Traditionally, this type of intervention concentrates on behaviour and the delivery is a top down approach. By contrast, the mode of delivery in this intervention is de-centralised, meaning there is a community development approach. For example, the setting leader is sensitive to their particular setting and can adapt the programme as required. Again, this is similar to Estabrooks and Gyurcsik (2003) whereby interventions need to be sensitive to local conditions. The evidence for change includes; self-completed questionnaires on physical activity and food intake. There are eight controls so there is an element of comparison.

This next part outlines the distinctive features of the intervention. The setting leaders develop a healthy place in conjunction with other settings leaders. To engender collaboration the setting leaders meet face to face four times a year and there is collaboration between sites through virtual learning facilities including an interactive web site and monthly conference calls. Essentially meetings and web based materials encourages collaboration without creating dependency on experts. Dzewaltowski et al. (2002) encouraged the production of community resources such as the creation of videotapes to show how young people manage their own physical activity and nutrition. The production of the videotape might also encourage elements of autonomy and skill–building. Dzewaltowski et al. (2002) consider the videotapes useful for vicarious learning in other centres in relation to modelling, citing what motivates, what is a driver to engaging in physical activity? What is a barrier? In addition, the videotapes aim to improve a sense of being part of the intervention and creating healthy norms.

In relation to the evaluation, the self-completed questionnaires offer one piece of evidence for change and the control group provide a comparison. Although a control group has shades of being a medical model, I would argue that in the current working environment it is worth considering the option to measure the effect of an intervention by comparing it with a control group.

Conclusion

In relation to the articles, issues on physical activity, the connecting issues are the inclusion of individual, social and environmental determinants in the research and evaluation of interventions. This requires clear definitions of health and health promotion on the part of the health promoter, and an approach that understands the different value positions that may be involved. The different components in research and evaluation include the individual skills that people need to take physical activity and their social environment. Therefore, health promoters need to make use of a range of methods in their research and evaluation. The following is a dialogue between the author and her colleague Alyson Learmonth:

Alyson, in the context of health promotion how do you understand the difference between research and evaluation?

I would like to start my response to this question with three definitions:

1. *'Research is the organised quest for new knowledge' (Last, 1995).*
2. *'Evaluation is the process by which we judge the worth or value of something' (Suchman, 1967).*
3. *'Health promotion is the process of enabling people to increase their control over, and to improve, their health' (WHO, 1986).*

Health promotion has frequently been criticised for the lack of 'rigorous evaluation'. For example, the Health Education Authority used this phrase in writing about the increase of projects designed to promote physical activity through general practice, usually using the exercise prescription model (G. Simmonds in Perkins et al., 1999). Yet in other aspects of General Practice there is not an expectation of rigorous evaluation. There may be clinical audit to ensure that a programme is being implemented in accordance with protocols and to develop action plans if the protocol is not evidence based, or is not being followed appropriately. There may be quality assurance to ascertain the views of users about the treatment or service in question. There may be participation in research, usually as part of multi-centre trials, after ethical approval has been sought and gained. But if 'rigorous evaluation' means making judgements about the effectiveness of the activity in terms of health improvement, that work is carried out away from the practical site of implementation.

I believe the process of evaluation is an important one for health promotion and sports practitioners to engage in, and my experience of gathering 55 evaluations from health promotion specialists in one department 1994–1997 was that this could be utilised to demonstrate useful effects, encourage good practice, prompt questions that generate larger scale research and influence other stakeholders (Learmonth, 2000b). Nonetheless, the task of generating new knowledge requires an interface with independent researchers. For example, this would be essential to tackle the problems of control groups, controlling variables and measuring outcomes that you quote as advocated by Raphael (2000). I think this interface between academic health promotion and the activity in practice is one benefit from writing this chapter.

Nevertheless, there are three other points I would like to make before moving on. One is that there are times when evaluation is not appropriate. Wright suggests the following: you do not have enough time, skills or funding; the work you are doing already has been researched elsewhere; the successes and failures are well documented and the reasons are well understood; the results are likely to be ignored; you do not have the support of your manager/organisation. (Perkins et al., 1999: 396). I would add one more: when the resource invested is too small to justify the time spent on evaluating its impact.

Secondly, the time to start evaluating is at the initial planning stage. In setting appropriate objectives the question 'how will we measure success?' is always critical.

Finally, there are exciting developments in relation to developing methods of realistic evaluation that are designed with complex community interventions in mind (Pawson and Tilley, 1997). The most major example of this applied in the UK to date is the Health Action Zones evaluation which engaged stakeholders in identifying the context/environment and units effect on the proposed change, the mechanism by which change was anticipated to happen, and therefore finally the predicted-outcome measurement. The aim is to increase knowledge about what works for whom in what circumstances. The challenge is to create an analytic stance among practitioners, whilst using their local knowledge and understanding (Bauld and Judge, 1999). This developing methodology may offer exciting opportunities for application in relation to physical activity that clearly engages with so many stakeholders in a complex environment. This also provides a way in which the goal of health promotion, which is to empower people and communities, can be brought in to the core of the evaluation process rather than being seen as a methodological difficulty interfering with the efficacy of the prescribed exercise.

So finally, to reflect on the writing of this chapter I have returned to the original brief, and to the four versions of the action learning problem written at approximately monthly intervals since we began work. My central dialogue has remained constant, how to use my role as Director of Public Health to lead, support and enable work to increase levels of physical activity in the communities of Sedgefield. Around this I have been learning and thinking, with the meetings and the action learning record acting as a prompt to take action and to reflect on what is happening around me. At the same time writing the chapter has stimulated another aspect for me in terms of ways this experience could be made useful and interesting to sports students specialising in health and physical activity.

In this chapter, we have tried to convey the way plans evolve. The development of plans involves drawing on theories and research to inform our next steps, while staying flexible and using the process of action learning to maintain our own motivation and learning as a core part of the process.

References

Active England (2003) Active England Awards http://www.sportengland.org/active_england_main.htm

Bandura, A. (1971) *Social Learning Theory*, Morristown, New Jersey: General Learning Press.

Bauld, L. and Judge, K. (1999) Evaluating policies to tackle inequalities in health: The contribution of health action zones. Paper presented at the European Health Forum Gastein, Austria, October 6–9, www.ukc.ac.uk

Bercovitz, K. L. (2000) A Critical Analysis of Canada's Active Living: Science or politics? *Critical Public Health*, 10, 1, 19–39.

Cowan, J. (1998) *On Becoming an Innovative University Teacher: Reflection in Action.* The Society for Research into Higher Education and Open University Press: Buckingham.

Dzewaltowski, D. A., Estabrooks, P. A. and Johnson, J. A. (2002) Healthy youth places promoting nutrition and physical activity, *Health Education Research*, 17, 5, 541–551.

Estabrooks, P. A. and Gyurcsik, N. C. (2003) Evaluating the impact of behavioural interventions that target physical activity: issues of generalizability and public health, *Psychology of Sport and Exercise*, 4, 41–55.

Health Canada, Population health directorate (1996) guide to project participatory evaluation a participatory approach. http://www.hc-sc.gc.ca/hppb/phdd/resources/guide/visited May 2002

Hunt, K., Ford, G. and Mutrie, N. (2001) Is sport for all? Exercise and physical activity patterns in early and late middle age in the West of Scotland, *Health Education*, 101, 4, 151–158.

Kerr, J., Eves, F. and Carroll, D. (2001) Six-month observational study of prompted stair climbing, *Preventive Medicine*, 33, 5, 422–427.

Kolb, D. A. (1984) *Experiential Learning.* Englewood Cliffs: Prentice Hall.

Last J. M. (1995) *A Dictionary of Epidemiology.* Oxford: Oxford University Press.

Learmonth, A. M. (1999) Evidence-based health promotion: the contribution of qualitative research methods, *International Journal of Health Promotion and Education*, 37, 11–18.

Learmonth, A. M. (2000a) Utilizing research in practice and generating evidence from practice, *Health Education Research*, 15, 6, 743–756.

Learmonth, A. M. (2000b) Evaluating effectiveness in health promotion: A case of re-inventing the millstone? Co-author Phil Mackie *Health Education Journal*, 59, 3, 267–280.

Linstone, H. A. and Turoff, M. Eds. (1975) *The Delphi Method: Techniques and Applications.* Reading MA: Addison-Wesley.

Mulvihill, C., Rivers, K. and Aggleton, P. (2000) Views of young people towards physical activity: determinants and barriers to involvement, *Health Education*, 100, 5, 190–199.

Øvretveit, J. (1998) *Evaluating Health Interventions.* Open University: Milton Keynes.

Park, P. (1993) What is participatory research? A theoretical and methodological perspective in Park, P., Brydon-Miller, M., Hall, B. and Jackson T. (Eds) *Voices of Change: Participatory Research in the United States and Canada.* Toronto: Greenwood Publishing group, 1–20.

Pawson, R. and Tilley N. (1997) *Realistic Evaluation.* London: Sage Publications.

Perkins E. R., Simnett I. and Wright L. (1999) *Evidence-based Health Promotion.* Chichester: Wiley.

Pikora, T., Giles-Corti, B., Bull, F., Jamrozik, K. and Donovan, R. (2003) Developing a framework for assessment of the environmental determinants of walking and cycling, *Social Science and Medicine,* 56, 1693–1703.

Raphael, D. (2000) The question of evidence in health promotion, *Health Promotion International,* 15, 4, 355–367.

Seedhouse, D. (1997) *Health Promotion Philosophy, Prejudice and Practice.* Chichester: Wiley.

Spence, J. C. and Lee, R. E. (2003) Toward a comprehensive model of physical activity, *Psychology of Sport and Exercise*, 4, 7–24.

Suchman, E. A. (1967) *Evaluation Research.* New York: Russell Sage Foundation.

Swain, J. (2000) 'The money's good, the fame's good, the girls are good': the role of the playground football in the construction of young boys' masculinity in a junior school, *British Journal of the Sociology of Education*, 21, 1, 95–109.

The European Heart Network (1999) *Physical Activity and Cardiovascular Disease Prevention in the European Union.* http://www.ehnheart.org/files/physical%20 activity%202-085948A.pdf

Vilhjalmsson, R. and Kristjandottir, G. (2003) Gender differences in physical activity in older children and adolescents: the central role of organized sport, *Social Science and Medicine*, 56, 2, 363–374.

Williams, C. (1999) *Physical Activity and Cardiovascular Disease Prevention in the European Union*, European Heart Network. http://www.ehnheart.org/files/ physical%20activity%202-085948A.pdf

WHO (World Health Organization) (1986) *Ottawa Charter for Health Promotion.* Geneva: WHO.

PART II

HEALTH OF THE INDIVIDUAL

CHAPTER 5

Health Benefits of Physical Activity across the Lifespan

DAVID BLACKWELL

This chapter is written from a biological perspective. It focuses on the benefi-cial effects upon the body that can be produced as a result of physical activity. These effects are viewed in terms of both bodily structure and function and thus the evidence reviewed and reported here is derived from the study of human physiology. The emphasis of this chapter is upon later life and how exercise can benefit the older person. The effect of physical activity upon the ageing process is therefore the primary focus of the chapter. The period after adulthood is however only one phase of the lifespan. All three phases are linked in a chronological sequence. As well as direct benefits from physical; activity within each lifespan stage there are carry over effects from each phase to that which follows. The effects of exercise in childhood and adolescence, when growth and development are taking place, and upon adulthood, when main-tenance of the body and reproductive processes are at their optimum, are also examined. This permits contextualisation of the third phase, old age, when the body's structures, processes and functions are in a period of decline.

Introduction

To live a long and healthy life is surely at the top of everyone's wish list. The hope of living longer is becoming reality for the majority of people in the major developed countries of the world. Life expectancy and age of death have risen steadily and significantly over the last century. Advances in medicine and associated technology, along with developments in health and social care have been responsible for this rise. With this extension of life span, however, has come an increase in the frequency of age-related chronic diseases. Many of these are painful and debilitating and certainly compromise the hope of health and well-being in older age. Although the technological revolution of the last fifty years has allowed people to live longer and experience a much better standard of living during most phases of their lives, with it have come disorders associated with overindulgence and lack of mobility. These have become apparent in all phases of the lifespan. Obesity and its concomitant morbidities such as type-2 diabetes have risen to epidemic proportions in the developed countries and have been identified in children as young as two years of age. There is however a possible alleviator for these problems. It is free, relatively painless, can be fun, and an investment in it will pay back 300 to 400 per cent in terms of adding years to life and life to years. It will produce an immediate effect at any stage of the lifespan and as long as it is continued will produce carry over benefits to the next phase. The alleviator is exercise.

Human ageing: The process and causes

The ageing process is a universal trait that, sooner or later, affects all members of the human species. The changes within the body caused by the process of ageing, which are collectively termed senescence, happen gradually and pro-gressively. These changes are deleterious in nature since they cause a decline in the functional ability of all of the systems that make up the human body. The effects of the changes are summative with the greatest reductions in functional capacity being found in those functions involving a coordinated role of several systems. The changes in functional capacities can be measured using various physiological parameters. Examples can be seen in the respiratory system where Maximal Breathing Capacity is reduced by 60 per cent between 30 and 80 years of age, within the urinary system Glomerular Filtration Rate is reduced by 40 per cent, in the cardiovascular system Cardiac Index decreases 30 per cent and within the nervous system Nerve Conduction Velocity shows a 10 per cent reduction over the same time period (Arking, 1998). Collectively these functional changes are characterised by a reduced ability to maintain homeostasis, a steady internal environment, and an increased vulnerability of the body to challenges by external and internal factors. The ageing process affects the body at all levels from molecular to organ system.

Ageing is intrinsic in nature and is due to a combination of the expression of the genetic information in an individual, resulting in changes at the molecu-lar and cellular levels, along with stochastic changes resulting from the decline in functional capacity. The changes associated with ageing have been explained in evolutionary biological terms by Kirkwood (1994) who posits the idea that the genetic information in humans programmes them to maintain the body using the available energy supplies until reproductive potential has been achieved. After this the energy is not devoted to maintaining the body and so it declines in functional ability and the various forms of damage occur because of this change of upkeep. Kirkwood calls this the Disposable Soma Theory (throw-away body theory) of biological ageing (Kirkwood, 1994). It is has been proven that there is a genetic component to the ageing process and to longevity itself. Studies on accelerated ageing syndromes such as Progeria (Erikson et al., 2003) and Werner's Syndrome (Goto et al., 1992; Yu et al., 1996) have illustrated the involvement of a genetic component and the signs of ageing are shown in these disorders at an early age. Indeed longevity itself has been demonstrated to have a genetic component to it. Work with other animals such as yeast (Egilmez et al., 1989; D'Mello et al., 1994), the nematode worm, Caenorhabditis elegans (Brenner, 1974; Johnson, 1987), and the fruit fly, Drosophila melanogaster (Rose 1984; Arking and Wells, 1990) has shown that maximal lifespan can be increased up to four times using genetic manipulation techniques. Recent studies have demonstrated the involvement of a specific gene, known as Sir2, in the regulation of lifespan of yeast, worms and mice (Brunet et al., 2004). In humans it has been shown that long-lived individuals are most likely to be descended from long-lived ancestors so it is good advice to 'choose your grandparents well'.

Care must be taken to distinguish between the genetic causal factors of the ageing process, also termed intrinsic or programmed ageing, and so called extrinsic ageing brought about by external environmental factors. An illustration of this can be seen in the processes involved in the ageing of human skin. Intrinsic ageing processes affecting the skin at the cellular or tissue level can be seen occurring progressively in the skin in all regions of the body. This causes wrinkling, laxity, dryness and fragility of the skin. The sun protected areas, for example, buttocks or ventral surface of arms, show these age-related changes in the skin of older people. The skin is also subjected to external factors, most notably U-V radiation, that bring about extrinsic or photo-ageing. In sun-exposed regions of the body, for example, face and dorsal surface of forearms, the intrinsic effects are increased or accelerated by U-V exposure. Prolonged exposure to U-V radiation, however, also brings about effects that are different from those caused by intrinsic factors. This can cause chronologically younger sun-exposed skin to have the same appearance as older, in terms of chronological age, sun protected regions.

Age-related disorders

Although ageing is not itself a disease there are a variety of disorders that can be considered as being age-related since they occur more frequently in the older subject than in younger people. The frequency of occurrence of these age-related diseases is also directly related to chronological age of person after 45 years of age. Examples of these age-related disorders are malignant neoplasms (cancers), cardio-vascular disease and autoimmune diseases. Since humans in general are now living to increasingly older age, these age-related disorders, which are often painful and debilitating, are becoming increasingly common within the population.

Mediation of the ageing process by exercise

Even though the process of ageing is inevitable and is subject to genetic control its progress can be mediated in a variety of ways. The rate of progression of the changes associated with ageing can be influenced by a group of external environmental factors which can be attributed to a person's life-style. The lifestyle factors form a complex and are interactive and summative in nature. The complex includes diet, alcohol consumption, tobacco smoking, along with diverse cultural and social factors and very importantly physical activity. The terms physical activity and exercise are sometimes used inter-changeably even though they represent different entities. Physical activity refers to any movement produced by muscular contractions whereas exercise is a specific type of physical activity including planned structured and repetitive bodily movement. The amount of physical activity associated with a person's occupation or leisure time activities lead to people being classified as active or sedentary.

Exercise and the older person

It has been demonstrated that, within the elderly population, regular physical activity can promote and prolong health and well-being. In addition, it can retard the ageing process and even reverse some of the deleterious effects (Svanborg, 1993). The beneficial effects of appropriate exercise can be pro-duced regardless of age. Exercise can positively affect functional ability and help defend against the diseases associated with older age. Physical activity has been shown to aid in the prevention of age-related disorders such as heart disease, diabetes and osteoporosis (McGuire et al., 2001). It is also a key ingredient for losing or maintaining a healthy weight. Exercise, therefore, can play an influential role in improving the chances of living longer and healthier. Higher levels of regular physical activity are associated with lower mortality rates for both older and younger adults. Even those who are moderately active on a regular basis have lower mortality rates than those who are least active. Schnohr et al., (2003) carried out a study on more than 7000 Danish subjects aged between 20 and 79 to determine the effect of regular exercise on the risk of death. They found that regular moderate physical activity lowers death risk. For men there was a 29 per cent and for women a 36 per cent lower risk compared with those reporting low levels of physical activity. The researchers also found that increasing physical activity levels from low to moderate levels produced a lower risk of death. For men in this category there was a 36 per cent reduction and for women a 25 per cent lower risk.

In a survey of over 9000 older adults found that those who were regularly active in their fifties and sixties were about 35 per cent less likely to die in the next eight years than those were sedentary. Those who were identified as having a high heart-disease risk, due to several underlying conditions, showed a reduction of 45 per cent. The health improvement was seen even among those who carried out relatively little physical activity. Individuals who catego-rised their activities as walking, gardening or dancing a few times a week benefited. The improvements were not confined to those who pursued more vigorous activities. Even individuals defined as being obese were found to have a lower risk of death if they were regularly active (Richardson et al., 2004).

Effects of exercise on the ageing cardiovascular system

Regular physical activity has been found to reduce the risk of cardiovascular disease in general and of coronary heart disease mortality in particular. There may also be a link between physical activity and the occurrence of stroke. Regular physical activity across the lifespan aids in the prevention or delay of the development of high blood pressure. In addition it can help in its reduction of hypertension in cases where it already exists. Since high blood pressure and increased blood cholesterol levels are precursors to heart disease exercise can be influential in reducing risk. On average the risk of developing heart disease is reduced by about a third in people who exercise regularly (Patient UK, 2004).

The senescence of the cardiovascular system, along with its potential deterioration, is one area in which exercise intervention can be rewarding. If a regular programme of exercise has been an integral part of someone's life the effects of ageing in the heart and blood vessels are much less pronounced. Even if instituted in later life the programme of exercise can have highly beneficial effects. Age related losses in Aerobic Capacity, a measure of maximum oxygen consumption, have been shown to be retarded when a programme of moderate aerobic exercise has been initiated. Those who have maintained an active athletic life throughout adulthood show the highest overall capacity within their age group. Even in the most physically fit however there is an age-related reduction in this measurement. Improvements in functional measures such as cardiac output, left ventricular contractility, and peripheral blood supply have all been shown to be improved with exercise in older people who maintain exercise levels. Chen et al. (2004) found that resting heart rate could be significantly decreased by the introduction of a regular step based physical activity programme.

The changes in circulation efficiency and blood composition can be felt system wide. Damage to our tissues due to a loss of nutrient supply and inefficient waste disposal removal is greatly reduced when regular exercise is initiated. Conversely there are benefits to the skin, digestive organs, excretory organs and reproductive organs brought about by improvements in the circulatory system as a result of physical activity in later life. It should be noted, however, that lung tissue cannot be affected by respiratory exercise. This is due to the fact that the respiratory membrane is composed of epithelial tissue and contains no muscle layers. Gaseous exchange cannot therefore be enhanced by exercise. The amount of air available for gaseous exchange can be increased by exercise due to the action of the muscular diaphragm and intercostal muscles which are amenable to the effects of increased physical activity. Gaseous exchange also relies on efficient blood supply for the transport of oxygen and carbon dioxide to and from the respiratory membrane and this can be enhanced by exercise.

A medical-social intervention was carried out in a 70-year-old Swedish population (Svanborg, 1993) who found that physical activity could influence the rate and functional consequences of ageing. Some of the most important ageing effects were found to occur in the heart, and blood vessels. Svanborg (1993) found that since the tissues in these organs are extremely resilient they could be strengthened by exercise programmes even if commenced in old age. Boreham et al. (2004) found that cardiovascular fitness could be significantly improved and arterial stiffness significantly reduced by the introduction of a regular programme of physical activity. Shephard (1997) in a review of the evidence reports that regular, moderate physical activity has significant value in the primary and secondary prevention of a number of cardiovascular conditions including ischaemic heart disease, stroke, hypertension and peripheral vascular disease.

Blood composition

Lipid metabolism is enhanced in older adults who exercise due primarily to increases in high density lipoprotein (HDL) the function of which is to transport lipids from peripheral tissues to the liver for storage. Exercise promotes the manufacture of HDL and hence lipid is transported more efficiently and removed from the bloodstream more effectively. Thus there is less likelihood of lipid deposition on the blood vessel walls which is an integral part of the production of atherosclerotic plaques. Atherosclerosis of blood vessels is linked with the development of coronary heart disease, angina, myocardial infarction, peripheral vascular disease, ischemia, intermittent claudication and cerebral vascular accident (stroke). Regular exercise can reduce the serum levels of cholesterol, triglycerides and other molecules associated with cardiovascular disease. Lee et al. (1999) carried out a longitudinal study on 22,000 men aged 30 to 83 over 8 years and found that physical activity was highly beneficial in all aspects of health regardless of whether or not weight was lost.

Researchers at the University of Minnesota carried out a 20 week exercise programme on 675 sedentary people with normal cholesterol levels. Findings were that Total Cholesterol and Low density Lipoprotein levels remained unchanged but HDL was increased by 3 per cent. In another study a group of women undertook a three to 6 months of regular exercise programme. It was found that their Total Cholesterol was reduced by 5 per cent, their LDL by 10 per cent and their HDL was raised by 17 per cent. Another study showed increased HDL levels and lowered Total Cholesterol as a result of a regulated programme of physical activity based on step classes. All of these studies show that good cholesterol can be boosted and bad cholesterol reduced by physical activity programmes.

Effects of physical activity on the ageing skeletomuscular system

There is a normal loss of muscle mass in later adulthood that is at least partly due to decrease in neuronal responses or to a reduction in blood flow. This causes muscle inactivity and wastage. Muscles, however, are amenable to the effects of exercise and the rate of deterioration can be slowed if muscle remains active. Indeed skeletal muscle tissue can maintain or even increase overall strength regardless of age. Ageing adults can benefit as much as younger adults from exercise. One research study showed that 69–74 year old men can gain 22 per cent in strength. Svanborg (1993) reported that physical activity could influence the rate and functional consequences of ageing particularly on bone strength and reduction of fractures of the femur.

Regular physical activity is necessary for maintaining normal muscle strength along with joint structure and function. Physical activity, within the recommended range, is not associated with joint damage or osteoarthritis and has been found to be beneficial for many people with arthritis by helping to relieve pain and stiffness and hence promote greater mobility. Joint swelling and pain caused by arthritis may be control by regular exercise (Hughes et al., 2004; Kettunen and Kujala, 2004). Weight bearing physical activity is essential for normal skeletal development during childhood and adolescence and for achieving and maintaining peak bone mass in young adults. The peak bone mass in premenopausal women has been shown to have a strong influence on the development of osteoporosis in later life. Strength training and other exercise in older adults have been found to preserve the abilities to maintain independent living and reduce the risk of falling. Increase in bone mineral content has been found to increase with moderate exercise particularly if the diet is supplemented with calcium (Beck and Snow, 2003). Age-related joint damage represents a process which is the least amenable to the effects of exercise. Light exercise can keep help with lubrication by synovial fluid and increased blood supply stimulated by exercise can help maintenance of joint structure and aid damage repair. In addition, physical activity has been shown to protect against falling and consequent bone fractures in older adults (Stevens and Olson, 2004; Suzuki et al., 2004; Thornton et al., 2004). Shephard (1997) reviewing the evidence, reports that programmes of moderate physical activity have been used successfully in the prevention and treatment of sarcopenia, osteoporosis, muscular dystrophies and rheumatoid arthritis.

Exercise, weight control and obesity in later life

Low levels of activity, resulting in fewer calories being used than are consumed, is a major contributor to the high prevalence of obesity found currently in the United States and across much of Western Europe and other developed nations. Physical activity can favourably affect body fat distribution since increased levels will cause the fat deposits to be broken down and respired. The redistribution of fat depots in the adipose tissue underlying skin can be influenced by exercise. Physical activity affects the amount and placement of fat and measurements such as abdominal girth and Body Mass Index can be favourably reduced by exercise programmes. Alterations in aspects of physical appearance that are due to fat deposition are completely reversible with exercise. Physical activity is a successful route to weight loss since it increases calorie burn and weight loss results when calorie output exceeds calorie intake. It has been estimated that exercise can increase calorie burn at a rate five or six times greater than at rest. Moreover, active individuals have been found to have slightly higher resting metabolic rates than sedentary individuals. Regular physical activity therefore increases calorie burn both during exercise and at rest (Poehlman, 1989).

Physical activity maintains the Fat Free Mass (FFM), or lean body mass, during dieting. FFM is important for the maintenance of resting metabolic rate. When FFM is lost metabolic rate dips and calorie output decreases. Exercise attenuates but cannot totally prevent loss of FFM when weight loss occurs. Ballor and Poehlman (1995) conducted a meta-analysis to examine the effects of exercise training on preservation of FFM during diet induced weight loss. They found that 24 per cent to 28 per cent of weight loss came from FFM in the non-exercising dieter whilst only 11 per cent to 13 per cent of weight loss came from the FFM in the dieter who engaged in aerobic and resistance exercise. It is therefore important to note that dieting alone is not solution for weight loss and it must be accompanied by appropriate physical activity. Significant reductions in waist girth and BMI have been reported in studies on late middle age women who have taken part in programmes of physical activity (Chen et al., 2004; Sternfeld et al., 2004; He and Baker, 2004).

Exercise, ageing and mental health

Physical activity appears to relieve symptoms of depression and anxiety and to improve mood. It can play a major role in the maintenance of mental health into older life. Regular physical exercise may also reduce the risk of developing depression and the symptoms of anxiety. It can promote the feeling of well-being and self-esteem. Physical activity appears to improve health related quality of life by enhancing psychological well-being and improving physical functioning in persons compromised by poor health.

Byrne and Byrne (1993) found that individuals who exercised regularly were less likely to feel depressed, had a higher self-esteem and a much improved body image when compared with their sedentary counterparts. It has been shown that an hour of aerobics reduces tension anger and fatigue (Kin Isler et al., 2001).

Harada et al. (2004) carried out a research study on individuals who embarked on a programme of regular jogging. They found that they scored consistently higher on intellectual tests than non-exercisers. These improvements, however, quickly disappeared when the joggers stopped training. Researchers have shown that older people embarking on a four month exercise programme showed significant improvement in memory and cognitive function. Weuve et al. (2004) found that any form of physical activity including light exercise such as walking has a significant effect on cognitive function in older adults.

In a recent review of physical activity in the older adult, Taylor et al. (2004) reported that there were significant beneficial effects of increased exercise that affected the cardiovascular and musculoskeletal systems as well as psychosocial aspects of daily living.

Physical activity and age-related disorders

Non-communicable diseases have become a major epidemic in all societies. This has occurred concurrently with modernisation of lifestyle and increasingly widespread adoption of more sedentary lifestyles. The WHO (2003) estimated that lack of activity leads to more than 2 million deaths per year. Physical inactivity is a cause of increasing morbidity and mortality. Regular physical activity is associated with a decreased risk of developing certain forms of cancer. It has been estimated that the chance of developing cancer of the colon is approximately halved if a programme of regular exercise has been followed. Bauman (2004) showed that there is also evidence that breast cancer is less common in women who exercise regularly. Lagerros et al. (2004) have demonstrated a relationship between levels of physical activity in adolescent and young adulthood and development of breast cancer in later life. The researchers found that physically active women have been shown to have a 20–30 per cent reduced risk of developing breast cancer. These findings have also been corroborated by Dorn et al. (2003) who found significantly beneficial effects of exercise on the development of breast cancer in pre- and post-menopausal women. Lee (2003) reported that regular exercise can reduce the risk of colon cancer by 40–50 per cent. Recent studies have also shown beneficial gains of exercise in lessening the risk of prostate (Torti and Matheson, 2004), endometrial (Purdie and Green, 2001) and lung cancer (Mao et al., 2003).

The risk of developing non insulin dependent diabetes mellitus is reduced by regular physical exercise across the lifespan and in addition it helps in the prevention of type-2 diabetes (adult-onset diabetes). Exercise programmes can also be effective in aiding the control of type-2 diabetes with reductions of 50–60 per cent reported by Bauman (2004).

Lees and Booth (2004) refer to all the chronic disorders associated with inactivity throughout life that come to play in older age as Sedentary Death Syndrome (SeDS). They report the beneficial effects of regular physical exercise in combating SeDS and state that many of the symptoms can be significantly prevented or postponed by exercise.

Effects of physical activity levels on overall longevity

Work on laboratory rats by Goodrick (1980) suggests that both mean and maximum life span may be extended by exercise. The study also showed that the values were increased when a regular exercise regime was established early in life. However life extension is of little matter unless quality of life is maintained in the extra years. Paffenbarger (1986) carried out a longitudinal study tracking the health and lifestyles of 17,000 Harvard graduates over twenty years. The conclusions from the study were that for each hour of physical activity undertaken there would be a reward of three of four times as much time in extra lifespan. In 1993 Paffenbarger et al., followed up their research on the same group and reported that those who were sedentary before 1977 but who started participating in regular physical activity had a 23 per cent lower risk of death than men who remained inactive (Paffenbarger et al., 1993). It can be seen that the health maintenance and therapeutic aspects of continuing physical; activity throughout the lifespan can add years to lives and life to years.

Appropriate amount and type of physical activity

Physical activity has been described as a miracle drug (Tanescu et al., 2002) that, if performed regularly, can administer many health benefits. To gain these benefits 30 minutes of moderate exercise on at least five days a week is recommended (US Department of Health and Human Services, 1996). Several short bursts of activity are thought to be equally as good as the half hour per day. Any type of exercise that increases the heart rate and makes the person at least mildly out of breath are appropriate for producing beneficial effects on health and well-being. Brisk walking, jogging, swimming, cycling, dancing have all been identified as suitable activities. The physical activity does not have to be specifically different from normal. Fairly heavy housework, and gardening can make the person out of breath and sweaty and thus are appropriate activities to provide benefits. Higher levels of exercise can be built into the normal routine. A brisk walk to work instead of using the car or bus, getting off the bus one stop before normal and walking, taking the stairs instead of the lift are all appropriate and useful examples. Sedentary people embarking on a physical activity programme should start with short durations of moderate-intensity activity and gradually increase the duration or intensity.

Various studies have demonstrated that walking, a simple form of exercise can substantially reduce the chances of developing heart disease, stroke and diabetes in different populations. Lee (et al., 2001) carried out a study on slow walking for only one hour per week in 40,000 women and found that it halved the risk of heart disease. Weuve et al. (2004) found that cognitive functioning could be improved by walking on a regular basis. Gentle exercise such as Tai Chi has also been found to be effective (Tsang and Hui-Chan, 2004; Wang et al., 2004). It has also been acknowledged that for most people engaging in physical activity of more vigorous intensity or of longer duration can produce greater health benefits. Recent recommendations suggest that cardiovascular endurance activity should be supplemented with strength developing exercises at least twice a week for adults in order to improve musculoskeletal health maintain independence in performing the activities of daily life. The activities of daily life include, transferring, continence, dressing mobility, feeding and washing Svanborg (1993). Increased physical activity has also been shown to benefit the maintenance of balance and to reduce the risk of falling (Thornton et al., 2004; Suzuki et al., 2004).

Risks associated with increasing physical activity

There are risks associated with the engagement in physical activity particularly if the person has previously led a sedentary lifestyle. The most common risks are musculoskeletal injuries such as sprains and more serious injuries to muscles, bones and joints are possible. This is particularly the case with some types of competitive sports. Warming up before vigorous exercise and correct footwear can help reduce some of the risks. Endurance sports such as marathon running can cause stress fractures fat and cessation of menstrual periods in some women.

Rarely there can be much more serious cardiovascular events. Sudden death sometimes occurs in people who are exercising; although this is rare with moderate exercise. It is more likely to occur in the person who does little exercise and then suddenly engages in a sudden bout of vigorous exercise such as an intense game of squash. As long as there is a gradual and progressive build up to regular moderate exercise the potential health gains greatly outweigh the risks involved. It is of the utmost importance that the type of exercise along with the intensity and duration of physical activity should be appropriate to the individual. Notwithstanding this, however, as Melzer et al. (2004) state, the health benefits of physical activity far outweigh the risks involved.

Exercise benefits in childhood and adolescence

The beneficial effects of exercise in adulthood and the later years have been outlined above. Exercise, however, is important at all ages across the life span. From infancy through childhood, adolescence and the various phases of adulthood physical activity can produce beneficial effects. These effects are not only immediate but also produce protective or carry over benefits for subsequent stages of the lifestyle. Regular exercise has been recommended as an important health maintenance strategy for children and adults (Ganley and Sherman, 2000). Benefits cited include the facilitation of weight control, bone strengthening, reduction of cardiovascular risk factors and improvement of mental health. Physical activity can therefore produce an immediate benefit but is also an investment for the future well-being and health of the individual.

Infancy, childhood and adolescence are the phases of the human lifespan in which growth and development are taking place. Physical activity is essential for these processes to take proceed effectively. Rarick (1974) for example suggests that there are a certain minima of muscular activity that are essential for supporting normal growth and maintaining the integrity of the tissues. The skeleton-muscular systems can be properly developed and strengthened by exercise. The fibres in skeletal muscle multiply and function more efficiently with the stimulus of regular exercise. Exercise is essential for the production of healthy bone and peak bone mass, developed by late adolescence, is a strong protective agent for osteoporosis in later life. Cardiac muscle is amenable to the effects of exercise. The ventricular wall can be strengthened with consequent improvement in Stroke Volume and Cardiac Output both of which are measures of heart function. A variety of other parameters such as lung function, fat distribution, stamina, blood composition, blood pressure and mental health can all be positively influenced by physical activity in the formative phases of development. These developments in early life have long term benefits for later phases of the life span.

Exercise, weight control and childhood obesity

Childhood and adolescent obesity has doubled in the last five years and the need for intervention in childhood obesity is clear. Overweight children are at increased risk of many health problem including hypertension, hyperlipidemia, type 2 diabetes, growth hormone deregulation, respiratory problems and orthopaedic problems. Self-esteem and socialisation often suffer leading to bullying, social exclusion, self-harm and even suicide (Must et al., 1992). Continuation of obesity into adulthood is also a high probability with 40 per cent of overweight children and 70 per cent of overweight adolescents become obese adults. Obesity in adolescence is independently associated with chronic diseases that develop in adulthood.

Many cross-sectional studies suggest that obese children and youths are less active than their leaner peers. (Bar-Orr and Baranowski, 1994). There is little evidence, however, that inactivity is a cause of juvenile obesity (Roberts, 1993). Training studies with non-obese adolescents have shown little or no reduction in body adiposity (Wilmore, 1983). Enhanced physical activity with or without a low calorie diet has been shown to reduce percentage body fat or excess body weight in obese children and adolescents (Alpert and Wilmore,

1994). Lower body fat levels have been found in physically active children than their sedentary contemporaries (Madsen et al., 1993). Studies investigating the relationship between levels of physical activity and adiposity in children have shown inconsistent results. This may be due to the complex nature of the relationship particularly at earlier ages. It has been shown, however, that increases in physical activity whilst reducing caloric intake has been shown to be an effective strategy for weight loss.

Effects of exercise on the cardiovascular system in childhood and adolescence

Although cardiovascular disease manifests itself in adulthood, risk factors appear much earlier in life and typically persist. Evidence links lipid and lipoprotein profiles in childhood and adolescence with the development of atherosclerotic lesions and higher than normal blood pressure in young people. These conditions significantly increase the risk of essential hypertension in adulthood and the concomitant risk of developing cardiovascular disease. Some cross sectional studies show slightly higher resting blood pressure among sedentary adolescents compared with their active peers although most studies do not show a difference particular. For children, the evidence that there are beneficial effects of physical activity, particularly at aerobic levels on cardiovascular risk factors is more limited and equivocal. Nevertheless, some well designed studies suggest that aerobic exercise is beneficial in this age-group particularly in individuals at high risk. Children who are active and physically fit demonstrate fewer cadiovascular risk factors than less active children and there are lower rates of coronary heart diseases (Ross and Pate, 1987) in this group.

Research has shown that physically active children have lower blood pressure (Fraser et al., 1983). The introduction of exercise programmes, however, in healthy previously inactive children or adolescents with blood pressure values within the normal range has been shown to induce little or no drop in blood pressure. Indeed decreases of only 1–6 mm Hg, change have been reported. In hypertensive adolescents, however, exercise over several months has been shown to reduce both systolic and diastolic blood pressure. Although the reported reduction is modest, around 10 mm Hg, it has been shown to have beneficial effects on individuals with mild hypertension. Haghratrt et al. (1984) found that a 5 month weight training programme followed by a 6 month aerobic programme reduced the blood pressure values of adolescents with hypertension. Such beneficial effects disappeared within several months if the termination of the programme.

A study by Ewart et al. (1998) found positive effects on blood pressure of 99 adolescent schoolgirls who had systolic and diastolic blood pressures in the top third for their cohort. The girls were randomised to a semester of either aerobic exercise or standard PE classes. Among the 88 who completed the study, systolic BP dropped significantly more in the aerobic exercise group than in the standard PE group (6 mm Hg compared with 3.7 mm Hg) though decreases were modest the decreases were notable taking into consideration that the girls were not hypertensive.

Children and adolescents who are physically active or whose aerobic fitness is high have a more favourable blood lipid profile than their sedentary or less fit peers. The difference is particularly apparent in HDL high density. One trial compared 28 prepubescent children who took part in a 12 week exercise programme (stationary cycling for 30 minutes, three times a week) with 20 controls who did not. It was found that exercise produced significantly favourable improvements in reduction of LDL and increase in HDL cholesterol ratios (Armstong and Simmond Morton, 1994).

Exercise and skeletal health in children and adolescents

Physical activity in childhood and adolescence can produce lasting effects on bone development. Exercise may lower the risk of osteoporosis by increasing bone mineral density (BMD). Although most research in this area has been focused on later years to reduce bone loss, the skeleton appears to be most responsive to the effects of activity during the periods of the lifespan in which growth is taking place, i.e. childhood and adolescence (Welton et al., 1994).

Physically active post-menopausal women and elderly populations in general have a higher bone mineral density (BMD) and less osteoporosis than less active controls. One of the determinants of bone health in old age is the peak BMD reached by young adulthood. Bone mass and BMD subsequently and inevitably decline with the years until the bone become fragile. This has important paediatric relevance since the majority of bone build up occurs during adolescence. Increased physical activity during childhood and adolescence has been shown to result in a higher peak BMD. Cross sectional studies have shown that participants in weight bearing sporting activities have a higher BMD than non-athletes (Bradney et al., 1998). Conversely limbs demobilised for several weeks or months have lower BND. Retrospective studies in which adults were asked about their PA during childhood suggest that women who had been physically active during childhood have a higher BMD in the third and fourth decades of life than women who had been less active as children. Girls are at a greater risk of inactivity than boys particularly during and after puberty (Ganley and Sherman, 2000). Bass et al. (1998) found that pre-pubescent physical activity in females could significantly increase BMD and reduce fractures after the menopause.

The effects of physical activity on mental health in children and adolescents

Active adolescents tend to feel less lonely, shy and hopeless than do their physically inactive peers (Page, 1994). Physical activity has been used as a treatment for hyperactive behaviour by McGimsby and Favell (1988) who showed that increased exercise was an efficient means of reducing rates of aggression and hyperactivity in 80 per cent of mentally retarded subjects. Some studies suggest that the positive effect of exercise is limited and that exercise improves children's physical self-image but not academic or general self-worth (Biddle, 1993) Exercise may improve the ability of young people to cope with stress. A study of 220 adolescent girls (Brown and Lawton, 1986) during a high stress period found that those who adhered to a rigorous exercise programme reported less physical and emotional distress than those who exercised less.

In a study on 500 school children researchers found a strong correlation between levels of physical fitness and academic achievement. Behaviourally they found that fit children made fewer errors than their more sedentary contemporaries (Hillman et al., 2004). It has been shown that children engaged in daily physical activity show better motor activity, academic performance and attitude towards school as compared to their counterparts who do not participate in regular physical activity (Pollatschek and Hagen, 1996). Brink (1995) identifies physical exercise as one of the best ways to stimulate the brain and learning. Exercise has the potential to act positively on both physical and mental health of the patient (Leith and Taylor, 1990). Research investigating the psychological effects of exercise has been carried out by Leith and Taylor (1990) who found a 70 per cent improvement on the psychological constructs under consideration as a result of participation in exercise programmes.

Endorphins are chemicals produced within the body that produce morphine like effects such as euphoria and other behavioural effects. Endorphins may play a positive role in memory and learning (Harrison, 1994). Goldfarb et al. (1987) and Donevan and Andrew (1986) have shown that endorphin levels can be raised as a response to exercise. Since endorphins are heavily involved in the emotion charged body changes that take place during adolescence, increases in their levels resultant from increased physical activity, may have a positive effect on emotional development (Moyers, 1992).

Conclusion

Exercise can have a profound positive effect on health and well-being at all phases of the lifespan. Physical activity is essential for successful ageing. It helps maintain cardiovascular fitness, reduces the risk of morbidity of osteoporosis and morbidity and mortality of other age related disorders and increases the sense of equilibrium. The effects can be direct in improving functional capacity of all systems as well as protecting against a variety of disorders. The carry over effect to the next phase must not be neglected. These seeds therefore need to be sown in childhood carried on through adolescence into adult life. Physical exercise needs to become an intrinsic part of the everyday life to produce maximum benefit. It is a small investment which produced both short and long-term gains which are directly related to the amount of investment. Even if the initial investment is not made it is never too late to start as short-term benefit will always take place, even in later life. For successful ageing, to have along and health life and to promote well-being and self-esteem throughout the lifespan a mixture of healthy eating and appropriate regular exercise is the key.

References

Alpert, B. S. and Wilmore, J. H. (1994) Physical activity and blood pressure in adolescents. *Paediatric Exercise Science*, 6, 361–380.

Arking, R. (1998) *Biology of Aging: Observations and Principles*. Sunderland MA: Sinauer Associates.

Arking, R. and Wells, R. A. (1990) Genetic alterations of normal aging processes is responsible for extended longevity in Drosophila, *Developmental Genetics*, 11, 141–148.

Ballor, D. L. and Poehlman, E. T. (1995) A meta-analysis of the effects of exercise on resting metabolic rate, *European Journal of Applied Physiology*, 71(6), 535–542.

Bar-Orr, O. and Baranowski, T. (1994) Physical activity, adiposity, and obesity among adolescents, *Pediatric Exercise Science*, 6, 348–360.

Bass, S., Pearce, G. and Bradney, M. (1998) Exercise before puberty may confer residual benefits in bone density in adulthood: studies in active prepubescent and retired female gymnasts, *Journal of Bone Mineral Research*, 13(3), 500–507.

Bauman, A. E. (2004) Updating the evidence that physical activity is good for health: an epidemiological review 2000–2003. *Journal of Science, Medicine and Sport*, 7(1), 6–19.

Beck, B. R. and Snow, C. M. (2003) Bone health across the lifespan: exercising our options. *Exercise Sport Science Review*, 31(3), 117–122.

Biddle, S. (1993) Children, exercise and mental health, *International Journal of Sports Psychology*, 24, 200–216.

Bradney, M., Pearce, G., Naughton, G., Sullivan, C., Bass, S., Beck, T., Carlson, J. and Seeman, E. (1998) Moderate exercise during growth in prepubertal boys: changes in bone mass, size, volumetric density, *Journal of Bone and Mineral Research*, December, 13, 1814.

Brenner, S. (1974) The genetics of Caenorhabditis elegans, *Genetics*, 77, 71–94.

Brink, S. (1995) *Smart Moves*. U.S. News and World Report. Online Database, 5, 15.

Brown, J. D. and Lawton, M. (1986) Stress and well-being in adolescence: the moderating role of physical exercise, *Journal of Human Stress*, 12(3), 125–131.

Brunet, A., Sweeney, L. B., Sturgill, J. F., Chua, K. F., Greer, P. C., Lin, Y., Tran, H., Ross, S. E., Mostoslavsky, R., Cohen, H. Y., Hu, L. S., Cheng, H. L., Jedrychowski, M. P., Gygi, S. P., Sinclair, D. A., Alt, F. W. and Greenberg, M. E.

(2004) Stress dependent regulation of FOXO transcription factor by SIR1 deacetylase, *Science*, 26, 303(5666), 2011–2015.

Byrne, A. and Byrne, D. G. (1993) The effect of exercise on depression anxiety and other mood states: a review, *Journal of Psychsomatic Research*, 37(6), 565–574.

Chen, C. B., Ryan, D. A. and Tudor-Locke, C. (2004) Health benefits of a pedometer-based physical activity intervention in sedentary workers, *Preventive Medicine*, 39(6), 1215–1222.

Donevan, R. H. and Andrew, G. M. (1986) Plasma B-endorphin immunoreactivity during graded cycle ergometry, *Medicine and Science in Sports and Exercise*, 19, 3.

Egilmez, N. K., Chen, J. B. and Jazwinski, S. M. (1989) Specific alterations in transcript prevalence during the yeast life span, *Journal of Biological Chemistry*, 264, 14312–14317.

Eriksson, M., Brown, W. T., Gordon, L. B., Glynn, M. W., Singer, J., Scott, L., Erdos, M. R., Robbins, C. M., Moses, T. Y., Berglund, P., Dutra, A., Pak, E., Durkin, S., Csoka, A. B., Boehnke, M., Glover, T. W. and Collins, F. S. (2003) Recurrent de novo point mutations in lamin: A cause Hutchinson-Gilford progeria syndrome, *Nature*, 423, 293.

Ewart, C. K., Young, D. R. and Hagberg, J. M. (1998) Effects of school-based aerobic exercise on blood pressure in adolescent girls at risk of hypertension, *American Journal Public Health*, 88(6), 949–951.

Fraser et al. (1983) Physical fitness and blood pressure in school children, *Journal of the American Heart Association*, 67, 405–412.

Ganley, T. and Sherman, C. (2000) Exercise and children's health: a little counselling can pay lasting dividends, *Physical Sports Medicine*, 28(2), 2002–2008.

Goldfarb, A. H., Bradley, D., Hatfield, S. G. A. and Flynn, M. G. (1987) Serum B-endorphin levels during a graded exercise test to exhaustion, *Medicine and Science in Sports and Exercise*, 19, 2.

Goodrick, C. L. (1980) Effects of long-term voluntary wheel exercise on male and female Water rats, *Gerontology*, 26, 22–23.

Goto, M., Rubenstein, M., Weber, J., Woods, K., Drayna, D. (1992) Genetic linkage of Werner's syndrome to five markers on chromosome 8, *Nature*, 355, 735–738.

Harada, T., Okagawa, S. and Kubota, K. (2004) Jogging improved performance of a behavioral branching task: implications for prefrontal activation, *Neuroscience Research*, Jul, 49(3), 325–37.

Harrison, S. (1994) *Principles of Internal Medicine*, 13th ed. St. Louis Mo: Mcgraw Hill.

He, X. Z. and Baker, D. W. (2004) Body mass index, physical activity, and the risk of decline in overall health and physical functioning in late middle age. *American Journal of Public Health*, 94(9), 1567–1573.

Hillman, C. H., Castelli, D. M. and Buck, S. M. (2005) Aerobic fitness and neuro-cognitive function in health preadolescent children, *Medicine and Science in Sports and Exercise*, November, 37, 11.

Hughes, S. L., Seymour, R. B., Campbell, R., Pollak, N., Huber, G. and Sharma, L. (2004) Impact of the fit and strong intervention on older adults with osteoarthritis, *Gerontologist*, 44(2), 217–228.

Johnson, T. E. (1987) Aging can be genetically dissected into component processes using long lived lines of Caenorhabditis elegans, *Proceedings of National Academy of Sciences of the United States of America*, 79, 6603–6607.

Kettunen, J. A. and Kujala, U. M. (2004) Exercise therapy for people with rheumatoid arthritis and osteoarthritis, *Scandanavian Journal of Medical Sports Science*, 14(3), 138–142.

Kin Isler, A., Kosar, S. N. and Korkusuz, F. (2001) Step aerobics may raise 'good cholesterol' level, *Journal of Sports Medicine and Physical Fitness*, 41, 539–545.

Kirkwood, T. (1994) The biological basis of ageing, *Medical Research Council News*, 3, 14–18.

Lagerros, Y. T., Hseish, S. F. and Hseish, C. C. (2004) Physical activity in adolescence and young adulthood and breast cancer risk: a quantitative review, *European Journal of Cancer Prevention*, 13(1), 5–12.

Lee, C. D., Blair, S. N. and Jackson, A. S. (1999) Cardiresiratory fitness, body composition and all-cause and cardiovascular disease mortality in men, *American Journal of Clinical Nutrition*, 69(3), 372–380.

Lee, I. M. (2003) Physical activity and cancer prevention: data from epidemiologic studies, *Medical Science Sports Exercise*, 35(11), 823–827.

Lee, I. M., Rexrode, K. M., Cook, N. R., Manson, J. E. and Buring, J. E. (2001) Physical activity and coronary heart disease in women: is 'no pain, no gain' passé?, *Journal of American Medical Association*, 285, 1447–1454.

Leith, L. M. and Taylor, A. H. (1990) Psychological aspects of exercise: A decade literature review, *Journal of Sport Behavior*, 13, 219–239.

D'Mallo, N. P., Childress, A. M., Franklin, D. S., Kale, S. P., Pinswadi, C. and Jazwinski, S. M. (1994) Cloning and characterisation of LAG1, a longevity assurance gene in yeast, *Journal of Biological Chemistry*, 269, 15451–15459.

Madsen, J., Sallis, J. F., Rupp, J. W., Senn, T. L. (1993) Relationship between self-monitoring of diet and exercise change and subsequent risk factor changes. *Patient Education and Counselling in a Changing Era of Health Care*. Jun, 21(1–2), 61–69.

Mao, Y., Pan, S., Wen, S. W. and Johnson, K. C. (2003) Physical activity and the risk of lung cancer in Canada, *American Journal of Epidemiology*, 158, 564–575.

McGimsey, J. F. and Favell, J. E. (1988) The effects of increased physical exercise on disruptive behaviour in retarded persons, *Journal of Autism and Developmental Disorders*, 18(2), June.

McGuire, D. K., Levine, B. D. and Williamson, J. W. (2001) A 30 year follow-up of the Dallas bed rest and training study: effect of age on the cardiovascular response to exercise, *Circulation*, 104, 1350–1358.

Moyers, B. (1992) *Healing and the Mind*. New York: Doubleday.

Must, A., Jacques, P. F. and Dallal, G. E. (1992) Long-term morbidity and mortality of overweight adolescents; a follow up of the Harvard growth study, *New England Journal of Medicine*, 327(19), 1350–1355.

Paffenbarger, R. S. (1986) Physical activity, other life-style patterns, cardiovascular disease and longevity, *Acta Medica Scandinavica Supplement*, 711, 85–91.

Paffenbarger, R. S., Blair, S. N., Lee, I. M., and Hyde, R. T. (1993) Measurement of physical activity to assess health effects in free-living populations, *Medical Science Sports Exercise*, Jan, 25(1), 60–70.

Page, R. and Tucker, L. (1994) Psycholosocial discomfort and exercise frequency: An epidemiological study of adolescents, *Adolescence*, 29.

Pate, R. R. and Ross, J. G. (1987) Factors associated with health-related fitness. The National Children and Youth Fitness Study II, *The Journal of Physical Education, Recreation and Dance*, 58, 93–95.

Patient, UK (2004) *Preventing Heart Disease and Stroke*. London: EMIS and Patient Information Publications.

Poehlman, E. T. (1989) A review: exercise and its influence on resting metabolism in man, *Medical Science Sports Exercise*, 21(5), 515–525.

Pollatschek, J. and Hagen, F. (1996) Smarter, healthier, happier, *International Health, Racquet, and Sportsclub Association Booklet*, Boston, Mass.

Pratt, M., Macera, C. A. and Wang, G. (2000) Higher direct costs associated with physical inactivity, *Physiological Sports Medicine*, 28, 63–70.

Purdie, D. M. and Green, A. C. (2001) Epidemiology of endometrial cancer, *Best Practice Research Clinical Obstetrics Gynaecology*, 15, 341–354.

Rarick, G. L. (1974) Exercise and growth in Johnson, W. R. and Busrick, E. R. (Eds.) *Science and Medicine of Exercise and Sport*. New York: Harper and Rowe, 306–321.

Richardson, C. R., Kriska, A. M., Lantz, P. M. and Hayward, R. A. (2004) Physical activity and mortality across cardiovascular disease risk groups, *Medicine and Science in Sports and Exercise*, 36(11), 1923–1929.

Roberts, S. B. (1993) Energy expenditure and the developments of early obesity, *Annals of the New York Academy of Medicine*, 699, 18–25.

Rose, M. R. (1984) Laboratory evolution of postpones senescence in drosophila melanogaster, *Evolution*, 38, 1004–1010.

Schnohr, P., Scharling, H. and Jenson, J. S. (2003) Changes in leisure-time physical activity and risk of death: an observational study of 7,000 men and women, *American Journal of Epidemiology*, 158, 639–644.

Shepherd, R. J. (1997) Aging, physical activity and health, *Human Kinetics* Champaign IL.

Sternfeld, B., Wang, H., Quesenberry, C. P. Jr, Abrams, B., Everson-Rose, S. A., Greendale, G. A., Matthews, K. A., Torrens, J. I. and Sowers, M. (2004) Physical activity and changes in weight circumference in midlife women: Findings from the Study of women's Health across the Nation, *American Journal of Epidemiology*, 160(9), 912–922.

Stevens, J. A. and Olson, S. (2004) Reducing falls and resulting hip fractures among older women. *Morbidy and Mortality Weekly Report Recommendations and Reports*, 31(49), 3–12.

Suzuki, T., Kim, H., Yoshida, H. and Ishizaki, T. (2004) Randomized controlled trial of exercise intervention for the prevention of falls in community-dwelling elderly Japanese women. *Journal of Bone and Mineral Metabolism*, 22(6), 912–922.

SvanBorg, A. (1993) A medical-social intervention in a 70-year-old Swedish population: Is it possible to postpone functional decline in ageing, *Journal of Gerontology*, 48, 84.

Tanescu, M., Leitzmann, M. F., Rimm, E. B., Willett, W. C., Stampfer, M. J. and Hu, F. B. (2002) Exercise type and intensity in relation to coronary heart disease in men, *Journal of American Medical Association*, 288.

Taylor, A. H., Cable, N. T., Faulkner, G., Hillsdon, M., Narici, M. and Van Der Bij, A. K. (2004) Physical activity and older adults: a review of health benefits and the effectiveness of interventions, *Journal of Sports Science*, 22(8), 703–725.

Thoren, P., Floras, J. S., Hoffman, P. and Seals, D. R., (1990) Endorphins and exercise: physiological mechanisms and clinical implications, *Medical Science Sports Exercise*, 22(4), 417–428.

Thornton, E. W., Sykes, K. S. and Tang, W. K. (2004) Health benefits of Tai Chi exercise: improved balance and blood pressure in middle aged women, *Health Promotion International*, 19(1), 33–38.

Torti, D. C. and Matheson, G. O. (2004) Exercise and prostrate cancer, *Sports Medicine*, 34(6), 363–369.

Tsang, W. W. and Hui-Chan, C. W. (2004) Effect of a 4–8-week intensive Tsai Chi training on balance control in the elderly, *Medical Science Sports Exercise*, 36(4), 648–657.

US Department of Health and Human Services (1996) *Physical Activity and Health: A Report of the Surgeon General*, Atlanta: DHSS, Center for Disease Control and Prevention, National Center for Chronic Disease Prevention and Health Promotion.

Wang, Y. T., Taylor, L., Pearl, M. and Chang, L. S. (2004) Effects of Tai Chi exercise on physical and mental health of college students, *American Journal of Chinese Medicine*, 32(3), 453–459.

Welton, D. C., Kemper, H. C. and Post, G. B. (1994) Weight bearing activity during youth is a more important factor for peak bone mass than calcium intake, *Journal of Bone Mineral Research*, 9(7), 1089–1096.

Weuve, J., Kang, J. H., Manson, J. E., Breteler, M. M., Ware, J. H. and Grodstein, F. (2004) Physical activity, including walking, and cognitive function in older women, *Journal of American Medical Association*, 292(12), 1454–1461.

Wilmore, J. H., Keogh, J. F. (Eds.) (1983) *Exercise and Sport Science Reviews* in Finch, C. E., Hayflick, E., Schneider, L. and Rowe, J. W. (1991) *Handbook of the Biology of Ageing*. California: Academic Press.

World Health Organization (2004) *Global Strategy on Diet, Physical Activity and Health*. Geneva: WHO.

Yu, C. E. J., Oshima, Y. H., Fu, E. M., Wijsman, F., Hisama, R., Matthews, S., Nakura, J., Miki, T., Ouais, S., Martin, G. M., N. A. D. and Schellenberg, G. D. (1996) Positional cloning of the Werner's syndrome gene, *Science*, 272, 258–262.

CHAPTER 6

Drug Use in Sport

ALISON MCINNES, RALPH HERON AND MARK HARRISON

Introduction

The content of this chapter will address the use of ergogenic aids, in particular performance enhancing drugs (i.e. anabolic/androgenic steroids) and performance continuation drugs (i.e. narcotic analgesics). Doping classes and methods (International Olympic Committee, 1999) will, therefore, be defined. The constraints to health promotion that these drugs present will be the main focus of this chapter. The health promotion constraints to the individual may include, for example, social harm or the deterioration of interpersonal relationships with family and friends. The constraints to the community may include, for instance, community harm including the transmission of blood born viruses, i.e. HIV and Hepatitis, etc. These constraints are often reduced by harm minimisation strategies. Harm minimisation can be defined as a strategy to reduce the harm caused by drugs, to its lowest level to maximise health (Petersen and McBride, 2002). Therefore, the management of these drugs by bodybuilders and others, and the identification of side effects and other detrimental effects on health when taken above the therapeutic dose, will be examined. Harm minimisation will be discussed in detail, and reference to individual case studies from a dynamic and innovative Drugs in Sport Clinic and User's Support (DISCUS) in the North East of England will be focused upon. The clinic/service was established in 1994, as a response to the expressed needs of performance enhancing drug users and offers harm minimisation interventions.

Definitions

Ergogenic aids have been defined as 'agents which are used in an attempt to increase the capacity to work' (Mottram, 1996: 26). Ergogenic aids can include performance enhancing drugs (PEDS), which can be defined as the 'deliberate, illegitimate use of drugs in an attempt to gain an unfair advantage over fellow competitors' (Verroken, 1996: 44). The use of performance continuation drugs '*enables the athlete to continue to train and even compete during the period of recovery from injury*' (Verroken, 1996: 41). Related to these terms, the International Olympic Committee (IOC) defines doping as:

> the use of an expedient (substance or method) which is potentially harmful to athletes' health and capable of enhancing their performance, or the presence in the athlete's body of a prohibited substance or evidence of the use of a prohibited method. (IOC, 1999: 1).

History

Doping in sport and the use of PEDS is not a new phenomenon. It can be argued that throughout history, athletes have sought a magic potion to give them a sporting edge (Verroken, 1996). Galen in Ancient Greece in the third century BC, reported athletes using stimulants to enhance their performance (Waddington, 2000). In Egyptian times, it was alleged that pharaohs boiled the hind hooves of an ass to give them a sporting edge. In the late nineteenth century, doping was widely associated with cycling (Houlihan, 1999). It can be argued, however, that doping drug scandals in athletics have only provoked condemnation and stigmatisation (via the media) since the Cold War era. During this time Eastern European countries initiated national doping programmes for their athletes, including the use of anabolic/androgenic steroids (ASS) (Crace, 2003). Another seminal point involved a cyclist dying after alleged amphetamine use during the 1960 Rome Olympic Games (Wilson and Derse, 2001).

Anti-doping and testing

Following on from this, anti-doping policy and testing of athletes was introduced in the 1960s. In 1967, the IOC decided upon a definition of doping and developed a list of doping classes and methods, which have gradually evolved and grown. In 1999, the World Anti-Doping Agency (WADA) was established to harmonise the way individual sport organisations, as well as nations approach anti-doping. In the UK, the responsibility of doping falls to the Ethics and Anti-Doping Unit of UK Sport (BMA, 2002). The unit tests approximately 5,000 sportsmen and women, each year (O'Leary, 2001). Amateur sports are also covered by the same rules as professional sports (BMA, 2002). The banned substances list is often deemed confusing as the use of certain cough and cold remedies can also appear on the list. The processes involved in anti-doping are prohibitive and aim to punish the athlete. After the 1998 Tour De France, Williams wrote that doping is 'generally felt to be the worst of sporting crimes' (Williams, 1998: 50).

Officials would argue, however, that drugs in sport are banned in the belief that they are harmful to health and that drug taking undermines the values of fair play and the concept of a level playing field (BMA, 2002). On the other hand, it can be argued that elite level sport itself can be injurious to health and that athletes may only use drugs to continue to compete and not just win. This issue is further complicated, in that athletes may use other performance enhancing techniques, which although not banned, may put an athlete's health at risk. These can include the process of carbohydrate loading, which can result in hypoglycaemia, nausea, fatigue and dizziness (Vernacchia, 1990).

It can be argued that a '*medicalisation of sport*' (Waddington, 2000: 121) and the '*pharmacological revolution*' (Verroken, 1996: 19), which developed ideologies justifying increasing medical intervention have taken place. Donohoe and Johnson (1986: 126–7) highlight the relation between illicit drug use and processes of medicalisation,

> We live in a drug-oriented society. Drugs are used to soothe pain, relieve anxiety, help us to sleep, keep us awake, lose or gain weight. For many problems, people rely on drugs rather than seeking alternative coping strategies. It is not surprising that athletes should adopt similar attitudes.
> (Donohoe and Johnson, 1986: 126–7)

The testing procedure itself involves the athlete selecting a sealed jar for the sample. In full view of the doping control officer (DCO) they must expose their midriff and provide a sample. The athlete then chooses, checks and opens a sealed doping kit containing two bottles, marked A and B. The sample is then divided between the two bottles, which are then sealed, placed in a secure bag and sent to a laboratory. The athlete is then asked to declare all supplements and medicines used in the last week, which are documented and then checked and signed by the athlete. If a banned substance is found in sample A, then sample B can be tested at the request of the athlete (Crace, 2003).

All national governing bodies provide a system of appeals and hearings. Nevertheless, the penalties given to sportsmen and women need to be consistent. Recently in Premier League football, Rio Ferdinand of Manchester United was given an 8 month ban for failing to turn up for a doping test. This contrasted sharply with Christian Negouai of Manchester City who only 8 months earlier, missed a drugs test appointment and was fined £2,000 and given no suspension. Moreover, Edgar Davids and Jaap Stam were only banned for 5 months for failing tests for the banned substance Nandrolone. However, Dick Pound (the World Anti-Doping Agency Chairman), claimed Ferdinand's sentence was lenient, compared to most other sports in which he would have been awarded an automatic 2 year ban.

Harm reduction/minimisation

In contrast to the punitive stance of anti-doping, Coomber (1997: 16) suggests that there are 'many lessons to be learned about drugs, drug users and methods of control from the non-sporting world' particularly in relation to harm reduction/minimisation. Harm reduction has been defined as 'trying to reduce the harm that people do to themselves or other people, from their drug use' (www.drugscope.org.uk). Nevertheless, harm reduction/minimisation and anti-doping programmes appear to be worlds apart, complicated by policy ambiguities among the sporting organisations themselves (Houlihan, 1999).

There is also a considerable unmet demand for harm minimisation and medical support at the level below elite sport, i.e. amateur bodybuilding (referred to later in this chapter). Indeed,

> Drug misusers have the same entitlement as other patients to the services provided by the National Health Service. It is the responsibility of all doctors to provide care for both the general health needs and drug related problems, whether or not the patient is ready to withdraw from drugs.
> (DoH, 1999: 1)

Health promotion for performance enhancing drug users

Harm reduction strategies were legitimised and strengthened in the mid 1980s, following a report published by the Advisory Council on the Misuse of Drugs (ACMD). The report identified the threat of HIV amongst the general population. 'HIV is a greater threat to public health than drug misuse' (ACMD, 1988: 1). This led to a proliferation of services targeting injecting drug users, with the provision of sterile injecting equipment and harm reduction/minimisation advice.

The DISCUS service was established in 1994, in response to the increased numbers of Performance Enhancing Drug (PEDS) users attending needle exchange outlets, who did not feel able to approach/utilise 'traditional' substance misuse services. They also felt unable to approach general practice to address concerns associated with their drug use. DISCUS offers a specific service aimed at PED users and focuses on the reduction of harm associated with their drugs of choice. In order to deliver these services a specialist team was established, which consists of a Clinical Co-ordinator, Responsible Medical Officer (RMO), Sports Dietician, Women's Worker and Drugs Worker. The services offered include:

- Instruction/promotion of harm minimisation techniques.
- Needle exchange facilities.
- Medical assessment.
- Nursing assessment of drug use and risk behaviour.
- Dietetic assessment, review and goal planning.
- Bodyfat analysis.

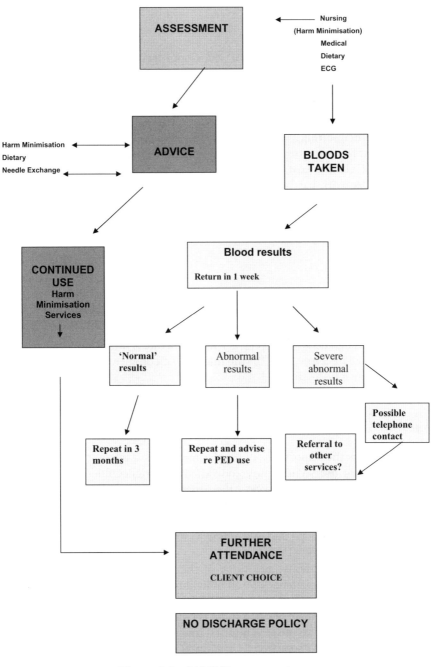

Figure 6.1 DISCUS – care pathway

- Full range of blood tests.
- ECG.
- Hepatitis B vaccination.
- Signposting and onward referral where appropriate.

The DISCUS service operates weekly for a 2-hour period on a 'drop in' basis and has provided treatment to over 600 individuals with an average attendance of 10 individuals per week. The service is delivered in an informal and confidential setting, which is valued by service users and is highlighted as an important factor in attracting and retaining individuals in treatment (Heron, 2003). DISCUS is one of only a few specific services, nationally, for this client group and its work has been identified as a model of good practice (BMA, 2002; Waddington, 2000). See Figure 6.1 for the care pathway that a service user at DISCUS is offered.

Case studies

The following three case studies provide an example of some of the physical, psychological, social and legal implications associated with the use of PEDS. The way PEDS are generally used is in 'cycles', where an 'on cycle' means someone is using and an 'off cycle' is when someone is not using, or maintaining themselves on a low dose. In the interests of confidentiality, the names of individuals have been changed.

Case study 1

This highlights the importance of regular medical and nursing reviews during periods of drug use. Whilst most individuals experience fluctuations in liver functioning during an 'on cycle', there have been on occasions, instances where Liver Function Test (LFT) results have been elevated enough, to cause concern to the RMO. Elevated LFT results in individuals using PEDS, have been previously identified and recognised as an adverse effect of using anabolic steroids (Hickson et al., 1989).

This case study demonstrates some of the physical implications that have been observed and experienced by an individual attending the DISCUS clinic. Alan's attendance at the clinic was sporadic and generally dependent upon levels of use, consumption of new products/substances and his level of concern about the effect upon his physical health status. He was extremely well informed about his drug use and appeared to have an 'if high doses are good, then more is better' attitude to his substance use. Alan's training and drug taking schedule was designed to give him the best chance of success within his chosen sport. This resulted in him, generally being the first to experiment with new products and combinations of drugs. These could be 'stacked' together to achieve optimal results in relation to increased strength and muscle mass. Alan presented to the clinic with concerns relating to his physical health status and described feeling generally '*run down*' and fatigued. He also claimed to have experienced a reduction in performance and ability to train at his usual level was proving to be problematic.

Upon assessment Alan did in fact, appear generally run down and blood samples were taken and investigations requested to determine the potential underlying causes. Prior to identification of increased LFTs, Alan had increased his levels of drug use and on presentation described his use as follows:

- Dianabol (Anabolic androgenic steroid) 4 × 20 mg orally daily
- Tamoxifen (Hormone antagonist) 20 mg daily
- Human Growth Hormone (Growth Hormone) 4 i.u twice a day
- Anavar (Anabolic androgenic steroid) 9 × 25 mg daily
- Proviron (Anabolic androgenic steroid) 8 × 2.5 mg orally
- Halotestin (Anabolic androgenic steroid) 4 × 2.5 mg orally
- Orimetin (Anabolic androgenic steroid) 2 × 250 mg daily for 4 days
- Primabolan (Anabolic androgenic steroid) 3 × 50 mg orally daily

As identified in Table 6.1, in Week 1, the clinic received the abnormal LFT results. Tests for Hepatitis were also requested at week 1 (after the abnormal LFT results were identified), to rule out viral infection and/or damage. Nevertheless, these tests proved negative for all previous or current Hepatitis infection, although a previous Hepatitis B vaccination was identified.

Alan was given the immediate advice to discontinue his use of PEDS, to avoid other substances that would place additional stress on the liver (i.e. alcohol) and to attend on a weekly basis for review. This would enable staff to monitor his LFT results. The following 6 weeks showed an immediate improvement to the LFT results, once the PEDS had been discontinued. Nevertheless, in week 8 his LFT results showed a further increase, following his decision to restart (at a much reduced level), his use of PEDS. Alan continues to attend the clinic on a regular basis, particularly when he is 'on

Table 6.1 Weekly Liver Function Test results

Results Normal Values	AST (u/L) 2–40	ALT (u/L) 2–40	GGT (u/L) 11–50
Week 1	260	852	52
Week 2	287	476	77
Week 3	137	165	51
Week 4	108	70	33
Week 5	85	53	27
Week 6	84	46	19
Week 7	35	27	21
Week 8	62	59	30

'cycle', to ensure his LFT results remain as close as possible to his 'normal range'.

This case study clearly demonstrates the direct link between the levels of PED use and their effect on LFT results. Nonetheless, the clinic believes that for Alan, harm minimisation interventions such as regular screening and attendance, were instrumental in identifying these difficulties. This enabled action to be taken immediately, resulting in a rapid improvement in his health and a reduction in the level of risk associated with continued drug use. Generally, within DISCUS there appears to be an increase in LFT results whilst service users are 'on cycle' and an improvement when 'off cycle'.

Case study 2

This second case study demonstrates some of the psychological and social implications that have been observed and experienced by an individual attending the DISCUS clinic. Frank was a regular attendee at the clinic and appeared to be well informed about his drug use and the risks associated. He was using PEDS; however, in contrast to Alan, trained for aesthetic reasons and not for success in amateur sport. He would organise his on/off cycles to coincide with his visits to the clinic. He, could therefore, monitor his LFTs to reduce the risks to his health and generally described himself as a very easy going '*laid back*' person. He had been living with his current partner for over two years and described his relationship as '*very good*'.

Frank was clear about how many PEDS to use during his cycles and trained almost on a daily basis. He described using no other drugs or alcohol whilst 'on cycle'. Nevertheless, Frank attended the clinic at one point following a holiday in Europe and described an extremely traumatic event (involving his partner) that had occurred whilst on holiday. He had planned to weight train most days whilst he was on holiday but did not want to carry his PEDS through Customs.

He decided that whilst on holiday the best thing for him to do, to enable him to train better and harder, was to take the same amount of PEDS he would normally take over a 2 week period. He took these PEDS before he went on holiday in one large dose. Within two days of arriving at his destination he had experienced an episode of paranoid ideation, which led to a prolonged, aggressive outburst. During this time he repeatedly demonstrated paranoid thoughts which led to him subjecting his partner to intense questioning in relation to a past relationship. Throughout the remainder of the holiday, Frank continued to question his partner until she gave him the information he requested. This resulted in him attacking her and causing extensive injuries.

Upon his return, he claimed that his behaviour had been '*totally out of character*' and that he had never done anything like this before. The social consequences of his action had resulted, however, in the break up of his relationship. He believed that his aggressive and paranoid behaviour had been as a direct result of his '*overdose*' of testosterone.

Case study 3

This last case study looks at some of the legal implications of the current status of anabolic steroids as defined within the Misuse of Drugs Act (The Advisory Council for the Misuse of Drugs, 1971).

Legal status

Anabolic steroids are Prescription Only Drugs under the Medicines Act (1968). They were reclassified as Class C drugs in 1997, under the Misuse of Drugs Act (1971). It is not an offence to possess them for personal use. Nonetheless, it is an offence to supply anabolic steroids (Cohen, 2002). With the changes in the law some users were concerned that they could be classed as suppliers, if they were caught with large amounts of steroids in their possession.

In some European countries anabolic steroids are available over the counter (OTC) in pharmacies. This has attracted PED users from the DISCUS clinic to travel regularly to Europe for holidays to acquire enough supplies to last for 4–5 months. Nevertheless, in order to ensure that they are not identified as suppliers of anabolic steroids, some users carry a plan of their training schedule and the exact amounts of steroids, which they themselves will use in a 4–5 month period. This allows them to identify themselves as individual users, if stopped by Customs. This could be seen as a harm minimisation strategy to reduce the risks of being arrested and charged with intent to supply.

The case study of Terry, a service user at DISCUS highlights the lengths PED users will go to obtain drugs. He travels to different areas of Greece every 3 months alternating between particular towns, where he knows he will be able to buy authentic anabolic/androgenic steroids in large enough amounts to last his training and drug using regime. His action maintains that he does not have to rely on counterfeit or veterinary products as they are difficult to distinguish from legitimate pharmaceutical products. His drug of choice is Viramone (anabolic/androgenic steroid) and he has been stopped at Customs on one occasion where he was able to produce a comprehensive and detailed training and drug schedule for a full 3 month period. He became acquainted with this practice of purchasing PEDS abroad, after accessing information from an 'underground' network of local amateur sports enthusiasts.

Service users' perceptions of PEDS

As part of the assessment process carried out when an individual first attends the DISCUS service, service users are asked to identify the positive and negative aspects of their drug use. The following list in Box 6.1 shows the positive and negative aspects identified by service users. Some consequences appear in both lists as they are sometimes viewed differently by individuals, that is, increased aggression may be frowned upon by some users, whilst others see it as a positive aspect, enabling them to train harder and longer.

Box 6.1   Positive and negative aspects or drug we: user reflections

POSITIVE	NEGATIVE
Increased aggression	Increased aggression
Appearance	Acne
Strength	Tissue scarring
Size	Reduced libido
Train harder/longer	Gynecomastia
Body image	Mood variations
Increased libido	Possibility of counterfeits
Increased confidence	

Other reported effects from service users

Side effects from the use of PEDS have been widely reported for a number of years, (Yesalis, 2000). The following list of side effects are those that have been experienced personally by users of the DISCUS service (Dawson, 2001). Some side effects may have alternative/contributory causes, but these effects were assumed by service users to be caused by their use of PEDS.

- Acne.
- Changes in libido.
- Fertility problems.
- Testicular shrinkage.
- Clitoral hypertrophy.
- Male pattern baldness.
- Hypertension.
- Jaundice.
- Abscesses at injection sites.
- Irritability.
- Gynecomastia.
- Pituitary access shutdown.
- Biggrexia.

Other recognised side effects

Side effects from the use of PEDS, from other references (Yesalis 2000) include:

Box 6.2   Side effects of drug use

Physical	**Psychological**
Gynecomastia	Psychosis
Acne	Hypomania
Altered lipid profile	Euphoria
Abnormal liver function	Emotional lability
Cholestatic jaundice	Aggression
Cardiomyopathy	Irritability
Acromegaly	Reckless behaviour
Altered blood coagulation	Increased libido
Increased haematocrit	Paranoid reactions
Testicular shrinkage	
Clitoral hypertrophy	
Infertility	
Menstrual irregularities	
Headaches	

Conclusion

It can be argued that given the success of the DISCUS clinic with it's philosophy of harm minimisation (rather than facilitating an approach which demands abstinence), a philosophy along these lines needs to be discussed nationally. The use of PEDS is becoming widespread in all sporting arenas, both amateur and professional and, therefore, some acknowledgement and thoughtful debate, rather than purely punitive measures needs to be implemented. There is a danger that athletes are being targeted in anti-doping programmes, not just because they are guilty of using PEDS, but because they are the easiest targets in what is a much more complex and widespread pattern of culpability. Further research needs to be carried out to address the effects and needs of the people using PEDS, rather than only taking national and international punitive stances. If athletes and other people are going to continue to use PEDS in the future, it is paramount that the effects on their health are minimised and casualties are limited, as the full extent of the health costs of using these drugs is uncertain. 'Drug misusers have the same entitlement as other patients to the services provided by the National Health Service' (DoH, 1999: 1).

References

ACMD Report (1988) *Aids and Drug Misuse*. Part One. London: HMSO.
British Medical Association (2002) *Drugs in Sport: The Pressure to Perform*. London: BMJ Books.
Cohen, J. (2002) *Understanding Drugs and the Law*. London: DrugScope.
Coomber, R. (1997) Effect of drug use in sport, *Journal of Performance Enhancing Drugs*, 1, 16–20.
Crace, J. (2003) Sprinting error, *Guardian Education*, 28th October, 64.
Dawson, R. T. (2001) Drugs in sport – the role of the physician, *Journal of Endocrinology*, 170(1), 55–61.
Department of Health (1999) *Drug Misuse and Dependence Guidelines on Clinical Management*. London: HMSO.
Donohoe, T. and Johnson, N. (1986) *Foul Play: Drug Abuse in Sports*. Oxford: Blackwell Scientific Publications.
Drugscope, www.drugscope.org.uk
Heron, R. (2003) *Audit of Service User Satisfaction*. County Durham and Darlington: Priority Services NHS Trust.
Hickson, R. C., Ball, K. L. and Falduto, M. T. (1989) *Adverse Effects of Anabolic Steroids*. Chicago: University of Chicago.
Houlihan, B. (1999) *Dying to Win. Doping in Sport and the Development of Anti-doping Policy*. Strasbourg: Council of Europe Publishing.
International Olympic Committee Medical Commission (1999) *Olympic Movement Anti-Doping Code*. Lausanne: IOC.
Mottram, D. R. (1996) *Drugs in Sport* (2nd ed), London: E and FN Spon.
O'Leary, J. (2001) *Drugs and Doping in Sport. Socio-legal Perspectives*. London: Cavendish Publishing Ltd.
Petersen, T. and McBride, A. (2002) *Working with Substance Users. A Practical Guide*. London: Routledge.
Petersen, M. and McBride, A. (2002) *Working with Substance Misusers*. London: Routledge.
The Advisory Council for the Misuse of Drugs (1971) *The Misuse of Drugs Act*, London: The Stationery Office.
The Medicines Act (1968) (Commencement No. 8) Order 1989.
Vernacchia, R. A. (1990) Ethical issues of drug use in sport in Tricker, R. and Cook, D. L. (Eds.) *Athletes at Risk: Drugs and Sport*. Dubuqe I. A: R. A. C. Brown.
Verroken, M. (1996) Drug use and abuse in sport in Mottram, D. R. (Ed.) *Drugs in Sport*, (2nd Ed.). London: E and FN Spon.
Waddington, I. (2000) *Sport, Health and Drugs, a Critical Sociological Perspective*. London: Spon Press.
Wilson, W. and Derse, E. (2001) *Doping in Elite Sport. The Politics of Drugs in the Olympic Movement*. Champaign: Human Kinetics Publishers.
Williams, R. (1998) Plague pulls peddlers from their pedestal. *The Guardian*, 30, 12.
Yesalis, C. E. (2000) *Anabolic Steroids in Sport and Exercise*. Illinois: Human Kinetics Champaign.

CHAPTER 7

Culture, Lifestyle and Identity: Constructing the Healthy You

NIGEL WATSON

Introduction: Can you be what you want to be?

In this chapter we are going to look at the contribution of cultural studies to our understanding of contemporary experiences of sport, fitness and health in the advanced capitalist societies. In doing this we will need to consider the interplay between a number of related aspects of modern contemporary life. These include the emphasis on the consumption of goods and services, the predominance of leisure as a source of meaning and identity, and the domination in visual culture of images of perfect bodies.

In their book *Sport Worlds*, Joseph Maguire and his co-authors (Maguire et al., 2002) remind us of the extent to which sport (and I would argue health and fitness) are social products. By this they mean that '*sport . . . is deeply embedded in cultural processes*' (ibid. p. xiii) and that it can only be fully understood by recognising the social context in which sport is developed and engaged with. Our pursuit of excellence in our chosen sport, or our desires to achieve the perfect embodiment of fitness, are not simply individual activities, they occur within cultures, which shape and direct these ambitions and desires, leading us to historically and socially specific outcomes. To this extent our aims and wishes are socially constructed.

An example of this is the ways in which our engagement with physical activity has changed in the last 50 years. It has been particularly affected by shifting patterns of work and also by the differing expectations placed upon men and women as gender roles have changed. Prior to the decline of the heavy industries, which dominated the North East of England, where this chapter is being written, men defined a significant part of their identities through their daily engagement with hard physical work in the mines and shipyards. Sport, if they took part at all, was a recreational activity undertaken for the enjoyment of the game and not primarily for its connotations of fitness or health. Their bodies developed through their use in the physical labour, which was at the core of their lives. The idea of the leisure gym in which men now spend hours working out would have seemed very strange indeed. If they did go to a gym it would have been an all male preserve, possibly devoted to boxing. Similarly, for women, the gender roles then in play would have restricted their daily experiences to the largely domestic. It is unlikely that working class women would have participated in sport very much at all. The unisex leisure gym would have been even more alien to them than to their men.

I hope that this example, whilst general, points to the ways in which large changes in social structures and social processes impact upon the individual lived experiences of us all. The relocation of heavy manufacturing away from Europe to Asia has indirectly and partially altered the decisions made by individuals in the North East of England as to how they pursue fitness regimes and spend their leisure time. It has also impacted upon the kinds of work and leisure, which is associated with our gender identities. At the core of this discussion is the idea of embodiment. All of us live our lives through physical bodies and it is perhaps strange to think that these apparently fixed material entities are also socially constructed. The ideals of masculinity and femininity, which change with history and culture, find their way into the ways our bodies look and the efforts that we give to reconstructing them through diet, exercise and even surgery. A number of feminist authors (for a useful summary see Kay, 2003, and for a full coverage of the UK context see Hargreaves, 1994) have pointed to the specific power which the institutions of sport have exercised in maintaining differences in power between men and women, and they have also shown us how this extends into our experiences of embodiment and physicality. In this context it is interesting to remember that the International Olympic Committee did not include a 1500 m event for women until 1972, and it was 1984 before there was a women's Olympic Champion in the marathon. The widely held belief had been that women were not physically strong enough to undertake a tough endurance event. The point is, of course, that the regulatory framework was not just a neutral set of rules, but also a moral one, symbolic of social and cultural beliefs, which both reflected and further constructed gender expectations.

The remainder of this chapter will go on to explore these issues in more depth. In particular, I want to show how the overlapping discourses associated with sport, health and fitness all contribute in a significant way to constructing our lived expectations of normality in the contemporary world. The fitness and health industries in all their various manifestations serve as a locus for aspects of the modern experience of consumption, gender, lifestyle and identity.

Lifestyle and consumption: making the healthy you

Our everyday lives are dominated in one way or another by the need and desire to buy goods and to consume services. In the richest parts of the world we are surrounded by opportunities to consume, which are unthinkable in the poor countries and which would have been inconceivable even in the northern countries 50 years ago. That is not to say of course that everyone, even in the richest countries is able, or actively chooses to define their identity through consumer goods. Large numbers of people choose not to participate in the rigours of shopping or are excluded by their social status or income. It has become commonplace for consumption in general, however, to be a leisure activity for millions, as a visit to any shopping mall on Saturdays or Sundays will show. Our lives are surrounded by aspirational images of products and by images of how we should look in order to be wholly acceptable to others. These images often focus upon desirable bodies for both men and women, accompanied by the service or gadget, which helps the achievement of the ideal. Just a glance through lifestyle magazines, the Sunday papers or a casual look at day time television will provide a dozen or more adverts for slimming products, weight gain products, home fitness equipment and surgical techniques, all of which promise to create the perfect you.

A theme of this book is that the contemporary approach to health promotion focuses on lifestyle issues. The way that we lead our lives is both a source of ill health because of 'bad' behaviours and the opportunity for redemption by following appropriate regimes of sanctioned 'good' behaviours. Concerns for our lifestyles bring together public, political and commercial interests in a common effort to convince us of the shifts that we need to make in order to achieve betterment and even 'perfection'.

Featherstone has pointed out how the term lifestyle assumes a meaning within commodity culture such that it is associated with '*individuality, self-expression and a stylistic self-consciousness*' (Featherstone, 1991: 83). It is as if in following the prescriptions for good health and fitness, we believe that each of us is acting with individual freewill in order to construct a sense of our self, which is unique. The construction of the healthy self becomes an aesthetic project in pursuit of the perfect person.

The extent, to which we have the freedom to be who we want to be, and to construct our desired image of ourselves for others, is at the heart of a basic issue in the social sciences. It was traditionally referred to as the nature/ nurture debate and essentially the question is: are our significant characteristics biologically determined or socially constructed? Most, though not all writers on either side of the argument recognise that our social selves are the outcome of a complex interaction between society, biology and environment. From the cultural side of the debate the process of achieving social competence and appropriate behaviours is a learned one and is referred to as socialisation. This process continues through life, although during childhood primary socialisation builds our basic vocabulary for survival in our culture. We adopt, or at least become familiar with the values and beliefs, which are characteristic of our family, community and society. These values will change over time and may be drastically revised through a change of place or community. Travelling to another country or changing jobs will often throw into relief our basic assumptions about the 'normal' way of doing things.

To illustrate this further and specifically in relation to sport, we can look at the arguments which used to be put forward to explain the achievements of black athletes. Ellis Cashmore summarises a once commonly held position that black athletes were successful because of their inherited and genetic capacities, which would have been attributed to 'race' (Cashmore, 2000). He gives the example of the journalist Martin Kane who was writing for *Sports Illustrated* in the early 1970s. Kane argued that the physical characteristics of black people gave inherent advantages when participating in sports which required speed and power, whilst their psychological disposition towards calmness helped when under competitive pressure. As Cashmore says:

> Kane's arguments border on the absurd, especially when we consider anthropologist's dismissal of the concept of race itself as having any analytical value at all. Black people are descended from African populations, but, over the centuries, their genetic heritage has become diversified and complicated . . . There is no 'pure' race. (Cashmore, 2000: 119)

From a social constructionist viewpoint, discrimination against black people elsewhere in society and their exclusion from wider socio-economic opportunities has focused attention upon the achievements of black athletes in public life. Nevertheless, even in sport, let alone in politics or in business their participation is still limited by social stratification and structures. It is only recently, for example, that black competitors have achieved international status in golf or tennis, and we are a long way from the first black British prime minister. In summary then, the values and beliefs of our cultures do much to construct and channel our opportunities and expectations. In our complex consumer society, the greatest level of freedom often appears to be at the level of buying an image for ourselves. We can acquire the latest fitness or sports wear, irrespective of our levels of fitness or sporting achievement, and in doing so buy into the celebrity associated with it.

If we focus this discussion on the health related aspects of fitness and exercise we can see that there is an application here as well. Different communities place differential value upon participation in sport and exercise. Lupton (1995) makes an important, if rather oversimplified distinction, between the typical aspects of middle class and working cultures when engaging with sport and physical activity. She suggests that exercise for its own sake, for example, working out or jogging fit more closely with the middle class values of self-discipline and asceticism derived in part from the nineteenth century public school system. Middle class people are, therefore, more likely to take part in activities which link exercise with regulating their bodies in order to create and accomplish a newly desired self. Traditionally, the working classes on the other hand, would prefer organised activities that were sociable and often associated with drinking. It is true that the status of darts, snooker and pool as sports is in a different social space from golf or croquet. There are dangers in this kind of stereotyping, but nevertheless it does provide an insight into the ways in which we accept the relative worth of different forms of sport and physical activity. Perhaps the dominance of consumer culture in contemporary society has contributed to a lessening of traditional social class boundaries and introduced greater equality in the pursuit of perfect bodies. As she says:

> From this perspective, engaging in sporting act activities or exercise is strongly associated with the construction of subjectivity. The terms 'fitness' and 'health' have generally become synonymous in everyday discourse, especially for members of the middle class. Fitness activities represent the attempt of individuals to find their 'true' selves, to uncover the 'fit' and lean individual hiding beneath the layers of flesh, to bring together the mind and the body, to cope with the seemingly chaotic nature of life in the late twentieth century by mastering the body.
> (Lupton, 1995: 143)

To summarise then, whilst we like to think of ourselves as free and autonomous beings, our lives are in part structured for us by the prevailing values and beliefs of our time. In relation to the contemporary world, our access to the resources that allow us to construct our desired image to others is through a consumer culture, and this is equally true for our access to fitness and to health. I want to go on now to look in more detail at the ways in which a concern for the shape and size of the physical body is associated with the pursuit of health and fitness, and consider as well the part which sport plays in this.

Perfect bodies and perfect health

Although, the historical origins of health promotion lie in programmes for environmental change and improvement (see Ashton and Seymour, 1988), the contemporary approach focuses upon individual lifestyles and associated consumption and physical activity. This is partly because the changes to infrastructure needed to secure good health indicators and the provision of comprehensive health care systems are now in place in the advanced capitalist societies and in even in many poorer countries. This has, therefore, moved the locus of attention away from general societal issues and onto individuals. It is also the case that the ideal of individualism is at the core of advanced capitalist economies.

Over the last 50 years or so, significant change has occurred in the work leisure balance in people's lives, releasing more time to pursue activities of choice. This, combined with generally greater levels of disposable income, has meant that individual discretion has increased significantly in the ways in which we can occupy our time. The plethora of contemporary consumer choice focuses this time on spending available income on goods and services, including those that are marketed as health and fitness related. (For an introduction to contemporary issues in understanding leisure see Roberts, 1999.) We should remember, though, that in the main, these comments apply only to the richest parts of the world, and for millions of people life is still characterised by grinding poverty and the absence of even the most basic aspects of a healthy life such as clean reliable water supplies.

These material changes, however, are not the whole story. From a cultural perspective, there have also been significant shifts in the related values and social meanings that inform our day-to-day lives. Contemporary social experience is characterised by imagery, which is saturated with the notion of individual gratification and its achievement through the development of the ways in which we represent ourselves to others. The best illustration of this lies in the unrelenting media attention given to celebrities. If we take the obvious example of David Beckham, the worlds of advertising and gossip journalism provide a constant focus on the minutiae of his everyday activities and so, if we do it like Beckham, we will by association, become a little like him. Advertisers and public relations specialists are able to exploit our desires for celebrity status. They encourage us to think that by buying a pair of endorsed boots, changing our hairstyles, wearing a tattoo or drinking a cola we become a little more like Beckham. (For an introduction to the topic of consumption see Bocock, 1993.)

Given the ways in which consumption and lifestyle have achieved centrality in contemporary discourse, it is no surprise that health promotion too has focused in recent years upon the regulation of consumption activities. The agenda for change treats lifestyle as a source of pathological behaviours, which need correction or treatment through prescriptions for altering our exposure to the banned list of risky activity. A link is commonly established, for example, between body weight and exercise. Health promotion discourse thus forms a sub-set of the commercial discourses that promote exercise and slimming products as the way to achieve a perfect body. It so happens that the perfect bodies are often, though not always, exemplified by successful sports men and women or other celebrities.

Lupton (2003) points out though, that health promoters are often quiet on the questions of adherence to lifestyle choice, preferring to assume that if the public is presented with rational choices then they will choose to change in line with the advocated healthy option. She argues that this ignores the ways in which lifestyle within commodity culture has assumed a centrality in the creation of subjectivity and meaning. Lifestyle is at the centre of how we see ourselves (Lupton, ibid: 110). She goes on to say that sport and exercise are in this way, associated with the creation of personal meaning and that in everyday discourse the resulting fitness is linked to health such that the terms become synonymous. We, therefore, find that the pursuit of the perfect body is linked to both commercial and health promoting narratives. Certain parts of the body become defined as problems. For men this is the stomach that should be flat and demonstrate the 'six-pack', whilst for women thighs and buttocks require toning and reduction in size. Gym based workouts take on the status of corrective and self-regulatory practices aimed at taming an undisciplined body in pursuit of the ideal image, with specific equipment designed to correct the problem parts of the body.

In social and cultural studies this process is generally called medicalisation. This term is a way of summarising the ways in which medicine has extended its sphere of influence beyond the simple treatment of illness and into the regulation of social behaviour and even moral conduct. Turner (1984) argues that since the late eighteenth century there has been gradual shift of responsibility for the control and regulation of moral conduct, in its widest sense, from the activities of the church and theology to the professions of medicine and law.

By reminding us of the moral basis for lifestyle changes Turner is directing our attention to the ways in which science has come to support the normative imperative behind medical interventions. In terms of health promotion and the overweight, for example, there are embedded assumptions about the social worth of people who, it is implied, must eat too much and exercise too little. Health promotion discourse implicitly validates certain appearances over others, and devalues those who do not conform to the prescriptions of normality. In this respect health promotion sits along side the commercial advocates of ideal bodies, though its legitimation for change lies in science and medicine rather than the self-regarding perfection of the body for its own sake.

In summary then, body modification has taken place in most cultures throughout history. In contemporary society the drive behind change and the drive to establish what is 'normal', comes from a set of overlapping discourses. In particular, there is a significant overlap between health promotion prescriptions for weight loss and exercise and commercial ones. The former embeds its authority in the language of sciences and medicine and the latter in images of celebrity and desirable social status. The outcome of both is to establish notions of ideal bodies, bringing social approval for those who achieve the ideal and possible social exclusion for those who do not.

Conclusion

In this chapter, we have explored a number of overlapping issues in relation to exercise, fitness and health, and these have been illustrated through contemporary concepts and ideas from cultural studies. Central to this discussion has been the recognition that exercise and health have become wrapped up within consumer discourse, which is associated with a range of consumer products and services that are marketed as ways of achieving a more desirable image and sense of self. Health promotion initiatives both draw upon the methods used to sell these products and services, as well as maintaining a counter discourse aimed at controlling the excesses of an unregulated consumer lifestyle.

An analysis of this function for health promotion has been developed by Armstrong (1995). Drawing on the work of Foucault, he has used the concept of surveillance to show how health promotion contributes to the definitions of normal and abnormal in human behaviours. Supported by the combined authority of science and medicine the discourse of health promotion can create the legitimisation for the inclusion and exclusion of whole social groups, and it can be the basis for the exercise of bio-power over individual bodies.

Throughout this chapter one theme in particular has been explored. It has been argued that the value that is attached to social behaviours and to social groups is the outcome of a complex process of social differentiation. In the human sciences this is called social constructionism. From this perspective, there are no natural behaviours. All social action carries with it a meaning that is specific to time and to place and to culture. This is not to deny the existence of biological differences, but rather to argue that in trying to understand others it is important to step back and to acknowledge that there are no universal meanings attached to the differences between social groups. If programmes for social change ignore this principle than their effectiveness is likely to be compromised. As Susan Birrell has said when discussing the place of black women in sport:

. . . . . We need to work not towards unity and synthesis but towards affinity – always sensitive to the subordinate and dominant relations, but, for now, privileging the most overlooked example of those relations. The new insights produced through these connections will enrich our analyses of cultural relations. . . . . . (Birrell, 1990: 199).

References

Armstrong, D. (1995) The rise of surveillance medicine, *Sociology of Health and Illness*, 17, 3: 393–404.

Ashton, J. and Seymour H. (1988) *The New Public Health*. Milton Keynes: Open University Press.

Birrell, S. (1990) Women of color, critical autobiography, and sport in Messner, M. and Sabo, D. (Eds.) *Sport, Men, and the Gender Order: Critical Feminist Perspectives*. Illinois: Human Kinetics Books.

Bocock, R. (1993) *Consumption*. London: Routledge.

Cashmore, E. (2000) *Making Sense of Sports* (3rd edition). London: Routledge.

Featherstone, M. (1991) *Consumer Culture and Postmodernism*. London: Sage.

Hargeaves, J. (1994) *Sporting Females: Critical Issues in the History and Sociology of Women's Sports*. London: Routledge.

Kay, T. (2003) Sport and gender in Houlihan, B. (Ed.) *Sport and Society: A Student Introduction*. London: Sage.

Lupton, D. (2003) 2nd edition *The Imperative of Health*. London: Sage.

Maguire, J., Jarvie, G., Mansfield, L. and Bradley, J. (Eds.) (2002) *Sport Worlds: A Sociological Perspective*. Illinois: Human Kinetics Books.

Roberts, K. (1999) *Leisure in Contemporary Society*. Oxford: CABI Publishing.

Turner, B. S. (1984) *Body and Society*. Oxford: Blackwell Sage.

CHAPTER 8

Health Promotion and Healthy Lifestyles: Motivating Individuals to Become Physically Active

ISTVÁN SOÓS, JARMO LIUKKONEN, AND REX W. THOMSON

Introduction

Motivating individuals to become physically active is one of the major tasks confronting those who wish to promote good health through participation in sport and physical activity. The purpose of this chapter is to highlight the links between health promotion, motivation and physical activity. This chapter provides a brief overview and an introduction to theories of motivation, which have particular relevance to participation in sport and physical activity. Practical applications such as models to support active lifestyles, and to promote physical and mental health in different cultures are also considered. The chapter concludes with a summary of the relationships between health promotion, motivation and participation in physical activity.

Overview

The vocabulary of health promotion reflects the perspectives of varying scholars – philosophers, medical practitioners, educationalists, and exercise psychologists – and the general public. The World Health Organization (1946) defined health as 'an ideal state of physical, psychological, and social wellbeing and not just the absence of illness.' For the public, health is often considered as an optimal state of body functions providing immunity from simple health problems such as colds and influenza, or as the avoidance of accidents. Medical practitioners using 'traditional western methods' have tended to concentrate on healing, while those adopting a 'holistic approach' to medicine have attempted to treat the 'person as a whole', and have included

103

a focus on the prevention of illness and disease. Educators and sport and exercise psychologists have largely focused on prevention as part of active health promotion. The goal of health promotion is to enhance positive health and prevent ill health, and this includes the fields of health education, disease prevention, and health protection (Downie et al., 1995). Educators and sport and exercise psychologists attempt to motivate individuals to participate in physical activity to promote positive health.

According to Downie et al. (1995), the following factors interact and influence the health of individuals: biological factors (including ageing and genetic changes), lifestyle (including health behaviour, physical activity, exercise and sport, as well as fitness levels), environmental conditions (including air and water pollution, food safety, communicable diseases, and availability and use of health services), and economic factors (including economic resources to pay for exercise facilities, healthy food, and preventive health care such as medical and dental examinations).

Health promotion targets the lowering of mortality and morbidity rates, increasing the uptake of immunisation, and changes in lifestyle, and consequently provides steps to improving health and the quality of life. Future generations will be able to judge the outcome of current health promotion programmes, but it is clear that many individuals do not realise the importance of good health until they are confronted with illness (Killoran et al., 1994; Sallis and Owen, 1999). Health and illness should be seen to be on a continuum and not as isolated concepts, since health cannot be explained without illness. In other words, health is a state which can be constantly improved (Downie et al., 1995).

Theoretical approaches

There is a Gaelic phrase which suggests that 'health is an inheritance', and the maintenance of good health and the prevention of ill health is clearly a worthwhile commitment for both individuals and the state. There are many approaches to health from the point of view of well-being or wellness (Hoeger and Hoeger, 1995; Pruitt and Stein, 1994), and some give practical advice on how to achieve a healthy and physically active lifestyle (Biddle, 1991; Biddle et al., 1998). Many also focus on the psychological benefits of physical activity (Biddle, 1995; Biddle et al., 2000; Biddle and Mutrie, 2001; Faulkner and Biddle, 2002).

Several national and cross-cultural studies support the importance of a favourable motivational climate (including task-involvement, autonomy and social relatedness support) in preventing the sedentary behaviour of individuals, especially adolescents (Biddle et al., 1999; Liukkonen, 1998). Not just the strength but also the direction and type of motivation play a major role in promoting physically active and healthy lifestyles for young people. The stability of internal regulation during the teenage years is a good predictor of whether an individual is likely to remain physically active in later life.

Development of motivation theories

According to Franken (1998), the study of motivation has traditionally been concerned with the arousal, direction and persistence of behaviour. Motivation can be directed by both internal and external forces. In early research on motivation, instincts, needs and drives were seen as being beyond human control. This represented a mechanistic view and the main emphasis was on a homeostatic, stability-maintaining mechanism. The early theories were linked to arousal reduction, self-preservation and need satisfaction, while the human capacity for self-direction or self-regulation was not seen as relevant.

Later, the concept of motivation became associated with cognitive concepts such as a realistic level of decision-making, rather than emotions and desires (Ford, 1992). The role of self-evaluative thought increased, and the focus turned to motivational qualities (for example, incremental, transformational change processes, behaviour shaping, and hope for success and mastery). The explanation of the cognitive concept was based on expectancy, causal attribution and locus of control. Today, the cognitive orientation remains the dominant approach, although it has often been combined with various emotional processes.

Relevant theories of motivation

The *theory of reasoned action* (Ajzen, 1991) attempts to explain how people move from global thoughts and expected outcomes (attitudes and beliefs) to specific, concrete thoughts and expected outcomes (intentions and expectations). This theory provides the most direct predictors of a person's actions, and is congruent with other motivation theories that focus on goal-setting processes and personal agency beliefs. Nevertheless, it fails to take into account emotional arousal processes, and it defines the action as the primary dependent variable of interest.

Learned helplessness, hopelessness, or optimism theory is linked to pessimistic thinking and interprets an event in a negative way (for example, 'I'll never be successful', 'I can't do anything right'), and it can lead to depression and/or hopelessness. These personal beliefs are associated with capability and personal goals, which have affective consequences and contain a demotivating pattern. A similar interpretation can be found in *self-worth theory*, which explains self-defeating, or self-destructive behaviour patterns such as avoiding reasonable challenges, setting unrealistic goals and ignoring valued goals. Personal value or worth is associated with competition failure or negative social feedback. *Effectance motivation theory* (White, 1959) significantly contributed to *self-worth theory* and focused on competence across the lifespan, using the arousal – reduction approaches and the optimal challenge concept. The attainment of this concept requires a significant and reasonable investment of personal effort through personal efficacy and the feelings of pleasure.

Self-determination theory (Deci and Ryan, 1985; Ryan and Connell, 1989) and *goal orientation theory* (Nicholls, 1989) are motivational predictors of the physical activity intentions of individuals. Deci and Ryan distinguish between the autonomous or intrinsic motivational orientation, internal locus of causality and the control of extrinsic motivational orientation. The person's lack of competence leads to reducing both intrinsic and extrinsic motivation, and ends in amotivational experiences that promote impersonal motivational orientation. *Goal orientation theory* (Nicholls, 1989) focuses on the two personal orientations of perception of competence, an ego or normative referenced, and a task or self-referenced orientation, which have different motivationally relevant cognitive, affective, and behavioural outcomes.

According to Bandura's (1977) *self-efficacy theory*, thoughts are much more likely to have a direct and substantial impact on behaviour. It links to capability beliefs, or in other words to how people think about their capabilities in certain behaviour episodes. Locke and Latham's (1990) *goal setting theory, or high performance cycle theory*, has a leading role in work motivation, and describes capable people's behaviour in a responsive environment, where they commit themselves to challenging goals and believe that they can attain these. Csikszentmihalyi (1990) contributed a new theoretical element to *optimal experience theory*. He identified the concept of flow, which is the subjective experience of a sense of control, focused attention, personal meaning and pleasure. Ford's (1992) *motivational systems theory* has also provided a useful integrative conceptual framework for understanding and influencing human motivation.

Intrinsic motivation in sport and exercise

Intrinsic motivation is part of a motivational continuum, and represents the highest level of self-determinism. People pursue activities that interest them and in which they can freely participate. They need the feeling of personal control, without the sense of engaging the activity for material award, and spontaneous involvement in the activity (Cox, 2002). Intrinsic motivation can be directed toward knowledge, if someone wants to learn a new skill, toward accomplishment, when a person desires to master a particular skill, or toward stimulation when performers are physically and mentally experiencing sensations innate to a specific task ('enjoy doing'). Every individual has the basic need to be an originator rather than a 'pawn' in the activity (DeCharms and Carpenter, 1968).

For many individuals, 'why they play' determines 'how they play' a sport. They should feel as if they are participating in sport and exercise for reasons that they have chosen or internalised, and not for reasons that others have imposed on them (Cox, 2002). If people are pawns in sport and exercise, they are more likely to behave as machines, less likely to have fun and to play without enthusiasm. People need to have a choice in their actions, which leads to the perception of their autonomy. The other basic need for humans is to interact with other individuals in a positive way. This kind of cooperation leads to enjoyment in physical activity. The sense of care for others or having others care for us is an important aspect of relatedness. Perceived competence is a major component in gaining self-confidence and a prerequisite for motivated behaviour. Without competence and autonomy, self-determination is impossible, and without self-determination there is no intrinsic motivation (Cox, 2002).

Theories and models explaining physical activity

Precede-proceed model

According to the *precede-proceed model* (see Figure 8.1), health behaviour is affected, in addition to environmental factors, by various predisposing, enabling and strengthening factors (Green and Kreuter, 1999).

Predisposing factors include individual values, attitudes, experiences, opinions and knowledge, which may increase or decrease motivation towards behavioural changes. Enabling factors include such skills, resources and hindrances that facilitate or hinder wanted behavioural and environmental changes. Social support from peers, feedback and encouragement, and possible rewards after adopting a new behaviour style are examples of strengthening factors. Strengthening factors either encourage continuing adopted behaviour or may hinder the continuation of it. Environmental factors include all physical, social and economical factors related to the individual which may support wanted behaviour.

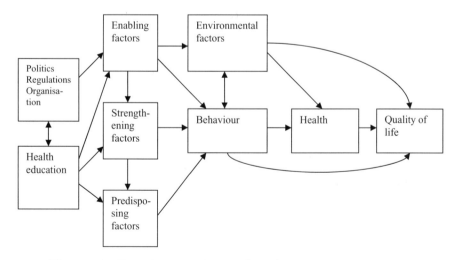

Figure 8.1　Precede-proceed model from Green and Kreuter: Health Promotion planning 3/e, 1999, McGraw-Hill Companies Reproduced with permission of the McGraw-Hill Companies

Enabling factors include intrinsic expectations and attitudes as well as external stimuli such as someone reminding the individual about the advantages of exercise. Research findings have revealed that perceived risk of heart disease or perceived easiness of exercise are associated with physical activity. Enabling factors of the model include the accessibility to sport facilities and equipment, high motor skill level and sufficiency of time. Strengthening factors include external support and positive feedback as well as the intrinsic rewards of physical activity such as joy, satisfaction and perceptions of the meaning of exercise. The probability of physical activity is greatest if enabling, predisposing and strengthening factors are versatile, intensive and have an effect simultaneously. For physical activity, the optimal situation would be when a person is aware of the importance of physical activity, has the possibility to exercise near their home and their family supports exercise activities.

Exercise behaviour model

The *exercise behaviour model* (see Figure 8.2) has been modified from the health belief model (Rosenstock, 1974). Noland and Feldman (1984) created a theoretical model of exercise behaviour which clarifies the role of various

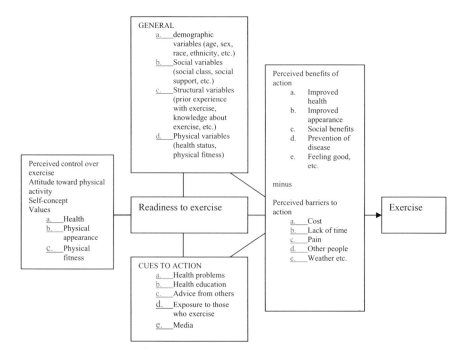

Figure 8.2 Exercise behaviour model (Noland and Feldman, 1984)

factors affecting the human decision-making related to participation in physical activity. According to the model, four predispositions influence readiness for exercise. These are perceived locus of control for exercise, attitude toward physical activity, self-concept and exercise-related values such as physical fitness, health and appearance.

Modifying factors affecting readiness to exercise include demographic, social, structural and physical variables, as well as cues to action such as health problems, health education, advice from others, exposure to those who exercise and the media. The final decision about exercise is made as a result of the comparison process of perceived benefits of, and barriers to action. According to the model, individuals will not be physically active if they perceive the barriers stronger than the possible benefits of exercise. The exercise behaviour model can be utilised in the planning for promoting physical activity. If one succeeds in increasing readiness to exercise, even minor stimuli may result in the individual commencing physical activity. In addition, removing any perceived barriers may help to lower the threshold for starting to exercise.

Stages of change model

One of the most popular contemporary topics in exercise and health psychology is the behavioural determinants at various stages of health behaviours. The *stages of change model* (see Figure 8.3) by Buckworth and Dishman (2002)

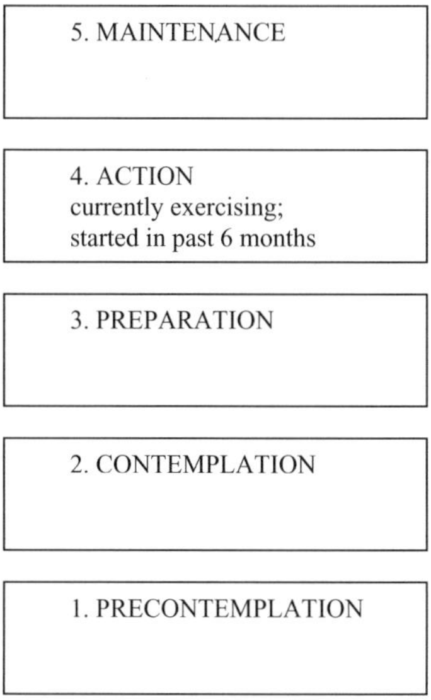

5. MAINTENANCE

4. ACTION
currently exercising;
started in past 6 months

3. PREPARATION

2. CONTEMPLATION

1. PRECONTEMPLATION

Figure 8.3 Prochaska and DiClemente's (1985) stages of change model applied to physical activity (Marcus and Forsyth, 2003)

was developed on the basis of studies of Prochaska and DiClemente (1983; 1985), who named it the transtheoretical model. The model defines the processes of change as the cognitive, affective and behavioural strategies and techniques people use as they progress through the different stages of change over time. It has proven to be a relevant frame of reference in research of behavioural changes in the context of physical activity and health.

The model was created when Prochaska and DiClemente studied individuals who tried to quit smoking. They found that individuals go through certain stages when trying to change their behaviour. The model identifies five stages of change (Marcus and Forsyth, 2003). In the precontemplation stage the person is not currently exercising and has no intention of doing so in the near future. In the contemplation stage the person is not currently exercising, but intends doing so in the near future. In the preparation phase the person is currently exercising, but not regularly. The involvement is sporadic. In the action phase the person is currently exercising according to the recommended amount and intensity, but the involvement has continued for less than half a year and exercise is not yet habitual. In the final maintenance stage, the person has been exercising more than half a year and exercise has become a stable custom.

When planning exercise consultancy and interventions, it is important to take into account the individual needs of those in various stages of change. These needs may vary considerably. For those in the precontemplation phase, an appropriate goal could be to get them acquainted with articles about healthy behaviour, and to get them involved in a short walk, two to three times a week. Similarly, for those in the preparation phase, a satisfactory recommendation could be to gradually participate in longer periods of exercise in order to achieve the recommended level for health-promoting exercise.

Theory of reasoned action

Ajzen and Fishbein (1980) hypothesise in the *theory of reasoned action* that human behaviour in a certain situation is affected by both the individual's own attitudes and by social pressure from the community towards the activity. The *theory of planned behaviour* (see Figure 8.4), which also aims to explain behaviour is a continuation of the theory of reasoned action. These theories suggest that starting and continuing physical activity are associated with the expectations an individual has about the outcomes of exercising and how much they value the assumed outcomes (Smith and Biddle, 1995).

The individual's beliefs about physical activity and how deeply that individual wants to adapt to these beliefs also affect commitment to physical exercise. In addition, the perceived difficulty of the activity is related to commitment. It is hypothesised that commitment is associated with positive emotions towards the activity and the perception that one is able to control the situation (Doganis and Theodorakis, 1995).

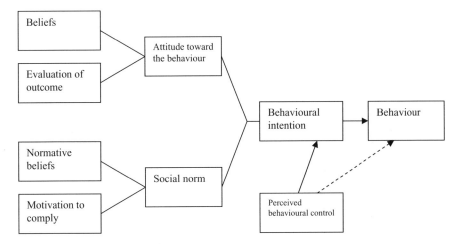

Figure 8.4 Theory of planned behaviour from Biddle and Mutrie Psychology of Physical Activity and Exercise: A Health Related Perspective, 1991. With kind permission of Springer Science and Business Media

Locus of control theory

Rotter's (1975) *theory of locus of control* has a close connection to attribution theory. Locus of control theory also helps to investigate how people explain their behaviour. Based on previous experiences and the conclusions drawn from them we adopt a certain view about our own possibility to influence life events. If individuals perceive that they cannot achieve wanted outcomes with their own acts, they believe that events are not under their own control. In such a case, they perceive intensive external control. Similarly, individuals perceiving intensive internal control have a view that events are under their own control and that they can achieve wanted outcomes. The dimensions of internal and external reasons are orthogonal, which means that a person may simultaneously perceive both strong internal and external control.

Sport commitment model

Scanlan and Lewthwaite (1986) have presented a model integrating factors underlying sport commitment (see Figure 8.5). The model, which can be also used in exercise settings, has been modified and extended to examine the specific nature of commitment to sport from Rusbult's (1980) social psychological commitment model, which has proven effective in predicting commitment to work and personal relationships. Greater enjoyment is believed to promote greater commitment in sports (Scanlan and Simons, 1992). Nevertheless, although enjoyment and joy are important elements for the continuation of exercise, and they give exercise participants a positive sense about the

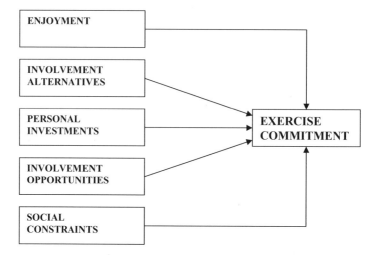

Figure 8.5   Sport commitment model (Scanlan and Simons, 1992) modified to exercise

activity, in the case of adults there are also several other intrinsic and extrinsic factors associated with physical activity.

Other factors predicting commitment in the model are the attractiveness of involvement alternatives, personal investment in participation, the involvement opportunities afforded by continued participation and social constraints to continue participation. Social expectations and norms may cause feelings of responsibility to continue exercise activities. These feelings may, however, decrease individual perceptions of self-determination, and thus for commitment the social pressure to participate in exercise activities should be as low as possible. Furthermore, commitment is also influenced by the possible outcomes that can only be achieved if the participation continues, such as the chance to achieve success or to be with friends.

Health promotion through motivated physical activity: practical applications

One of the main causes of a number of global public health problems is sedentary lifestyles. The lack of physical activity can be a contributor to death, disease and disability. A sedentary lifestyle enhances the risk of mortality and morbidity, doubles the risk of cardiovascular diseases, diabetes and obesity and also increases the risk of cancer (e.g. colon cancer), high blood pressure, osteoporosis, depression and anxiety (NCD Prevention and Health Promotion, 2004; Soós and Biddle, 1997). Physical activity is a difficult choice in some instances because of barriers such as poverty, the lack of sport and recreation facilities and safe play areas. The World Health Organization recommends at least 30 minutes of moderate physical activity every day, which may include not only a great variety of leisure and recreational sports, but everyday activities such as walking, climbing stairs, gardening, dancing, etc. Weight control requires more physical activity, and children also need additional physical activity. Continuity and regularity are essential, as the cholesterol and triglyceride-lowering effect of a 30-minute walk or a 20-minute jog may last for 50 hours only (NCD Prevention and Health Promotion, 2004).

Programmes of health-enhancing physical activity are promoted through education, the media, the fitness industry, sports organisations, etc., and by a number of agencies and governing bodies. A number of countries are involved in such programmes – in the United States, 'America is on the move' (America is on the move, 2004), 'Going for the goal' (Danish, 1998) and 'SUPER' (Danish, 2002); in New Zealand, 'Push play' (Push play, 2004); and in Europe, 'The European Network for Health-Enhancing Physical Activity' (the HEPA Network) (Foster, 2000). Other national programmes include 'Allez Hop' (Movement for everybody, Switzerland), 'Fit for life' (Finland), and 'Active for life' (England). In the North East of England, the 'BASE Activity Programme' was developed for increasing sport participation, and its philosophy closely reflects the Sport England philosophy for increasing participation in sport (Coulson, 2004).

The 'America is on the move' campaign claims that 60 per cent of American adults do less than 30 minutes physical activity a day, and 25 per cent of American adults are not physically active at all. The 'America is on the move' message targets the adult population to make two daily changes – to take 2000 more steps (about 1 mile), and to eat 100 fewer calories (about a pat of butter). 'Going for the goal' (Danish, 1998) is a goal-setting programme, and 'SUPER' (Sports United to Promote Education and Recreation) (Danish, 2002) is a skill development programme. Both of the latter were designed for young people. The aim of each programme is to build health-enhancing activity into the lifestyle and to improve physical shape (for example, weight control).

'Push play' considers that young people should be the first priority, and the programme aims to ensure that they enjoy the benefits of healthy active lifestyles. The initiative is to promote and encourage 30 minutes of physical activity a day. This improves young people's health and fitness and makes them more confident and better prepared for life. 'Kiwiwalks' is another initiative – these are a series of short, accessible walks throughout New Zealand to be enjoyed by people of all ages and fitness levels. In the HEPA network strategy (Foster, 2000), the 'Netherlands on the move programme' used an epidemiological approach to target different age groups. The prevalence of physical inactivity as well as smoking contributes to high blood cholesterol levels and hypertension. Only 23 per cent of the Dutch population (16 years and older) are physically active, with 34 per cent being completely inactive, based on a 1990 survey. The authorities supported intervention methods, and health educators employed social-cognitive theory, the transtheoretical model and social marketing in the intervention strategies. 'Allez Hop' also used the transtheoretical model to identify and target different groups of inactive adults for participation in its courses. The groups included sedentary adults and adults who were only slightly active. Particular strategies were used to support and encourage participants to become more active.

The 'Fit for life' programme in Finland aimed to increase the number of regularly active, 40 to 60-year old men and women by 10 per cent in the year of 2000. The 'Active for life' programme In England used a media campaign based on social marketing. The sedentary adult population was segmented into specific groups, including young women (16–24 years of age), middle-aged men (45–55 years of age) and older men and women (50 years of age and older). Ethnic minority groups and people with disabilities were also identified. The programme aimed to reduce the numbers of adults who were sedentary, and at the same period to increase the number of adults who participated in moderate-intensity physical activity for 30 minutes five times per week (Cavill, 1998; Foster, 2000).

The 'BASE Activity Programme' in the North East of England focuses on the participation of young people in sport and physical activity within the national physical education curriculum. It attempts to tackle peer pressure by emphasising that to participate in physical activity and sport for enjoyment is more important than competing or winning. Motivation is a major element of the programme, because research suggests that there is a strong correlation between lack of motivation and decreased participation. Perceived competence is another psychological indicator which needs to be considered, as it is widely acknowledged that those children who experience repeated lack of success or failure avoid such activities. BASE is a highly innovative programme of activities which is designed for children and youth of both genders, all age ranges and which is suitable for all ability ranges. It is highly individualised in nature and delivered with the emphasis on enjoyment. The programme aims to increase children's confidence in their physical competence, to increase confidence in their ability to carry out regular activity, to help children experience success, to develop a positive self-image and to encourage positive interaction among the participants (Coulson, 2004).

Conclusion

There is no doubt that the ability to motivate individuals to become involved in physical activity and sport is an important part of health promotion. Beyond the direct medical benefits, increasing physical activity may provide recreational enjoyment, and physical and mental well-being. Participation in physical activity improves musculoskeletal health, controls body weight, reduces symptoms of depression, anxiety and distress, and lowers the risk of diabetes, cardiovascular disease, cancer (for example, breast cancer, colon cancer), thus positively effecting hormonal metabolism. The psychological benefits may involve positive attitude and lifestyle changes and increased self-efficacy resulting in motivated behaviour towards physical activity (Foster, 2000). In addition, physical activity has economic benefits in terms of health care costs, increased productivity, and healthier physical and social environments. In line with other societal strategies, physical activity encourages the adoption of a healthy diet, discourages the use of tobacco, alcohol, and drugs, helps to reduce violence, enhances functional capacity and promotes social interaction and integration (America is on the move, 2004).

The different programmes attempt to involve the inactive global population (estimated at 60 per cent) in the 30-minutes recommended moderate intensity daily physical activity. This may be achieved at work (walking or cycling to work; using the stairs instead of the elevator; getting off the bus one stop early and walking, and so on), housework (including gardening), leisure time (sports and recreational activities in sports fields, parks, and so on), and curricular and extra-curricular physical education at school. Physical activity can be promoted in all life settings and will clearly support the cause of positive health promotion.

References

Ajzen, I. (1991) The theory of planned behaviour, *Organizational Behaviour and Human Decision Processes*, 50, 179–211.

Ajzen, I. and Fishbein, M. (1980) *Understanding Attitudes and Predicting Behaviour.* Englewoods Cliffs, NJ: Prentice Hall.

America is on the move (2004) www.americaonthemove.org.

Bandura, A. (1977) Self-efficacy: Toward a unifying theory of behavioural change. *Psychological Review*, 84, 191–215.

Biddle, S. J. H. (1991) *A Practical Guide to a Physically Active Life.* Exeter: F.I.T. Systems Ltd.

Biddle, S. J. H. (1995) Exercise and psychosocial health, *Research Quarterly for Exercise and Sport*, 66, 4, 292–302.

Biddle, S. J. H., Fox, K. R. and Boutcher, S. H. (2000) *Physical Activity and Psychological Well-Being.* London: Routledge.

Biddle, S. J. H. and Mutrie, N. (1991) *Psychology of Physical Activity and Exercise: A Health-Related Perspective.* London: Springer.

Biddle, S. J. H. and Mutrie, N. (2001) *Psychology of Physical Activity. Determinants, Well-Being and Interventions.* London: Routledge.

Biddle, S. J. H., Sallis, J. and Cavill, N. (1998) *Young and Active? Young People and Health-enhancing Physical Activity – Evidence and implications.* London: Health Education Authority.

Biddle, S. J. H., Soos, I. and Chatzisarantis, N. (1999) Predicting physical activity intentions using a goal perspective approach: A study of Hungarian youth. *Scandinavian Journal of Medicine and Science in Sports*, 9, pp. 353–357.

Buckworth, J. and Dishman, R. K. (2002) *Exercise Psychology.* Champaign, IL: Human Kinetics.

Cavill, N. (1998) National campaigns – Can they make a difference? *International Journal of Obesity*, 22, suppl 2, 48–51.

Coulson, M. (2004) *BASE Activity Programme. Initial Proposal.* Unpublished manuscript.

Cox, R. H. (2002) *Sport Psychology. Concepts and Applications.* New York: McGraw-Hill.

Csikszentmihalyi, M. (1990) *Flow: The Psychology of Optimal Experience.* New York: Harper and Row.

Danish, S. (Ed.) (1998) *Going for the Goal.* Richmond: Life Skills Center, Virginia Commonwealth University.

Danish, S. (2002) *SUPER. Sports United to Promote Education and Recreation.* Richmond: Life Skills Center, Virginia Commonwealth University.

Deci, E. L. and Ryan, R. M. (1985) *Intrinsic Motivation and Self-Determination in Human Behaviour.* New York: Plenum Press.

DeCharms, R. C. and Carpenter, V. (1968) Measuring motivation in culturally disadvantaged school children. *Journal of Experimental Education*, 37, 31–41.

Doganis, G. and Theodorakis, Y. (1995) The influence of attitude on exercise participation in Biddle, S. J. H. (Ed.) *European Perspectives on Exercise and Sport Psychology.* Champaign, IL: Human Kinetics, 26–49.

Downie, R. S., Fyfe, C. and Tannahill, A. (1995) *Health Promotion Models and Values.* Oxford: Oxford University Press.

Faulkner, G. and Biddle, S. J. H. (2002) Exercise and mental health: It's just not psychology!, *Journal of Sports Sciences*, 19, 433–444.

Ford, M. E. (1992) *Motivating Humans. Goals, Emotions, and Personal Agency Beliefs.* New York: Sage Publications.

Foster, C. (2000) *Guidelines for Health-Enhancing Physical Activity (HEPA) Promotion Programmes.* British Heart Foundation Health Promotion Research Group: University of Oxford.

Franken, R. E. (1998) *Human Motivation.* Pacific Grove, CA: Brooks/Cole Publishing Company.

Green, L. W. and Kreuter, M. W. (1999) *Health Promotion Planning: An Educational and Ecological Approach.* Volume 3. Mountain View, CA: Mayfield.

Hoeger, W. W. K. and Hoeger, S. A. (1995) *Lifetime Physical Fitness and Wellness: A Personalized Plan.* Englewood, CO: Morton Publishing Company.

Killoran, A. J., Fentem, P. and Caspersen, C. (Eds.) (1994) *Moving On. International Perspectives on Promoting Physical Activity.* London: Health Education Authority, Great Britain.

Liukkonen, J. (1998) *Enjoyment in Youth Sports: A Goal Perspectives Approach.* Jyväskylä: LIKES-Research Center for Sport and Health Sciences.

Locke, E. A. and Latham, G. P. (1990) *A Theory of Goal-Setting and Task Performance.* Englewood Cliffs, New Jersey: Prentice-Hall.

Marcus, B. H. and Forsyth, L. H. (2003) *Motivating People to be Physically Active.* Champaign, IL: Human Kinetics.

NCD Prevention and Health Promotion (2004) *Physical Activity and Health. www.who.int/hpr/physactiv/index/shtml.*

Nicholls, J. G. (1989) *The Competitive Ethos and Democratic Education.* Cambridge, Mass: Harward University Press.

Noland, M. P. and Feldman, R. H. L. (1984) Factors related to the leisure exercise behaviour of returning women college students, *Health Education*, 15(2), 32–36.

Prochaska, J. O. and DiClemente, C. C. (1983) Stages and processes of self-change of smoking: Toward an integrative model of change, *Journal of Consulting and Clinical Psychology*, 51, 390–395.

Prohaska, J. O. and DiClemente, C. C. (1985) Common processes of self-change in smoking, weight control, and psychological distress in Shiffman, S. and Willis, T. (Eds.) *Coping and Substance Use*. New York: Academic Press, 345–363.

Pruitt, B. E. and Stein, J. J. (1994) *Health Styles. Decisions for Living Well*. Orlando, FLO: Saunders College Publishing.

Push play (2004) *http://www.sparc.org.nz/whatwedo/active.php*.

Rosenstock, I. M. (1974) The health belief model and preventative health behaviour, *Health Education Monographs*, 2(4), 355–387.

Rotter, J. B. (1975) Some problems and misconceptions related to the construct of internal versus external control of reinforcement, *Journal of Consulting and Clinical Psychology*, 43(1), 56–67.

Rusbult, C. E. (1980) Commitment and satisfaction to romantic associations: A test of the investment model, *Journal of Experimental Social Psychology*, 16, 172–186.

Ryan, R. and Connell, J. (1989) Perceived locus of causality and internalization: Examining reasons for acting in two domains, *Journal of Personality and Social Psychology*, 63, 397–429.

Sallis, J. F. and Owen, N. (1999) *Physical Activity and Behavioural Medicine*. London: Sage Publications.

Scanlan, T. K. and Lewthwaite, R. (1986) Social psychological aspects of competition for male youth sport participants: IV. Predictors of enjoyment, *Journal of Sport Psychology*, 8, 25–35.

Scanlan, T. K. and Simons, J. P. (1992) The construct of sport enjoyment in Roberts, G. C. (Ed.) *Motivation in Sport and Exercise*. Champaign, IL: Human Kinetics, 199–215.

Smith, R. A. and Biddle, S. J. H. (1995) Psychological factors in the promotion of physical activity in Biddle, S. J. H. (Ed.) *European Perspectives on Exercise and Sport Psychology*. Champaign, IL: Human Kinetics, 85–108.

Soós, I. and Biddle, S. J. H. (1997) Motivating physical activity for disease prevention. *Acta Universitatis Carolinae Kinanthropologica*, 33, 2, 55–59.

White, R. W. (1959) Motivation reconsidered: The motivation of competence, *Psychological Review*, 66, 297–333.

World Health Organization (1946) Constitution. Geneva: World Health Organization.

CHAPTER 9

Psychology and Home Exercise Prescription

SANDRA DARKINGS AND ANNE CHARNOCK

Introduction

Home-based exercise programmes are regularly prescribed for individuals who have a range of health problems. It is often assumed that they will have the necessary repertoire of skills and available resources to enable them to effectively undertake the agreed course, an assumption often falsely based. One major role for health promotion is to help people develop the skills necessary to gain control over their lifestyle and health, in order, to lead a fulfilling social and economically productive life (Tones, 2001). One of the key principles as described in the Ottawa Charter (WHO, 1986) is 'empowerment' and strategies that strengthen an individual's personal competency and resources are, therefore, necessary. Tones (2001) identifies communication, motivation and support as key elements in the role of the health professional in an empowering encounter with an individual. We aim to elaborate on some of these strategies using a social cognitive framework. Specifically, this chapter explores some of the major issues that influence both the delivery, adoption and maintenance of individual home based exercise programmes. We will commence with a discussion of the rationale for home exercise, and discuss psychological strategies that have been found to be effective in assisting individuals to adopt physical activity as part of a healthy lifestyle. In order, to facilitate individual adherence to a prescribed home-based exercise programme, it is argued that we need to focus on the development of self-regulatory skills that can be called upon when the health professional is not present.

High demand on resources has led to increasing pressure on health care professionals to move clients quickly through the health care system, whilst maintaining high quality client care and positive treatment outcomes (Selker, 1995). This movement has led to further health care treatment being continued in both the home and primary health care environment. Self-management programmes have, therefore, become an increasingly popular intervention. Home-based exercise programmes are seen as a low-cost option that have been shown to be as effective as centre-based programmes in relation to, for example, physical function and risk reduction for cardiovascular disease (Brubacker et al., 2000); and maintenance of physical, cognitive and psychological functioning in patients with chronic obstructive pulmonary disease (Emery et al., 2003) Emphasis on home exercise is also reflected in the 'Active Living' messages advocated in national strategies for physical activity promotion during the past ten years in the UK and USA (Killoran et al., 1994).

The problem of adherence

One would expect that those prescribed exercises that are beneficial as both treatment and prevention of illness recurrence would be highly motivated to adhere. Research with a range of patient and non-patient groups indicates, however, that even amongst those who value exercise and are aware of its benefits, adherence is problematic. Physiotherapists, for example, estimate that on average approximately two thirds of patients with chronic back pain comply with exercise prescription during the treatment period, but just over 20 per cent adhere to home exercise recommendations after treatment has stopped. This drop is associated with the moment of discharge and continues to decrease as time passes (Sluijs et al., 1998). A similar problem is found in cardiac rehabilitation (Burke et al., 1997) and chronic obstructive pulmonary disease (Emery et al., 2003). Even individuals one would expect to be highly motivated such as those recovering from sports injury or undergoing physiotherapy have problems adhering to prescribed exercise at home, for example, reports of non-adherence to sport injury rehabilitation are frequent even among elite performers (Lawson et al., 1996). Adherence to long-term home exercise in which there is no supervision, therefore, appears to be particularly problematic.

The terms compliance and adherence are often used interchangeably, nevertheless, a number of fundamental differences exist. First, if the condition is chronic and degenerative, the goal of treatment after discharge from health care is typically prevention of recurrent symptoms rather than treatment aimed at recovery. Secondly, in such cases expectation of recovery, which is a strong motivational force in acute conditions such as those in sport injury rehabilitation, is not present. Furthermore, symptoms that act as cues to remind patients to exercise may no longer be present, particularly, in conditions with long periods of remission. Finally, the presence of a stimulating and supportive therapist is absent in long-term treatment. Compliant behaviour, therefore, reflects willingness to follow or consent to the wishes of another person. Adherence, on the other hand, is the action of sticking to, supporting, or following a person or idea that conceptually is the result of a deeper internalised motivation (Buchmann, 1997). This conceptual shift from compliance to adherence is central to an empowerment approach that emphasises the role of self-regulatory activity on the patient's part.

There are a number of books and articles that summarise effective health promotion strategies; for example, Ley (1997) outlines a series of factors important in influencing adherence to health care interventions, which can be seen in Bennett (2000: 109). A fairly comprehensive list of skills required by health professionals involved in GP-referral schemes can also be found in Biddle and Mutrie (2001: 279). Many of the strategies available to increase adherence to behavioural regimens such as home exercise, are centred on models of social cognition. Basically, it is suggested that if we want to help someone to make a behavioural change such as maintaining a home exercise plan or a physically active lifestyle, we need to first understand and if need be bring about a change in that individuals beliefs. The following section will discuss some of the important issues related to these social cognitive approaches.

Social cognitive models

In order, to develop effective strategies that facilitate adherence to home exercise we need to first understand how and why individuals adopt or refrain from health behaviour. There are a number of theoretical models offering useful frameworks and practical advice regarding strategies for health promotion and motivation for exercise behaviour (Ogden, 2003). To date, no single model has provided a full explanation for exercise adherence. Overlaps between concepts can be confusing and theories are continually augmented and integrated. A number of explanatory models have been developed and utilised in the health domain and useful summary models are provided by Abraham and Sheeran (2000: 8) and Bandura (2000: 301). These Social Cognitive Models share a common assumption that cognitive factors such as values and beliefs and self-regulatory processes such as planning are major determinants of intention and behaviour.

Most Social Cognitive Models suggest that we engage in rational, conscious processes when deciding whether to take a course of action. There are two basic processes required for successful behaviour change, motivation and volition. Motivation is concerned with the development of an 'intention' to exercise. The concept is usually operationalised as 'I will try to', or 'I plan to'. Research on intention formation is more prevalent than research on factors that facilitate behaviour change as an understanding of the antecedents of *intention* is important, based on the well-documented finding that once an intention is formed a person is more likely to act (see, theory of reasoned action in Kaplan et al., 1993: 53–54, also outlined in Chapter 8 of this book). The values and beliefs that underpin intention formation are, therefore, the focus of much of the current health promotion communication targeted at individuals.

The second process, volition is the process of translating intention into behaviour. One challenge encountered all too often by health professionals is that many people have well formed 'intentions' to start an exercise regimen or to comply with recommendations from a health professional but fail to act on this. For them the problem is one of turning these good intentions into action. The process of volition is often the most problematic and involves considerable self-regulation on the part of the client, particularly in the long-term (Abraham and Sheeran, 2000). The distinction between motivation and volition is recognised in action phase theories such as the Health Action Process Approach (HAPA), (see Schwarzer, 1992) and the Model of Action Phases (see Gollwitzer and Oettingen, 2000). Both offer a self-regulatory view and suggest that individuals who successfully pursue health goals do so because they utilise self-regulatory strategies such as 'implementation intentions' when planning, initiating and maintaining exercise behaviour. One key role for health promotion is, therefore, to identify and facilitate the development of supportive resources and skills tailored to the needs of the individual.

It is suggested that elements of a number of different models when combined together may have practical utility in exercise adherence enhancing strategies with patient groups (Thomson, 1999). The two most often cited in the exercise domain are the Theory of Planned Behaviour, (Ajzen and Fishbein, 1980; Ajzen, 1985) and Self-efficacy Theory (Bandura, 1997). A discussion of theories of exercise behaviour can be found in Biddle and Nigg (2000). Self-efficacy Theory suggests that a person must believe that they are capable of performing recommended exercise (exercise self-efficacy) and also perceive an incentive to do so, termed outcome efficacy (Bandura, 1997). In the theory of planned behaviour, perceived behavioural control, which incorporates the concept of self-efficacy (Ajzen, 2002) and outcome expectations that underpin attitudes are motivational factors, having the greatest impact on exercise intention and behaviour. Generally, it is agreed that whilst outcome expectations predict intention, self-efficacy strengthened by positive past experience predicts actual performance, particularly in the long-term.

Promoting adherence to home exercise prescription

Much of the current research highlights behavioural strategies and characteristics of the therapist and therapy environment. Nevertheless, the focus here is the development of motivation and self-regulation, as both are necessary when the ultimate aim is promotion of adherence without the presence of a health professional. One strategy that has become a popular approach and been found to be an effective means of promoting physical activity with both patient and none patient samples (for example, Laitakari and Asikainen, 1998) is physical activity counselling. In the USA for example, 'Project PACE' (Physician-based Assessment and Counselling for Exercise) has been shown to be an effective tool for promoting adherence (Marcus et al., 1997). The approach is very humanistic or person-centred involving (see Rogers, 1967) the use of basic counselling skills. Active listening skills and empathy are used to enhance barrier and benefit identification, increased self-efficacy and social support. Guidelines for effective consultation in the general population are provided by Loughlan and Mutrie (1995).

Promoting strategies

The following section discusses a selection of strategies that are often incorporated within physical activity counselling. All have a sound theoretical base and empirical support and focus on a self-regulatory perspective. They should all be effective when presented within a client-centred approach that focuses on the needs, expectations, resources and general lifestyle of the individual as well as their readiness to change, and may be useful when promoting home exercise adherence with individuals in the context of exercise referral, physiotherapy and sport injury rehabilitation. Examples of these are: education, increasing awareness of risk, increasing positive outcome expectations, increasing self-efficacy, implementation intentions with goal setting, increasing barrier self-efficacy, social support and follow-up home based exit strategies. Each of these strategies, together with an assessment of their effectiveness will be discussed in the following section.

During a consultation process the basic principles of *motivational interviewing* developed by Miller and Rollnick (1991) may be utilised. The aim is to help clients explore conflicting beliefs and ambivalent attitudes by using a non-directive, empathic approach (Bennett, 2000: 146–147). This process is found to be particularly effective with individuals who have not yet started exercising (Lowther et al., 1996). Within the framework of the Transtheoretical Model of Behaviour Change (see Prochaska and Markus, 1994) advocated by the Health Education Authority (1995a; 1995b) motivational interviewing may be a useful strategy when helping individuals move from precontemplation to contemplation and eventually to the action stage of exercise change.

Education plays a major role in the initial phase of any consultation or treatment programme, as patients may not fully understand their condition, or the rationale for physical activity and skills involved in performing exercise. The main role of the exercise professional or physiotherapist is to instruct and advise on safe and effective physical activity. Exercise instruction and advice about home exercise and keeping fit are typically given in at least two thirds of all physiotherapy treatment sessions (Sluijs, 1991). Nevertheless, knowing why and how to undertake exercise does not necessarily lead to adherence. A secondary and perhaps more important role in relation to adherence is one of motivation. Motivating patients' to undertake home exercise both during the treatment phase and after the treatment has stopped is an essential element of the consultation process. Counselling, motivation, behaviour management and goal setting, for example, are typically the focus of attention following on from initial consultation in physiotherapy, GP referral, and so on.

Increasing an individual's awareness of risk has also been seen as an important strategy related to behaviour change. Health promotion strategies often include educational information about risk and risk reduction. This can be effective at enhancing awareness. Knowledge and awareness of risk, however, does not necessarily lead to intention formation or behaviour change. Many individuals in rehabilitation are well informed about the nature of their condition and the consequences of not exercising. Contrary to popular belief fear appeals, for example, do not necessarily lead to behaviour change and can in fact have the opposite effect in those who choose to remain non-compliant. Fifty-eight per cent of athletes asked what injury rehabilitation strategies would not be effective methods of enhancing adherence said, 'threats and scare tactics', (Fisher and Hoisington, 1993). Scaring people into healthy behaviour by arousing fear of disease or increasing perceived vulnerability is less effective than increasing personal efficacy beliefs (see Ruiter et al., 2001).

Increasing positive outcome expectations in an individual has also been seen as an important strategy related to behaviour change. Outcome expectations reflect the belief that a course of action will lead to anticipated outcomes and act as an incentive provided the person values the outcome (Bandura, 1997). The concept is closely related to behavioural beliefs that make up attitudes in the Theory of Planned Behaviour (TpB). According to TpB, intention to engage in exercise and subsequent behaviour will be largely influenced by the person's attitude to the activity in question. Attitude according to this model is composed of behavioural beliefs regarding perceived outcomes and the value placed on each. Individuals who perceive many advantages and few disadvantages are more likely to engage in and maintain health behaviour. The Health Education Authority (1995a; 1995b, currently named the Health Development Agency) now recommends weighing up pros and cons or 'decisional balance' as a way of influencing behaviour change and this is found to be particularly useful with individuals who have not yet formed a strong intention. It is, therefore, important to find out a number of factors affecting an individual's perception of undertaking home-based exercise programmes, such as: What physical activities are attractive to the individual? Why are these attractive? What do they find enjoyable and stimulating? What do they dislike or fear? What have they enjoyed in the past? What opportunities are available to them now? The aim is to enhance intrinsic motivation, as this is a stronger motivational influence than more tangible, extrinsic rewards.

Increasing self-efficacy in the individual is another important strategy related to behaviour change. During consultation, strategies should be adopted that enhance exercise self-efficacy in the client. Self-efficacy is primarily enhanced by positive past and present experience. Guided mastery practice and informative feedback are, consequently, important elements of the consultation process. It is important, therefore, to aim to develop a strong sense of exercise self-efficacy, alongside motor skill. Vicarious experience from observation of realistic role models and verbal persuasion also play a role when a person is judging their capability (Bandura, 1986). The final source of self-efficacy is physiological arousal. This may be particularly important to consider when patients are anxious or feel pain and discomfort during exercise. An individual's self-efficacy can, therefore, be increased by optimizing their vicarious experiences, together, with verbal persuasion and by facilitating the development of a physically active self-identity. It is, therefore, important to ensure that experiences are positive in terms of the individual's physical, mental, physical and physiological state. The aim is to develop a feeling of competence in ability (exercise self-efficacy) in the individual.

Goal setting is another important strategy related to behaviour change. It is an approach that has been adopted by health professionals to help translate *intention* into *action*. It is important, nevertheless, to distinguish between 'goal intention' and 'goal pursuit' when setting goals with clients. The former is concerned with making a decision to pursue a goal and is similar to the motivational phase of intention formation within the Theory of Planned Behaviour. The latter with the volitional processes involved in turning this intention into initiation, maintenance and relapse prevention. To successfully maintain exercise at home your client must implement the self-regulatory skill of planning. 'Implementation intentions' are specific plans that specify when, where and how an activity is to be carried out (Gollwitzer, 1993). Evidence suggests that specifying when and where exercises will take place will significantly increase the likelihood of initiating exercise activity (volition) provided the person already intends (motivation) to do it (Milne et al., 2002). It is, therefore, important to empower your client by using a questioning approach. For example, by asking when and where specific exercises will take place, what preparatory activities need to be in place and drawing up a contract to enhance their commitment.

Identifying and reducing barriers is another important strategy. Maintaining exercise activity requires a range of self-regulatory skills such as adjusting goals, creating incentives, seeking social support and coping with difficulties. Exercise activity can be made difficult, for example, due to the presence of disabling symptoms, exacerbation of pain and discomfort or increased anxiety. In situations where barriers arise it may be more appropriate to focus implementation intentions on the actions needed to cope with barriers rather than the exercise itself. In accordance with Bandura (1997), we can differentiate between belief in ability to carry out a task (exercise self-efficacy) and belief in ability to cope with barriers (coping or barrier self-efficacy). It is extremely important, therefore, to identify barriers and perceived ability to overcome barriers, and to develop action plans for coping with barriers alongside carefully structured exercise plans. In this way action plans can be made that focus not only on where and when (implementation intentions), but also on 'what' needs to be done, or 'how' home exercise will be maintained under specific adverse conditions. Strategies can be developed that identify and deconstruct barriers, thereby, enabling the client cope with these adverse factors. The aim, therefore, is to develop a sense of control over any barriers (barrier or coping self-efficacy) as they arise.

Social support is also a key factor influencing exercise behaviour, as it is important that we feel important when others support our activity. Its dimensions include social interaction, subjective support and instrumental support. Close relatives are an important source of social support. Positive feedback from GPs, nurses and fellow exercisers and attendance at self-help group meetings all play an important role in successful rehabilitation. Individuals attending group physical therapy sessions are more likely to continue with exercises at home than those who do not attend. A group-mediated counselling intervention was more effective than a traditional cardiac rehabilitation exercise training programme in relation to physical activity adherence with a sample of older adults (Schneiderman et al., 2001). On occasions, however, the social influence may not necessarily be supportive. The presence of others, for example, can be intimidating for some. It is important to ensure that the support is proactive and to include the support agent or relative at all stages of education and motivation. The aim is to facilitate seeking out of others who can actively support the individual. Telephone support and mail reminders, for example, can act as sources of information, *aide-mémoire* and also offer a message of support.

Follow-up home-based exit strategies have also been found to be particularly important in physical exercise adherence. A review of interventions for promoting physical activity adherence in the UK in 1996, for example, suggested that the most successful strategies involved behaviour modification strategies concerning goal-setting but also regular follow-up (Hillsdon and Thorogood, 1996). Use of video, newsletters, partner participation and telephone contact are strategies thought to enhance participation in rehabilitation involving home exercise (Stevens et al., 2003). The mediating processes thought to link strategy to exercise behaviour are education, increased self-efficacy and increase social support.

Summary

Perhaps the most frustrating issue for health professionals promoting adherence to home exercise is the fact that knowing 'how' and 'why' exercise should be carried out does not necessarily lead, however, to formation of a strong intention to exercise. Furthermore, even when a person is knowledgeable, exercise is valued and a strong intention is formed, this does not necessarily lead to successful exercise behaviour. Both initiation and maintenance require considerable behaviour change. Educating patients is apparently not sufficient to increase behaviour change. Although, education, reinforcements and cues may be useful in short-term treatment, approaches that focus on the self-regulatory nature of adherence may be more appropriate with individuals managing their own exercise at home. Scare tactics are not particularly effective. Focus should be on developing awareness of self-regulatory capabilities and coping resources that aid the implementation of self-regulatory skills.

Conclusion

In conclusion, the following are suggested to be effective strategies to use when promoting home exercise adherence:

- Communicate using basic counselling skills in order to develop empathy with your client and perhaps motivational interviewing when attitude change is the aim.
- Use cognitive-behaviour strategies that:
  - Educate to increase knowledge of the rationale for exercise recommendations in order to challenge values and beliefs.
  - Increase awareness of benefits and reduce perceptions of cost to enhance outcome expectations.
  - Set goals for exercise performance with the aim of maximising perceptions of competence in order to increase self-efficacy.
  - Utilise action planning to help develop the implementation intentions that will aid the translation of an intention into action.
  - Identify and develop strategies for overcoming barriers when they arise in order to enhance barrier self-efficacy.
  - Encourage efforts to increase support from the client's own social network as well as self-help groups.
  - Utilise direct or mediated follow up when possible.

All are based on social cognitive models shown to be effective in a variety of settings with a range of target groups and should be used alongside exercise instruction and advice.

References

Abraham, C. and Sheeran, P. (2000) Understanding and changing health behaviour: From health beliefs to self-regulation in Norman, P., Abraham, C. and Conner, M. (Eds.) *Understanding and Changing Health Behaviour: From Beliefs to Self-Regulation*. Amsterdam: Harwood Academic Publishers, 3–24.

Ajzen, I. (1985) From intentions to actions: A theory of planned behaviour in Kuhl, J. and Beckham, J. (Eds.) *Action Control: From Cognition to Behaviour*. New York: Springer-Verlag.

Ajzen, I. (2002) Perceived behavioural control, self-efficacy, locus of control, and the theory of planned behaviour, *Journal of Applied Social Psychology*, 32(4), 665–683.

Ajzen, I. and Fishbein, M. (1980) *Understanding Attitudes and Predicting Social Behaviour.* Englewood Cliffs, NJ: Prentice-Hall.

Bandura, A. (2000) Health promotion from the perspective of social cognitive theory in Norman, P., Abraham, C. and Conner, M. (Eds.) *Understanding and Changing Health Behaviour: From Beliefs to Self-regulation.* Amsterdam: Harwood Academic Publisher.

Bandura, A. (1997) *Self-efficacy: The Exercise of Control.* New York: Freeman.

Bandura, A. (1986) *Social Foundations of Thought and Action: A Social Cognitive Theory.* Englewood Cliffs, NJ: Prentice-Hall.

Bennet, P. (2000) *Introduction to Clinical Health Psychology.* Buckingham: Open University Press.

Biddle, S. J. H. and Mutrie, N. (2001) *Psychology of Physical Activity: Determinants, Well-Being and Interventions.* London: Routledge.

Biddle, S. J. H. and Nigg, C. (2000) Theories of exercise behaviour, *International Journal of Sport Psychology*, 31, 290–304.

Brubacker, P. H., Rejeski, W. J., Smith, M. J., Sevensky, K. H., Lamb, K. A., Sotile, W. M. and Miller, H. S. (2000) A home-based maintenance exercise programme after centre-based cardiac rehabilitation: Effects on blood lipids, body composition, and functional capacity, *Journal of Cardiopulmonary Rehabilitation*, 20, 50–56.

Buchmann, W. F. (1997) Adherence: A matter of self-efficacy and power, *Journal of Advanced Nursing*, 26, 132–137.

Burke, L. E., Dunbar-Jacob, J. M. and Hill, M. N. (1997) Compliance with cardiovascular disease prevention strategies: A review of the research, *Annals of Behavioural Medicine*, 19, 239–263.

Emery, C., Shermer, R., Hauck, E., Hsiao, E. and MacIntyre, N. (2003) Cognitive and psychological outcomes of exercise in a 1-year follow-up study of patients with chronic obstructive pulmonary diseases, *Health Psychology*, 22(6), 598–604.

Fisher, A. C. and Hoisington, L. L. (1993) Injured athletes' attitudes and judgements toward rehabilitation adherence, *Journal of Athletic Training*, 28(1), 48–54.

Gollwitzer, P. M. (1993) Goal achievement: The role of intentions, *European Review of Social Psychology*, 4, 141–185.

Gollwitzer, P. M. and Oettingen, G. (2000) The emergence and implementation of health goals in Norman, P., Abraham, C. and Conner, M. (Eds.) *Understanding and Changing Health Behaviour: From Self-Beliefs to Self-Regulation*, 229–260. Amsterdam: Harwood.

Health Education Authority (1995a; 1995b) in Biddle, S. J. H. and Mutrie, N. (2001) *Psychology of physical activity: Determinants, Well-Being and Interventions.* London: Routledge, 335.

Hillsdon, M. and Thorogood, M. (1996) A systematic review of physical activity promotion strategies, *British Journal of Sports Medicine*, 30: 84–89.

Kaplan, R., Sallis, J. and Patterson, T. (1993) *Health and Human Behaviour.* New York: McGraw-Hill International Editions, Psychology Series.

Killoran, A. J., Fentem, P. and Caspersen, C. (Eds.) (1994) *Moving On. International Perspectives in Promoting Physical Activity.* London: HEA.

Laitakari, J. and Asikainen, T. (1998) How to promote physical activity through individual counselling: A proposal for a practical model of counselling on health related physical activity, *Patient Education and Counselling*, 33: S13–S24.

Lawson, G. A., Starkey, C. A. and Zaichowsky, L. D. (1996) Psychological aspects of athletic injuries as perceived by athletic trainers, *The Sports Psychologist*, 10, 37–47.

Ley, P. (1997) Compliance among patients in Baum, A., Newman, S., Weinman, J., West, R. and McManus, C. (Eds.) *Cambridge Handbook of Psychology, Health and Medicine.* Cambridge: Cambridge University Press.

Loughlan, C. and Mutrie, N. (1995) Conducting and exercise consultation: Guidelines for health professionals, *Journal of the Institute of Health Education*, 33(3), 78–82.

Loughlan, C. and Mutrie, N. (1997) An evaluation of the effectiveness of three interventions in promoting physical activity in a sedentary population, *Health Education Journal*, 56, 154–164.

Lowther, M., Mutrie, N. and Scott, M. (1999) Attracting the general public to physical activity interventions: A comparison of fitness assessment and exercise consultations, *Journal of Sports Sciences*, 17, 62–63.

Ogden, J. (2003) Brief reports. Some problems with social cognition models: A pragmatic and conceptual analysis, *Health Psychology*, 22(4), 424–428.

Marcus, B., Goldstein, M. G., Jette, A., Simkin-Silverman, L., Pinto, B. M., Milan, F., Wahburn, R., Smith, K., Rakowski, W. and Dob, C. E. (1997) Training physicians to conduct physical activity counseling, *Preventive Medicine*, 26, 382–388.

Miller, W. R. and Rollnick, S. (1991) *Motivational Interviewing: Preparing People to Change Addictive Behaviour.* New York: Guilford Press.

Milne, S., Orbell, S. and Sheeran, P. (2002) Combining motivational and volitional interventions to promote exercise participation: Protection motivation theory and implementation intentions, *British Journal of Health Psychology*, 7(2), 163–184.

Prochaska, J. O. and Markus, B. H. (1994) The transtheoretical model: Applications to exercise in Dishman, R. K. (Ed.) *Advances in Exercise Adherence*, 161–180. Champaign, IL: Human Kinetics.

Rogers, C. R. (1967) *The Therapeutic Relationship and its Impact.* Madison WI: University of Wisconsin Press.

Ruiter, R. A. C., Abraham, C. and Kok, G. (2001) Scary warnings and rational precautions: A review of the psychology of fear appeals, *Psychology and Health*, 17, 405–416.

Schneiderman, N., Antoni, M. H., Saab, P. G. and Ironson, G. (2001) Health psychology: Psychosocial and biobehavioural aspects of chronic disease management, *Annual Review of Psychology*, 52, 555–580.

Schwarzer, R. (1992) Self-efficacy in the adoption and maintenance of health behaviours: Theoretical approaches and a new model in Schwarzer, R. (Ed.) *Self Efficacy: Thought Control of Action.* Washington DC: Hemisphere.

Sluijs, E. M. (1991) Patient education in physiotherapy: Towards a planned approach, *Physiotherapy*, 77, 503–508.

Sluijs, E. M., Kerssens, J. J., van der Zee, J. and Myers, L. B. (1998) Adherence to physiotherapy in Myers, L. B. and Midence, K. (Eds.) *Adherence to Treatment in Medical Conditions.* Amsterdam: Harwood Academic Publishers: 363–382.

Selker, L. (1995) Human resources in physical therapy: Opportunities for service in a rapidly changing health system, *Physical Therapy*, 75, 31–37.

Stevens, M., van den Akker-Scheek, I., Spriensma, A., Boss, N. A. D., Diercks, R. L. and van Horn, J. R. (2004) The Groningen orthopedic exit strategy (GOES): a home-based support programme for total hip and knee arthroplasty patients after shortened hospital stay, *Patient Education and Counselling*, 54(1), July, 95–99.

Tones, K. (2001) Health promotion: The empowerment imperative in Scriven, A. and Orme, J. (Eds.) *Health Promotion: Professional Perspectives.* Basingstoke: Palgrave: 3–18.

Thomson, P. (1999) A review of behavioural change theories in patient compliance to exercise-based rehabilitation following acute myocardial infarction, *Coronary Health Care*, 3(1), 18–24.

Turk, D. C. and Rudy, T. E. (1991) Neglected topics in the treatment of chronic pain patients: Relapse, non-compliance and adherence enhancement, *Pain*, 44, 5–28.

World Health Organization (1986) Ottawa Charter for Health Promotion: An International Conference on Health Promotion, November 17–21. Copenhagen: WHO.

PART III
HEALTH OF COMMUNITIES

Physical Activity across the Lifespan: Establishing Community-Based Classes for the Older Person

LORRAINE HUGHES

Introduction

The aim of this chapter is to introduce you to some of the issues and processes that may need to be addressed by practitioners concerned with using physical activity to promote health and well-being in the older population. This will be achieved through drawing upon examples from work that I have been involved with, which focused upon the older adult. For the purpose of this work, an older person was classified as someone aged 50 years or more, in accordance with the guidelines of the National Ageing Well United Kingdom programme, which was delivered through Age Concern England.

The first part of the chapter will provide an overview of the context in which the work took place, including the influence of national health policy. The second part will look in more detail at the emergence of accident prevention, as a focus of public health and the programme of work itself, exploring how models of health promotion were used to develop the intervention. The third and final part of the chapter will reflect on the current context regarding health, physical activity and the older person.

The intervention that will be used as a framework to explore the role of community-based classes in supporting activity across the lifespan, took place during my time working in the voluntary sector in the North East. My role was project co-ordinator of an Ageing Well United Kingdom Project, with a particular focus on accident prevention. It is worth reflecting at this point on the national Ageing Well United Kingdom Programme, which is delivered through Age Concern England. Ageing Well United Kingdom is a national health promotion programme delivered with and for older people. The aim of Ageing Well United Kingdom is to recruit older volunteers to work within local communities promoting healthy ageing initiatives, maximising the potential of older people to act as a health resource for their peers, with a focus on coronary heart disease, stroke, mental health and accidents. In 1993, the programme provided support to a wide range of work being carried out under the banner of health (Bernard, 2000; Age Concern, 2005).

The Ageing Well Project that I was involved with was developed in response to the Health of the Nation (Department of Health, 1992), local epidemiological data and a feasibility study commissioned in 1996. The Health of the Nation (Department of Health, 1992) identified accident prevention amongst older people as a priority, with a target set for a reduction in mortality amongst people aged 65 and over, as a result of accidents, to a rate of 37.9 per 100,000 by the year 2000 (Department of Health, 1992). Nationally and locally, there was recognition that accidents were a major cause of mortality, morbidity and ill health among older people and that accidental falls are a major contributing factor (Everitt et al., 1996). The feasibility study undertaken by the Social Welfare Unit, at the University of Northumbria in September 1996 found that in the area under study, falls accounted for nearly 60 per cent of reported external causes of accidental injury among people aged 65 and over. No accident prevention schemes were currently in existence and there was acknowledgement amongst primary health care staff that there were gaps in the services provided where the issue of accident prevention was concerned (Everitt et al., 1996).

The importance of healthy ageing and the profile of accident prevention and the older person have persisted as strong themes within national policy, most notably in the National Service Framework for Older People published in 2001. The document identifies eight standards pertinent to the older person, including falls and the promotion of health and active life in older age, outlining a programme of action and reform to address the needs of older people and deliver high quality services (Department of Health, 2001).

The ageing population: health and physical activity

The Office for National Statistics (2000) recognises that the United Kingdom has an 'ageing population', but what does this actually mean in practice? The term 'ageing population' has two characteristics. First, the number and proportions of older people have experienced a dramatic increase during the twentieth century; secondly, the older population is itself ageing, with projections that between 1995 and 2025 the number of people over the age of 80 will increase by almost half, and the number of people over the age of 90 will double. Such trends are attributable to a number of factors, including declining fertility that leads to fewer young people in the population, declining mortality rates and greater life expectancy (Bernard, 2000). The statistics give credence to these statements, with predictions that between 1996 and 2021, the number of people aged 65 and over will increase by 30 per cent, whilst the number of children aged under 14 will decline by 9 per cent (Health Promotion England, 2001).

More recent data from the Office for National Statistics (2004) describes a similar picture. There were 19.8 million people aged 50 and over in the United Kingdom in 2002, a 24 per cent increase over four decades, from 16.0 million in 1961. The number of people aged 50 and over is projected to increase by a further 37 per cent by 2031, when there will be near to 27 million people aged 50 and over. Projections for 2031 also indicate a more rapid ageing of the population, with people aged 85 and over comprising 3.8 per cent of the UK population.

Older people are not a homogenous group, but a group with a wide range of needs (Bernard, 2000). Three distinct groups of older people have been identified, which may be helpful or limiting when considering the older population (Department of Health, 2001). These three groups are:

1. Entering old age – people who have completed their career in paid employment and/or child rearing. This is a socially constructed definition of old age and could include people as young as 50. This group tend to be active and independent, with many remaining so into late old age.
2. Transitional phase – a group of older people in transition between healthy, active life and frailty, often occurring in the seventh or eighth decades.
3. Frail older people – people who are vulnerable as a result of health problems, social care needs or a combination of both.

An ageing population has huge implications for health and social care, and presents a challenge to all those with a role in promoting health and well-being. The physiological process of growing older has been consistently associated with disease and disability, resulting in a perception that old age is synonymous with pain, discomfort, illness, disease, sickness and increased immobility and dependency (Bernard, 2000). Nevertheless, individually held beliefs and attitudes about health are complex, and varied. The lay population identify the absence of disease/not being ill, as being functionally fit/coping with daily activities and a state of positive fitness as dimensions of health (Bernard, 2000; Reed et al., 2004). For older people specifically, there is a greater emphasis on health being viewed in functional terms, highlighting the importance of being able to cope, undertaking important daily activities and maintaining a level of independence (Bernard, 2000; Hughes, 2002).

Physical activity has an integral role to play in supporting older people to achieve greater longevity, and a period of old age that brings with it a healthy and fulfilling life (Department of Health, 2001). As people get older, functional capacity declines: strength, endurance, bone density, flexibility and muscle power are all affected (Skelton and McLaughlin, 1996). This results in daily activities such as rising from a chair, getting up from the floor or climbing stairs, becoming difficult, if not impossible. Participation in regular physical activity can help to limit or reverse such decline (see Chapter 5). It has been shown that it is possible to achieve the equivalent of 15 years rejuvenation of muscle strength in 3 months, among people aged over 75, from strength training, consisting of one supervised class a week, and home exercises (Skelton and McLaughlin, 1996). Regular physical activity can also provide other health benefits for older people, including:

- Reduction in coronary heart disease and stroke.
- Management of type II diabetes.
- Prevention and management of osteoporosis.
- Weight control and management.
- Relief of arthritis.
- Prevention and control of high blood pressure.
- Improved quality of sleep.
- Reduced risk of colon cancer.
- Maintenance of independence and mobility.

(United States Surgeon General, 1996; Health Promotion England, 2001)

It is impossible, as health promoters to ignore the overwhelming strength of evidence for a physically active lifestyle for any age group, including the older person. Accepting that physical activity can enhance mobility and independence, and improve quality of life, presents a challenge to us all to develop and promote opportunities for physical activity (Department of Health, 2001). The significance of this is even greater, given that a large proportion of people over the age of 50 are sedentary, and few participate in the recommended levels of physical activity for improving health (Department of Health, 2001; Health Promotion England, 2001).

Public health and accident prevention

Green (1999) argues that accidents have not always been regarded as a public health issue, but as an event for which responsibility should be accepted at the micro, individual level. By the middle of the twentieth century, health planners no longer regarded accidents as random misfortunes, but as something constructed and preventable (Green, 1997; Green, 1999). This is an approach that has been reflected within health policy, which prioritised accident prevention as a public health issue (Green, 1997; Department of Health, 1999; Green, 1999; Department of Health, 2001). This led to the emergence of a 'professional' view of accidents, located within a discourse of risk management, increased epidemiological mapping and the development of a body of knowledge for the purpose of prevention (Blaxter, 1999).

Contemporary health promotion practice mainly focuses on primary and secondary prevention, and highlights the role of education as a key strategy for accident prevention (Green, 1997). Most recently, the National Service Framework for Older People (Department of Health, 2001) has emphasised the importance of both falls prevention and the need to promote health and well-being (Department of Health, 2001).

Box 10.1   Activity identifying main links between health, physical activity and accident prevention

Activity
Identify what you think are the main links between health, physical activity and accident prevention.

Feedback
Appropriate physical activity can help to improve balance and co-ordination and maintain or build muscle strength, all of which can play an important role in preventing accidental falls in the older person.

  Physical activity can also promote positive mental well-being and provide opportunities for social interaction, which can be beneficial to a person's overall state of health.

The relationship between physical activity and the prevention of accidents (seen in Box 10.1), particularly falls is well documented, and any literature search will highlight a plethora of articles available on the topic (Health Promotion England, 2001). It is recognised that strength, balance and endurance training has an important role to play in reducing the risk of falling, as does Tai Chi as an exercise (Health Promotion England, 2001). Nonetheless, there are debates about the type, intensity and frequency of physical activity that is of benefit to preventing falls, or minimising the resulting morbidity from an accidental fall. Whilst it is important to be aware of such debates when considering the evidence base for specific interventions, it is important to reflect at this point that the target age group for the project allowed for flexibility, and a broader approach to physical activity and the older adult.

  The need to support community programmes of physical activity was identified because of the acceptance of the wide range of potential benefits resulting from an increase in levels of physical activity. In addition, the importance placed on primary prevention (that provides an opportunity to work with older people who had not yet fallen, and had a reasonable level of health and mobility, for the purpose of preventing falls in the future) and promoting the ageing well message.

Development of a community-based programme of physical activity

Recognising that physical activity has a wide range of benefits, and is important to physical, emotional and social well-being (Finch, 1997; Victor and Howse,

2000; Health Promotion England, 2001), does not overcome the issue that when developing community based programmes of work you need to consider the needs and values of your target audience. In this instance, the target group can be defined as the older adult; they should not be regarded as a homogeneous group (Bernard, 2000). Accepting that people will have different perceptions, previous experiences and attitudes towards physical activity, it is important to consider a number of issues before implementing a physical activity programme.

A qualitative study conducted by Finch (1997) provides a useful insight into the experiences, attitudes, barriers and motivations of the older person towards physical activity, and is useful to consider prior to planning any intervention. The research found that people held some strong beliefs about the relationship between physical activity and health. People did recognise that physical activity was beneficial to health, general fitness and well-being, and there was an emphasis on the social benefits of physical activity. Nevertheless, there was also a sense that physical activity could be dangerous, necessitating the need for moderation (Finch, 1997).

In exploring people's reasons for participating in physical activity, Finch (1997) summarised that people had to want to do it, and that there was often a desire to counter the effects of ageing, maintain suppleness, and manage weight. Finch (1997) identified many barriers to participation in physical activity including embarrassment, lack of confidence, safety concerns, lack of interest, and potential risks to health (Box 10.2).

In planning an activity, it is important to use any information available for familiarising yourself with the target group. If no such information is available, it may be possible to gather your own, by conducting a small-scale needs assessment. See for instance, examples in the handbook by the Scottish Community Development Centre (2000).

Box 10.2   Activity identifying the issues to consider when planning a community based programme of physical activity

Activity
What issues do you think are important to consider when planning a community-based programme of physical activity?

Feedback
Some important issues to consider include venue, timing, cost and the type of activity on offer, to ensure the programme appeals to as many of the target group as possible. To support this you would want to speak to interested parties first, to find out what would appeal to them. It would also be important to consider publicity, transport and insurance.

The aim of the programme was to support older people in becoming more physically active, and to provide opportunities for physical activity in an environment that was supportive and encouraging, recognising the importance of social support networks.

Beattie's model of health promotion (Figure 10.1), which was adapted in 1991 to support analysis of the theoretical underpinnings of health promotion (Jones and Naidoo, 1997), is a useful tool for consideration in the development of community based health promotion activity. This is because it encourages practitioners to reflect on how and why they are following a particular path.

The model considers the 'mode of intervention' and the 'focus of intervention'. When considering the mode of intervention it is important to reflect on whether it is to be 'top down', that is imposed and authoritative, or whether it is driven more by a 'bottom up' approach, and as such is negotiated and hopefully owned by the target group. The focus of the intervention is also an important consideration at the outset. Is the focus to be on the individual, and by implication small scale in nature? Or is it to be targeted more at the collective level: an approach inherent within the population approach of many health promotion campaigns? Whilst it is important to give attention to such considerations, it is also important to reflect at this point that 'health promotion' and an individual's understanding of health are not always synonymous (Ewles and Simnett, 1999). Many interventions may draw on more than one mode or focus of intervention, or maybe used in a diluted way to greater effect.

In the example drawn upon here, the intention was to develop a community-based programme for a group of older people in a way that

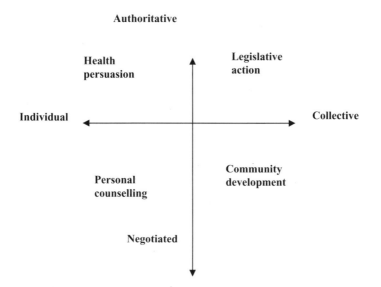

Figure 10.1 Beattie's model of health promotion (1991)

enabled them to shape the development and delivery of the programme. Translated to Beattie's model, the intention was to develop the programme utilising a community development approach. Whilst the aim was to establish an ongoing programme of physical activity in the community, the decision was taken not to impose upon older people what this activity would be. Rather, the aim was to provide people with an opportunity to try different types of activity in a non-threatening environment, and for them to provide feedback about whether they liked it, and if they would like it to be a permanent activity. In planning this programme a whole range of issues needed to be considered. These included types of physical activity on offer, location and venue cost, timing, day of delivery, issues of access, transport and publicity. It was also important to find out what people preferred, especially if the activity was to become sustainable. This was supported through providing opportunities for discussion and interaction amongst the group.

It was decided that a short programme of taster sessions would be delivered in a local community centre that had a large sport hall, a smaller informal room that could be used at the beginning and end of the session, and facilities for refreshments. The sessions would run once a week for four weeks on a morning, taking into account the times of public transport. These sessions were publicised in the local paper and through posters and flyers, which were displayed in the community centre and at other key sites in the area, including the library, post office, sheltered accommodation and shops. Following consideration of planning issues, a four-week programme was devised, which offered different sessions: dance, chair-based exercise, gentle aerobics and Tai Chi. The sessions were offered free of charge to all participants and the number of participants was monitored, including gender split. At each session information was gathered from participants through a short questionnaire, which asked information about age, what they had enjoyed about the session, what could be improved, if they would be interested in attending such a class on a more permanent basis, if so, how much they would be willing to pay, and what their preferred day of the week and time would be. This was done each week as different participants came to the sessions, although many attended all four.

At each of the sessions refreshments were made available at the end and a room was available for people to relax in. This became very popular with lots of people discussing the sessions, as well as providing further opportunity to talk to people informally and find out their thoughts about the activity and the tutor.

Following analysis of the questionnaires submitted, a decision was taken to establish a Tai Chi group in the community centre. Whilst the gentle aerobics session was popular, the Ageing Well Programme had recently started such a group in a neighbouring community centre, and from local knowledge, no other Tai Chi group ran nearby. Information was sent to all those who had attended and supplied their contact details, explaining which session would be continued and why. It was necessary at this stage to introduce a fee for the session, as although it was possible to subsidise it by a small amount initially, it was also important to consider the long-term sustainability of the group. Using a small amount of funding to support the group in the early stages, alongside the money that was paid by participants each week, which went back into supporting the group, it was possible to run the class on an ongoing basis. It was also important to attract other members to the class, as the nature of any group is that some people will continue, whilst others will withdraw or attend intermittingly. The goal was to get enough participants to cover the costs of hiring the hall and the tutor. To support this, group members were encouraged to continue with refreshments at the end of the session and volunteers were identified to undertake this role. The group ran very successfully for many months with a large number of people on the register, although there were only 15 regular participants.

Beattie's model of health promotion (Beattie, 1991) is useful as it emphasises the importance of social and political values, and provides an opportunity to reflect as a practitioner on some of the ethical dilemmas implicit within health promotion. Whilst I can argue that the project recognised the importance of involving the target group as much as possible, and following community development principles my professional role also required me to meet particular objectives. Recognising the health benefits of physical activity for prevention and health improvement, coupled with the need to demonstrate at least the short-term impacts of the wider programme, it could also be argued that the health persuasion approach was dominant. The desired long-term outcome was for people to maintain a change in their behaviour, in this instance being physically active, and for health gains to be evident. For me this presents an ethical dilemma in terms of how far professional aims can be pursued, before becoming detrimental to an approach grounded in the principles of negotiation and joint ownership.

Over time, the sessions continued with an identifiable core group, although it did not become self-sufficient, primarily due to the high costs of the tutor coupled with the room hire. There was ongoing publicity of the sessions to try to attract more members, although attending an established group can be a barrier for many people, due to embarrassment, fear and not wanting to enter a strange environment alone (Finch, 1997). I continued to visit the group on a regular basis, sometimes taking part, to see how things were developing and meet and talk to the members. This helped to develop a rapport with the members, and I was able to begin to talk to them about the future of the class. The intention had always been that the group should be able to run independently, so I began to discuss the finances of the group with key members, asking them for suggestions as to how they would like to proceed, and emphasising the importance of attracting new members to the group. In a further effort to continue the group, I also negotiated tutor costs and was able to reduce this by a quarter, on the agreement that if numbers rose again for a continued period there would be the possibility to re-negotiate. Through addressing the sustainability of the group in this way it was possible to encourage the participants and the tutor to consider the future of the group, and to take responsibility for it. Financial support for the group was not withdrawn in totality at this point but it was emphasised that it would not be able to continue at the present level. Whilst in hindsight there were disadvantages to this approach in that members of the group may not have been ready for the responsibility of meeting the costs for the session the group did continue for over two years (see activity Box 10.3).

Box 10.3   Activity identifying what needs to be done to ensure the sustainability of the group

Activity

What would you have done at this point to ensure the sustainability of the group?

Feedback

One solution would have been to continue to support the group, whilst also working with a local agency experienced in fundraising. This would have provided the group with support and expertise to apply for additional funding in their own right, beginning with the process of becoming a constituted group.

Ensuring the continuous publicity of the group to a wide audience would also support the sustainability of the group, through the attraction of new members.

As with any work undertaken it is always valuable to look back upon it and reflect on how things could have been done differently. Whilst the intention for establishing the group was to support health improvement, and the approach used meant that a degree of choice was given to participants, this was still in the context of set parameters, one of which was time. Upon reflection the work would have benefited from more developmental time, as this would have enabled more work to be undertaken prior to the commencement of the taster sessions to consult with the community. More time should have also been spent on considering the short and long-term goals of the intervention, with the support of other agencies, including one with expertise on fundraising. It was also unrealistic to expect the group to become self-sustaining in such a short timescale, and more support and time should have been given to developing the group toward independent status. This would have enabled the group to apply for financial support in its own right, and enabled members of the group to take it forward in a way, which was reflective of the wishes of the group. To help support this it may have been beneficial to liase with staff from leisure services at an early stage, as they may have been able to provide support with tuition fees.

Conclusion

The need to promote the health and well-being of older people and reduce accidents has continued to be emphasised, with an emphasis on the injuries resulting from accidental falls (Department of Health, 1999; Department of Health, 2001). The National Service Framework for Older People (Department of Health, 2001) contained two standards relevant to this discussion, one of which was concerned with falls, whilst the other looked at the promotion of health and active life in older age. The aim of the latter standard is 'to extend the healthy life expectancy of older people' through a co-ordinated programme of action (Department of Health, 2001: 107). A search of local NHS bodies and Local Authorities will illustrate that the issue of physical activity continues to be taken seriously, with the development of many local Physical Activity Strategies, many of which identify the older person as a distinct group with particular needs and motivators separate to that of the general adult population. It is important, however, to remember that within this, the older population are not a homogenous group (Bernard, 2000). The challenge for us all, therefore, is to encourage and support older people to become more physically active, by listening to their views. In addition, by providing a range of accessible and enjoyable opportunities for physical activity, and resisting the temptation to concord with 'disengagement theory', which argues that as people grow older they will withdraw from society, disengaging from everyday experiences and activities (Reed, Stanley and Clark, 2004).

References

Age Concern (2005) www.ageconcern.org.uk

Beattie, A. (1991) Knowledge and control in health promotion: a test case for social policy and theory in Gable, J., Calnan, M. and Bury, M. (Eds.) *The Sociology of the Health Service*. London: Routledge, Taylor and Francis.

Bernard, M. (2000) *Promoting Health in Old Age*. Buckingham: Open University Press.

Blaxter, M. (1999) Risk, health and social research: Lessons from the ESRC programme on risk and human behaviour, *Health Risk and Society*, 1(1): 11–24.

Department of Health (1992) *The Health of the Nation*. London: HMSO.

Department of Health (1999) *Saving Lives: Our Healthier Nation*. London: HMSO.

Department of Health (2001) *National Service Framework for Older People*. London: HMSO.

Everitt, A., Zataar, A. and Stevenet, L. (1996) 'Ageing well campaign': Accident prevention for older people in Gateshead – a feasibility study for a project to be undertaken by Age Concern.

Ewles, L. and Simnett, I. (1999) *Promoting Health: A Practical Guide*, 4th Edition. London: Bailiere Tindall.

Finch, H. (1997) *Physical Activity 'At Our Age': Qualitative Research Among People Over the Age of 50*. London: Health Education Authority.

Green, J. (1997) *Risk and Misfortune: A Social Construction of Accidents*. London: UCL Press.

Green, J. (1999) From accidents to risk: Public health and preventable injury, *Health, Risk and Society*, 1(1): 25–39.

Health Promotion England (2001) *Older People and Physical Activity*. Physical education factsheet, London: Health Promotion England.

Hughes, L. (2002) *When is a Fall not a Fall: the Older Person's Perspective?* Unpublished MSc, Northumbria University.

Jones, L. and Naidoo, J. (1997) Theories and models in health promotion in Katz, J. and Peberdy, A. (Eds.) *Promoting Health: Knowledge and Practice*. London: Macmillan, 75–88.

Office for National Statistics (2004) http://www.statistics.gov.uk/cci/nugget. asp?id=874 accessed 14/08/04 Office for National Statistics *Population Trends*, London: HMSO.

Reed, J., Stanley, D. and Clarke, C. (2004) *Health, Well-Being and Older People*. Bristol: The Policy Press.

Scottish Community Development Centre (2000) *Learning Evaluation and Planning: A Handbook for Partners in Community Learning*. Glasgow: The Centre.

Skelton, D. A. and McLaughlin, A. W. (1996) Training functional ability in old age, *Physiotherapy*, 82(3), 159–67.

United States Surgeon General (1996) *Physical Activity and Health: A Report of the Surgeon General*. Atlanta, GA, USA: Centres for Disease Control and Prevention, US Department of Health and Human Services.

Victor, C. and Howse, K. (2000) *Promoting the Health of Older People: Setting a Research Agenda*. London: Health Education Authority.

CHAPTER 11

How Understanding Community Development Will Help Your Career

MARK BURNS AND BARBARA L. GRIFFIN

Introduction

This chapter addresses the issue of community development and the promotion of physical activity. It will help you understand how a grasp of community development is essential to everyone wanting a career promoting physical activity. It links to Chapter 1, in terms of exploring your views and values about the nature of human beings, society and physical activity. Drawing these issues together raises one question, that is, what kind of community are you trying to develop? This question places community development into an arena that changes in relation to public policies and different values held within different communities. Current public policy encourages physical activity and community development workers to work together in order to develop communities (Coatler, 2002). This chapter analyses what community development workers have to gain from one another by examining definitions of community and approaches to working in, and with communities. Finally, an example of a job description aims to bring together the different elements facing physical activity workers in community development. The job description aims to throw light on how community development and physical activity come together in a workplace. It illustrates how community development principles and skills can contribute to promoting sport and physical activity. In addition, there are further boxes providing information, including new games, an example of a successful project and an example of a job description.

An underpinning issue in this chapter relates to values, as outlined in the first chapter. Understanding values is critical in helping you decide the best form of physical activity to promote in different communities and the most appropriate approach. If we accept current public health policy that physical activity is, beneficial for health then we are accepting that we all need physical activity to help us remain healthy. Nevertheless, the kinds of physical activity people have promoted have depended on their values, and views of human nature and society. The following questions illuminate different issues concerning the promotion of physical activity and the link to values. What do you believe?

- Are people full of anti-social urges? Do they need to be disciplined through sport teaching them about rules and authority? Alternatively, is sport somewhere to let their hair down?
- Do you believe that life is about competition? Moreover, if you do, is this because it is good for society and the individual? Do you think it makes countries more successful to have workers who know how to compete with the rest of the world? If you take this view, to promote your values, it would make most sense to encourage competitive sport, with its winners and losers.
- Do you think that the world is a hostile place? In which case, you might want to promote physical activities that are useful in terms of self-defence. Even the Boy Scouts owe their origins in part to Baden-Powell's belief in the need to prepare for war (Girouard, 1981).
- Do you think it is safer if people obey the rules? Traditional sports do not change the rules to suit the players. You have to fit in, regardless if you are too small or too slow. The New Games Movement encouraged players to change the rules if this was more fun for more people. (Fluegelman, 1976) What sort of society would develop if this were the dominant pastime? How would you feel about it? (see Box 11.1 on New Games)
- Is life about community? Do you worry about society breaking down and people becoming distant from each other? You would want to promote sporting activities, therefore, that bring people together. For example, team sports, leagues or ceildhs encourage social activities rather than solitary jogging or exercise machines.
- Do you think that it is important to promote different cultures? In Ireland, in the past, Gaelic games such as hurling were encouraged to stop English culture dominating. With the global take over of soccer in much of the world, will other cultures begin to feel the same way?

Another dimension to promoting physical activity in a community, as Popple (1995) argues, is that the word community is a contested concept. The word incorporates elements of description and value. For example, the word community can mean a group in a particular place such as a town or city from similar socio-economic backgrounds. It may also describe people with the same background, for instance, ethnicity, beliefs or a disability they share. In addition, Popple (1995) suggests the word community engenders a sense of warmth. This means that when people use the word community, it is rarely used negatively. Rather, the word conveys positive elements about people living, working or being together as part of a group.

In the context of health promotion, community means a site for a variety of interventions and approaches that bring together public policies and community values within particular locations or within particular groups of people. Nonetheless, the word remains contested because different people apply it to a variety of types of work such as community police, community development worker, or a community school; however, despite the variety of meanings of the word community there are principles that contribute to the work of community development.

Community work: background

An early example of promoting physical activity for community development was in Victorian times. In 1884, Harrow teacher Edward Bowen said, 'I had rather regenerate England with the football elevens than with average members of parliament' (Bowen, 1902 in Girouard, 1981: 233). This example illustrates the moral value of sport within the public schools.

Thomas (1983) argues community development in Europe has evolved from colonial programmes in the Third world. During the 1960s, workers from former colonies were returning to Europe and had skills in working with local people in implementing changes. Thomas (1983) suggested the combined influences of the skill base in colonial workers, the social work techniques in American social programmes and the UNESCO initiatives developed community based work in Europe, and helped to establish community development in the United Kingdom.

Approaches in community work

To explain the approaches available in community work, the categories draw on Popple's (1995) 'Analysing Community Work'. He uses the term 'community work' to cover a number of different approaches. One of these he calls 'community development'. This is an example of where the terminology is fuzzy as the terms can mean the same thing.

Community care

This involves paid workers, local residents and/or volunteers to help people in need. These could include older people, those with disabilities or young children. Once these self-help networks are up and running successfully, the paid worker may move on to repeat the process elsewhere. As a physical activity worker, you may be able to offer help and training to the groups involved.

Community organisation

This approach is about co-ordination and aims to make sure that project worker use resources efficiently. In recent years, there has been much greater partnership working between the various parts of the state and the voluntary sector. This ties in well with the ideas of community organisation.

Community development

The approach of the workers is to help people in local neighbourhoods decide what they need as a group. They then support them to meet these needs. If, for example, the need was to help young people have something useful to do, they might help them bid for money for a sports centre. If you are promoting physical activity, then you are making a decision for the people, but offering a choice about the type of physical activity.

Community planning

The role of the community worker here is to ensure that the views of local people are heard when plans are being made to redevelop an area. This could be a large-scale economic regeneration. Alternatively, it could simply be how to improve local services. Physical activity workers have an interest in both of these areas.

Community education

Community education is about helping people to take charge of their own lives. This involves giving them the necessary ideas, tools and confidence. Different projects may have different values. They may promote how to fit more successfully into the world. Alternatively, they may enable people to change it. Physical activity workers can also help people improve their health. In turn, this may help them find work, if they have a poor sick record or it improves their self-confidence.

Community action

The state pays for most community work. Nevertheless, local people may want to challenge what is going on. Community activists may organise petitions, marches or direct action. It is difficult to see what role a paid physical activity worker could have here. Except perhaps to listen and take note if the conflict was concerned with their organisation.

Feminist community work

The growth of the Women's Movement created new organisations. It also pushed a new set of values, about the equality of the sexes. The growth of women in sport is one result of both of these.

Black and anti-racist community work

The key issue here is how to meet the needs of black people. This is partly by ensuring that community projects welcome everybody. Nonetheless, racism still exists in the United Kingdom so there is also a need for separate projects. One example is the 'Kick it Out' campaign (Council for Racial Equality, 1993). This international project supports community initiatives that raise awareness about racism within all levels of football, including being a fan, or establishing football related projects in deprived areas. For example, physical activity workers may, therefore, develop centres or classes to raise awareness about racism in established teams and promoting football within ethnically diverse areas.

It is also worth pointing out, the downside of sport. In North America, for example, many young black men are poor because of racism. They are attracted to sport as a way out of poverty. Very few have successful professional careers. Another argument is that they would have been better off doing other things with their lives, such as getting an education (Cashmore, 2000).

Box 11.1   New games

New games

In 1966, anti-Vietnam protestors planned World War IV. It resulted in slaughter. Slaughter being the first activity of this peacenik event. It was four balls, two baskets and forty people wrestling, laughing and making it up as they went along. Steward Brand, the organiser, felt that the pacifists needed to let out their own anger and aggression safely, rather than denying it existed. It was a great success. Other games followed and they were dubbed 'soft war' (Fluegelman, 1976). Soft War developed into New Games. Though soft war is still part of this, people interested in 'soft' games introduced other non-competitive games. The focus is on altering the game, so that everyone could be included if they wanted to be. This is the opposite of traditional sport. Traditional sport possesses systems to exclude people, such as those who lack ability in a particular sport. None-theless, often in New Games, there is a referee to look after safety. Everyone is encouraged to contribute a game or create new rules. This last point also encourages people's creativity. In this sense, New Games is much more like children's play than traditional sport where an outside authority sets the rules, often many generations ago. Perhaps because of this link with child-hood, acting games are also part of the mix. This also allows a change of pace, if people need a rest.

The point is that Victorians established most of our games. What if Hippies had invented all our favourite team games instead of the Victorians?

Maybe then, we would all be playing games ourselves rather than just watching other people play games on TV. The Open University brought New Games over to the United Kingdom in 1976. A body was formed to promote them, particularly with disabled groups. Though only a small organisation, they were part of a wider social movement that popularised things like parachute games for play workers, team-building exercises for youth workers and icebreakers for community workers. 1966 was the start of a challenge to Victorian ideals of physical activity.

You may want to promote non-competitive physical activity because you believe in it or simply because it meets the needs of a particular community group you are working with, see Sport Psychologist Terry Orlick's (1982) *The Second Co-operative Sports and Games Book*. Read his suggestions and adapt them to meet your own needs.

What does community development offer you in your role as a physical activity worker?

An integral element of community development is collaboration. In a health promotion context, collaboration means working with other agencies or people to resolve particular health issue or issues. Gray (1985: 912) stated, 'collaboration is the pooling of perceived or tangible resources . . . by two or more stakeholders, to solve a set of problems which neither can solve individu-ally.' Naidoo and Wills (2000) confirm this by suggesting inter-sectoral collaboration goes beyond any one sector, and may include public, private businesses and voluntary groups. Inter-sectoral action challenges traditional patterns of organisation and management in the public sector. In addition, working within community development offers physical activity workers access to a range of funding sources, such as mainstream funding or single fund for a specific project. For instance, in the United Kingdom it is possible to apply for 'Kick Racism out of Football' community projects through the Commu-nity Chest (Kick it Out, 2006).

The concept of collaboration underpins the notion that much of community work requires active partnerships. For example, the Healthy City movement that the World Health Organisation promotes takes a very holistic approach. It sees how a wide range of things affects health in a local community. Some of these are listed below.

1. *Regeneration and unemployment*
   Towns and cities need good sports facilities if they want to persuade com-panies to set up business there. High profile stadiums or events may even

be used to improve the image of an area. In rural areas, walking and other outdoor activities may help the local economy. Physical activity projects and businesses themselves may also create work for people. All this is important to the National Health Service too, as high employment is linked with good health. Similarly, physical activity can be provided to communities with high rates of unemployment in an attempt to offer meaning to people's lives. This could be seen as a way of distracting them from fighting the system that causes unemployment. On the other hand, without subsidies, it may be hard for poor people to afford to exercise.

2. *Social cohesion*
   The United States academic, Robert Putnam (2001) in 'Bowling Alone: The Collapse and Revival of American Community', shows how Americans join fewer groups than they used to. His classic example is bowling clubs. This shift has been bad for community spirit in that people become more isolated and less willing to help each other. His book has influenced politicians in the United Kingdom. Physical activity workers can encourage people to do more things together. This could be sport or events to promote racial integration, such as multicultural dancing.

3. *Crime and disorder*
   Sport can be used as a way to divert young offenders away from crime. This is good both for them and for potential victims. Sport can also be a way of people letting out aggression and frustration safely. Even watching sport may do this. Sport can also be used to help people develop new skills and values.

4. *Education*
   Sport can be 'a way in' to reach certain groups. In Sunderland, for example, the NHS has worked with the football club to produce drug education resources. Sport may also be offered as a reward to encourage pupils to do well as school or to keep out of trouble. This is sometimes controversial if it is only for 'difficult' and not 'good kids'.

5. *Equal opportunities*
   Sport and physical activity should offer opportunities for everybody to develop. This means tackling barriers that get in the way of any group exercising because of factors such as ethnicity, sex, age, wealth or age.

6. *Culture and local pride*
   Dance and the beauty created by gardening both involve hard physical work. In certain places, specific physical activities are part of the local identity and a source of pride. For example, in Scotland, ceilidhs and traditional dancing seem to be associated with the country more than in England.

7. *Physical and mental health*
   Physical activity can be good for mental health. Together, with the obvious physical health benefits of being fitter, you can also help communities be less at risk of death or danger in other ways. In particular parts of the country, being able to swim may be vitally important.

8. *Environment*

To improve the environment and tackle health problems like pollution and asthma means fewer cars. Physical activity workers can help to develop and action plans for people to walk or cycle more.

Box 11.2 Learn from the Groningen Active Living Model; an award winning physical activity project

The Groningen Active Living Model, (GALM) won a European Health Promotion Award in 2000. It targets older people who could benefit from more exercise. The project is Dutch but offers many tips for community physical activity workers in the United Kingdom. The following points help to shape physical activity projects in a community

- See things from the point of view of the people you are targeting.
- The project aimed to make older people healthier. Nevertheless, they engaged the community by promoting the idea that it would be a fun, social activity.
- Give them plenty of things to choose to do.

Some exercise schemes in the United Kingdom have only offered gym work or perhaps swimming. As far as possible let people be able to pick what they fancy.

- Let them be with their friends.

GALM recruited people from quite small areas. People may well have known each other already. Living locally new friendships could develop easily. If people wanted to bring a friend with them, they could. Even if that friend did not need GALMs, help to be fit.

- Give them plenty of support and then move on.

The GALM programme runs for many weeks. In the end; however, the group are expected to continue on their own with the help of a local sports club. The GALM workers move on to form new groups elsewhere.

- Recognise that there is no one right answer.

GALM does not work for everyone. Other projects have been set up for people who prefer not to be in a group or are too sick to take part such as specific projects for people with disabilities.

'What would you bring to the job of a physical activity development worker?' There are four key issues to understand in community development today:

1. *Partnerships with other agencies*

   All major Government projects now demand that organisations work in partnership with each other, and often with the people, they are providing a service to, as well. The partnership may be at a planning level, or be more concerned with getting things done on the ground as for example in Box 11.2. The Groningen Active Living Model contributes to how a community action project can shape physical activity in local areas. Partners might include the Voluntary sector, community groups, the National Health Service, the Local Authority, other state bodies such as schools as well as businesses, such as the local professional football club or private gym. Partnership offers advantages, but also challenges. The organisations involved may all have different aims and ways of doing things. The need for extra meetings may slow things down. If you want a successful career in the community development area then it is useful to brush up on your people skills. Research (Higgs and Dulewicz, 1999) shows that dealing with your own and others feelings is twice as important as technical skills for high job performance. Seventy-five per cent of the reason for career failure is because of lack of skills in dealing with emotions.

2. *Partnerships with local people and other service users*

   How do you involve local people with the services that they use? Traditionally, voting in council elections has been the main way. Recently projects have often tried to get local people more actively involved. This is not easy. Public meetings can be boring and may only attract a small number of people. Asking a few local people to join a planning group may not give you a true picture of what most people think. Putting money aside from your budget for local people to bid for is another option. For example, when a group of agencies interested in health promotion did this in Sunderland, they found that about a third of the money went on physical activities. This included things such as dancing, sport and swimming. Anecdotally, the group discovered that the same proportion seemed to be true across the United Kingdom. One observation is that local people are more likely to ask for money for their children's football teams, rather than for health promotion leaflets on skin cancer or fibre.

3. *Sustainability*

   In the United Kingdom, the national government provides all kinds of funding to improve poor areas. Usually, this is for a limited length of time. This could be as little as three years or could be more nine or more. When the cash runs out does this mean that services are cut down and the area is back to square one? Short-term funding raises the issue of what happens to the project when the funding stops? Contemporary government programmes usually ask how projects will continue once funding ends. Again, this is not easy. In terms of physical activity projects, one way is to try to train up local people as volunteers to carry on after the paid workers have left. Another is to give them the skills to look for new sources of cash. Alternatively, projects can invest in property that will bring in rent. It may even be possible for projects to become part of the normal services offered by the local authority or health services in that area.

4. *Evaluation*

This subject is covered in Chapter 4 of this book. Nonetheless, as this chapter is about community development the comments refer to this topic. Power is often a key issue in community development theory. Who has it and how do they use it? In terms of evaluation the questions then are:

● Who decides what needs to be found out?
● Who is paid for being involved in the evaluation?
● Who obtains the results and decides what to do with them?

In the past, the answer for all of these questions has usually been paid professionals. This does not have to be the only method of evaluation in a community. For instance, if necessary, local people can often be involved and offered training. This also helps if the project is to be sustained after the paid workers have left. It may also help create work in the community and give people new skills to get new jobs. For further reading see Coatler (2002) who provides a manual about sport and community development.

If you visit www.philosophyfootball.com one of their T-shirts quotes Albert Camus, the Existentialist writer. It says, 'All that I know most surely about morality and obligations, I owe to football.' This illustrates a key point of this chapter that physical activity is not value free. What kind of physical activity you decide to promote in the community will depend on your view of both how the world is and how it should be. This in turn will affect what direction your career takes and how successful you are. Box 11.3 provides an example of the type of job description illustrating the responsibilities of a physical activity development worker. It aims to draw together elements of this chapter and help offer an example of how sports, physical activity and community development work in practice. A sports development person needs to be flexible and learn appropriate skills as Robins (1990) argues it is easier for a trained youth worker to learn sports skills rather than a sports person to learn community development skills. Nonetheless, Coatler (2002) argues that leadership skills are critical in the management of successful sport and physical activity work in communities.

Box 11. 3 Sports development project manager: equity in communities

Are you able to inspire others?

You need to be enthusiastic about developing sport, recreation and physical activity opportunities for others, in particular concerning disability sport. You need to have a working knowledge of the partners and key agencies that contribute to sport nationally and locally.

You will need to develop and maintain networks of partners who can assist in sustaining local projects drawing on statutory, voluntary and business organisations.

You will be expected to plan, develop, monitor and review projects that have equity as a core value.

You will be expected to support the national and local federations of disability sport to ensure equity and cohesion with other partners and community structures.

You will need to identify barriers to under represented groups by engaging with sport coaches, advocates to develop innovative interventions.

Conclusion

In conclusion, this chapter provides insight into how physical activity workers locate their work in communities. It makes connections with other chapters in the book, namely, values in Chapter 1, and planning and evaluation in Chapter 4. Measuring success in community projects is not easy; however, Coatler (2002) suggests that understanding the varied role of sport in communities contributes to delivering sustainable projects in them. Community sport development workers require specific skills that need to be acknowledged within the broader structure of professional development.

References

Bowen, W. E. (1902) Edward Bowen: A memoir in Girouard, M. (1981) *The Return to Camelot: Chivalry and the English Gentlemen*. New York and London: Yale University Press.

Cashmore, E. (2000) *Making Sense of Sport* (3rd Edition). London and New York: Routledge.

Coatler, F. (2002) *Sport and Community Development: A Manual*, Research Report No. 86, University of Edinburgh http://sportdevelopment.org.uk/sportcom2002.pdf

Council for Racial Equality (1993) *Kick it Out*, http://www.kickitout.org/

Fluegelman, A. (1976) *The New Games Book*. New York: Headlands Press.

Girouard, M. (1981) *The Return to Camelot: Chivalry and the English Gentlemen*. New York and London: Yale University Press.

Gray, B. (1985) Conditions facilitating inter-organisational collaboration, *Human Relations*, 38, 911–936.

Groningen Active Living Model, http://www.isapa.org/Regional_Web_Pages/netherlands.pdf

Higgs, M. and Dulewicz, V. (1999) *Making Sense of Emotional Intelligence*. Berkshire: NFER-Nelson.

Kick it Out (2006) *Kick it Out*, http://www.kickitout.org/

Naidoo, J. and Wills, J. (2000) *Health Promotion Foundations for Practice* (2nd Edition). London: Bailliere and Tindall.

Orlick, T. (1982) *The Second Co-operative Sports and Games Book*. New York: Pantheon Books.

Popple, K. (1995) *Analysing Community Work*. Milton Keynes: Open University.

Putnam, R. (2001) *Bowling Alone: the Collapse and Revival of American Community*. New York: Simon and Schuster.

Robins, D. (1990) *Sport as Prevention: The Role of Sport in Crime Prevention Programmes Aimed at Young People*. University of Oxford, Centre for Criminological Research occasional paper No. 12. Oxford: The Centre.

Thomas, D. (1983) *The Making of Community Work*, London: Allen and Unwin.

CHAPTER 12

From 'Personal Exercise on Prescription' to 'HELP': Evolution of an Exercise on Referral System

SUE COLLINS AND GEORGE GOODSON

Introduction

This chapter aims to illustrate by a detailed case study a four-staged process of introducing an exercise on prescription scheme titled 'Personal Exercise on Prescription' in the City of Sunderland.

The first section reviews the background to stage I of exercise on prescription, setting the scene by considering the political climate, and identifying the challenges associated with the early years of the scheme. Included is a description of the practicalities of setting up, and running the scheme providing an overview of emerging evidence together with the lessons learnt over the seven-year period of developing the scheme. Throughout the chapter, we will explore the relationship of theory and practice to provide a means of contextualising the complex issues surrounding exercise on prescription, including the development of stage II and III. The chapter ends with a summary of the elements that constitute a successful scheme, including stage IV, future developments and conclusions.

Background – setting the scene

The early 1990s saw the publication of the Health of the Nation document (Department of Health, 1992). This was one of the first government strategies that attempted to define National Health Service health targets, including reducing death rates from coronary heart disease and stroke (Department of Health, 1992).

At that time, the Allied Dunbar National Fitness Survey indicated that although the majority of people felt that they were sufficiently active, in reality approximately 70 per cent of men and 80 per cent women in the United Kingdom did not take enough physical activity to benefit their health (Sports Council and Health Education Authority, 1992). Furthermore, those individuals who reported inactive, sedentary lifestyles showed poorer health records; this suggested that engaging a small proportion of this target group in regular physical activity may be a viable way of improving population health. The priorities of central government focused on:

- Common causes of death or major illness in the population.
- How to reduce the health problem and how it would be achieved.
- How could health improvements be monitored, measured and evaluated effectively?

Exercise was embedded within the Health of the Nation's (Department of Health, 1992) target for heart disease and stroke and had not yet become a priority in its own right. This was, in part, because Health of the Nation (Department of Health, 1992) targets concentrated on disease and personal behaviour, with little about how targets were to be achieved and where the extra resources were coming from (Kemm and Close, 1995).

Exercise on prescription, as a concept was a relatively new phenomenon. It emerged as an innovative way to promote physical activity in response to the need for proactive, community-based interventions. Whilst there were a variety of ways that schemes operated, they typically involved partnerships between community health trusts and local leisure services, with general practitioners referring patients to the local leisure centre for a specific exercise scheme. The underpinning principle for exercise on prescription was that primary health care teams play a significant role in facilitating health behaviour change. More than 70 per cent of people see their general practitioner at least once in any given year and 95 per cent do so within a three-year period (Biddle et al., 1994). Furthermore, the public perceives doctors as credible sources of information, and as the preferred source of health information for advice on physical activity (Booth et al., 1997).

Early pioneers of exercise on prescription in England were the Wealden District Council with their Oasis programme, and the Stockport Exercise on Prescription scheme. The internal evaluation framework of these schemes highlighted their effectiveness, demonstrating improvements in participant's physical and mental health. Anecdotal evidence gathered from referring agents and participants supported the programmes (Wealden Leisure, 1993; Caroll and Green, 1993; Lord and Green, 1994).

In 1994, there were approximately 121 schemes in operation in the United Kingdom (Biddle et al., 1994). After nearly a decade, the number has increased seven-fold with 816 schemes currently identified (Wright Foundation, 2004). This is probably an underestimation, as these are the schemes that have contacted the Wright Foundation to take part in their three-year United Kingdom wide study of exercise on referral.

An area, which proved beneficial for exercise on prescription, was the increasing emphasis from central government on multi-agency/partnership working, or 'Healthy Alliances'. This was primarily to minimise duplication and fragmentation, facilitate joint funding, and maximise health gains by utilising available resources in the most effective manner.

At this time, the Local Authority leisure departments were very specific in their target audience. Studies showed that the majority of the general public were not accessing leisure facilities (Department of Culture, Media and Society, 2002). This triggered a wide spread consultation process leading to a plethora of strategies designed to build on community infrastructure.

What we did – in the beginning

In 1990, the National Health Service and Community Care Act signalled a turning point resulting in a 'managed' system with the emphasis on getting results and value for money (Heyman, 1995). The subsequent National Health Service restructure had 'purchasers' responsible for contracting services and 'provider' functions delivering the services (Simnett, 1997). Government and local funding had identified heart disease as a priority and under 'purchaser/provider' arrangements, the health promotion department was asked to plan projects to address lifestyle behaviour changes. It was felt that the exercise on prescription model addressed a number of coronary heart disease risk factors, such as, exercise, diet, smoking and alcohol consumption.

This process highlighted a common problem with prevention-based initiatives, which was essentially about the lack of proper consultation with the target group. Effectively, this creates a 'top down' process where direction comes from the authorities instead of the people (Kemm and Close, 1995). For example, once health or local authorities took the decision to adopt the exercise on prescription concept, its arrival was communicated to the target audience.

Evidence base

Evidence-based literature on the most effective way of increasing physical activity levels was scarce at this time (Biddle et al., 1994). Exploration of similar initiatives within the United Kingdom identified some models that incorporated elements of good practice, which resulted in the Sunderland scheme modelling itself on the Stockport scheme.

Pilot scheme (October 1994–September 1995)

A partnership between the community National Health Service Trust (Priority Healthcare Wearside) and the Local Authority (City Leisure Services

Department) led to the scheme being piloted in the West area of Sunderland. This area covered the district of Washington and its outlying areas, as part of a wider coronary heart disease prevention programme.

Stage I

Stage I addresses the early development, management and recruitment elements of the scheme. A steering group was formed (with representatives from the community trust, primary care and local authority) to agree to participating in the scheme, identify resources, and produce a plan of action (Table 12.1).

Marketing strategy

In order for a health promotion initiative to be effective, a marketing strategy is essential to stimulate demand for the 'services' on offer (Alcalay and Bell, 2000). The multi-agency partnership felt that exercise on prescription was too impersonal. Therefore, it was decided to adopt the acronym physical educationP, standing for Personal Exercise on Prescription and this created a catchy strap line 'physical educationP up your life'.

As part of the marketing plan, leaflets and posters were designed for the target group, and seminars were organised for professionals. The seminars provided an opportunity to:

1. Discuss the evidence base for exercise on prescription.
2. Explain the scheme in detail, and address the potential physical, psychological and social benefits for participants.

Table 12.1 Overview of setting up personal exercise on prescription

Objective	Action

Establish steering group	Steering group established, comprising:
	    Health Promotion Officer
	    Leisure Centre Manager
	    Community Fitness Officer
	    Community Nurse

Develop scheme design and operation	The scheme operated from Washington Leisure Centre offering a 10-week personalised exercise scheme Identify exclusive room within the centre Purchase computer hardware / software package for monitoring participants Develop protocol
Identify staff	Community Nurse to deal with lifestyle issues Community Fitness Officer with specialist fitness qualifications
Develop marketing strategy designed to engage the general practitioners	Contact general practitioners in area Set up workshops / seminars for general practitioners and health professionals Produce leaflets / posters Ensure local media / newspaper cover
Launch scheme	Arrange launch with local celebrity Distribute specifically designed leaflets and posters across the target area

3. Update general practitioners, health professionals and residents on current research relating to the prevalence of exercise in the adult population.
4. Answer questions and elicit feedback.

Subsequently, the scheme was publicised through the local media (radio and newspaper), and a formal launch was conducted with a local celebrity. Personal Exercise on Prescription was promoted, and included stressing the increased enjoyment and social contact rather than placing it within a traditional medical model that isolates a particular condition, for example, reducing blood pressure with medication. Embedded in the scheme were the inclusive qualities that addressed issues such as social isolation and exclusion; these became priorities in later government strategic thinking (Department of Health, 1999).

Stage II

Stage II involved evaluation and reflection. Table 12.2 provides an overview of the actions needed to develop the scheme.

Evaluation

Griffin and Learmonth discussed the importance of evaluation in Chapter 4, it is a vital component of any health promotion practice, and is an essential part of the planning and review process; it is primarily aimed at assessing what has been achieved, or judging the worth of the activity (Jones et al., 2002).

Table 12.2   Scheme structure

Action	Outcome
Establishment of scheme	Protocols and referral literature distributed to committed general practitioners and health professionals February 1995 first referrals received
Cost to participants	Activity card allowing 3 free activities per week for 10 weeks (30 visits)
Activities	Individualised gym programme Swimming and 'Aquafit' Additional activities: badminton and table tennis
Access times Gym Pool Additional activities	Mon. / Wed. / Fri. between 9.00–10.00 am As centre time-table Mon.–Fri. between 9.00–10.00 am Initial assessment / interview Supervision throughout the scheme
Support System – contact with community fitness officer	Re-assessment / interview
Evaluation – quantitative and qualitative	Initial, 10-week and 6-month questionnaires to participants Initial and final interviews Focus groups and semi-structured individual interviews
Exit strategy in place	Referring agent questionnaire 2-month free leisure card allowing subsidised access (for individuals who are unemployed / on benefit / old age pensioners)

Evaluation helps provide evidence of the success of the scheme, and provides structure and accountability for money and resources used. Early criticism of exercise prescription schemes centred on the lack of systematic evaluation, and the small numbers of individuals referred (Iliffe et al., 1994; Biddle et al., 1994).

The participants' feedback from interviews and questionnaires provided a deeper understanding of facilitators. The feedback identified barriers to activity, and potentially captures the wider social impact of the scheme. A community nurse would be in a good position as a primary care link, to reassure general practitioners that the scheme was running well, and to influence them to refer patients to the scheme.

The clients completed questionnaires at the initial assessment stage, scheme completion (10-weeks) and follow up (six-months from completion of referral). The questionnaires provided an indication of perceived health, general well-being by incorporating the General Health Questionnaire12 (Golderberg and Williams, 1988) and long-term adherence to activity. For individuals leaving the scheme before completion, an exit questionnaire provided the reason for 'dropping out'. Similarly, all referring agents completed a questionnaire to ascertain their views of the scheme.

Lessons learnt

Table 12.3 explains the measures put in place to reflect and address issues during stage II.

Table 12.3 Solutions to issues highlighted from information seminars

Point	Issue	Solution
1	Cost	Free assessment and activity card allowing three free activities per week for 10-weeks (30 free sessions)
2	Monitoring / evaluation	Evaluation questionnaires; medical questionnaire; initial and final interviews; interim and final report
	Monitoring of patients	Screening and risk stratification; supervision and monitoring and qualitative interviews
3	Confidentiality	Health promotion standard protocols such as keeping records for seven years
4	Feedback to referring agents	Regular updates on patient status
5	Long-term adherence (exit strategy)	Free 2-month leisure card allowing subsidised access
6	Sustainability	Exploration of other avenues of funding, including Health Improvement Programmes (HImP), Neighbourhood Renewal Funding
7	Liability / safety issues	Protocol with clear roles and responsibilities of all involved
		Specific forms for transfer of data from general practitioner to community fitness officer

Positive aspects

- Within six months, 90 per cent of general practitioners of target area were referring into the scheme.
- The first referral was February 1995, with 279 people attending by the end of the pilot scheme.
- The scheme guidelines were updated, revised and distributed to participating health professionals.
- The well-equipped leisure centre is central to the town and accessible (located near main bus station).
- The scheme utilised existing expertise and recruited a community fitness officer.

Negative aspects

- Concerns over lack of income generated during the one-year pilot due to the free sessions.
- *Action* – identified activities would be subsidised, with participants paying a nominal fee for chosen activities.
- A main issue was the cost of the sessions once the subsidy ended, for those on low income this was a particular worry.
- *Action* – the free leisure card extended to 6-months.
- Non-adherence after the initial fitness assessment, due to low motivation.
- *Action* – encourage continued involvement by regular telephone or letter.
- The instructor led gym sessions were restricted to off-peak periods, which limited patient access.
- *Action* – explore the possibility of extending support activities during peak periods.
- Prescriptions did not always communicate the correct information.
- *Action* – organise training on referral guidelines.
- Participants had preconceived ideas about the leisure centre.
- *Action* – Leisure centre staff training on new clientele such as having an inclusive attitude and supportive approach. Fox et al. (1997) identified that where staff made such changes the scheme experienced higher compliance and attendance.
- Capacity issues if the scheme was successful then there might be waiting lists.
- *Action* – seek funding to expand the scheme and recruit additional staff.

Summary from 1996–2001

Over the next five years, the majority of participants enjoyed their involvement, and the evaluation indicated promising results. Nevertheless, during this period the scheme experienced a major set back, due to Local Authority restructuring facilities being withdrawn, resulting in a reduction in the number of activities on offer, and a general deterioration in the quality of services provided. These difficulties persisted for over a year, with the turning point being the successful negotiation of access to the newly re-furbished fitness suite. On reflection, the survival of the scheme, during this difficult time, depended on the dedication and commitment of its staff.

Furthermore, the scheme had a number of elements that helped provide justification for the continuation of the scheme. For instance, the ongoing government interest in 'healthy alliances' and pressure on local authorities to change its culture meant that physical activity was on the health agenda. For example, the publication of the 'Game Plan' (Department of Culture, Media and Society, 2002), identified targets including increasing the current 30 per cent participation rate (numbers of people attaining the 30 minutes of moderate activity on at least five days a week) to 70 per cent by 2020.

At a local level, commitment from key stakeholders included investing time and resources into the scheme. For instance, 'in-kind' contributions from the local authority included office space, administration support, subsidised and free activities, and contribution towards the community fitness officer's wages. Nevertheless, limited funding remained a major barrier to the expansion of the scheme into other areas of the City.

Evidence base

During this time, evidence was accumulating for and against exercise on prescription schemes. Research indicating negative outcomes included Taylor (1996) who suggested that exercise referral schemes, although popular, had failed to make a long-term impact on people's levels of physical activity. Moreover, a review of exercise promotion initiatives by Hillsdon and Thorogood (1996) concluded that common factors, which achieved sustained levels of participation (such as using unsupervised, informal exercise), are not typical of general practitioner referral schemes, and did not, therefore, provide evidence of effectiveness of such schemes.

In contrast, a review by Riddock et al. (1998) concluded such schemes demonstrate small but possibly meaningful improvements in physical activity patterns and associated health improvements. In addition, Taylor (1999) suggested that for sedentary patients exercise on prescription schemes provide an important exercise experience, but strategies need to be in place to promote long-term behaviour change.

One particularly negative article in the British Medical Journal called into question the effectiveness of United Kingdom schemes; with the heading 'Exercise on Prescription is a waste of scarce resources' (Harland et al., 1999). This was to cause suspicion amongst some general practitioners regarding the efficacy of the scheme, their suspicion impacted on securing future funding. The article came from a study by Harland and colleagues, who had conducted a randomised controlled trial, comparing different methods of promoting physical activity in a primary care setting. The authors concluded that even the most intensive intervention (information pack, 6 motivational interviews, and 30 free vouchers to a leisure centre), did not promote long-term adherence (Harland et al., 1999).

The article provoked a number of responses (*British Medical Journal,* 2000), and the consensus was that the study had made a valuable contribution to the evidence base regarding physical activity promotion; however, respondents perceived methodological flaws, resulting in imprecise conclusions. For example, Smith and Sims (2000) suggested that the headline was discouraging to funding authorities and researchers. Whereas, Craig et al. (2000), authors of the National Quality Assurance Framework for Exercise Referral Systems, commented on the ambiguity of the term 'exercise on prescription' and suggested that the study in question did not fit the current guidelines.

In response to these criticisms, the authors of the Harland study pointed out that the programme in question was not an exercise on prescription scheme, but an exploration of what would motivate individuals to take up physical activity, rather than recommending/prescribing specific activities (Harland et al., 2000).

Ongoing scheme evaluation

In 1998, an external evaluation of the scheme was carried out in 1998 by Priority Healthcare Wearside Clinical Psychology Directorate to strengthen the evidence. Their report showed significant improvements in physical and mental well being for the target sample of 200 people. A summary of average improvements is in Figure 12.1.

The results of a series of t-tests showed that significant improvements on all measures except peak flow. For some measures (such as blood pressure), a negative change is favourable, whereas for others (such as grip strength) a positive change is favourable.

A number of changes followed the evaluation. The main one was the extension of the scheme from 10 to 15-weeks, serving two purposes. First, the available literature indicated that it takes between 12 to 16 weeks for training adaptations to take place, so that physiological improvements could be satisfactorily measured (DeVries and Housh, 1994).

Secondly, long-term adherence (to regular exercise) and 'drop out' were recognised problems for exercise on prescription. Extending the length of the scheme was a response from patients, who had been asked for practical solutions that would help maintain their activity programme. Lastly, the extension

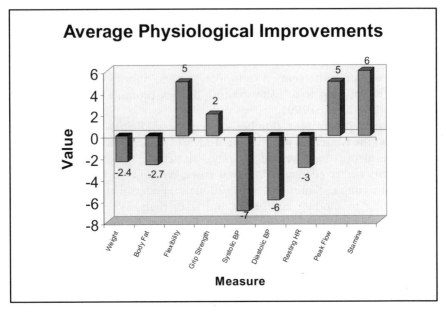

Figure 12.1 Data summary of average results comparing physical measures at baseline and follow up (10-weeks)

provided more support with the community fitness officer. Patients identified this as one of the most attractive elements of the scheme.

Stage III – development of HELP (2001–to date)

By the start of stage III, the reputation of the Exercise on Referral amongst the many referring agents had peaked. The scheme had expanded into the hospital setting taking referrals from Coronary Care and Rheumatology; this brought a new element to the scheme, necessitating updating the scheme operational manual to deal with moderate and high-risk patients. This would identify a need for additional specialist qualifications for the community fitness officers, ensuring a high quality of expertise, and professional registration to ensure accountability and continued professional development.

Updating the manual corresponded to the publication of the National Quality Assured Framework for Exercise on Referral Systems (Department of Health, 2001). This required all existing schemes to conduct an internal audit to ensure they meet the recommendations regarding quality assurance. Table 12.4 outlines the chronological developments leading to the emergence of the Healthy Exercise and Lifestyle Programme (HELP).

Table 12.4   Chronological sequence of events in setting up the
HELP programme

Objective	Action
Multi-agency Strategy Group	City wide consultation resulted in 54 per cent of general practitioners wanted a district wide programme Successful funding secured from October 2001–September 2004
Establishment of HELP programme	Develop professional marketing strategy to engage general practitioners and health professionals.
Identify key areas of development	Operating from four health and fitness centres, with four community fitness officers (two full-time, two part-time)
Increase capacity	Inclusion of a range of additional activities: home-based programme, local community activities such as 'Health Walks', offering
Additional activities	Step-O-meters for loan, Heart Smart classes, linking with Healthy Living Centre activities such as alternative therapy and 'fitness takeaway'.
Adopt behaviour change model	Transtheoretical – Stages of Change Model incorporated into the programme
Long-term evaluation	Develop one year evaluation questionnaire Track Active 8+ card and corporate membership uptake

Establishment of HELP

The Strategy Group developed the Exercise and Lifestyle Programme – HELP incorporating strategic development, continuity of provision, and including the recommendations from the National Quality Assurance Framework document, and to comply with the terms and conditions attached to the funding bid.

HELP utilised the established Exercise on Referral model, but focused on a client centred approach incorporating a recognised model of behaviour change, see Figure 12.2 for diagrammatical representation.

Key areas of development

A high profile advertising agency produced a number of images that encapsulated a holistic lifestyle approach, complementing the traditional centre-based activities with wider physical activity messages, for example, images of gardening and dancing. The distribution of the promotion literature used the Healthy Living Centre Network and local community groups.

All participating staff received motivational interviewing training to address the problems associated with long-term adherence and dropout. This was to ensure they had the necessary skills to implement the principles of behaviour modification (Rollnick and Miller, 1995). A number of strategies were used

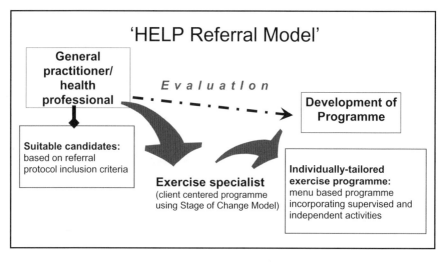

Figure 12.2   Revised Exercise on Referral model adopted by the
Sunderland programme

throughout the programme to build confidence and skills, and enhance motivation in order to foster a commitment to continuing the activity. One limitation of the Behaviour Change Model is that most research studies have used
very sophisticated interventions. These may require more time, technology
and counselling skills than may be available in typical Exercise on Referral
programmes (Buxton et al., 1996).

Although, all general practitioners and health professionals were enthusiastic
about the scheme and supported the concept, unlike the original Personal
Exercise on Prescription scheme, the majority were reluctant to commit to
the programme and refer patients. This resulted in slow progress. Two
major areas of concern were: funding constraints, and issues of clinical
responsibility.

Funding for the expansion of the programme linked to two specific geographical areas. This meant that health professionals could only refer patients
from the target areas into the programme, creating a two-tier service, resulting
in what was termed a 'post code lottery'. This was eventually resolved with
the funding authority, and within 6 months, 20 referrals per month were
received on average from each area.

Developments in evidence base

Findings from Wormald (2003) suggest that the support and supervision
offered on well-structured exercise referral schemes can be crucial in maintaining motivation and adherence. Corbett (2003) supports the notion of

structured schemes and identified that 'Exercise on Referral' was particularly beneficial for individuals recovering from knee or hip replacement operations. Furthermore, a qualitative study by Stathi et al. (2004) exploring the perceptions of older people at various stages of the referral programme, found that participants experienced a variety of benefits, including improvements in mood and well-being, feelings of accomplishment and success, and for some, expanding their social networks.

Government documents and strategies were now making explicit reference to 'Exercise on Referral' as a preferred intervention to increase physical activity levels in certain vulnerable populations, for example, the National Service Framework for Coronary Heart Disease (Department of Health, 2000). Recently, a report from the Chief Medical Officer (Department of Health, 2004) provides evidence on the benefits of physical activity in relation to health. This document suggests that Primary Care Trusts provide local leadership working closely with sport and leisure to develop sustainable, cost-effective physical activity strategies, such as exercise referral and pedometer initiatives, and providing advice and support on active lifestyles.

A number of attempts were made to introduce research and development into the scheme in collaboration with local universities, for instance, supervising final year students completing their dissertation around Exercise on Referral. The University of Teesside conducted research around motivational interviewing, and resulted in its research findings being accepted for presentation at the IOC World Congress in Athens (Breckon et al., 2003). Results from this work highlighted the benefits of using motivational interviewing to develop a more client centred approach. Figure 12.3 provides diagrammatical representation of the main issues experienced during the evolution of the Sunderland scheme. These are important factors that need to be taken into consideration when setting up an Exercise on Referral scheme.

The main developments influencing this stage include the introduction of government guidelines, through the National Quality Assurance Framework, outlining clear roles and responsibilities for professional staff, and the commitment to continual professional development. Additional factors of influence are the ability of this initiative to demonstrate year on year improvements in physical and mental health, increased adherence rates, and the successful engagement of hard to reach groups.

Stage IV future developments

Stage IV outlines the plan of action for future development, and expansion of the scheme informed by the evaluation and experiences gained through the evolution of the scheme.

1. Expansion of city-wide scheme linking to local networks and building on existing community infrastructures.

Figure 12.3   Issues that need considering when setting up an Exercise on Referral scheme

2. Secure mainstream funding.
3. Long-term tracking of patients, including the development of a 'one year follow up' questionnaire and monitoring uptake and use of free leisure card and subsidised corporate membership.
4. Set up 'Lifestyle Clubs' to address issues such as weight management, and smoking cessation.
5. Move into specialist areas, such as accepting patients awaiting orthopaedic surgery (replacement hip/knee) who are at risk due to other medical conditions (obesity, hypertension).
6. Sharing good practice – the HELP manual is being converted into a 'Toolkit' for use by other organisations who wish to set up the HELP programme their area.

Elements of a successful exercise on referral scheme

This chapter highlights a number of challenges that organisations may encounter when setting up or running an Exercise on Referral scheme, key elements include:

- Offering a quality assured scheme.
- Appropriately qualified, dedicated, enthusiastic staff.
- Offering a client centred approach with a wide variety of activities.
- Individualised exercise programmes with high levels of support and supervision.
- Low cost (especially for individuals on low income).
- Exit strategy to promote long-term activity.
- Evidence of effectiveness.

Conclusion

The concept of Exercise on Referral had been warmly welcomed by patients from the onset, but more so in the later years with dedicated staff support, and detailed support structures in the scheme design. These improvements have been developed over several years, through extensive consultation with referring agents and patients alike.

Exercise on Referral has slowly gained acceptance from the medical profession. They have increasing support from central government, as well as from the available mainstream evidence.

The scheme has facilitated major behaviour and lifestyle changes for many of the participants, in the face of concern over the efficacy of behaviour change models, and the historical problems relating to the under funding of Primary Care preventative strategies in favour of treatment based services.

A major strength of the Exercise on Referral scheme in Sunderland is the way it operates; the community fitness officers are employed by the National Health Service, and ensure a dedicated service with high quality standards. The majority of patients have contact with the community fitness officers on a weekly basis. This is an intensive, but crucial support structure in helping patients make the transition to a healthier lifestyle.

The evolution from Personal Exercise on Prescription to HELP demonstrates how work undertaken within a traditional medical model of risk factor reduction and treatment of disease can be enhanced by the application of health promotion principles around equity, collaboration, participation and prevention. The embodiment of these principles allow the scheme to engage many patients from 'hard to reach' groups, who would not normally take up activity of their own accord.

This chapter highlights the crucial role that a quality assured Exercise on Referral scheme can play in supporting individuals to address the complex behaviour change needed to enable them to start and maintain an activity programme. Making such schemes an integral component of a broader physical activity strategy contributes to moving towards increasing physical activity levels in the general population.

References

Alcalay, R. and Bell, R. A. (2000) *Promoting Nutrition and Physical Activity Through Social Marketing: Current Practices and Recommendations.* University of California, California: Centre for Advanced Studies in Nutrition and Social Marketing.

Biddle, S. J. H., Fox, K. and Edmunds, L. (1994) *Physical Activity Promotion in Primary Health Care in England.* London: Health Education Authority.

British Medical Journal (2000) Letters in response to 'Exercise on prescription is a waste of scarce resources', *British Medical Journal*, 320, 1470.

Booth, M. K., Bauman, A. Owen, N. and Gore, J. G. (1997) Physical activity preferences, preferred sources of assistance, and perceived barriers to increased activity among physically inactive Australians. *Preventive Medicine*, 26, 131–137.

Breckon, J. D., Lavallee, D. and Golby, J. (2003) Motivational interviewing in an exercise referral programme: Exercise motives and the effects on adherence to physical activity programming. 7th IOC Olympic World Congress on Sport Sciences, Athens. *Current Pharmaceutical Design*, 9(13).

Buxton, K., Wyne, J. and Mercer, T. (1996) How applicable is the stages of change model to exercise behaviour? *Health Education Journal*, 55, 239–257.

Caroll, J. and Green, F. (1993) *Exercise Prescription: A Report of a Pilot Scheme to Prescribe Exercise as Part of a Coronary Heart Disease Prevention Programme.* HMSO: Stockport Health Authorities.

Corbett, C. (2003) Exercise on prescription, *Professional Nurse*, 18(12), 666–667.

Craig, A., Dinan, S., Smith, A. and Taylor, A. (2000) The Newcastle exercise project: National quality assurance framework will guide best value and practice in GP exercise referral schemes (letter), *British Medical Journal*, 320, 1470.

Department of Culture, Media and Society (2002) *Game Plan: A Strategy for Delivery of Sport and Physical Activity Department for Culture.* HMSO: Media and Sport Strategy Unit.

Department of Health (1992) *The Health of the Nation.* London: HMSO Publications.

Department of Health (1999) *Saving Lives: Our Healthier Nation White Paper and Reducing Health Inequalities: An Action Report.* London: HMSO Publications.

Department of Health (2000) *National Service Framework for Coronary Heart Disease.* London: HMSO Publications.

Department of Health (2001) *National Quality Assurance Framework: Guidelines for Exercise on Referral Schemes.* London: HMSO Publications.

Department of Health (2004) *At Least Five a Week: Evidence on the Impact of Physical Activity and its Relationship to Health.* London: Department of Health, HMSO Publications.

DeVries, H. A. and Housh, T. J. (1994) *Physiology of Exercise for Physical Education, Athletics and Exercise Science* (5th Ed.) USA: Brown and Benchmark.

Fox, K., Biddle, S., Edmunds, L., Bowler, I. and Killoran, A. (1997) Physical activity promotion through primary health care in England, *British Journal of General Practice*, 47(419), 367–369.

Golderberg, D. and Williams, P. (1988) *A User's Guide to the General Health Question-naire*. Windsor, United Kingdom: NFER-Nelson.

Harland, J., White, M., Drinkwater, C., Chinn, D., Farr, L. and Howel, D. (1999) The Newcastle exercise project: a randomized controlled trial of methods to promote physical activity in primary care, *British Medical Journal*, 319, 828–832.

Harland, J., White, M., Howel, D., Drinkwater, C. and Chinn, D. (2000). Authors' reply. *British Medical Journal*, 320, 1470–1483.

Heyman, B. (1995) Matters of definition in Heyman, B. (Ed.) *Researching User Perspectives on Community Healthcare*. London: Chapman and Hall, 11.

Hillsdon, M. and Thorogood, M. (1996) A systematic review of physical activity promotion strategies, *British Journal of Sports Medicine*, 30, 84–90.

Jones, L., Sidell, M. and Douglas, J. (Eds.) (2002) *The Challenge of Promoting Health: Exploration and Action* (2nd Ed.). London: The Open University.

Kemm, J. and Close A. (1995). *Health Promotion Theory and Practice*. London: Macmillan.

Lord J., and Green F. (1994) Letter in response to prescribing exercise in general practice: Encourage active community life. *British Medical Journal*, 309, 872–873.

Riddock, C., Puig-Ribera, A. and Cooper, A. (1998) Effectiveness of physical activity promotion schemes in primary care: a review, *Health Promotion Effectiveness Reviews*, No. 14, Health Education Authority.

Rollnick, S. and Miller, W. (1995) What is motivational interviewing? *Behavioural Cognitive Psychotherapy*, 23, 325–334.

Simnett, I. (1997) *Managing Health Promotion: Developing Healthy Organisations and Communities*. Wiltshire: Wiley.

Smith, D. and Simms, S. (2000) Exercise prescription in primary care (letter), *British Medical Journal*, 320(7247), 1470.

Sports Council and Health Education Authority (1992) *Allied Dunbar National Fitness Survey: a Summary Report*. London: Health Education Authority.

Stathi, A. McKenna, J. and Fox, K. R. (2004) The experiences of older people participating in exercise on referral schemes, *The Journal of the Royal Society for the Promotion of Health*, 124(1), 18–23.

Taylor, A. H. (1996) Evaluating general practitioner referral schemes: findings from a randomised controlled study, *Chelsea School Topic Report*, No. 6, University of Brighton.

Taylor. A. H. (1999) Adherence in primary health care exercise promotion schemes in Bull, S. J. (Ed.) *Adherence Issues in Sport and Exercise*. Chichester: John Wiley and Sons Ltd (Chapter 3, 47–74).

Wealden Leisure (1993) *The Oasis Project: Project Manual*. Hailsham, East Sussex: Wealden District Council.

Wright Foundation, (2004) United Kingdom Research Study (webpage) http://www.wrightfoundation.com/uk_research_study.htm.

Wormald, H. (2003) *Exercise Referral Schemes: Improving the Patient's Experience*. Hull and East Riding: Community Health National Health Service Trust.

CHAPTER 13

Ethnicity and Health Promotion

REX W. THOMSON AND ISTVÁN SOÓS

Introduction

In multicultural societies, increasing interest is being paid to differences in the health experience of individuals from different ethnic groups (Macbeth and Shetty, 2001). Many contemporary societies are painfully aware that such differences exist, and that these differences often translate into negative experiences for such groups. Measures to deal with the negative aspects of these differences, however, are not easily achieved. One of the problems is that these multicultural societies may be facing considerable difficulties in the wake of a rebirth of ethnic nationalism, religious fundamentalism and group antagonisms. In order to utilise the power of collective identity as a tool for positive change in contemporary multicultural societies, we need to understand the concepts of ethnicity and ethnic identity, to appreciate ethnic differences, and to determine how these ethnic identities might be used in the cause of health promotion for ethnic minority groups.

Ethnicity and identity

According to Cornell and Hartmann (1997), and contrary to all predictions, the twentieth century was characterised by ethnic conflict and division on a scale that surprised academics and political commentators. Some countries with considerable ethnic diversity, such as the former Yugoslavia, completely disintegrated under the pressure of these ethnic conflicts. Nevertheless, as Cornell and Hartmann (1997: 3) point out, 'ethnic and racial diversity and identity have [also] been sources of pride, unity, and achievement.' In contemporary society, such identities have emerged as a potent force for dividing or bonding groups.

Streiff-Fenart (1999) describes ethnicity as a social construction of membership that is determined and manipulated in given situations by the individuals concerned, and clearly ethnic identity is something that is both personal and significant. Nonetheless, the form that ethnicity takes in a specific society may also be determined by structural conditions in that society, including relationships between social classes, and the distribution of social status, and power.

As Cornell and Hartman (1997: 20–21) suggest, ethnicity is identification in ethnic terms, but this may simply be a group that has been assigned an ethnic identity by outsiders. Nevertheless, 'once that identity becomes subjective – that is, once that population sees itself in ethnic terms . . . it becomes an ethnic group'. This proposition leads to a number of potential problems identified by Cronin and Mayall (1998) such as is an ethnic group and an ethnic identity something formed and then imposed by outsiders (usually the majority society), or is it a self-forming process by the group themselves? What role does opposition or antagonism play in this process?

According to Chapman (1993), the term ethnicity has been one concerned with opposition. It draws attention to the nature of differences between groups. Ethnicity is clearly a powerful form of collective identification in contemporary society, and as MacClancy (1996b: 9) suggests, 'it is a remarkably powerful means of mustering large groups of people for particular social ends.' While the oppositional nature of ethnicity and the problems and conflicts created by a desire for ethnic sovereignty are plain for all to see throughout the world, the concept of using ethnicity to achieve certain positive social or political ends is not so obvious.

Cronin and Mayall (1998: 3) maintain that there is 'considerable interest in those collectivities within the larger societies generally termed "ethnic groups"'. They are of particular interest because their ethnicity and ethnic identity is not necessarily defined by the nation state. Nonetheless, a nation and a national identity 'might directly coincide with an ethnic group and a sense of distinctive identity, thereby forming the majority element of that society' (Cronin and Mayall, 1998: 3). It is more commonly used to refer to minority groups, whether indigenous (such as Australian Aborigines) or immigrant (such as Roma (Gypsies) in Europe, Pacific Islanders in New Zealand), within the larger population.

It is these three ethnic groups, indigenous Aborigines in Australia, the Roma population in Europe, and Pacific Island immigrants in New Zealand, which will be used as examples of how the relationship between ethnicity and health promotion might well be positively influenced through participation in sport and physical activity.

Ethnicity and health

It is becoming increasingly obvious that the physical and social environments in which people live determine to a large degree their ability to live productive lives free of serious illness. The indigenous population in Australia, the Aborigines and Torres Strait Islanders, make up around 2.5 per cent of the total Australian population, and a significant majority of these are in age groups under 20 years (Trewin and Madden, 2003). Clear economic disadvantage, poor and overcrowded housing, poor quality water supplies, and sewage problems are common features of their physical and social environment, and all contribute to poor health; as Tatz (1995: 337–338) has suggested, there is an 'appalling pattern of ill health in almost all Aboriginal societies'. Onset of disease occurs at earlier ages, and there is a much shorter life expectancy than for the general Australian population, with figures for both indigenous males and females being 19–21 years lower than for other Australians (Trewin and Madden, 2003).

Cardiovascular disease ranks as the greatest cause of death among Aborigines, while the most common reason for hospitalisation of indigenous people is for the treatment of diabetes, associated with a lack of exercise, obesity, and rapid changes to lifestyle and diet. Death from non-natural or external causes such as accidents, intentional self-harm, and assaults also rank highly. Tatz's (1995) research into Aboriginal violence and delinquency suggests that 60 per cent of men aged between 20 and 30 are involved in violence of some kind. Aborigines are significantly over-represented in group violence and gang violence, in patterns that are almost universal.

Teenage suicide, and especially male suicide, has reached dramatic proportions in many Western societies in the past few decades, 'but the leap in Aboriginal suicide and attempted suicide rates is staggering' (Tatz, 1995: 320). With a suicide rate of 128–148 per 100,000 of the population (Tatz, in Radmer, 2002), suicide among Aboriginal children is off the scale in comparison to the rate of 19–20 for males and 7–8 per 100,000 for females in New Zealand, which has the highest national youth suicide rate in the world.

The overall state of health amongst Roma (Gypsy) populations, the largest minority group in Europe, is also far from satisfactory. Roma became one of the peoples of Europe around one thousand years ago, when they first arrived from India via the Balkans, and the current Roma population in Europe of around 12 million is roughly equivalent to that of an average European country. Hancock (2002: 89) points out that in both Eastern and Western Europe 'the life expectancy [of Roma] is generally lower than the national average, and the rate of infant mortality is higher'. The limited research that exists suggests that Roma life expectancy is significantly below national averages; the life expectancy of between 50–60 years is up to 10 years less than the neighbouring European non-Roma. In many parts of Europe, the life expectancy for most Roma is under 50 years (Reyniers et al., 2000), an appallingly short life span.

Infant mortality might be up to four times higher (Braham, 1993), although other sources would suggest that even this is a considerable underestimate (Médecins du Monde-International and Save the Children Alliance, 2001). The overall health of Roma is undoubtedly influenced by their often appalling living conditions, much higher levels of poverty, lack of education, overcrowding, and unemployment (McKee, 1997). Evictions, because of their inability to pay rent, mortgages or utility bills, increasing homelessness, internal displacement and increasing tensions with local authorities have been major issues for many European Roma groups.

The Romani culture itself may bring an increased risk for certain illnesses. Dietary habits include a high fat and salt content in foods, and social (or societal) isolation, resulting in lower participation in health screening, all create significant health issues. Binnie (1998: 1824) suggests that the unofficial caravan sites of Roma in Britain today mirror the conditions that prevailed a couple of centuries earlier – 'no clean or adequate water supply, no sewage disposal system, no rubbish collection, and certainly totally inadequate education, immunisation, and medical attention.'

The recent report from Save the Children (2001) paints a disturbing picture with regard to Roma communities in Europe. Andruszkiewicz (2001: 27) notes these communities 'continue to encounter discrimination, lower-quality service provision and a lack of personal security, freedom of movement and choice'. In many of these communities, poverty exacerbates this powerlessness, and 'successive generations find themselves excluded from educational opportunity and trapped in insecure, marginal and low-paid employment'.

With respect to more recent immigrant ethnic groups, leaving one's homeland in response to pressures at home 'raises potential questions about culture, community and identity and processes of change, both for those who leave and for their children' (Mayo, 2000: 133). For minority ethnic groups within a foreign (and sometimes hostile) society, the socio-economic environment may have a negative impact on the health of the minority group, and there may also be problems with regard to alcohol and drug abuse, violence and many other negative behaviours.

The Pacific Islands immigrant population in New Zealand is particularly heterogeneous, comprising people from Samoa, Tonga, Cook Islands, Tokelau, Niue, Fiji and Tuvalau (the largest ethnic groups), along with people from Melanesian countries such as Papua New Guinea, Vanuatu and the Solomon Islands, and those from Kiribati and several other small countries in Micronesia. These migrants are from population pools characterised by a diet that includes more imported Western foods, and a rise in diabetes, heart disease and cancer (Bathgate et al., 1994).

Pacific Island people living in New Zealand; however, may well be worse off than those who have remained at home, for example, they have:

> A less healthy diet than their counterparts in the Islands, having poorer access to traditional foods . . . , being more dependent on red meat, bread and potatoes, and consuming more salt, sugar and fat.
> (Bathgate et al., 1994: 23)

In addition, cigarette consumption and the use of alcohol were considered to be much higher by the Pacific Island community in New Zealand because of their ready availability and the higher incomes earned. Further, the violent consequences of over-use of alcohol were much better controlled through village support structures in the Islands than they were in New Zealand (Bathgate et al., 1994).

The picture that emerges is that Pacific Island people in New Zealand suffer from increases in physical health conditions such as diabetes, heart problems and high blood pressure, and from increases in specific adverse behaviours such as violence, suicide, and drug and alcohol abuse. This is a picture that to a large extent mirrors similar patterns within the Aboriginal and Roma groups and other ethnic minority groups (both aboriginal [native] and immigrant) around the world (see for example, Anand and Yusuf, 2001; Bandaranyake, 1986; McMichael, 2001).

Health promotion through sport and physical activity

'Ethnicity and race . . . appear to have striking potency as bases of collective identity and action' (Cornell and Hartmann, 1997: 12), and for this reason a focus on ethnicity may well bring positive results with regard to health promotion through sport and physical activity. Sport has been used by nation states for many different purposes since the development of modern sport in the nineteenth century, and it has also been used by those wishing to promote the idea of separate ethnicities. For example:

> The most common practical embodiment of this has been amongst immigrants as they seek either to preserve the cultural separateness of their own ethnic group, or as they strive to assimilate themselves into their host community.
> (Cronin and Mayall, 1998: 4)

There is no doubt that for many ethnic groups, sport has contributed to their sense of unity, but it has also been frequently used as a point of differentiation within an ethnic group, particularly with respect to age (cf. Werbner, 1996) or gender.

Research into ethnicity and sport involvement has frequently adopted the assimilation/acculturation paradigm, which 'suggests that differing recipient ethnic groups will eventually adopt the values and hence behavioral repertoires of a host or donor culture' (Allison, 1979: 90). Henderson (2002) has observed that there is a popular belief that organised sport fosters integration and creates an environment of equality for minority groups. As Cronin and Mayall (1998: 3) put it, 'a national identity can permit the blurring of differences and serve to unite a multi-ethnic people behind a single national ideal.'

On the other hand, as MacClancy (1996b: 2) suggests, sport can be a vehicle of identity, and help to provide people 'with a sense of difference and a way of classifying both themselves and others . . .' Fleming (1991) is one who concludes that sport participation often has outcomes that are quite the opposite from the assumptions of the assimilation/acculturation paradigm. As Floyd et al. (1994: 159) explain:

> the ethnicity or subcultural hypothesis states that minority underparticipation or intergroup variation results from differences between racial or ethnic groups in values systems, norms, and socialization patterns. This explanation suggests that regardless of socioeconomic standing, cultural processes are more important in explaining variation . . . in leisure participation patterns.

Allison (1988) also concluded that empirical evidence favors the ethnicity hypothesis. Although members of different ethnic groups may adopt mainstream sporting activities, Allison suggests that these groups often use these sports as clear expressions of their own ethnic identity.

Participating in sport generally ranks highly as a youth leisure activity in most developed societies (see for example: Brandl-Bredenbeck, 1994; Haleem, 2002; Rees and Brettschneider, 1994; Thomson, 2000; Thomson and Soós, 2000; Thomson and Soós, 2005), and a focus on such involvement might well pay significant dividends in the promotion of a healthy, active lifestyle for ethnic minority groups.

With regard to Australian Aborigines, Tatz (1995: 4) suggests that sport already plays a significant role in assisting Aboriginal communities that are in danger of social disintegration because of the 'deep inner meaning that sport has in Aboriginal existence'. In the absence of an 'inner faith or philosophy', such as the black consciousness movement in the United States, or an ethnic-based nationalism such as the Zulu Inkatha movement in Natal, Tatz maintains that there is a desperate need for a cement that produces a sense of cohesion. For Australian Aborigines sport may well provide a partial answer to some of the major problems faced by this group.

There is considerable strength of Aboriginal participation in and achievement in sport in rural areas of Australia, and what grudging respect Australians do accord Aborigines comes mostly from their sporting prowess. Tatz maintains that psychological, sociological and political needs give Aboriginal sport a centrality that rarely occurs in other societies, and this centrality suggests that sport could play a key role in health promotion for this group. The 'internal breakdown' in Aboriginal communities and the personal violence within groups and even within families is a major cause for concern. Sport is a key factor in sustaining and nurturing group identity for Aborigines, and there is sufficient evidence to suggest that successful sport experiences reduce community crime rates and significantly reduce the incidence of violence (Tatz, 1995).

Tatz (in Radmer, 2002) has also suggested that participation in sport can be a powerful force in the prevention of suicide amongst Aboriginal children. Sport tends to have much more significance for Aborigines:

Because much of the Aboriginal society is fatherless. There are no elders, very few Christian marriages, no beliefs and far too many funerals. Rituals have simply disappeared. But the ritual of belonging in sport is unchanged.
(Radmer, 2002: 21)

'Sport can, and does, have more important functions in Aboriginal societies than it does in the lives of other Australians' (Tatz, 1995: 315), and while sport is not a *cure* for the ills that beset the Aboriginal people, 'a full sporting life is a *partial* answer to some of the major problems' (Tatz, 1995: 324). Government spending on sport is clearly not just expenditure on play and recreation – it is expenditure on something that is a major facet of Aboriginal survival and should be treated as such (Tatz, 1995).

When we examine the second of our ethnic groups, the Roma of Europe, it is difficult to locate literature concerning their involvement in sport or physical activity, other than that activity associated with physical occupations and with lifestyles that may incorporate considerable physical activity. There has been a tradition of Roma involvement in boxing, particularly in Great Britain, while bare-knuckle fighting has been described as 'a passion among gypsies' (Stockin et al., 2000).

Nevertheless, it is clear that, unlike Aborigines and a number of other ethnic minority groups, Roma adolescents have not been as enthusiastic in their attitudes toward sport and physical activity (Thomson and Soós, 2005). While much of the data are based on the involvement in sport and physical activity of young Roma in Hungary, there is little in the literature to suggest that their situation is atypical of Roma youth throughout Europe. This would seem to indicate a significant point of difference between Roma youth and other adolescent groups, and it may well be linked to the fact that Roma as an ethnic group are spread across numerous national boundaries, while other ethnic groups largely share a common national sporting identity.

Outside of school hours, there are a significant number of Roma students who have no involvement in sport, and this is clearly a cause for some concern. It seems that while Roma youth acknowledge that sport and physical recreation is important for health and fitness, they are much less likely than adolescents in other countries to see it as an 'enjoyable' activity (Thomson and Soós, 2005). Nonetheless, there is a suggestion that the martial arts and combat sports are becoming more popular with Roma boys, and the interest in these two activities is in line with traditional Roma involvement in such sports (see for example, Remias, 2000; Stockin et al., 2000).

There is also evidence to suggest that the process of cross-fertilisation between Roma and Hungarian culture evident in literature and the theatre (Kerékgyártó, 2000) may also be occurring in sport and physical activity (Thomson and Sóos, 2005). The improved educational opportunities for Roma youth, provided by such schools as Gandhi Secondary Grammar School in Pécs, Hungary is a positive pointer to an improved situation for Roma in the future. If such improved educational opportunities can be mirrored throughout Europe for Roma youth, there will also be improving opportunities to participate in school sport. This may well lead to improved attitudes toward, and patterns of involvement in, sport and physical activity, with consequent benefits to Roma health (Thomson and Sóos, 2005).

For the Pacific Island immigrant population in New Zealand, sport has a particularly high profile. In New Zealand's 'national game', rugby football, more than 5 per cent of the participants in the national provincial champion-ship have Pacific Island ethnicity (Melnick and Thomson, 1996), with such famous names as Jonah Lomu (Tonga) and current national team captain, Tana Umaga (Samoa) and a number of other high profile current All Blacks being members of this group. The emergence in more recent times of gifted Pacific Island athletes on the New Zealand sporting scene has been one of the consequences of change brought about by New Zealand's immigration policies. Another significant factor is that while the relative proportion of the country's European population is decreasing, the number of people of Pacific Island descent continues to grow (Hyde, 1993). With the greater proportion of Pacific Islanders being from the younger age groups, it is not surprising that they are considerably over-represented at the top levels of a number of sports.

While such sporting success should be cause for celebration, the fact remains that there are major health concerns for Pacific Islanders in New Zealand, and the numbers who remain active and progress through to the top levels of sport are clearly a small minority. Pacific Island youth (in common with Maori) rate sporting participation more highly than pakeha (Caucasian) adolescents and significantly higher than ethnic Asian youth. While this might be seen as a positive factor, there is also the concern that such a focus leaves them less time for study, and this clearly has a negative impact on their academic success (Thomson, 2000). Perhaps, the most striking feature; however, is that signifi-cantly more Pacific Island students play sport because they hope to make a career out of their participation. Such aspirations are doomed to failure for the majority, and if a successful career in sport is no longer possible, the major-ity cease to participate, and end up as adults with lower than desirable levels of physical activity.

Pacific Island youth also tend to have higher levels of involvement in team sports (basketball, rugby, touch rugby, rugby league and netball are most popular). It is the social factors and the sense of community that are empha-sised in such participation, rather than a focus on health and fitness, that individual sports and activities might better promote (Thomson, 2000). In all age groups and for both males and females, Pacific Island people have showed the lowest levels of physical activity in comparison to other New Zealanders, and with some surveys showing that 60 per cent of Pacific Islanders had not exercised at all in the previous seven days (Public Health Commission, 1994). Recommended levels of physical activity for cardiovascular fitness are clearly not being reached by the majority of this population. With diabetes and coro-nary heart disease in particular being major health problems for this group, a focus on increasing Pacific Island involvement in individual sports and physical activities could well prove beneficial.

Conclusion

As Stuart (1996) has indicated, sport can provide cohesion and community to ethnic groups, and as such maybe used in an attempt to improve the physical and psychological health of such groups. In specific instances where such minorities face considerable discrimination, sport may provide the 'cement that produces a sense of cohesion' (Tatz, 1995: 324). In this chapter, all three ethnic groups considered have had to cope with discrimination and/or deprivation, and each group is confronted with a number of highly significant health problems.

For ethnicity to play a role in health promotion, a sense of community through involvement in team sports may also be seen as a vital factor. MacClancy (1996a: 197) maintains that the introduced sport of football has become a 'traditional' part of Basque modernity, and rugby league and Australian rules football could similarly play an increasingly important part in modern Aboriginal life. While the magnificent athlete, Cathy Freeman, has been the international flag bearer for Aboriginal sport in recent times, the people have a proud sporting history and have made a wonderful contribution to Australian sport. Sport, conversely, makes a great contribution to 'Aboriginality', as Tatz (1995) puts it – it is not a frivolous activity, but a vital component of the public perception of a people.

For Roma in Europe, the problem of being a 'people without a nation' is an extra difficulty to overcome. Discrimination against Roma throughout Europe remains one of the most pressing social problems to be faced by the European Community, and perhaps the most urgent need is for improved access to appropriate education for Roma children. If educational opportunities are increased, so too, will opportunities be provided for their involvement in sport. While sport involvement may often provide an avenue for the participants to be successfully integrated into the host or dominant society, the specific nature of that sporting involvement can also continue to provide a point of difference between Roma youth and the dominant culture (Thomson and Soós, 2005). For Roma culture to continue to exist, that point of difference might well be essential.

It would be wrong to suggest that sport and physical activity will provide the complete answer to the health problems of any particular social or ethnic group, but increased physical activity may well bring with it a sense of increased well-being. This could prove invaluable, particularly for displaced groups such as Pacific Islanders in New Zealand, where problems caused by a change in diet and lifestyle must be overcome. The multiple health benefits of regular physical activity are not debated, independent of the presence of other risk factors. The 'consistent trend for Pacific Islands people in different age groups to have substantially lower levels of physical activity than other people' (Bathgate et al., 1994: 119) is a challenge for educators and sports administrators in New Zealand, but one which must be accepted. The costs of failing to act, in both social and economic terms, are simply too high.

References

Allison, M. T. (1979) On the ethnicity of ethnic minorities in sport, *International Review of Sport Sociology*, 14(1), 89–96.

Allison, M. T. (1988) Breaking boundaries: Future directions in cross-cultural research. *Leisure Sciences*, 10, 247–259.

Anand, S. and Yusef, S. (2001) Ethnic variations and cardiovascular disease in Macbeth, H. and Shetty, P. (Eds.) *Health and Ethnicity*. London: Taylor and Francis, 164–186.

Andruszkiewicz, M. (2001). Summary of findings and conclusions in *Denied a Future? The Right to Education of Roma/Gypsy and Traveller Children in Europe. Summary*. London: Save the Children.

Bandaranyake, R. (1986) Ethnic differences in disease – an epidemiological perspective in Rathwell, T. and Phillips, D. (Eds.) *Health, Race and Ethnicity*. London: Croom Helm, 80–99.

Bathgate, M., Alexander, D., Mitikulena, A., Borman, B., Roberts, A. and Grigg, M. (1994) *The Health of Pacific Islands People in New Zealand*. Wellington: Public Health Commission.

Binnie, G. A. C. (1998) The health of Gypsies, *British Medical Journal*, 316, 1824.

Braham, M. (1993) *The Untouchables: A Survey of the Roma People of Central and Eastern Europe*. Geneva: UNHCR.

Brandl-Bredenbeck, H. P. (1994) A cross-cultural comparison of selected aspects of adolescent sports culture – USA/Germany. Paper presented at the annual conference of the North American Society for the Sociology of Sport, Savannah, Georgia, November 9–12.

Chapman, M. (1993) *Social and Biological Aspects of Ethnicity*. Oxford: Oxford University Press.

Cornell, S. and Hartmann, D. (1997) *Ethnicity and Race: Making Identities in a Changing World*. California: Pine Forge Press.

Cronin, M. and Mayall, D. (1998) Sport and ethnicity: Some introductory remarks in Cronin, M. and Mayall, D. (Eds.) *Sporting Nationalisms: Identity, Ethnicity, Immigration and Assimilation*. London: Frank Cass.

Fleming, S. (1991) Sport, schooling and Asian male youth culture in Jarvie, G. (Ed.) *Sport, Racism and Ethnicity*. London: Falmer.

Floyd, M. F., Shinew, K. J., McGuire, F. A. and Noe, F. P. (1994) Race, class, and leisure activity preferences: Marginality and ethnicity revisited, *Journal of Leisure Research*, 26(2), 158–173.

Haleem, H. (2002) *Adolescent Sports Participation: A Case Study of the Maldives*. Thesis (MPhEd). Dunedin, New Zealand: University of Otago.

Hancock, I. (2002) *We are the Romani People. Ame Sam e Rromane Džene*. Hertfordshire: University of Hertfordshire Press.

Henderson, D. A. (2002) Sport, racism and ethnicity (Review), *Sociology of Sport Journal*, 19(1), 99–100.

Hyde, T. (1993) White men can't jump: The Polynesianisation of sport, *Metro*, September, 62–69.

Kerékgyártó, I. (2000) Culture in Kállai, E. and Tõrzõl, E. (Eds.) *A Roma's Life in Hungary. Report 2000.* Translated by T. Wilkinson. Budapest, Hungary: Bureau for European Comparative Minority Research.

Macbeth, H. and Shetty, P. (2001) *Health and Ethnicity.* London: Taylor and Francis.

MacClancy, J. (1996a) Nationalism at play: The Basques of Vizcaya and Athletic Club de Bilbao in MacClancy, J. (Ed.) *Sport, Identity and Ethnicity.* Oxford, UK: Berg, 181–199.

MacClancy, J. (1996b) Sport, identity and ethnicity in MacClancy, J. (Ed.) *Sport, Identity and Ethnicity.* Oxford, UK: Berg, 1–20.

McKee, M. (1997) The health of Roma (Gypsies) in Europe, *The British Medical Journal, 315,* 1172–1173.

McMichael, A. J. (2001) Diabetes, ancestral diets and dairy foods: An evolutionary perspective on population differences in susceptibility to diabetes in Macbeth, H. and Shetty, P. (Eds.) *Health and Ethnicity.* London: Taylor and Francis, 133–146.

Mayo, M. (2000) *Cultures, Communities, Identities. Cultural Strategies for Participation and Empowerment.* Hampshire, UK: Palgrave.

Médecins du Monde-International and Save the Children Alliance (2001) *Human Rights of the Roma/Gypsies.* Joint declaration to the Sub-Commission for the Promotion and the Protection of Human Rights, Doctors of the World Secrétariat International, Geneva, 10 August.

Melnick, M. J. and Thomson, R. W. (1996) The Maori people and positional segregation in New Zealand rugby football: A test of the anglocentric hypothesis, *International Review for the Sociology of Sport, 31*(2), 139–154.

Public Health Commission (1994) *Our Health – Our Future (Hauora pakari, koiora roa).* Wellington: Public Health Commission.

Radmer, K. B. (2002) Prevent the young from suicide, *Play the Game, 2002,* 21.

Rees, C. R. and Brettschneider, W.-D. (1994) The meaning of sport for German and American adolescents. Paper presented at the ISCphysical education Conference, Prague, 4 July.

Remias, I. (2000) Mean streets, *The Prague Post,* 26 January.

Reyniers, A., Solimano, N. and Mori, T. (2000) Gypsies: Trapped on the fringes of Europe, *UNESCO Courier, 53*(6), 38–40.

Save the Children (2001) *Denied a Future? The Right to Education of Roma/Gypsy and Traveller Children in Europe.* London: Save the Children.

Stockin, J., with King, M. and Knight, M. (2000) *On the Cobbles. The Life of a Bareknuckle Gypsy Warrior.* Edinburgh: Mainstream Publishing.

Streiff-Fenart, J. (1999) *Théories de l'ethnicité.* Paris: PUF.

Stuart, O. (1996) Players, workers, protestors: Social change and soccer in colonial Zimbabwe in MacClancy, J. (Ed.) *Sport, Identity and Ethnicity.* Oxford, UK: Berg, 167–180.

Tatz, C. (1995) *Obstacle Race. Aborigines in Sport.* Sydney: University of New South Wales Press.

Thomson, R. W. (2000) Globalization and national differences: The changing face of youth sport, *New Zealand Sociology, 15*(1), 30–45.

Thomson, R. W. and Soós, I. (2000) Youth sport in New Zealand and Hungary: Globalisation versus local resistance, *International Sports Studies, 22*(2), 74–82.

Thomson, R. W. and Soós, I. (2005) Rroma culture and physical culture in Hungary, *International Review for the Sociology of Sport*, 40(2), 255–263, ISSN 1012–6902.

Trewin, D. and Madden, R. (2003) *The Health and Welfare of Australia's Aboriginal and Torres Strait Islander Peoples*. Canberra: Australian Bureau of Statistics.

Werbner, P. (1996) 'Our blood is green': Cricket, identity and social empowerment among British Pakistanis in MacClancy, J. (Ed.) *Sport, Identity and Ethnicity*. Oxford, UK: Berg, 87–111.

CHAPTER 14

Gender and Sport: Promoting/ Preventing Health in our Schools

KATE M. RUSSELL

Introduction

The aim of this chapter is to identify how schools promote and/or prevent health through the medium of physical activity and sport. I explore not only the factors that can create barriers to active participation in school-based activities, but also how such experiences can lead to long-term health-related problems. Specifically, I will be looking at the role of physical education lessons in the construction of meaningful experiences of being active, and how it could be used to mediate health within the wider school environment. There will be a focus on the gendered structures of physical education, in the hope of understanding how and why girls, in particular, participate in school activities far less than boys. The chapter draws on a variety of research, to highlight the gendered position that teachers and pupils find themselves in relation to physical education. While sport is used as the context to promote health, it will become clear that it may actually act as a hindrance for many girls trying to maintain a healthy approach to life. There are several key factors that support this argument: physical education and sport at school are gender constructed activities; girls are physically less active than boys. Both within and outside of school lessons, girls are given limited opportunities for sport participation, and girls are more likely than boys to suffer from poor body image. Subsequently, girls could be at a greater risk for developing eating disorders. I want to explore how sport and physical activity are constructed within the school environment, which factors drive positive and negative perceptions of the purpose of sport, and the programmes that have proved successful in actively engaging girls in sport and physical activity.

Setting the context for health promotion

The prevalence of obesity among children and adolescents is steadily increasing throughout the world (World Health Organization, 2003), with the level of

American children being classed as overweight (Body Mass Index over 25) trebling since 1980. Within the United Kingdom, recent estimates of obesity indicate a range of between 6 per cent in pre-school children (Reilly et al., 1999) to 17 per cent by the age of 15 (Fruhbeck, 2000; Rudolf et al., 2001). In 2002, The Health Survey for England (Sproston and Primatesta, 2002) indicated that 30.3 per cent of boys and 30.7 per cent of girls aged 2–15 years were at least overweight, and 16 per cent of boys and 15.9 per cent of girls aged 2–15 were obese. There are also indicators for ethnic differences in obesity levels. The 1999 Health Survey for England (Saxena et al., 2004) produced data to indicate that compared with the general population, Indian and Pakistani boys were more likely to be overweight or obese, and Bangladeshi and Chinese boys were less likely to be overweight or obese. Among girls, it was found that more girls from an Afro-Caribbean background were overweight or obese than the general population, and Chinese girls were less likely to be overweight or obese (report from Chief Medical Officer, Department of Health, 2004). When considering the increased likelihood of obese children developing into obese adults (Freedman et al., 1999; Sinaiko et al., 1999; Twisk et al., 1997), the human, as well as, resource costs are staggering. The Chief Medical Officer (Department of Health, 2004) estimates that the cost to both the National Health Service and the economy, in terms of absence from work, is £2.5 billion annually. At current levels, a third of all adults will be obese by 2010, bringing levels of obesity up to that currently experienced in the United States of America (National Audit Office, 2001).

The evidence for the role of physical activity and sport in public health is clear, as adults who engage in physical activity have '20–30 per cent reduced risk of premature death, and up to 50 per cent reduced risk of developing chronic diseases such as coronary heart disease, stroke, diabetes and cancers' (Chief Medical Officer, Department of Health, 2004: 1). The effects of physical activity and health for children are related more to the long-term benefits of avoiding excessive weight gain, which can lead to obesity related diseases as adults. Nevertheless, children who are obese are more likely to have certain cardiovascular risk factors (Freedman et al., 1999; Reich et al., 2003), are more likely to experience long-term social and economic discrimination (Gortmaker et al., 1993), and have a lower quality of life (Schwimmer et al., 2003). As such, the government has taken steps to promote the benefits of a more active lifestyle to both the adult and younger populations in an attempt to halt the obesity epidemic.

Recommendations for active life

The government has set out a series of recommended levels of physical activity for both adults and children that seek to clarify just what is required in order to gain a general health benefit. For adults, the recommendation is a total of at least 30 minutes a day of at least moderate intensity physical activity, on

5 or more days of the week. These recommendations follow those produced by the American College of Sports Medicine and the Centres for Disease Control (Pate et al., 1995) and endorsed by the USA Surgeon General (USA Department of Health and Human Service, 1996). The recommended levels can be achieved either by doing all the daily activity in one session, or through several shorter bouts of activity of 10 minutes or more. To prevent obesity; however, a level of 45–60 minutes a day would be necessary. For children and young people, the level of at least moderate intensity physical activity should be at least 60 minutes a day. At least twice a week these activities should seek to improve bone health, muscle strength and flexibility. These recommendations follow those produced by Biddle et al. (1997). Again, this target can be reached through the accumulation of activity throughout the day. It is expected that this requirement will be reached through the build up of short bursts of play during break times, and longer periods in physical education lessons. While it is recognised that many children do already participate at this level of activity (Sproston and Primatesta, 2003), childhood obesity continues to increase and levels may need to be raised in the near future.

The key question to address, therefore, is not only how we can encourage more children to be more active more of the time, but also, how do health care professionals and school teachers educate children in understanding, and accepting the long-term benefits of taking part in physical activity and sport, when there is little motivation to do so at such a young age?

Promoting physical activity and sport at schools

Schools do have physical activity programmes in place, either as part of the National Curriculum or as after school activities. The key concern, in particular, for teachers and health promoters alike, is the continued low participation rates of girls in these activities. A number of studies (Flintoff and Scraton, 2001; Sports Council for Wales, 1995; Youth Sport Trust/Nike, 1999, 2000) have shown that girls participate in sports and physical activity at school far less than boys, and have very negative perceptions of that experience. There has also been an increase in the percentage of young people who do not take part in *any* sport in school lessons on a regular basis (at least 10 occasions in the last 12 months) from 15 per cent in 1994 to 18 per cent in 2002 (Sport England, 2002). Nonetheless, women are participating in physical activities outside of the school environment (including activities such as aerobics, swimming and walking) far more than in previous decades (General Household Survey, 1998). There is also an increase in the number of women participating in sports traditionally considered male, such as rugby and football. Despite this increase in women's overall participation in out of school activities, the concern persists around girls and young women's engagement with sport and physical activity within the school environment. A number of factors have been identified as influencing the participation of girls and women in physical activity. These include biological and physical capabilities (Flintoff and Scraton, 2001), perceptions of femininity and masculinity (Krane et al., 2004; McDermott, 1996, 2000; Obel, 1996; Russell, 2004), body image (Krane et al., 2004; Russell, 2004), self-confidence (Graydon, 1997), parental influences (Deem and Gilroy, 1998: Kay, 1995), and the organisation and structure of physical education and sport (Harris and Penney, 2002). I intend to look closer at how the construction of physical education and sport creates an environment for girls that is often restrictive in terms of enjoyment and opportunity, but also one in which feelings of acceptable physical expression can be determined by peers and teachers.

The gendered construction of physical education and sport

Traditional structures of physical education and sport at school may be one of the key factors in why so many girls have negative experiences. It is clear that existing school physical education teachers, and those involved in the training of potential teachers, have some responsibility for this type of response. In a report delivered to the Nuffield foundation, Williams and Bedward (1999: 7) noted that:

> The disadvantaged position of girls would seem to have little to do with the recent implementation of policy and more to do with the remarkable resilience to change that physical education has demonstrated, particularly over the last 15 years. The failure to abandon a traditional gender differentiated approach has resulted in physical education being unique among subjects within British secondary education.

In the United Kingdom, physical education has been utilised for many years to reinforce traditional views of accepted versions of femininity and masculinity that only serve to present restricted opportunities of participation to girls at school. As such it is what Kirk (2002: 35) describes as a *'masculinised form of the subject'*, and with it inherently masculinised versions of acceptable physical expression that do not meet the 'needs of many girls and at least some boys'. Alongside this restricted version of what physical education should look like comes accepted ways of delivering physical education to schoolchildren. Kirk (1992) noted that traditional (masculine) forms of practice also drive this. This form of practice often included a reliance on command style teaching, competitive sport, particularly team sports, and an objectification of the body within biological and mechanical terms. Traditional forms of physical education delivery appeared to serve and enhance the control and direction of the teacher, at the expense of the individual.

Understanding where, and in what form, expected forms of physical education delivery come from, may bring some light onto the situation. The first aim of all subjects under the National Curriculum ensures that teachers should 'provide opportunities for all pupils to learn and to achieve'. Teachers work towards achieving this aim by developing 'enjoyment of, and commitment to: learning as a means of encouraging and stimulating the best possible progress and the highest attainment for all pupils. It should build on pupils' strengths, interests and experiences and develop their confidence in their capacity to learn and work independently and collaboratively' (National Curriculum, Online, 2005). The document also notes the active involvement of teachers in the development and implementation of the curriculum, in that they should 'reappraise their teaching in response to the changing *needs of their pupils and the impact of economic, social and cultural change'*. The suggestion is that teachers would adapt and develop schemes of work, through an understanding of the changing social and cultural world in which children exist. Whilst the aims of the National Curriculum provide an optimistic view for the advancement of physical education as a subject, the reality of the situation does not always merit this outlook.

Penney (2002) provides an excellent review of the development and implementation of the National Curriculum for Physical Education in England throughout the 1990s, and highlights a number of the key principles the National Council for Physical Education sought to address, such as equal opportunity. She pays particular attention to the Interim Report of 1991, in which some common practices and perceptions of physical education were noted worthy of further consideration. Two of these practices and perceptions have particular resonance to this chapter: the legacy of single-sex teaching and teacher education in physical education, and the barriers to young people's involvement, caused by restrictive ways some sports and forms of dance are portrayed and practised.

As part of our understanding of the ways in which physical education is constructed and delivered to schoolchildren, we must start with a recognition and exploration of how physical education teachers are trained. Brown and Rich (2002) examined how gender is positioned within a Postgraduate Certificate in Education course in an English University for teachers wanting to specialise in physical education. Their research takes a relational perspective of gender in physical education by following Messner and Sabo's (1990) *'Gender Order'*, in which femininity and masculinity are critically examined in relation to each other, within a given system of inequality. In this instance, Brown and Rich seek to show the ways in which 'gendered student teacher identities, masculine and feminine, are positioned and deployed as pedagogy' (Brown and Rich, 2002: 80). Humberstone (1990) noted that the physical education curriculum itself mediates the complicated interrelationships between our cultural values, and how we develop gender identity and gender based sport stereotypes. It does this in two key ways. First, physical education helps to define acceptable physical activities for girls and boys through the inclusion and exclusion of certain events throughout the sporting calendar. In doing so, it demarcates what is considered to be appropriately feminine and masculine behaviours. Sport is often regarded as a male preserve (Dunning, 1994), and an area in which images of ideal masculinity are constructed and promoted (Connell, 1987). In this environment boys learn what it is to become *'men'*, and notions of the differences between men and women, and between men who do and do not compete, are also developed (Connell, 1987). These differences often reflect notions of the differences between men and women's physical capabilities and the questioning of the sexuality of men who do not play competitive sport. Similarly, Connell (1987) argues, sport provides the avenue in which many girls construct their identities, forming boundaries for acceptable behaviour, future sporting career opportunities, and notions of their importance in the sporting world.

Secondly, the style of physical education teaching, rooted in Initial Teacher Training, also comes to define preferred methods of sport delivery. The construction of appropriate teaching practice is often predicated by concerns that not teaching traditionally female or male sport may have consequences, not only for the presumption of a teacher's ability/inability in that sport, but also fears over being identified as homosexual (Brown and Rich, 2002; Clarke, 2002; Griffin, 1992; Squires and Sparkes, 1996). In this way, individual choice, in terms of specialising in a particular sport, is limited. To accept traditional notions of what a female or male physical education teacher should specialise in, such as netball for women, and football for men, merely reinforces the gendered construction of sport. To reject these notions, teachers challenge the accepted ideal of being a female or male physical education teacher, and place themselves in a subordinate or *'other'* position (Brown and Rich, 2002). For women, it is the presence of supposed *'masculine'* qualities such as aggression and competitiveness, that often pre-empts the definition of homosexuality; whereas for men, it is often the absence of such qualities that can label themselves as homosexual (Russell, 2004).

This classification of female homosexuality mirrors much of the research into women's participation in sports traditionally deemed as masculine (Krane et al., 2004), such as boxing (Halbert, 1997), body building (Choi, 2000), football (Scraton et al., 1999; Kolnes, 1995; Pirinen, 1997), rugby (Russell, 2004; Russell, 2002) and wrestling (Sisjord, 1997). This research suggests that female participation in sports stereotyped as male, and in particular, those sports that require some display of power and strength, result in many women being perceived as aggressive, overly competitive, and ultimately 'unfeminine'. Veri (1999) points to the definition of the female athlete as deviant, because of its open defiance of the discipline of femininity. Any transgression from the traditional ideals of what the feminine body should be doing labels itself as deviant, masculine and thus homosexual.

The experiences of student teachers wanting to specialise in physical education (Brown and Rich, 2002: 86), can provide an excellent insight into how traditional structures of physical education often force students to take up positions that enforce the dominant ideals of masculinity and femininity. One example indicated a lack of opportunity for a male student to deliver a dance programme to boys. The comment from the head of department was simply that 'I don't believe boys should do that.' Not only does this prevent boys from having the opportunity to experience dance, but it also serves to limit the student's range of teaching techniques, and place of dance in the curriculum. Similarly, a more relaxed approach to teaching male pupils was criticised by another teacher for being 'too soft', indicating once again the presupposition that there is only one style of appropriate teaching, that being very regimented and structured. The student teacher in question then had to reposition his approach to teaching boys in a way that was more authoritarian, because that was how his work was considered to be of value. In this way, accepted versions of teaching practice are reinforced and maintained. On another occasion, a female student teacher (Christie) failed to speak out against a male teacher's derogatory comments about the dress of some of the girls in his class. This experience exemplifies what Brown and Rich (2002) call the 'double bind' of those wanting to challenge the Gender Order. The term 'Gender Order' was employed by Brown and Rich (2002) to determine a base from which issues of inclusion and exclusion, reproduction and change within the field of physical education and school sport can be viewed (they attribute the term to Messner and Sabo, 1990). The difficulty being that many students want to have a more inclusive perspective and practice to physical education lessons and education as a whole, but to do so, can often place them in a disadvantaged position. If Christie challenges the comments, she risks being stigmatised and identified as a non-complicit female and student teacher. If she does nothing, she is a willing participant in the process, and consequently merely reinforces the established order. For both men and women seeking to become physical education teachers, there is a clear barrier to openly challenging the status quo without negative consequence. Many student teachers abide by the expectations of their teaching mentors and programme advisors, in order to be successful. This may take place, even though this practice contradicts some of the National Curriculum's aims and objectives for equal opportunity.

It is also evident that female teachers often have to *'prove'* themselves, in order to be taken seriously by male pupils. Frequently, when taking an all boys group for football or basketball, Christie was only taken seriously when she was able to demonstrate a high level of skill to the class:

> I took an all-boys football group, and it was quite interesting the way that they [the boys] reacted. One of the balls rolled over to me, and naturally I did take a flick and then a few keepie-up and, you know, that was it, you know all the lads were like, 'Miss do you play football?' And I had my women's football top on, and then the lads started taking the mick out of one of the other boys in the group saying, 'Miss is better than you'.
> (cited from Brown and Rich, 2002: 92)

While Christie is able to demonstrate her ability to do the same things that the boys can do, she is also accepting that this is the only way in which to gain respect as a female teacher. What this account also indicates is that the boys in this group rated her performance initially as a woman playing 'their' sport, and an accomplished player second, when they used her performance as a method of peer ridicule. Being *'beaten by a girl'* is still utilised as one of the worst indicators of performance by young men and male teachers alike. Having to prove one's ability in sports considered to be in the male domain, such as cricket, football and rugby, is a consistent message in the sporting development of many girls and young women (Russell, 2002). Considering the often-restrictive forms of teaching practice accepted by mentors within the school environment, and the associated beliefs of limited physical capabilities of both girls and boys, it is not surprising to find that many girls have negative experiences of school sport.

Girl's experiences of physical education and sport

It should be recognised that girls and boys participate in sport and physical activity within a socially constructed environment. It is socially constructed in the sense that, while the National Curriculum sets guidelines for content and provision time for sport within schools, the delivery of this programme is based on long-standing ideals of accepted physical activity. It was noted earlier in this chapter that stereotypical notions of sports suitable for girls and boys are reinforced through teacher training. This training limits both opportunities for girls and boys to experience a greater variety of sports, and also restricts a teacher's capability to learn and deliver non-traditional activities, such as women teaching football and men teaching dance. The relative stability of this cultural practice (Kirk, 1999) is problematic, in the sense that while many educators may be critical of the way in which sports are delivered to school-children, there appears to be a limited opportunity for changing this. Recent research (Flintoff and Scraton, 2001; Hargreaves, 1994; Williams and Bedward, 1999, 2000, 2002; Youth Sport Trust/Nike, 1999, 2000) has highlighted that school sport often fails to provide a positive experience for girls, because of this limited view of physical education and how it should be delivered. Whilst Penney and Evans (1999) noted that there are often political frame-works that prevent many teachers from challenging and restructuring the way in which sport is delivered, it is important to consistently present material that highlights the dissatisfaction of both pupils and teachers alike in the hope that change will come. Some of the key factors, which influence the positive and negative experiences of girls include: the gendered structure of the cur-riculum, and the lack of choice of activities; a highly prescribed uniform, chosen by those in authority and not the pupils; sexist attitudes of teachers and pupils regarding participation in non-traditional sports; lack of awareness regarding body image and its consequences; and conformity to codes of conduct which have little relevance to recreational sports.

Many girls in Williams and Bedward's (2002) study noted the inequity of providing boys the opportunity to play football, while they were excluded. It was clear, from the accounts given to Williams and Bedward (2002) that the girls were very aware of the gendered structures of physical education, and critical of it. One reason for this may be that many girls had played football within the primary school environment, and were now unable to continue simply because they were at secondary school. Ravinder, one of the students interviewed by Williams and Bedward (2002: 151), highlighted this situation:

> Well, I don't really like hockey and I enjoy football because I've done football a lot in my primary school. I was going to join a team, but then, no. We were going to a team in Year 7 but then Mr Jacques says you can't.

The study also found that one of the reasons for the exclusion of girls from football maybe a lack of awareness by the teachers themselves, regarding the opportunities for girls to play football outside of the school setting. This reflects not only, traditional views of gender appropriate activities, but also, equally a failure to recognise the growth of new sports, and its opportunities for girls and women in the long term. Robert, a white male head of physical education, was clearly unaware of the recent growth in girl's football, and the knock-on effects that greater involvement produces:

> I feel that it is in their best interests for us to teach them games that they are actually more likely to be able to follow up after they leave school, so I actually feel that we're better sticking to the traditional range – that we teach rugby to boys and football to boys, basketball to boys, although we have done some mixed basketball, and netball and *hockey to girls*. [Author's emphasis]
> (Williams and Bedward, 2002: 152)

What Robert is demonstrating could be considered a realistic sport plan for girls. Boys and men may well have a greater opportunity to make a financially viable career from their chosen sports, such as cricket, rugby or football, but Robert is clearly missing the point. Girls should be provided the same opportunities to experience and enjoy a whole variety of sports and physical activity programmes, not simply cordoned off into sports that require little effort on his part. Such responses highlight what Williams and Bedward (2000) noted as the cultural and generational gap between current teachers and their pupils. This gap results in a lack of awareness, on the part of teachers, to what girls actually want to do, and are certainly capable of undertaking. Even when opportunities are made available for girls to participate in sports they enjoy, such as football and basketball, the results are often negative, because of the attitude of male peers and teachers (Flintoff and Scraton, 2001). In an examination of both student and teachers perceptions of physical education in middle and high school programmes within the United States, Ennis (1999) found co-educational lessons only served to decrease participation motivation

levels among girls. She noted numerous occasions where male students dominated mixed basketball sessions, through their aggressive and individualised
style of play. This practice, which relegated female students to observers, and
a nuisance, was often supported by male teachers and highlighted as a reason
to exclude girls from this activity. Ennis (1999) also noted that one of the key
reasons for this is the boys' belief that in order to be chosen for a preferred
team, and respected by their male peers, they had to demonstrate their aggression, regardless of the impact it had on other classmates:

> You gotta be in there fighting for the ball or the other guys won't want you. If you
> don't they be saying stuff like, 'You be sorry . . . you play like a mother'. I try to
> drive around the girls and not hit them, but they're in my way. I can't be backing
> down to no girl . . . no matter what. I would never be allowed to play on Sean's
> team again. And you know that's real important to me (Ennis, 1999: 34).

This research suggests the strength of the belief of these young men that in
order to be successful, they need and have to display appropriate aggressive
characteristics. This action not only reinforces preconceived ideas of what it
is to be a good basketball player, but also the position of girls in the physical
education school programme. Girls are provided an opportunity to play basketball, but on male terms.

The role of physical education uniforms

Physical education uniforms are often noted as key determinants in the negative experience of girls within physical education lessons, and this is closely
associated to observation by male peers. Many schools impose a uniform for
physical education for both girls and boys, in an attempt to present a school
identity, not only in competitive matches against other schools, but as a way
to promote an image of itself to a wider social environment. Within many
schools, this is seen in the preference of gym skirts or gym knickers with t-shirt
for girls, and shorts and t-shirt for boys. The biggest concern expressed was
related to the revealing state of the gym skirts and gym knickers:

> The physical education skirts are really short, but you have to deal with it because that's
> the school uniform for physical education. And you're not allowed to wear cycling
> shorts either. I don't think it's fair . . . We have to wear physical education pants. Even
> though it's not showing your other pants, it's still a bit revealing I think.
> (Diane, year 11 student, Williams and Bedward, 2002: 154)

There is clearly a conflict between the wishes of many girls to wear clothes that
are less restrictive and revealing, and that reflect more fashionable styles, and
the teachers need to maintain a traditional style of uniform that is 'smart'. The
Youth Sport Trust/Nike project (2000, 1999) highlighted this particular aspect

when addressing the resistance of teachers to change this fundamental aspect. One teacher commented:

> I'm a bit torn really, because I suppose, I'm a bit of a traditionalist and I think they do look very smart in gym skirts, but from a practical point of view I think it's maybe time to change.
> (Youth Sport Trust/Nike, 2000: 53)

The real concern, for this author, is the continued impact that restrictive and revealing clothes may have on girls and young women's body image. Restrictive and revealing physical education kits can often make girls very aware of their bodies, and how it does or does not fit a sporting ideal. More so, displaying your body in front of unsympathetic teachers and other students can often be a humiliating, degrading experience. Teresa, a student in Williams and Bedward's (2002: 155) study highlighted this factor:

> If, say, you're chubby and you want to wear shorts under your skirt because you get picked on, they (the teachers) don't understand. They always tell you to take them off, but you can't. Like today, we had to stand up whoever didn't have the right physical education kit, and I got a warning.

A lack of understanding or complacency concerning the impact of physically displaying your body, by the teachers, is certainly a disturbing trend. The Youth Sport Trust/Nike (Department of Culture, 2001) report noted many instances of the complacency of teachers in relation to this issue, arguing that they were addressing body image concerns in the physical education arena by paying particular attention to how they spoke to girls about their bodies, but often failed to demonstrate any real change in policy. Teachers need to recognise the alarming increase in girls who experience some form of body dissatisfaction, and provide alternative ways of delivering physical education that can reduce this anxiety. In particular, allowing girls to choose their own kit for participating in sport allows them the opportunity to be active in ways that make them feel comfortable. By emphasising, the requirement of a kit that restricts movement, because of a concern over how they feel they look, can lead to many girls engaging in unhealthy practices in order to obtain the 'ideal' physical shape. Research informs us that girls primarily desire a thinner body size than boys (Collins, 1991; Gardner et al., 1997; Lawrence and Thelen, 1995) and report greater body image concerns than boys (Mendelson et al., 1996; Wood et al., 1996). Over 57 per cent of girls as young as 5–7 wanted to look thinner (Ambrosi-Randic, 2000), with 77 per cent of girls aged 14–16 wanting to lose weight (Grigg et al., 1996). These indicators provide strong evidence that there must be a change in the way in which we deliver sporting opportunities for girls, so that there is a greater focus on the value of participation for health and social reasons, rather than being regarded as a means for critical observation.

One success story, in relation to increasing girls involvement in physical education, can be found in The Manor School and Specialist Sports College in Mansfield. This school took part in the Nike Girls in Sport research pilot project run by the Youth sport Trust (Youth Sport Trust/Nike, 1999). Teachers here wanted to explore the reasons behind girls' disengagement with physical education at school, and found that levels of self-esteem among the girls were very low. The low levels of confidence felt by the girls was often compounded by negative attitudes presented by the boys, and did not see sport as a positive influence. Key strategies that improved participation rates and positive experiences included: changing the physical education curriculum to one that met the desires of the girls to include football, aerobics, trampoline, street dance, self-defence and badminton; relaxing physical education kit to include tracksuit bottoms; abandoning showers; and providing alternative sporting roles such as leader, coach and administrator, to girls who did not want to be physically active (Bakewell, 2004). The Nike Girls in Sport scheme has been undertaken by a number of schools in England, and has shown that positive experiences of sport can be achieved for girls, by addressing how physical education and sport is delivered to them. A restructuring of the physical education curriculum, to include more girl friendly sports and activities, such as street dance, aerobics, self-defence and badminton, in addition to a relaxation of the physical education kit and changing policies can have a huge impact on participation rates for girls. What is more important is that girls will enjoy the experience of being physically active, and we can only hope that they will continue with this involvement, and develop a lifelong relationship with physical activity and/or sport.

Conclusion

We know from research (Pate et al., 1999) that encouraging participation in physical activity in children can lead to them becoming physically active adults. A recent longitudinal study (Thompson et al., 2003: 375) found a number of factors that influenced the continued participation in physical activity of children, as they became adults. In particular, adolescence was considered a critical time for developing a preference for physical activity or inactivity later in life. In men, the level of physical activity decreased when experiences were negatively recalled, such as,

> Playing only 10 per cent of the time when on a team, a feeling of inadequate skill development or size disadvantage, or teachers/coaches paying more attention to the more talented individuals.

In a similar vein, women whose physical activity level dropped as adults, recalled other negative experiences such as 'inequitable teacher/coach treatment, feelings of intimidation in physical education and when trying out for sport teams, and lack of parental support and encouragement' (Thompson et al., 2003: 375).

What this study and the other material presented in this chapter highlights is the need to act now, to change the way in which we think about and deliver physical education and sport to our children. We know that there are severe health implications for children who do not maintain a healthy lifestyle. The promotion of physical activity must be considered a priority for all professionals involved in care and guidance of children and young people. In particular, we need to address the low participation rates and drop out rates of girls in sport and physical activity. There are interventions out there such as the Nike Girls in Sport project that can have a positive influence on participation levels of girls, through simple but effective changes in the way in which physical education is delivered at school level. It is also essential that we re-evaluate the ways in which we train and mentor our physical education teachers. We need to encourage a rejection of the restricted gendered stereotypes of 'female' and 'male' sports, and create a more open environment, for trainees to question preconceived ideas of the best teaching methods. As part of this process, student teachers must be permitted to develop more socially and culturally specific programmes that will encourage greater participation of all pupils. Only by doing so, can we prevent disaffected students becoming disaffected adults, and halt the impending obesity epidemic.

References

Ambrosi-Randic, N. (2000) Perception of current and ideal body size in preschool age children, *Perceptual and Motor Skills*, 90(3), 885–889.

Bakewell, B. (2004) Girls can do: They just don't always want to, *Sportsteacher*, Spring, 38–40.

Biddle, S. J. H., Sallis, J. S. and Cavill, N. (Eds.) (1997) *The Young and Active? Young People and Health-Enhancing Physical Activity – Evidence and Implications.* 1st Edn. London: Health Education Authority.

Brown, D. and Rich, E. (2002) Gender positioning as pedagogical practice in teaching physical education in Penney, D. A. (Ed.) *Gender and Physical Education: Contemporary Issues and Future Directions.* London: Routledge, 80–100.

Choi, P. L. (2000) *Femininity and the Physically Active Woman.* London: Routledge.

Clarke, G. (2002) Difference matters; Sexuality and physical education in Penney, D. A. (Ed.) *Gender and Physical Education: Contemporary Issues and Future Directions.* London: Routledge, 41–56.

Collins, M. E. (1991) Body figure perceptions and preferences among preadolescent children, *International Journal of Eating Disorders*, 10, 199–208.

Connell, R. W. (1987) *Gender and Power: Society, the Person, and Sexual Politics.* Stanford, CA: Stanford University Press.

Deem, R. and Gilroy, S. (1998) Physical activity, life-long learning and empowerment – situating sport in women's leisure, *Sport, Education and Society*, 3, 89–104.

Department of Culture, Media and Sport (2001) *Youth Sport Trust/Nike Girls in Sport Initiative.* London: HMSO.

Department of Health, Physical Activity, Health Improvement and Prevention (2004) *At Least Five a Week: Evidence on the Impact of Physical Activity and its Relationship to Health. A Report from the Chief Medical Officer.* London: The Stationery Office.

Dunning, E. (1994) Sport as a male preserve: Notes on the sources of masculine identity and its transformations in Birrell, S. and Cole, C. L. (Eds.) *Women, Sport, and Culture.* Champaign, IL: Human Kinetics, 163–179.

Ennis, C. D. (1999) Creating a culturally relevant curriculum for disengaged girls, *Sport, Education and Society,* 4(1), 31–49.

Flintoff, A. and Scraton, S. (2001) Stepping into active leisure? Young women's perceptions of active lifestyles and their experiences of school physical education, *Sport, Education and Society,* 6(1), 5–21.

Freedman, D. S., Dietz, W. H., Srinivasan, S. R. and Berenson, G. S. (1999) The relation of overweight to cardiovascular risk factors among children and adolescents: The Bogalusa Heart Study, *Paediatrics,* 103, 1175–1182.

Fruhbeck, G. (2000) Childhood obesity: time for action, not complacency, *BMJ,* 320, 328–329.

Gardner, R. M., Sorter, R. G. and Friedman, B. N. (1997) Developmental changes in children's body images, *Journal of Social Behaviour and Personality,* 12, 1019–1036.

General Household Survey (GHS) (1998) *Living in Britain, Results From 1996 GHS.* London: Office for National Statistics.

Gortmaker, S. L., Must, A., Perrin, J. M., Sobol, A. M. and Dietz, W. H. (1993) Social and economic consequences in adolescence and young adulthood, *New England Journal of Medicine,* 329, 1008–1012.

Graydon, J. (1997) Self-confidence and self-esteem in physical education and sport in Clarke, G. and Humberstone, B. (Eds.) *Researching Women and Sport.* London: Macmillan Press.

Griffin, P. (1992) Changing the game: Homophobia, sexism, and lesbians in sport, *Quest,* 44, 251–265.

Grigg, M., Bowman, J. and Redman, S. (1996) Disordered eating and unhealthy weight reduction practices among adolescent females, *Preventive Medicine: An International Journal Devoted to Practice and Theory,* 25(6), 748–756.

Halbert, C. (1997) Tough enough and woman enough: Stereotypes, discrimination, and impression management among women professional boxers, *Journal of Sport and Social Issues,* 21(1), 7–36.

Hargreaves, J. (1994) *Sporting Females: Critical Issues in the History and Sociology of Women's Sports.* London: Routledge.

Harris, J. and Penney, D. (2002) Gender, health and physical education in Penney, D. A. (Ed.) *Gender and Physical Education: Contemporary Issues and Future Directions.* London: Routledge, 123–145.

Humberstone (1990) Warriors or wimps? Creating alternative forms of physical education in Messner, M. A. and Sabo, D. F. (Eds.) *Sport, Men and the Gender Order.* Champaign, IL: Human Kinetics, 201–210.

Kay, T. (1995) *Women in Sport: A Review of Research.* London: Sports Council.

Kirk, D. (1992) *Defining Physical Education: The Social Construction of a School Subject in Postwar Britain.* London: Falmer Press.

Kirk, D. (1999) Physical culture, physical education and relational analysis, *Sport, Education and Society,* 4(1), 63–73.

Kirk, D. (2002) Physical education: A gendered history in Penney, D. A. (Ed.) *Gender and Physical Education: Contemporary Issues and Future Directions.* London: Routledge, 24–37.

Kolnes, L. J. (1995) Heterosexuality as on ongoing principle in women's sport, *International Review for the Sociology of Sport*, 30(1), 61–75.

Krane, V., Choi, P. V. L., Baird, S. M., Aimar, C. M. and Kauer, K. J. (2004) Living the paradox: Female athletes negotiate femininity and masculinity, *Sex Roles*, 50, 315–329.

Lawrence, C. M. and Thelan, M. H. (1995) Body image, dieting, and self-concept: Their relation in African-American and Caucasian children, *Journal of Clinical Child Psychology*, 24, 41–48.

McDermott, L. (1996) Toward a feminist understanding of physicality within the context of women's physically active and sporting lives, *Sociology of Sport Journal*, 13(1), 12–30.

McDermott, L. (2000) A qualitative assessment of the significance of body perception to women's physical activity experiences: Revisiting discussions of physicalities, *Sociology of Sport Journal*, 17, 331–363.

McGill, H. C., McMahan, C. A., Zieske, A. W., Tracy, R. E., Malcolm, G. T. and Herderick, E. E. (2000) Association of coronary heart disease risk factors with microscopic qualities of atherosclerosis in youth, *Circulation*, 102, 374–379.

Mendelson, B. K., White, D. R. and Mendelson, M. J. (1996) Self-esteem and body esteem: Effects of gender, age, and weight, *Journal of Applied Developmental Psychology*, 17, 321–346.

Messner, M. A. and Sabo, D. F. (1990) Toward a critical feminist reappraisal of sport, men, and the gender order in Messner, M. A. and Sabo, D. F. (Eds.) *Sport, Men and the Gender Order*. Champaign, IL: Human Kinetics, 1–15.

National Audit Office (2001) *Tackling Obesity in England*. London: The Stationery Office.

National Curriculum Online (2005) http://www.nc.uk.net/nc_resources/html/valuesAimsPurposes.shtml.

Obel, C. (1996) Collapsing gender in competitive bodybuilding: Researching contradictions and ambiguity in sport, *Review for the Sociology of Sport*, 31, 183–202.

Pate, R., Pratt, M., Blair, S. N., Haskell, W. L., Macera, L. A., Bouchard, C., Buchner, D., Ettinger, W., Heath, G. W. and King, A. C. (1995) Physical activity and public health – recommendation from the centers for disease control and prevention and the American college of sports medicine, *The Journal of the American Medical Association*, 273(5), 402–407.

Pate, R. R., Trost, S. G., Dowda, M., Ott, A. E., Ward, D. S., Saunders, R. and River, W. (1999) Tracking of physical activity, physical inactivity, and health-related physical fitness in rural youth, *Paediatric Exercise Science*, 11(4), 364–376.

Penney, D. A. (2002) Gendered policies in Penney, D. A. (Ed.) *Gender and physical education: Contemporary Issues and Future Directions*. London: Routledge, 103–122.

Penney, D. A. and Evans, J. (1999) *Politics, Policy and Practice in Physical Education*. London: Routledge.

Pirinen, R. (1997) Catching up with men?: Finnish newspaper coverage of women's entry into traditionally male sports, *International Review for the Sociology of Sport*, 32(3), 239–249.

Reich, A., Muller, G., Gelbrich, G., Deutscher, K., Godicke, R. and Kiess, W. (2003) Obesity and blood pressure – results from the examination of 2365 schoolchildren in Germany, *International Journal of Obesity*, 27, 1459–1464.

Reilly, J. J., Dorotsy, A. R. and Emmett, P. M. (1999) Prevalence of overweight and obesity in British children: cohort study, *BMJ*, 319, 1039.

Rudolf, M. C. J., Sahota, P., Barth, J. H. and Walker, J. (2001) Increasing prevalence of obesity in primary school children: cohort study, *BMJ*, 322, 1094–1095.

Russell, K. M. (2002) *Women's Participation Motivation in Rugby, Cricket, and Netball: Body Satisfaction and Self-identity*. Unpublished doctoral dissertation. Coventry, UK: Coventry University.

Russell, K. M. (2004) On vs Off the pitch: The transiency of body satisfaction among female rugby players, cricketers, and netballers, *Sex Roles*, 51, 561–574.

Saxena, S., Ambler, G., Cole, T. J. and Majeed, A. (2004) Ethnic group differences in overweight and obese children and young people in England: cross sectional survey, *Archives of Disease in Childhood*, 98, 30–36.

Schwimmer, J. B., Burwinkle, T. M. and Varni, J. W. (2003) Health-related quality of life of severely obese children and adolescents, *Journal of the American Medical Association*, 289, 1813–1819.

Scraton, S., Fasting, K., Pfister, G. and Bunuel, A. (1999) It's still a man's game?: The experiences of top-level European women footballers, *International Review for the Sociology of Sport*, 34(2), 99–111.

Sinaiko, A. R., Donahue, R. P., Jacobs, D. R. and Prineas, R. J. (1999) Relation of weight and rate of increase of weight during childhood and adolescence and body size, blood pressure, fasting insulin and lipids in young adults. The Minneapolis Children's Blood Pressure Study, *Circulation*, 99, 1471–1476.

Sisjord, M. K. (1997) Wrestling with gender: A study of young female and male wrestlers' experiences of physicality, *International Review for the Sociology of Sport*, 32(4), 432–438.

Sport England (2002) *Young People and Sport National Survey 2002*. London: Sport England.

Sports Council for Wales (1995) *Changing the Rules: Women, Girls and Sport*. Cardiff: Sports Council for Wales.

Sproston, K. and Primestata, P. (2002) *Health Survey for England 2002. The Health of Children and Young People*. London: The Stationery Office.

Squires, S. L. and Sparkes, A. C. (1996) Circles of silence: Sexual identity in physical education and sport, *Sport, Education and Society*, 1(1), 77–101.

Thompson, A. M., Humbert, M. L. and Mirwald, R. L. (2003) A longitudinal study of the impact of childhood and adolescent physical activity experiences on adult physical activity perceptions and behaviours, *Qualitative Health Research*, 13(3), 358–377.

Twisk, J., Kemper, H. C., van Mechelen, W. and Post, G. B. (1997) Tracking the risks of coronary heart disease over a 14 year period: A comparison between lifestyle and biological risk factors with data from the Amsterdam Growth and Health Study, *American Journal of Epidemiology*, 145, 888–898.

USA Department of Health and Human Services (1996) *Physical Activity and Health: A report of the Surgeon General*. Pittsburgh, PA: USA Department of Health and Human Services, Centers for Disease Control and Prevention, National Center for Chronic Disease Prevention and Health Promotion.

Veri, M. J. (1999) Homophobic discourse surrounding the female athlete, *Quest*, 51, 355–368.

Williams, A. and Bedward, J. (1999) *Games for the girls: The Impact of Recent Policy on the Provision of Physical Education and Sporting Organisations for Female Adolescents*. Nuffield Foundation Study.

Williams, A. and Bedward, J. (2000) An inclusive national curriculum? The experience of adolescent girls, *European Journal of Physical Education*, 5(1), 4–18.

Williams, A. and Bedward, J. (2002) Understanding girls' experience of physical education: Relational analysis and situated learning in Penney, D. A. (Ed.) *Gender and Physical Education: Contemporary Issues and Future Directions*. London: Routledge, 146–159.

Wood, K. C., Becker, J. A. and Thompson, J. K. (1996) Body image dissatisfaction in preadolescent children, *Journal of Applied Developmental Psychology*, 17, 85–100.

World Health Organization (2003) *Global Strategy on Diet, Physical Activity and Health*. Geneva: WHO.

Youth Sport Trust/Nike (1999) *The Girls in Sport Partnership Project: Interim Report*. Loughborough Institute of Youth Sport: Loughborough University.

Youth Sport Trust/Nike (2000) *Towards Girl-friendly Physical Education: The Girls in Sport Partnership Project Final Report*. Loughborough Institute of Youth Sport: Loughborough University.

CHAPTER 15

Disability, Sport and Exercise

HAYLEY FITZGERALD AND DI BASS

Introduction

During the recent Olympics in Athens, millions of television viewers witnessed the most finely tuned athletes in the world compete for a coveted Olympic gold medal. The images portrayed through the popular media of these athletes illustrate immense ability, supreme physical prowess and highly motivated performers. Contrast this with the dominant images and understandings of disability evident in our society. Disabled people are frequently seen as in need of care, passive and defective in some way (Oliver, 1996), images that are very distant from those associated with sport. Nevertheless, those of us that managed to catch the brief televised glimpse of the Paralympics would have seen less stereotypical images of disabled people. We saw, the immense commitment of the wheelchair basketball players, as they played their shots, at any cost, even if this meant crashing down to the floor. During the Paralympics, we saw images that are very different to how most of society, all too often, view disabled people. These examples of sport and disability illustrate that the relationship between these two concepts is not a simple one, and is probably best described as contradictory and complex (Steadward, 1996). Nonetheless, it should be recognised that the value of exploring sport and disability, in combination, provide opportunities to critique the practices of sport. On this issue, (DePauw, 1997: 428) argued that, 'The lens of disability allows us to make problematic the socially constructed nature of sport and once we have done so, opens us to alternative constructions, and solutions'.

In this chapter, we explore a range of issues relating to disability and sport. We begin by positioning issues concerning sport for disabled people within a broader equity and inclusion context. After this, we consider four key developments that have strengthened the position of disability within sports equity and inclusion agendas. These are the social model of disability, legislation, national curriculum and sports policy. Next, we review the range of initiatives and programmes that have recently been developed to enhance the experiences of disabled people in sport. Consideration will be given to participation in sport by disabled people, and in particular, barriers limiting participation will be highlighted. This chapter focuses on the complex organisational structures from which sports provision is made for disabled people. The chapter considers elite disability sport, and presents two case studies of Paralympic swimmers. In concluding, we consider the extent to which agendas promoting equity and inclusion are impacting on disabled people's experiences of sport.

Equity and inclusion in sport

Within contemporary society, issues relating to equity and inclusion have become increasingly prominent in government agendas and public policy. Broadly speaking, understandings of equity and inclusion place emphasis on fairness and justice (Penney, 2002). Within a sports context, Sport England suggests sports equity is:

> Sports equity is about fairness in sport, equality of access, recognising inequalities and taking steps to address them. It is about changing the culture and structure of sport to ensure that it becomes equally accessible to all members of society, whatever their age, ability, gender, race, ethnicity, sexuality or social/economic status.
> (Sport England, 2000: 4)

Disabled people, then, are just one of a number of groups to which equity is promoted. The notion of inclusion is often used to describe the process through which equity can be worked towards and achieved. According to Cheminas (2000: 34) inclusion in the context of education is '. . . a process that develops ways of increasing the participation and learning of all pupils and minimises barriers to their learning and participation.' Within a sports setting, the process of inclusion can be addressed at a number of levels. For example, Sport England (2002) identify the following issues relating to the inclusion of disabled people at 'foundation' and 'participation' levels that National Governing Body development plans should address:

- Can disabled people access all awards schemes and modified games?
- Are there reasons why some are not accessible?
- Do clubs welcome disabled members, and can facilities be accessed appropriately?
- Has due consideration been given to technical modification and adaptation of the sport's rules, regulations and resources, to enable fair access for disabled people?
- Do coaching awards exist that provide coaches with the skills and knowledge required for working in this area?
- Has the governing body referred to the membership of disabled people in its publicity and advisory materials, and do disabled people feature in photographs or graphic illustrations in governing body presentations?
(Sport England, 2002: 20)

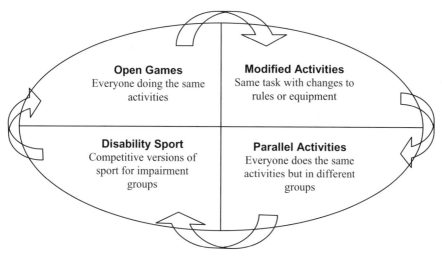

Figure 15.1 Inclusion spectrum (modified from Winnick, 1987)

Inclusion in the context of delivering sports sessions has been increasingly understood in terms of 'the inclusion spectrum' illustrated in Figure 15.1. In each quarter of the spectrum, different approaches to coaching are adopted.

Importantly, unlike understandings of 'integration', the assumption is not that disabled participants are necessarily best served if they are placed within the same setting as their peers. Instead, a range of different contexts is seen as inclusive. In supporting this approach, coaches and teachers are encouraged to adopt the particular strategy, or combination of strategies that best serve the needs of the disabled participants.

Developments strengthening the position of disability

In recent years, a number of developments have enhanced the position of disability within sports equity and inclusion agendas. Four key developments have been particularly influential: the social model of disability, legislation, the National Curriculum and sports policy.

Social model of disability

Understandings of disability have moved from an individualised medical model perspective to a social model approach. The medical model of disability is defined and legitimised within medical terms, and driven by a desire to diagnose and treat disabled people. Medical specialists, including those focusing on rehabilitation 'help' disabled people to cope, or fit in, with 'normal' life. In contrast to this view of disability, an alternative model has emerged that challenges the medicalised view of disability. The social model supports the view that people with impairments are disabled by a society that is not organised in ways that take account of their needs (Finkelstein, 1980; Oliver, 1996). From this perspective, sport is just one of many social experiences that is not structured or organised in ways that consider disabled people. Indeed, Barton (1993) argued that the very foundations of sport are based on 'ableist' assumptions, and little consideration is given to the consequences this may have on those that fail to match up to these ideals. Increasingly, sports organisations are claiming to support a social model perspective, and, in taking this position, are beginning to recognise that it is their responsibility, rather than that of disabled people, to make sporting opportunities (spectating, leadership, management and participation) more accessible.

Legislation

The Disability Discrimination Act (1995) (Department for Education and Employment, 1999) was passed in 1995, and makes it unlawful for disabled people to be discriminated against in employment, access to goods and services, property and education. This legislation has been introduced over time, and since October 2004, service providers have had to make 'reasonable' adjustments to the physical features of premises, to overcome physical barriers to access. Under the Disability Discrimination Act (1995), discrimination occurs when a disabled person is treated less favourably than someone else. Many sports organisations and facilities are now included within this legislation. Therefore, it is anticipated that a wider range of programmes and facilities will become more accessible to disabled people. As this legislation is relatively new, it has yet to be tested within a sports context. Nonetheless, concerns have already been expressed that many sports providers remain unaware of the duties they are required to fulfil, in order to satisfy the obligations of this legislation (Sport England, 2004a).

National Curriculum

With schools, the National Curriculum established that all pupils are entitled to a 'broad and balanced curriculum' (Department for Education and Employment/Qualifications and Curriculum Authority, 1999). The National Curriculum sets out that teachers must ensure pupils are enabled to participate and identifies three principles that are essential in developing a more inclusive curriculum:

● Setting suitable learning challenges.
● Responding to pupils' diverse learning needs.

- Overcoming potential barriers to learning and assessment for individuals and groups of pupils.

To overcome any potential barriers to learning in physical education, the statutory inclusion statement identifies that some pupils may require:

- Adapted, modified or alternative activities that have integrity and equivalence to the activities in the programmes of study and that enable the pupils to make progress.
- Specific support to enable them to participate in certain activities or types of movement.
- Careful management of their physical regime to allow for specific medical conditions.

Although the National Curriculum now provides pupils with an entitlement to physical education, some have argued that many young disabled people still do not have access to a full physical education curriculum (Penney and Evans, 1995). Indeed, as Kate Russell has outlined in the previous chapter, critics suggest that because physical education is resilient to change, many young people receive unfulfilling physical education experiences.

Sports policy

Since the 1970s, sports policy in the United Kingdom has continued to promote and encourage sport to a diverse range of groups, including disabled people. The principles underpinning the Sports Councils (now known as Sport England) original campaign for 'Sport for All' still remain central to practitioners working within sport development (Hylton and Totten, 2001). Indeed, the Government's recent strategy for sport over the next ten years reaffirms a commitment to sport for all, and seeks to 'ensure that every member of our society is offered opportunities and encouragement to play, lead and manage sport' (Department for Culture, Media and Sport, 2000: 7). In addition to promoting sport to disabled people through campaigns and policies promoting sport for all, Sport England have also continued to influence National Governing Bodies and National Disability Sport Organisations, in relation to the kinds of approaches advocated for provision. For example, in 1993, the Sports Council recommended a shift from a 'targeted' to a 'mainstreamed' approach to sports provision for disabled people (Sports Council, 1993). This recommendation represented a move from disability sport organisations solely supporting and providing sports opportunities, to mainstream governing bodies also taking responsibility and facilitating opportunities for disabled people. Since the 1990s, mainstream National Governing Bodies have been increasingly encouraged to provide sporting opportunities for disabled people. Indeed, National Government Bodies funding through Sport England now requires a commitment to equity. The consequences of failing to produce an equity action plan were clearly stated:

> . . . . it should be noted that offering equal opportunities is not an optional extra, as grant may be withheld if no progress is made in relation to the approved equity action plan [sic]
> (Sport England, 2000: 6)

More recently, thirty priority sport National Governing Bodies have also been asked to address issues relating to 'widening access' in their new Whole Sport Plans that represent National Governing Bodies activities for the next five years (Sport England, 2004b). Issues relating to equity and inclusion are increasingly becoming embedded within sports policy, and disabled people are now seen as one of many groups to benefit from this policy emphasis.

Programmes and initiatives targeting disabled people

As a consequence of the increasing prominence of disability within equity and inclusion agendas, a diverse range of programmes and initiatives have been developed, and continue to be developed, to enhance the experiences of disabled people in sport. These programmes and initiatives can be considered in relation to coach education and Continuing Professional Development, activity programmes, and advocacy and awareness initiatives.

Coach education and continuing professional development

A wider range of coaching and professional development opportunities is available to support coaches, volunteers, teachers and development officers in their work with disabled people in sport. The main providers of these opportunities include Sports Coach UK, the Youth Sport Trust, the English Federation of Disability Sport, National Governing Bodies and National Disability Sport Organisations. These opportunities are offered in a number of contexts including sports specific, disability sport specific and general disability and disability. Examples of these opportunities are illustrated in Table 15.1.

Activity programmes

Interrelated to a number of coach education and Continuing Professional Development opportunities are activity programmes. Similarly, in the training or coach education opportunities identified above, activity programmes usually have an element of training or development included within the programme. Activity programmes also include a number of additional dimensions such as

Table 15.1 Coach education and continuing professional development
opportunities

Context	Description	Awarding Body
Sports specific	**Swimming:** The Amateur Swimming Association run various courses specific to disability swimming including the Helper Certificate – swimming for People with Disabilities, Level 1 (Assistant Teacher Certificate) – Swimming for People with Disabilities and Teacher Certificate – Swimming for People with Disabilities.	Amateur Swimming Association
	Netball Introducing Netball to Disabled Players – for anyone with an interest in Disability Netball Introducing Netball to Disabled Players Adapted for Coaches – for All England Netball Association qualified Coaches – Level 1 Coaching Course Adapted for Disability workers or volunteers with some knowledge of Netball.	All England Netball Association
Disability sport	**Boccia** Currently CP Sport run a Level 1 Course (Assistant Teachers) which gives an introduction to the game and is designed for people who will be coaching Boccia within residential homes and schools. A Boccia Teachers Award is currently being developed in conjunction with Sportscoach UK.	CP sport
	Wheelchair basketball Preliminary Coach Award Basic introductory coaching qualification giving outline knowledge of wheelchair basketball. Coach Level II Award. Gives overview of all aspects of basketball as well as an introduction to sports coaching.	GBWBA
General sport and disability	**Coaching disabled performers** Focuses on developing coaching knowledge and skills to coach disabled people by exploring when integrated and segregate coaching might be most appropriate, considers safety and medical issues, explores how adaptation in coaching can meet the specific needs of disabled performers.	Sports Coach UK
	Including disabled pupils in physical education One day practical multi sport course including inclusive sessions and new teaching strategies in line with the NationalCurriculum physical education (2000).	English Federation of Disability Sport

equipment and resource cards. Table 15.2 highlights a number of current
national activity programmes.

Advocacy and awareness

The programmes and initiatives identified earlier are directly concerned with
enhancing active participation in sport by disabled people. In addition to these

Table 15.2   Activity programmes

Initiative/Programme	Description	Lead Organisation
Inclusive Fitness Initiative (IFI)	Following a successful two year pilot scheme Sport England are funding 150 IFI leisure centres nationally. Participating centres receive accessible fitness equipment, training and marketing support to enhance the targeting of promotional campaigns to disabled people.	English Federation of Disability Sport
TOP Sportsability	TOP Sportsability has been implemented nationally within schools, 'out-of-hours' learning and community settings. Participating schools and community groups receive games equipment, training, resource cards and a handbook providing illustrative examples of activities and games.	Youth Sport Trust
Soccability	Soccability is a national programme developed by the Football Association (FA) in partnership with the YST to provide football specific development opportunities to teachers, support workers and coaches on issues relating to including disabled people in football. Participating sites receive equipment, consisting of different sized football, training and a handbook.	Football Association

kinds of programmes, a range of initiatives have been developed that aim to empower disabled people to take on leadership, organisational or management roles within sports settings. This has also been coupled with increasing concerns to promote a greater awareness and understanding within society, of sport and disability. Table 15.3 provides a range of examples of the initiatives that have been developed to promote awareness.

Participation in sport by disabled people

Research specifically focusing on disabled people and sport has found that sport enables disabled people to experience their bodies in new and positive ways, improves perceptions of physical characteristics, increases confidence to participate in new activities and enhances social integration (Blinde and McClung, 1997; Blinde and Taub, 1999; Page et al., 2001). Duncan Wyeth, a wheelchair athlete, believes participation in sport can also be an effective means of developing a positive identity, and a way of escaping from the 'disability ghetto'. Here, the 'ghetto' is not an actual place, but rather a shared experience amongst disabled people which is characterised by 'poverty, unemployment, and limited socialisation' (Page et al., 2001). In contrast to the experience of Duncan, other disabled people believe their sporting experiences have reinforced dominant discourses of disability that emphasise lack and

Table 15.3 Advocacy and awareness initiatives

Initiative	Description	Lead Organisation
Sporting Voices	Sporting Voices aims to empower adults with learning disabilities to contribute and participate in sports related meetings. Participants with learning disabilities and 'enablers' attend an accredited course before their new skills are used in different sporting settings.	Federation of Disability Sports Organisations – Yorkshire
Athletes as Advocates	The Athletes as Advocates was initiated to address concerns that disabled athletes are often overlooked in sports coaching and leadership roles. Athletes as Advocates targets disabled people who are interested in sport and want to develop their skills and experiences to enable them to become role models, coaches, tutors or work in sports development.	English Federation of Disability Sport – East Midlands
Paralympic Schools Curricular resource	Paralympic Schools Curricular resources were developed for teachers in primary and secondary schools. The resource aims to raise awareness of the Paralymic movement and dispel myths about sport and disability. The resource includes guidance for teachers, case studies of Paralympic athletes and activities for pupils.	British Paralympic Association

inability. In some instances, rather than providing a positive experience, sport can contribute to a disabled person's sense of marginalisation. Indeed, this example shows how identity was constructed by others through physical education in negative terms.

> The reality of under achievement and exclusion from most sporting and other physical activities, within a school which placed great emphasis on competitive achievement, meant that I was unable to make my mark through officially sanctioned paths. There was, too, a sense of humiliation as my peers had their identities defined in terms of everything they could do, while I felt mine was being defined in terms of what I could not do.
> (Swain and Cameron, 1999: 72)

The account given by Swain and Cameron (1999) illustrates the negative consequences of participation in physical education. Research undertaken by the Health Education Authority (1999) and the Disability Rights Commission (2002) also concluded that low participation in physical activity and sport by disabled people is directly related to unfavourable experiences of school physical education. Many other reasons have been cited by disabled people for not participating in sport including:

- Lack of motivation or confidence to participate in sport.
- Limited family support.
- Lack of information about opportunities and support available.
- Limited or no accessible transport to sports facilities/ resources.
- Inaccessible facilities and equipment.
- Limited disposable income to spend on sports activities.
- Alternative preferences during free time.
- Stereotypical assumptions that disabled people will not be able to do sport.
  (Source: Health Education Authority, 1999; French and Hainsworth, 2001; Sport England, 2001; Sport England, 2002; Disability Rights Commission, 2002)

It is important to note that many of these issues have also been highlighted by non-disabled people, for non-participation in sport. Nevertheless, for many disabled people, a combination of these issues are often magnified to a greater degree, than for non-disabled people.

Sports organisations supporting disabled people

According to Thomas (2003), the historical development of disability sport organisations in the United Kingdom is best described as 'short but turbulent'. Today, the structure of disability sport is complex, and reflects a breadth of interests and concerns. Figure 15.2 provides a summary of the key organisations supporting disabled people in sport.

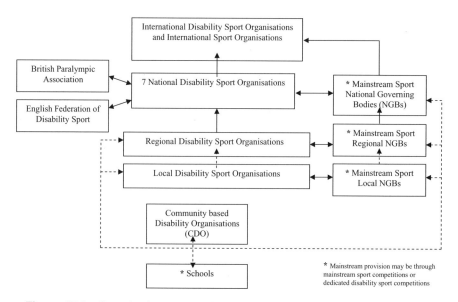

Figure 15.2 Organisations supporting sports participation by disabled people

Figure 15.2 illustrates that a disabled person can experience sport in four key organisational contexts: through schools, community based disability organisations providing a variety of opportunities including sport, through disability sport organisations and through mainstream sports organisations. Within mainstream organisations, disabled people may participate in mainstream competitions, or dedicated disability sport competitions that National Governing Bodies organise. Importantly, the pathway a disabled person takes, will not necessarily be linear, and is likely to reflect considerable crosscutting between these differing organisational contexts.

One of the key developments in recent years, relating to the structure and organisation of disability sport was the creation in 1998 of the English Federation of Disability Sport. The English Federation of Disability Sport was developed in response to the outcomes of a National Disability Sports Conference, and further wide-ranging consultations. The English Federation of Disability Sport has a mission 'to be the united voice of disability sport seeking to promote inclusion and achieve equality of sporting opportunities for disabled people'. In part, the English Federation of Disability Sport was formed to provide a more co-ordinated approach to the planning and provision of sport for disabled people. The seven National Disability Sports Organisations, identified above, continue to work towards their own development programme, while at the same time are represented within the English Federation of Disability Sport management structure. Increasingly, sport organisations are developing pathways and support mechanisms for talented performers. The next section considers performance pathways for disabled athletes.

Performance pathways in sport for gifted and talented disabled people

Within the disabled population, just as within the non-disabled, there will be talented athletes who wish to compete at the highest levels. This raises a number of questions about the extent to which support mechanisms are in place, to enable the potential of talented disabled performers to be achieved. Non-disabled elite athletes usually have access to a range of supports, including well-defined competitive structures, clear pathways for progression, extensive training opportunities, expert coaching, sports science support and financial assistance. In many cases, disabled athletes do not have access to these kinds of support mechanisms (Wyatt, 1999). Even though it is acknowledged that opportunities for participation and progression in sport at all levels will vary between sports, the remainder of this section will focus on swimming, and consider performance pathways by exploring the swimming career of two Paralympic athletes.

Organisations supporting elite disabled swimmers

In the first International Games for disabled people, held in 1948, swimming was a major sport. Subsequently, because of these games, disability groups began to appreciate the benefits of sporting competitions, and disability specific sports organisations began to form and develop their own competitive structures. The International Co-ordinating Committee had sole responsibility for the organisation of multi-disability Paralympic Games up to and including Barcelona in 1992. Following Barcelona, the International Paralympic Committee replaced the International Co-ordinating Committee as the governing body for international disabled sport, and today includes more than a hundred member nations.

Until 1989, disability specific organisations within Great Britain were responsible for preparing elite disabled swimmers for the Paralympic Games, but in that year the British Paralympic Association was formed to co-ordinate, administer and prepare elite disabled sports people for future games. Following the Barcelona Olympic Games in 1992, the Great Britain Paralympic Swim Squad was formed to prepare swimmers for future Paralympic Games. A strategy, and training programme was implemented and financed through funding from the British Paralympic Association, sponsorship agreements with British Telecom and fund raising events. In 1997, the responsibility for elite performance disability swimming passed from the British Paralympic Association to the branch of swimming's National Governing Bodies, responsible for international competition, the Amateur Swimming Federation of Great Britain. In 1998, Amateur Swimming Federation of Great Britain appointed a National Performance Director for disability swimming. In recent years, elite disabled swimmers have received many of the same benefits (although seldom to the same level, especially in terms of funding, and kit distribution) as their non-disabled counterparts such as sports science support, financial assistance, training camps at home and abroad and full-time professional coaches. In 2002, two new programmes were established within disability swimming: World Class Start Programme and World Class Potential. As in non-disabled swimming, these programmes underpin the World Class Performance Programme, and aim to identify and develop future international athletes.

Swimming classification

In order to adopt fair and equitable competition, swimmers are classified according to certain criteria. Prior to the 1990 World Championships, a medical classification was enforced, where swimmers with a physical impairment competed against other swimmers from their own disability group. In 1991, a functional classification system was introduced. This system allows all physically impaired swimmers with the same functional ability to compete against each other, regardless of their disability. Trained classifiers assess swimmers, both on land and in the water, to establish their classification. Swimming has ten classifications: S1–S10 for those with physical disabilities for the swimming strokes of freestyle, backstroke and butterfly, within this classification the lower the number, the more severe the impairment. The same swimmer may also be given a separate classification for breaststroke (SB), and for the individual medley (an event in which a swimmer swims three (lower classifications) or four of the competitive strokes (SM). Visually impaired swimmers are classified S11–S13, and those with learning difficulties are classified as S14.

The swimmers' stories: Sarah Bailey MBE

Sarah Bailey is Great Britain's most successful female Paralympic swimmer. Sarah won her first Paralympic gold medal in Barcelona, aged just 14, and since then she has won over 130 national swimming titles, broken 48 world records, and has 27 gold medals at international competition. As a schoolgirl, Sarah excelled at other sports such as table tennis, netball, cross country running and biathlon. On leaving school, Sarah obtained a Sports Science degree, and as well as her swimming commitments, she is a freelance journalist and speaker of renown.

Sarah became involved in swimming through her primary school. There was a strong move to teach children to swim following a drowning accident involving one of the school's pupils. As in other sports, Sarah quickly advanced in swimming, and encouraged by her parents, who themselves were keen sports people, she had obtained all her swimming badges by the time she was six years old, and by the age of eight, she was the fastest swimmer at the school.

She was introduced to Stockport Metro Swimming club at the age of 10 years and told that she was too old to start a swimming career, and that she would never be an elite swimmer. Nonetheless, Sarah persevered, spurred on by brief clips she had seen of the 1990 Disability World Championships. In particular, she remembers the 100 m freestyle final, which was won by an upper limb amputee. Sarah has a similar disability to this, and she thought that perhaps she could take part in disability swimming.

Nevertheless, becoming involved in disability swimming was not as easy as she had thought. One of her swimming coaches was a deaf Olympian, and had suggested that she contact the British Sports Association for the Disabled, one of the seven National Disability Sport Organisations, and now known as Disability Sport England. She contacted British Sports Association for the Disabled, but received no reply. She kept writing, and eventually received information about the 1991 Regional Championships: a competition she would have to compete in, if she wished to take part in the National Junior Championships. When she arrived at the meeting she was 'totally disillusioned' to quote Sarah, 'it was just like a load of disabled people splashing about in the pool.' There appeared to be little structure and she felt 'mortified', as she herself was at this time training for the mainstream national swimming championships. By chance, one of the athletic coaches spotted her, who suggested that she contacted 'Les Autres'. As a result of making contact with this organisation, Sarah attended one of their swim training weekends, and began to access other opportunities. At this time, it was evident that Sarah would achieve considerable success in disability swimming. Indeed, her personal bests were, in fact, faster than the current world records for the classification she was expected to receive. After excellent performances at the Junior Nationals, she was selected for the Barcelona Paralympics in 1992. Unusually, this was all before she had been officially classified. With the support of Lottery funding, Sarah has been a full-time swimmer now for 5 years. Sarah believes Lottery funding has 'made a huge difference' and enabled her to train hard for Athens. Sarah competes in the S10 category, and at the recent Athens Paralympics added more medals to her already extensive tally. Sarah remains committed and passionate about swimming and considers it to be an important part of her life.

> It's my whole life. I eat, sleep swimming . . . I can't say enough positive about it. It's about forging friendships, fun, excitement, and learning.

The swimmers' stories: Fiona Neale

Fiona was a strong competitive age-group swimmer and swam as a non-disabled child up to the age of twelve years; however, the effects of a congenital connective tissue disorder resulted in her giving up swimming. At this time, she believes she was not guided or supported at school to participation in any kind of physical activity.

> . . . the school I was at felt that it was best that I did no sport and so I went to the library for physical education lessons and the local swimming club didn't have any outlets for disabled swimmers, so that was it, that was my swimming gone, but I had swum for the A squad for the City of Cambridge. I had got to a reasonable standard swimming for the county.

It was not until Fiona was 17 that she discovered it was possible to swim, and compete as a disabled swimmer. Like Sarah, she contacted British Sports Association for the Disabled who informed her that she could not compete until she was classified. The news from the British Sports Association for the Disabled was discouraging, who went on to say that, classification was difficult to arrange and would not be organised in the near future. With no support or encouragement to participate in swimming, Fiona discounted it as an activity worth pursuing. Nevertheless, while rehabilitating after a car accident, Fiona decided to start swimming again. During this time, she took part in the 'Swimathon' and was spotted by the organiser of the disability swimming regional gala and invited to take part. Fiona admits, '. . . it was more by chance than anything else that I got back in [to swimming] again.' Fiona's feelings and experience of the regional gala were similar to Sarah's, and she came away feeling that she had not really achieved. After the regional gala, Fiona was invited to the Long Course National Championships. At this event, she felt she received little support, and the whole experience was particularly daunting, she recalls: 'everyone seemed to know what they were doing except me. . . . Had I been of a different personality you would have lost me at the very first gala.' Fiona's times were some way off the winning times, but she felt encouraged, and because of her earlier swimming career, believed she had potential to succeed.

Fiona was classified as S8, and after a period of dedicated training began to swim Paralympic qualifying times. Subsequent changes to her classification, from an S8 to an S9, meant that her times were no longer competitive for that class. She was 'gutted', but she continued to train and was eventually reclassified back to S8. Although, she just missed out on competing in the Paralympics in Atlanta, she qualified for Sydney, and benefited from lottery funding. According to Fiona, the introduction of lottery funding made a significant difference to herself and other disabled swimmers:

> [Lottery funding] made a huge difference. The whole ethos around swimming changed. There was more challenge – we felt like athletes . . . we were valued and from my point of view being able to afford to train and not having to balance part-time work with training and everything else made a difference.

Fiona has now given up competitive swimming, but for her the benefits have been 'massive, for me absolutely massive'. In particular, Fiona believes swimming has helped her to put life into perspective, and cope with her disability:

> I'd go and swim 6–100 lengths and feel better . . . sport provided me with health benefits in terms of physiologically. I lost weight and toned up. Psychologically I had more self-esteem and more self confidence . . . I have met a lot of people through the sport, and an identity – being part of a group and not having a great deal of self confidence being able to train at quite a high level and say 'I'm a swimmer and I am proud to be a swimmer'.

Both Fiona and Sarah's stories both show the need for perseverance and the role played by chance. The picture that emerges from both these swimmers stories, is that of a developing movement within swimming that over the years has become more structured and organised. Nonetheless, pathways to elite performance still require further changes and refinements. For example, swimming squads specifically for disabled people, such as 'Swim Northwest', are not available in every region. Consequently, the co-ordination and linkages between local, regional and national squads or groups remain fragmented in some parts of the country. In addition, in mainstream swimming clubs, lack of understanding and awareness of the abilities of disabled swimmers continue to create many real barriers. Furthermore, accessing information about the swimming opportunities available, and the kinds of organisations servicing these opportunities continues to be problematic for many disabled people, their coaches and teachers.

Conclusion

It is clear that over the last 10 years attitude changes, developments relating to new organisational structures, shifts in policy and new provisions for disabled people have enhanced, to some degree, the kinds of sporting opportunities disabled people are likely to experience. Nevertheless, it is difficult now to determine the extent to which disabled people's experiences of sport represent experiences that are founded on the principles underpinning equity and inclusion. In fact, Fiona provides us with a powerful reminder that our sporting society is probably a long distance away from achieving equity:

> [sporting excellence] done at a price . . . if I look at the able-bodied swimmers at a much less competitive level, competing say just at county or district level, the support they have and the structures they've been through and the battles I've had just to get simple access and to get coaches to take me seriously, especially at the start – it got better though through the four years, a lot better.

Continued and sustained efforts are needed to forward change in ways that will enable more people, including those that happen to be disabled, to participate and enjoy sport.

References

Barton, L. (1993) Disability, empowerment and physical education in Evans, J. (Ed.) *Equality, Education and Physical Education*. London: Falmer Press, 43–54.

Blinde, E. and McClung, L. (1997) Enhancing the physical and social self through recreational activity: accounts of individuals with physical disabilities, *Adapted Physical Activity Quarterly*, 14, 327–344.

Blinde, E. and Taub, D. (1999) Personal empowerment through physical fitness activity: Perspectives from male college students with physical and sensory disabilities, *Journal of Sport Behavior*, 22, 181–202.

Cheminas, R. (2000) *Special Education Needs for Newly Qualified and Student Teachers*. David Futon Publishers: London.

DePauw, K. P. (1997) The (in)Visibility of disAbility: Cultural contexts and 'sporting bodies', *Quest*, 49, 416–430.

Department for Culture, Media and Sport (2000) *A Sporting Future for All*. London: Department for Culture, Media and Sport.

Department for Education and Employment/Qualifications and Curriculum Authority (1999) *Physical Education. The National Curriculum for England*. London: HMSO.

Department for Education and Employment (1999) *Disability Discrimination Act 1995 Code of Practice: Rights of Access, Goods, Facilities, Services and Premises*. London: HMSO.

Disability Rights Commission (2002) *Survey of Young Disabled People aged 16–24.* London: Disability Rights Commission Research and Evaluation Unit.

Finkelstein, V. (1980) *Attitudes and Disabled People.* New York: World Rehabilitation Fund.

French, D. and Hainsworth, J. (2001) There aren't any buses and the swimming pool is always cold!: obstacles and opportunities in the provision of sport for disabled people, *Managing Leisure*, 6, 35–49.

Health Education Authority (1999) *Physical Activity 'in our lives': Qualitative Research among Disabled People.* Health Education Authority: London.

Hylton, K. and Totten, M. (2001) Developing 'Sport for All?' Addressing inequality in sport in Hylton, K., Bramham, P., Jackson, M. and Nesti, M. (Eds.) *Sports Development: Policy, Process and Practice.* London: Jessica Kingley Publishers Ltd.

Oliver, M. (1996) *Understanding Disability: from Theory to Practice.* Basingstoke: Macmillan.

Page, S. J., O'Connor, E. and Peterson, K. (2001) Leaving the Disability Ghetto: A Qualitative Study of Factors Underlying Achievement Motivation, *Journal of Sport and Social Issues*, 25(1), 40–55.

Penney, D. (2002) (Ed.) *Gender and Physical Education: Contemporary Issues and Future Direction.* London: Routledge.

Penney, D. and Evans, J. (1995) The National Curriculum for Physical Education: Entitlement for all?, *British Journal of Physical Education*, Winter, 6–13.

Sport England (2000) *Making Guidelines for Governing Bodies. Governing Body English Sport Inclusive: Equity Resource Pack Planning for Sport*, Factfile: Sports Equity. London: Sport England.

Sport England (2001) *Disability Survey 2000. Young People with a Disability and Sport, Headline Findings*, London: Sport England.

Sport England (2002) *Adults with a Disability and Sport National Survey 2000–2001 Headline Findings.* London: Sport England.

Sport England (2004a) *Disability Discrimination Legislation Information note for Sports Clubs.* Sport England: London.

Sport England (2004b) *National Governing Bodies and Whole School Plans*, London: Sport England [www.sportengland.org/index/get_resources/ngbs.htm]

Sports Council (1993) *People with Disabilities and Sport. Policy and Current/planned Action.* Sports Council: London.

Steadward, R. (1996) Integration and Sport in the Paralympic Movement, *Sports Science Review*, 5(1), 26–41.

Swain, J. and Cameron, C. (1999) Unless otherwise stated: discourses or labelling and identity in coming out in Corker, M. and French, S. (Eds.) *Disability Discourse.* Buckingham: Open University Press.

Thomas, N. (2003) Sport and disability in Houlihan, B. (Ed.) *Sport and Society: A Student Introduction.* London: Sage.

Winnick, J. P. (1987) An Integration Continuum for Sports Participation, *Adapted Physical Activity Quarterly*, 4(3), 157–161.

Wyatt, L. (1999) A study to compare and contrast the performance pathways of disabled and non-disabled swimmers. Unpublished undergraduate dissertation, Loughborough: Loughborough University.

PART IV

HEALTH OF SOCIETY

Social Inequalities, Social Exclusion and Health

JACQUELINE MERCHANT

Introduction

One of the key motivations for undertaking physical activity is that it makes us feel good, and exercise makes us feel healthy. Indeed, it is good for our health, both physically and psychologically. Then why is it that not everyone is able to enjoy the benefits of sport, exercise, and physical activity and the concomitant benefits which these yield upon one's health? Certain people may have barriers such as environmental, physical, psychological or cultural, or a mixture of any of these, which prevent them from entering into physical activity, in the sense that is defined within this book. Furthermore, if physical activity is promoted and taken up by those in most need, will it make a real difference to their health, in terms of altering or improving existent health inequalities according to social class (the key focus of this chapter)?

This chapter is divided into three broad areas. First, I outline the way in which health is unevenly distributed between people, depending upon the social class to which they belong. We will see how social class is measured, review the substantial and continuing evidence for widening differences in both morbidity (illness rates) and mortality (deaths rates).

Secondly, I will explore the explanations which have been identified to account for these inequalities, concluding with proposals for change which we have seen in recent years (e.g. Townsend et al., 1988; Drever and Whitehead, 1995; Drever et al., 1996; Department of Health, 1995, 2004; Acheson, 1998).

The third part of the chapter explores the relevance of the above for physical activity, together with some examples of government strategies and local initiatives which have been created to forge links between physical activity and social inclusion. It goes on to discuss the potential that health promotion may have in these areas.

What do we mean by inequalities in health and how do we measure them?

Evidence of an association between socio-economic position and health dates back to ancient China, Greece and Egypt, and is apparent today in societies for which data are available (Kreiger et al., 1997; Whitehead and Drever, 1997). This can be seen in Table 16.1, which shows the average age of death by social class and area of residence in mid-nineteenth century England. It also shows us how the scale of these socio-economic differences varied across the country. In Liverpool, for example, the average age of death for labourers was 15 years, less than half that recorded for gentry in the city (35 years) and for labourers in rural Rutland (38 years). Inequalities between places are matched by inequalities by individual socio-economic position, as each step down the social ladder brings an increased risk of premature death.

The Registrar General's scale of occupational classes

More recent UK studies have relied on occupation-based measures, most notably the registrar general's classification, to measure individual socio-economic status (SES). This classification (see Table 16.2) was developed 100 years ago, to capture the hierarchy of power, property and prestige among men. It has recently been updated (ONS, 2000) to take account of changes in the labour market, including the rise in the number of self-employed people, and presence of the long-term unemployed (see Table 16.3).

In recognition of the limitations of this scale, other measures of SES are increasingly used alongside occupation, housing tenure, car ownership, education and income. Nevertheless, the continued use of the registrar general's scale is justified for two reasons: occupation is the only socio-economic

Table 16.1   Average age of death by social class and area of residence, 1838–41

District	Gentry and Professional	Farmers and Tradesmen	Labourers and Artisans
Rutland	52	41	38
Bath	55	37	25
Leeds	44	27	19
Bethnal Green	45	26	16
Manchester	38	20	17
Liverpool	35	22	15

Source: Whitehead and Drever (1997) adapted from *Lancet* 1843, Office for National Statistics, Crown Copyright 1997. Crown copyright material in reproduced with the permission of the controller of HMSO and the Queen's Printer for Scotland

Table 16.2 Examples of occupations in their social class groupings

	Social Class	Occupations
I	Professional	Accountant, doctor, lawyer
II	Managerial and technical/ Intermediate	Sales manager, teacher, journalist, nurse
IIIN	Skilled non-manual	Secretary, shop assistant, cashier
IIIM	Skilled manual	Joiner, bus driver, cook
IV	Partly skilled manual	Security guard, machine tool operator
V	Unskilled manual	Building labourer, cleaner, laundry worker
VI	Armed Forces	

Source: Graham (2001) Understanding Health Inequalities, OUP
The scale has been greatly criticized, not least for assuming that women and children would earn their place through the occupation of the male 'breadwinner'

Table 16.3 The National Statistics Socio-economic Classifications (NS-SEC)

1. Higher managerial and professional occupations
   1.1 Employers and managers in larger organisations (e.g. company directors, senior company managers, senior civil servants, senior officers in police and armed forces)
   1.2 Higher professionals (e.g. doctors, lawyers, clergy, teachers and social workers)
2. Lower managerial and professional occupations (e.g. nurses and midwives, journalists, actors, musicians, prison officers, lower ranks of police and armed forces)
3. Intermediate occupations (e.g. clerks, secretaries, driving instructors, telephone fitters)
4. Small employers and own account workers (e.g. publicans, farmers, taxi drivers, window-cleaners, painters and decorators)
5. Lower supervisory, craft and related occupations (e.g. printers, plumbers, television engineers, train drivers, butchers)
6. Semi-routine occupations (e.g. shop assistants, hairdressers, bus drivers, cooks)
7. Routine occupations (e.g. couriers, labourers, waiters and refuse collectors)
8. Plus an eighth category to cover those who have never had paid work and the long-term unemployed

information that is recorded routinely at the census, and at birth and death registration, and occupation is regarded as a powerful determinant of income and life chances (Drever and Whitehead, 1995). The table above is the new occupational scale to replace the Registrar General's scale.

Evidence for inequalities in health according to SES

So how does SES affect and influence health? In the UK, perhaps the most influential findings of the twentieth century were those of the 1980 Report of the Working Group on Inequalities in Health, chaired by Sir Douglas Black (Townsend et al., 1988). This report examined standardised mortality ratios (SMRs) for different social classes in order to assess the scale of inequality and to monitor changes over time. The findings of the Black Report are now well known, although at the time the Thatcher Conservative government largely ignored the findings. These include a marked and persistent difference in mortality rate between the occupational classes, for both sexes and at all ages. A steep gradient, showing that the risk of death increases with lower social class was observed for most causes of death. The pattern for respiratory diseases was particularly strong. Babies born to parents in social class V (see Table 16.2) were found to be at double the risk of death in the first month of life, compared with babies of professional-class parents. The Black report concluded that the introduction of the NHS, that aimed to provide free health care to all regardless of income or social status, had not eliminated health inequalities. Despite an overall improvement in life expectancy, patterns of relative inequality seemed to have changed little over time. Inequalities were also found to exist in the utilisation of health services, working class people making less use of services, and receiving less good care, than their middle class counterparts.

What is meant by SMRs?

Class inequalities in health are not restricted to childhood but persist through-out adult life. By using SMRs (or standardised mortality rates), which were first calculated in 1931, it is possible to make comparisons between the dif-ferent occupational classes. The average for the population is 100, and there-fore an SMR below 100 indicates a lower than average chance of death, whereas a figure above 100 suggests a higher than average chance. Table 16.4 provides SMRs for all causes of death for adult males at three time periods between 1970 and 1993. The data not only illustrate the existence of a distinct gradient from class I through to class V but also reveals that class inequalities actually increased over the period in question. The SMR for class V was 1.8 times that of class I in 1970–72 and had risen almost three-fold by the early 1990s.

Table 16.4 SMRs for adult males, England and Wales (all causes of death)

Class	1970–72	1979–80 1982–83	1991–93
Professional (I)	77	66	66
Intermediate (II)	81	74	72
Skilled non-manual (IIIN)	99	93	100
Skilled manual (IIIM)	106	103	117
Semi-skilled manual (IV)	114	114	116
Unskilled manual (V)	137	159	189
England and Wales	100	100	100

Source: Adapted from Drever et al. (1996: 19)

More recent evidence of health inequalities and the intergenerational cycle it produces shows that:

- In Manchester, boys can expect to live almost eight years fewer, and girls almost seven years fewer than their contemporaries in Kensington, Chelsea and Westminster.
- Life expectancy for males in social class V is over 7 years less than for professional social classes: 71.1 years compared with 78.5 years. For women the gap is over 5.5 years.
- Some populations in this country have the same levels of early death as the national average occurring in the 1950s.
- Babies with fathers in social classes IV and V have a birth weight that is on average 130 grams lower than that of babies with fathers in classes I and II. Low birth weight (LBW) is closely associated with death in infancy, as well as being associated with coronary heart disease (CHD), diabetes and hypertension in later life. Low birth weight is used as a reliable indicator of poverty.
- Research shows that lower birth weight and father's social class can both increase your chance of dying of CHD over and above the impact of your own income and social class.
- An analysis of over 100 local education authority areas found educational attainment at age 15–16 to be significantly associated with both CHD and infant mortality. (Department of Health, 2002: 1)

The widening health gap

The patterns of health inequality identified in the Black Report continued into the 1990s. While the mortality rate for the whole population has declined, the differential between the lowest and the highest group seems to have increased. In the early 1990s, male mortality in social class V was almost three times that in social class I. During the preceding 20 year period, the difference between these groups in mortality from lung cancer, ischaemic heart disease, strokes, accidents and suicide had widened considerably (Drever and Bunting, 1997). Comparing data for 1981 and 1991, Roberts and Power (1996) found that socio-economic inequalities in child injury death rate had also increased during this period.

A study by Mitchell, Dorling and Shaw (2000) showed how the widening health gap could be narrowed if some of the key social policies of the Government prove to be successful. The researchers analysed every parliamentary constituency in Britain, and tested a number of different social policy scenarios, using statistical techniques. The research suggests that:

- Annually, some 7,500 deaths amongst people younger than 65 could be prevented if inequalities in wealth narrowed to their 1983 levels.
- The majority of lives saved from redistribution would be in the poorer areas of Britain, where 37 per cent of 'excess' deaths would be prevented.

- Some 2,500 deaths per year amongst those aged less than 65 would be prevented were full employment to be achieved. Two-thirds of these would be in areas which currently have higher than average levels of mortality, preventing 17 per cent of the 'excess' deaths in these areas.
- Some 1,400 lives would be saved per year amongst those under 15 if child poverty were eradicated (using the government's relative definition of child poverty). This represents 92 per cent of all 'excess' child deaths in areas of higher than average mortality.
- The researchers concluded that redistribution of wealth would have the greatest absolute effects (in terms of numbers of lives saved) because it would improve the lives of the largest number of people. Eradication of child poverty has the greatest relative effect (in terms of the proportion of lives saved).

Health behavioural differences

Socio-economic status (SES) is also linked to health-related behaviours such as cigarette smoking and dietary habits. The percentage of smokers among men in the unskilled manual classes is more than two and a half times that seen in professional classes. Similarly, the consumption of fats and sugars increases, and that of fruit decreases, with decreasing income (Drever and Bunting, 1997). Some discussion of reasons for this unhealthy behaviour can be seen below, as well as in the later section on Wilkinson's psychosocial causes of illness. The current government prioritise unhealthy behaviours in order to reach their health inequalities targets (Department of Health, 2002). Interventions which they see as being likely to make the major impact on achievement of the life expectancy target are:

- Reducing smoking in manual social groups through extended smoking cessation services, complementary tobacco education campaigns and other supporting interventions.
- Prevention and effective management of other risk factors in primary care (for example, through early identification and intervention on poor diet, physical inactivity, obesity and hypertension through lifestyle and therapeutic interventions, including use of statins and anti-hypertensives according to need).
- Environmental improvements to improve housing quality to tackle cold and dampness and increase safety at home (for example, smoke alarms, hand rails, and to prevent road accidents among old and young road users).
- Targeting over-50s where the greatest short-term impact on life expectancy will be made (Department of Health, 2002).

Explaining health inequalities

In order to provide an explanation for social class inequalities in health, many older sociology of health textbooks outline the four explanatory suggestions made in the Black Report (Department of Health 1980). These are the artefact explanation, social selection, behavioural/cultural explanation and structural/material explanation. Subsequent research, however, has dismissed or diminished the influence of the first three of these suggestions (see Table 16.5). Increasingly, research has pointed to material and structural causes. We will look, for example, at how poverty affects our lifestyle choices: diet, smoking and physical activity/exercise, and how material deprivation, in terms of living in deprived areas, affects health.

The Black Report's main recommendations centred on the need to reduce poverty. This was not, however, immediately accepted. Public health strategies up until the 1990s emphasised individual health education and lifestyle change in favour of addressing material and structural conditions (Department of Health, 1992).

Twenty years after the Black Report, an Independent Inquiry into Inequalities in Health was set up in 1998. The Acheson Report (named after its chair, Sir Donald Acheson, a former Chief Medical Officer) made

Table 16.5 The Black Report: class and health inequalities

Suggested Reasons for Health Inequalities	Subsequent Research
Artefact explanation The existence of health inequalities is due to the way in which the statistics are collected and the way we construct social class.	If anything, the statistics under-report the extent of class and health inequalities.
Social selection explanation It is poor health that assigns people to lower-class groups rather than any of the effects of belonging to a lower class group. Thus it is the other way around, health affects our class, rather than class affecting our health.	There may be some evidence of social selection at younger ages but the overall effect over a lifetime is very minor.
Behavioural/cultural explanations Ill health is due to people's choices and decisions; working class people tend to make the wrong choices to smoke, drink too much and eat the wrong foods.	Even among people who follow 'healthy lifestyles' we find similar patters of ill health. Lifestyle choices may only account for a quarter of social class inequalities between social classes.
Structural/material explanations Poor conditions, such as bad housing, and low incomes make it virtually impossible for working class people to lead a healthy lifestyle.	This perspective is the one currently most favoured by academics and leading researchers in this field.

Source: Kirby et al. (1997). Heinemann Educational Publishers

39 recommendations, this was to be a landmark occasion in the field of health inequalities research and policy, arguably the most important since the Black Report. Nonetheless, Shaw et al. (1999) argue that although the new report was welcomed and contained a comprehensive review of current knowledge on the extent and trends in health inequalities, it was not the definitive document that would set the government into action as many had hoped. Surprisingly, little media coverage and debate ensued, but three key criticisms were levied at the report (Davey Smith et al., 1998).

The first criticism was that there was not adequate prioritisation among the 39 sets of recommendations, which ranged from traffic curbing to water fluoridation. Sir Acheson responded by stating that the following three areas were considered by the advisory group as crucial:

- All policies likely to have an impact on health should be evaluated in terms of their impact on health inequalities.
- A high priority should be given to the health of families with children.
- Further steps should be taken to reduce income inequalities and improve the living standards of poor households (Acheson, 1998).

Despite the inevitable criticisms, the inquiry's report (Acheson, 1998) and its recommendations were, however, instrumental in fostering widespread recognition that health inequalities need to be addressed, and that tackling the wider determinants is crucial to this process. According to Exworthy (2003), who investigated the impact on policy-making of the Acheson Inquiry's recommendations, the report's four major impacts were that it:

- Acted as a prompt to new policies.
- Engendered a climate of opinion favouring policies to tackle health inequalities.
- Introduced a health inequalities dimension to current policies.
- Acted as a reference book.

Exworthy goes on to say that the report also provided the context for the public health strategy in England, *Saving Lives: Our Healthier Nation* (Department of Health, 1999a). Public health strategies in other parts of the UK have also drawn on the Acheson Inquiry's analysis and recommendations. Resulting policies have primarily focused on areas (mainly geographical zones) and on individual employment (through welfare-to-work strategies, mainly tax credits), and have involved some income redistribution (through tax and benefit reform). Most of these recommendations in the Acheson Inquiry's report have been addressed by these policies, which have sought to tackle the wider determinants of ill-health and to cover the lifespan.

Acheson also commented upon the value of exercise in relation to encouraging social inclusion of communities:

Opportunities afforded by exercise might also lead to wider networks and social cohesion . . . it has been suggested that people with good social networks live longer, are at reduced risk of coronary heart disease, are less likely to report being depressed or to suffer a recurrence of cancer, and are less susceptible to infectious illness than those with poor networks.
(quoted in Health Education Authority, 1999: 2–3)

For example, Jane Elster (2000) conducted a study on *Cycling and Social Inclusion*, in which she investigated and generated action on small-scale local cycling projects in the UK, with a focus on exploring the links between such projects and social inclusion. The aim was to increase action around cycling in low-income areas, and investigate how cycling projects can help to contribute to social inclusion, and how the potential social inclusion links can help to engage the interest of communities in cycling. The project achieved a wide range of positive outcomes, including engaging 'at risk' young people in challenging activities. The researcher summarised that small-scale cycling projects represent a way of engaging a much wider audience with cycling than the conventional approach of promoting cycling as transport. They are relevant to a range of high priority needs and priorities in many communities, for example crime diversion, activities for young people, and training. They also can be an effective tool for contributing to community development and social inclusion needs. The author concluded that a significant expansion of cycling project activity in the UK has the potential to contribute to several Government and non-government agendas, such as sustainable transport and the Social Inclusion Unit's work on neighbourhood renewal.

Wilkinson's psycho-social perspective

So far we have examined the effects of poverty and deprivation on health. Some researchers have recently been arguing that there are perhaps deeper factors at play. Richard Wilkinson (1996) and David Blane et al. (1996), for example, have broadened the debate and suggested a much richer and more complex basis to health inequalities. This 'psycho-social perspective' moves away from simply looking at how poor diet or so-called 'risk activities' affect and influence health, and concentrates on psychological stress, relative deprivation and how living in a society riddled with inequality affects the health of so many people. Wilkinson's sources of evidence for the psycho-social perspective involve looking at:

- Health and income deprivation.
- Social cohesion.
- Psychosocial causes of illness.

Health and income deprivation

In many ways, the evidence we have seen for class inequalities in health are both shocking and surprising, considering how developed and advanced society in Britain is, in comparison to other countries. It would seem to follow that as a country's economy improves, then, there would be a favourable knock-on effect for the health and life expectancy of that population. Yet Wilkinson challenges this assumption. He argues that countries that have a smaller gap between social classes tend to exhibit fewer health inequalities. Wilkinson proposes that it is relative, not average, income that affects health in affluent societies. For example, although the UK is the 5th richest nation, it recently ranked bottom of 21 industrialised countries in child well-being assessment (UNICEF, 2007).

If we compare the class and mortality rates for England and Wales with Sweden (an equally affluent Western country) we see some stark contrasts. England and Wales exhibit sharp differences between the social classes, while for Sweden, those differences are marginal. Wilkinson's explanation for this is that there is greater equality of income in Sweden, he suggests that the UK would see a dramatic improvement in the health of the lower classes if we had similar income distribution patterns to that of Sweden. Not only this, but greater income equality would benefit everybody, not just the most deprived. One stark and interesting fact is that the mortality rate of the lowest social class in Sweden is actually better than the mortality rate of the highest class in England and Wales (Wilkinson, 1996).

Social cohesion

Wilkinson further suggests that societies that exhibit high social cohesion tend to be the healthier ones. These societies typically emphasise mutual aid, narrow differences in income, and a shared sense of purpose or belief. One example given is that of Britain in the war years. Despite the tragedy which the two World Wars brought to the population of Britain in the twentieth century, ironically the health of the nation actually improved, whereby we saw the greatest increases in life expectancy. So why should this be? Wilkinson (1996) suggests that the narrowing of income differences, the reduction in poverty, and a sense of social solidarity were more likely to have influenced this increase in life expectancy. He proposes that in these times of difficulty we saw an example of how people who live in a more egalitarian society, with a common sense of identity and purpose, are healthier.

So, how cohesive is contemporary Western society? Is there more emphasis on the individual or on the wider social group. It should not be forgotten that between 1979 and 1998 the UK was governed by a political party whose leader, Margaret Thatcher, declared that 'There is no such thing as society; just individuals and their families'. Barry and Yuill (2002) suggest that if our society continues to become increasingly fragmented, with a widening gap between the rich and the poor, then we can expect the health of the poorest among us to worsen.

Social capital and health

More recently work in the UK has revealed a similar picture focusing upon social capital. There are many different ways to define 'social capital' but at a basic level we can understand it as the:

> social glue that holds people together in families and communities and gives them a sense of belonging in an increasingly fragmented and uncertain world. It is developed in our relationships, through doing things for one another and in the trust that we develop in one another.
> (Catts and Ozga, 2005: 1)

In the UK – following the US – policy makers have become interested in the extent to which the absence of social capital may be a cause of social exclusion and community decline. As Catts and Ozga (ibid) note, however, this focus on social capital 'may also be misused to distract attention from inequalities in wealth and resources in society and problems of poverty'. In relation to health, this is a concept that recognises that a range of social and community circumstances influence health-related behaviour, and that an individual's health and well-being can be affected by the way that they relate to social networks and communities.

> Social capital represents the degree of social cohesion which exists in communities. It refers to the processes between people which establish networks, norms and social trust, and facilitate co-ordination and co-operation for mutual benefit. Social capital is created from the myriad of interactions between people, and is embodied in such structures as civic and religious groups, family membership, informal community networks, and in norms of voluntarism, altruism and trust. The stronger these networks and bonds, the more likely it is that members of a community will co-operate for mutual benefit. In this way, social capital creates health, and may enhance the benefits of investment for health.
> (World Health Organization, Health Promotion Glossary, Geneva, 1998: 19)

Wilkinson (1997) cites research that identifies social trust (as indicated by membership of voluntary groups and levels of trust in the community) as a factor linking income distribution and health (Kawachi et al., 1997; Kawachi and Kennedy, 1997). Meanwhile, a study by Kaplan et al. (1996) found that the scale of investment in human and social capital paralleled variations in health outcomes and social indicators. In 2000, Rose found that social capital increased physical and emotional health in Russia, while McCulloch's (2001) study revealed that people in the lowest categories of social capital had increased risk of psychiatric morbidity. Others, while accepting that social networks might well play a role in promoting health, have been more cynical about the impact of social capital and in particular have expressed concern about the lack of clarity surrounding the term (see Muntaner et al., 2001; Cattell, 2001, 2004). Social capital is not new as a concept in health research, and Lynch et al. (2001) refers to it as 'a new and more fashionable label for investigations into what used to be called social support'.

Psycho-social causes of illness

Here, Richard Wilkinson (1996) acknowledges recent developments in epidemiology, and draws certain conclusions that relate the social to the biological, that is, how social factors interact with biological mechanisms, to result in deprived people becoming unwell. Wilkinson essentially argues that through deprivation comes stress, which ultimately has a detrimental effect on the body:

> . . . the poor suffer the psychosocial effects of deprivation as well as its direct material effects. Indeed, it is important to recognise that as well as the greatest material deprivation, those at the bottom of the social hierarchy also suffer the greatest social, psychological and emotional deprivation, and this may well have a greater impact on their health that the more direct effects of material deprivation.
> (Wilkinson, 1996: 176)

It is often argued that working class people do not help themselves in looking after their bodies, but rather abuse their bodies with lifestyle choices which have a damaging effect upon their bodies. This view was particularly prominent in the individualistic ethos of the last Conservative government. Wilkinson argues that lifestyle choices such as smoking, drinking, drug use and lack of physical activity are 'risk' behaviours which result from stress. He proposes that for the individual these risk activities function as substitutes for some form of status, or as mechanisms for much-needed social interaction. Indeed Hilary Graham (1987), who studied working class mothers and smoking behaviour labelled cigarettes 'drugs of solace' for the women, giving them a few moments of space, and control, in situations where they had little of either.

This constant bombardment of stress is also internalised leading to a detrimental effect on the body. Much research (for example, Brunner, 1996; Saplolsky, 1993) has shown that people who are continually stressed become biologically damaged. These authors propose that the continual build-up of stress chemicals, such as corticosteroids, can damage the body, diverting valuable biological resources away from repairing the body, and leaving the immune system depleted, and much more susceptible to infection and illness.

Therefore, people who experience stress on a variety of levels, on a daily basis, are more likely to become ill.

Physical activity and health

The lack of physical activity is a major underlying cause of death, disease and disability. Preliminary data from a WHO study on risk factors suggest that a sedentary lifestyle is one of the ten leading global causes of death and disability. More than two million deaths each year are attributable to physical inactivity.
(World Health Organization, Move for Health, 2002)

As has continuously been reported in previous chapters, there are numerous health benefits of regular physical activity. According to the British Heart Foundation, regular moderate physical activity:

- Reduces the risk of premature mortality.
- Reduces Cardiovascular diseases.
- Reduces the risks of developing some cancers.
- Reduces the risk of developing Type II diabetes.
- Helps prevent or reduce hypertension.
- Helps to prevent or reduce osteoporosis.
- Helps to control weight and lower the risk of becoming obese.
- Promotes psychological well-being (e.g. reduction of depression).
- Enhances and protects brain function.
- Can help in the management of painful conditions (for example, arthritis).
- Improves health-related quality of life.
- Physical activity also helps prevent or control risky behaviours, especially among children and young people, like tobacco, alcohol or other substance use, unhealthy diet or violence.
(British Heart Foundation, 2000)

In general, the major benefits of physical activity are to the heart and circulation, bones, joints and tendons, metabolism and hormones. In the case of other diseases associated with a sedentary lifestyle and a diet high in saturated fats (such as colorectal cancer – see White et al., 1996; Whittemore et al., 1990), physical activity has an important role in disease prevention. Given these numerous health benefits of physical activity, the hazards of being inactive are clear. Physical inactivity is a serious, nationwide problem. Further, there is evidence (Blair and Connelly, 1996) that the greatest population health gain would result from getting those who are inactive and at the greatest health risk to increase their activity levels, rather than promoting more intense activity among those who are already moderately active, and who have a lower morbidity and mortality rate.

Current activity and fitness levels

The *Health Survey for England* (DoH, 1998) gives the most accurate national data on current physical activity levels of the adult population.

- 37 per cent of men and 25 per cent of women participate in physical activity at the recommended level for health benefits; at least moderate intensity activity of at least 30 minutes' duration on most days (at least five days a week).
- This means that around 6 out of 10 men and 7 out of 10 women are not active enough to benefit their health.
- Activity declines dramatically with age: 58 per cent of men aged 16–24 were active at recommended levels compared to 7 per cent of men aged 75 and over. Among women, the proportion active at the recommended level was fairly steady at 30 per cent to 32 per cent in women aged 16–54, before falling to just 4 per cent among women aged 75 and over.
- 22 per cent of men and 26 per cent of women can be classed as completely sedentary.
- Among young people aged 2–15, 4 out of 10 boys and 6 out of 10 girls are not meeting the recommended 1 hour a day physical activity.
(Source: Department of Health (1998))

Physical activity and social class

The effect of social class and income on participation in physical activity is complicated. In summary:

- Men from manual social classes are more active overall than men from non-manual social classes. This is because of the greater contribution of occupational activity in the manual social classes. Among women there was no clear pattern according to income or social class.
- The pattern is reversed for leisure and sporting activity, where people from non-manual classes are more likely to participate.
- Participation in sports and exercise and walking is strongly related to household income, with men and women earning higher incomes being more likely to be regular participants.

Imogen Sharp, Head of CVD and Cancer Prevention at the Department of Health describes these inequalities in the following way:

Table 16.6 Trends in participation in sports, games and physical activities in the four weeks before interview by occupational social class, men and women (aged 16 and over, % participating), Britain (1987–96)

Year	I	II	IIIN	IIIM	IV	V	Total
			Occupational social class				
At least one activity (excluding walking)							
1987	65	52	45	48	34	26	45
1990	65	53	49	49	38	28	48
1993	64	53	49	46	36	31	47
1996	63	52	47	45	37	23	46
At least one activity							
1987	78	68	63	62	51	42	61
1990	79	71	67	66	55	46	65
1993	82	71	65	63	54	48	64
1996	80	69	66	63	55	45	64

Source: Adapted from GHS (1996)

- Rates of inactivity are higher among:
  - older people;
  - some ethnic minority communities;
  - people in rented council accommodation;
  - disabled people.
- Very marked social class differentials in sport participation exist: people from unskilled social classes are three times less likely to take part in sport than professionals

Table 16.6 shows the occupational social class differences in participation in sports, games and physical activities from the late 1980s to the late 1990s, showing very little change over this decade.

Physical activity participation among black and minority ethnic groups

When examining inequalities in health, ethnicity, along with gender, age, and geographical area, is an area where further inequalities exist. Ethnicity is discussed further within Chapter 13 of this book, but very briefly *The Health of Minority Ethnic Groups 1999* (Department of Health, 2000) measured participation in physical activity among the main minority ethnic groups in England. The survey found that compared with the general population, South Asian and Chinese men and women were much less likely to participate in physical activities, whether sport and exercise, walking, heavy housework or DIY. Bangladeshi men and women had the lowest level of physical activity: they were almost twice as likely than the general population to be classified as sedentary (see Chapter 17).

What is being done?

Social inclusion

The Labour Government has a strong philosophical commitment to social inclusion that underpins many of its strategic directions and policies. Therefore, it is encouraging to note that the role of physical activity, and not just sport, has been recognised as a means for Neighbourhood Renewal, and demonstrates how far into government thinking the physical activity message has penetrated. The strength of physical activity promotion in England is that there are a number of agencies with different strengths and resources determined to help more people be more active, more often.

These include:

- *The NHS plan* This was published in July 2002, and sets out comprehensive plans for investment in, and reform of, the NHS. Detailed plans included proposals on improving health and reducing inequality. This included the commitment to develop, by 2004 'local action to tackle obesity and physical inactivity, informed by advice from the Health Development Agency on what works'.
- *National Service Frameworks (NSFs)* The NHS Plan emphasised the role of NSFs as drivers in delivering the modernisation agenda. Physical activity has been a component of all the NSFs released to date which relate to CHD, cancer, diabetes, older people and mental health.
- *Local Exercise Action Pilots (LEAP)* In May 2002, the Department of Health (in collaboration with the Countryside Agency and Sport England) announced a programme of nine pilot projects to promote physical activity.
- The Department of Health is also involved in a number of initiatives with other government departments to promote physical activity. These include the *National Healthy Schools Standard (NHSS)* with the DfES and the *School Travel Advisory Group (STAG)* with the DfT.
- *Sport Action Zones* Instigated by the Department of Culture, Media and Sport (DCMS), and Sport England (SE), the aim of Sport Action Zones are 'To help bring the benefits of sport to deprived communities'. Sport Action Zones (SAZs) are a proactive initiative from Sport England in direct response to the need to address sporting deprivation in some of the most socially and economically deprived areas of the country. They have raised aspirations and help local communities to help themselves. They have also been instrumental in identifying what is really needed in each zone and involving local people in the planning process.

Sport Action Zones (SAZs) are a proactive initiative from Sport England in direct response to the need to address sporting deprivation in some of the most socially and economically deprived areas of the country. They have raised aspirations and help local communities to help themselves. They have also been instrumental in identifying what is really needed in each zone and involving local people in the planning process.

Examples of the kind of work the sports action zones are carrying out include:

- Working with young people involved in anti-social behaviour.
- Working with community health services to support people in poor health.
- Providing education, training and support for community sport workers and community workers in other sectors who might use sport to meet their objectives.
- Setting up local clubs where none exist.
- Making local sports centres more accessible.
- Engaging with local community groups especially ethnic minority groups.

Zone managers are also involved in:

- Getting sport and recreation integrated into existing and emerging programmes.
- Accessing funding from other sources.
- Influencing the wider strategic development of sport.
- Securing good press and media coverage.

In short, the government and government links are taking action at a national, regional and local level in order to increase physical activities within communities and especially within deprived communities.

Criticism: lifestyle, sport, fitness and health

Much of the evidence for health benefits, as discussed here, relates to general physical activity, and is often based on small-scale clinical evidence. There has been little large-scale longitudinal research into the relationship between sport participation, fitness and health, within the context of people's everyday lives. Roberts and Brodie (1992) undertook the only UK study. The study of 7000 people in six cities in the UK was conducted over 4 years and included non-participants and participants in activities provided in local authority sports and leisure centres (that is, largely recreational sports participants). The conclusions for the role of sport in the promotion of fitness and health are ambivalent. They found that playing sport did result in health benefits (especially increased muscular power and improved lung functions). Further, the health benefits were evident in all socio-demographic groups and these benefits were additional to those experienced as a result of other lifestyle practices. They conclude:

> Sport participation was certainly not the sole determinant of these people's health, but however favourable or unfavourable their other circumstances and living habits, playing sport was leading to measurable gains.
> (Roberts and Brodie, 1992: 138)

Nevertheless, they also conclude that, although sports participation was improving participants' self-assessment and strength, it was not improving their cardiovascular health or their freedom from illness (for example, those who played sport were remaining just as vulnerable to illnesses, infections, accidents and injuries). A major reason for this was that 'at low levels of sport activity, less than three times a week, only *self-assessments* showed statistically significant and consistent improvements within all socio-demographic groups [emphasis added]' (Roberts and Brodie, 1992: 139). They also state that even alongside favourable lifestyle practices, participation in sport was not eliminating or reducing the health inequalities associated with age, sex and socio-economic status, that is, all were improving but inequalities remained.

On the basis of this evidence, Roberts and Brodie conclude that if the 'aim of health promotion is to draw the less healthy sections of the population towards the norm, sport will not be an effective vehicle' (Roberts and Brodie, 1992: 140). They base this conclusion on three factors:

1. Evidence indicates that sports participation needs to be energetic and frequent to achieve changes in physical functioning, 'Improving one's health through sport is hard work. Weekly swimming is not enough.' Consequently, they question if it is possible to build the required level of sport activity into typical adult's lifestyle (when most surveys indicate that 'lack of time' constrains both participation and frequency of participation). Related to this, is the fact that, for many sports 'participants' the commitment is rather cyclical, with most dropping in and out of sport over time and only a minority of participants taking part regularly over time.
2. Lifestyles are not the basic source of health inequalities. 'Even when economically disadvantaged groups were making the healthiest of all possible leisure choices, their well-being remained handicapped by their low incomes, relatively poor housing and working conditions and vulnerability to unemployment' (Roberts and Brodie, 1992: 141). This is consistent with the 1999 Health White Paper (DoH, 1999), which states that life chances are an important determinant of health.
3. There are relatively persistent socio-demographic differences in sports participation patterns, which will require a fundamental and sustained change

in public policy to address (for example, a greater emphasis on sport in primary schools and increased facility provision).

This leads them to conclude that:

> the balance of all the evidence and arguments . . . points towards a niche rather than a foundation role for sport within health policy and promotion . . . its impact is focused on a limited number of health factors and it offers no solutions to socio-economic health inequalities.
> (Roberts and Brodie, 1992: 141–142)

Some may regard such arguments as rather over-stated – although in relative terms, inequalities remain, in absolute terms increased levels of activity benefit all participants. Nevertheless, the arguments raise important policy questions about:

- The health effects of current levels and frequency of sports participation.
- The ability of a purely sport-orientated strategy to have health goals.
- The ability to use sport for instrumental (that is, health promotion) rather than affective (enjoyment) aims.
- Whether the best strategy is to seek to solve such problems or simply 'concentrate on retaining existing players, encouraging them to persist and to participate at the frequency necessary to maximise health benefits'. (Roberts and Brodie, 1992: 143)

If this conclusion is accepted, then issues of health promotion among low participation groups might best be addressed via an 'active lifestyles' approach, in which sports will play a part for some people.

Psychological health benefits

The positive mental changes that occur as a consequence of long-term participation in physical activity may be caused by a number of factors – accumulation of short-term improvements to mood (Steptoe, 1992) and physiological benefits that improve individuals' psychological ability to deal with stressful situations. This ability to cope better with day-to-day problems can reduce the likelihood of depression and anxiety (Steptoe, 1992). The psychological effects often associated with participation in sport – improved self-esteem, self-efficacy and perceived competence – have also been identified as resulting from long-term participation in an exercise programme (King et al., 1989). Nevertheless, Roberts and Brodie (1992) in their longitudinal of recreational sports participants found no relationship between stress level and sport participation. They suggest that this finding may reflect the fact that the social and psychological pressures associated with certain activities, and related time pressures, could serve to increase stress levels.

Nonetheless, despite the absence of evidence of fitness and health-related outcome measures, the initiatives that have so far been carried out have illustrated that, within the context of concerns with community development and social inclusion, such issues of sociability and associated mental health benefits cannot be ignored. In terms of gender differences, qualitative information from the various case studies indicates that much of this appeal has been to women. Some involved in the promotion of programmes have felt that males' emphasis on competition, rather than sociability, and the desire for a sense of competence before entering such programmes, militated against their involvement.

Furthermore, those who have been involved in the health-orientated initiatives acknowledge that such short-term projects could have very limited impacts on deep-rooted health problems and attitudes to physical activity. Further, limited interview evidence suggests that without a commitment to ongoing provision, infrastructure (for example, crèches), local provision (transport issues and family responsibilities often restrict the time available), and social support, such exercise programmes are unlikely to be sustained (Loughlan and Mutrie, 1997). There is clearly a need to develop a more sophisticated understanding of inactive people's readiness and willingness for change (Wimbush, 1994; Loughlan and Mutrie, 1997) in the context of possible broader lifestyle constraints, and the types of activity that might be best for their individual needs.

Conclusion

The literature, research and case study evidence suggest that:

- There exists, in Britain, a marked, and persistent difference in mortality rate between the occupational classes, for both sexes and at all ages. A steep gradient is found, showing that the risk of death increases with lower social class, and this is observed for most causes of death.
- What is more, the health gap is widening. The patterns of health inequality identified in the Black Report continued into the 1990s and beyond into the twenty first century. While the mortality rate for the whole population has declined, the differential between the lowest and the highest group seems to have increased.
- By using SMRs (or standardised mortality rates), it is possible to make comparisons between the different occupational classes. The average for the population is 100, and therefore an SMR below 100 indicates a lower than average chance of death whereas a figure above 100 suggests a higher than average chance of death.

- Socio-economic status (SES) is also linked to health-related behaviours such as cigarette smoking and dietary habits. The percentage of smokers among men in the unskilled manual classes is more than two and a half times that seen in professional classes.
- The Acheson report (1998) and its recommendations were instrumental in fostering widespread recognition that health inequalities need to be addressed, and that tackling the wider determinants is crucial to this process.
- Richard Wilkinson's 'psycho-social perspective' (1996) moves away from simply looking at how poor diet or so-called 'risk activities' affect and influence health, and concentrates on psychological stress, relative deprivation and how living in a society riddled with inequality affects the health of so many people. Wilkinson's sources of evidence for the psycho-social perspective involve looking at: health and income deprivation; social cohesion; and psychosocial causes of illness.
- There are numerous health benefits of regular physical activity. In general, the major benefits of physical activity are to the heart and circulation, bones, joints and tendons, metabolism and hormones. In the case of other diseases associated with a sedentary lifestyle and a diet high in saturated fats (such as colorectal cancer – see White et al., 1996; Whittemore et al., 1990) physical activity has an important role in disease prevention. Given these numerous health benefits of physical activity, the hazards of being inactive are clear. Physical inactivity is a serious, nationwide problem.
- The effect of social class and income on participation in physical activity is complicated. In short, participation in sports, and exercise and walking is strongly related to household income, with men and women earning higher incomes being more likely to be regular participants.
- Much of the research evidence relates to the health benefits of *physical activity*, rather than sports *per se*. Further, the evidence suggests that, especially among many of the least active and least healthy groups the promotion of an 'active lifestyle' may be a more useful strategy than the promotion of sports (although much depends on the definitions used).
- Even among those predisposed to sport, the frequency of activity required to achieve and sustain health benefits is unlikely to be possible for many using sport as the sole focus
- Qualitative evidence suggests that the greatest gains from involvement in activity relate to psychological health and increased feelings of well-being. This outcome is related to such factors as 'getting out of the house' and 'meeting people' who are 'just like ourselves'.
- Formal activity provision can provide one way of socialising and can reduce feelings of isolation.
- Factors underpinning the success of activity provision have included, appropriate and convenient local facilities (not necessarily sports facilities); recognising the importance of participants' friendship groups in getting involved and staying involved; providing reassurance that 'people just like

us' are able to participate; acknowledging, particularly to older people, that some physical activity will be better than none; recognising that if the activity has some intrinsic value (good fun, enjoyable, a change of environment etc.) it may be more appealing and ensure adherence.

- Concern was expressed about the general absence of male participants in formal physical activity initiatives.
- There is a widespread absence of robust monitoring information on the health benefits of provision. Much of the rationale for this has rested on assumed beneficial outcomes of any increased activity. Further, there is little long-term monitoring of adherence to activity programmes. This reflects the short-term nature of most initiatives, the lack of funding for such monitoring and the lack of expertise to undertake such work.

Finally, as an update to government initiatives in this area, the most recent government white paper: 'Choosing Health: Making Healthier Choices Easier' (Department of Health, 2004), incorporates within it physical activity as a key element:

Choosing Activity: a physical activity action plan sets out Government's plans to encourage and co-ordinate the action of a range of departments and organisations to promote increased participation in physical activity across England. It is a summary of how we will deliver the commitments on physical activity presented in the public health white paper Choosing Health: making healthier choices easier. It brings together all the commitments relating to physical activity in Choosing Health as well as other action across government, which will contribute to increasing levels of physical activity. These include school PE and sport and local action to encourage activity through sport, transport plans, the use of green spaces and by the NHS providing advice to individuals on increasing activity through the use of pedometers.

(www.dh.gov.uk/. . ./PublicationsPolicyAndGuidanceArticle)

References

Acheson, D. (1998) *Independent Inquiry into Inequalities in Health.* London. The Stationery Office.

Barry, A-M. and Yuill, C. (2002) *Understanding Health: A Sociological Introduction.* London: Sage.

Blair, S. N. and Connelly, J. C. (1996) The case for moderate amounts and intensities of physical activity, *Research Quarterly for Exercise and Sport,* 67(2), 193–205.

Blane, D., Brunner, E. and Wilkinson, R. G. (Eds.) (1996) *Health and Social Organisation: Towards a Health Policy for the 21st Century.* London: Routledge.

British Heart Foundation (2000) *Couch Kids the Growing Epidemic: Looking at Physical Activity in Children in the UK,* British Heart Foundation. London: Taylor and Francis.

Brunner, E. (1996) The social and biological basis of cardiovascular disease in office workers in Brunner, E., Blane, D. and Wilkinson, R. G. (Eds.) (1996) *Health and Social Organisation*. London: Routledge.

Cattell, V. (2001) Poor people, poor places, and poor health: the mediating role of social networks and social capital, *Social Science and Medicine*, May, 52(10), 1501–1516.

Catts, R. and Ozga, J. (2005) *What is Social Capital and How Might it be Used in Scotland's Schools?* CES Briefing, No. 36, December, University of Edinburgh.

Cattell, V. (2004) Social Networks as Mediators between the Harsh circumstances of People's Lives, and their Lived Experience of Health and Well-being in Phillipson, C. and Allan, G. (Eds.) *Social Networks and Social Exclusion: Sociological and Policy Perspectives*. Hants: Ashgate.

Davey Smith, G., Morris, J. N. and Shaw, M. (1998) The Independent Enquiry into Inequalities in Health, *British Medical Journal*, 317, 1465–1466.

Department of Health (1980) *Inequalities in Health (The Black Report)*. London: HMSO.

Department of Health (1992) *The Health of the Nation: A Strategy for England*. Cm 1986. London: HMSO.

Department of Health (1995) *Variations in Health: What can the Department of Health and NHS do?* London: Department of Health.

Department of Health (1998) *Health Survey for England: The Health of Young People*. London: The Stationery Office.

Department of Health (1999) *Saving Lives: Our Healthier Nation*. Cm 4386. London: Stationery Office.

Department of Health (2000) *Health Survey for England: the Health of Minority Ethnic Groups 1999*. London: The Stationery Office.

Department of Health (2002) *Tackling Health Inequalities: Summary of the 2002 Cross-Cutting Review*. London: HM Treasury.

Department of Health (2004) *Choosing Health: Making Healthier Choices Easier*. London: Stationery Office. www.dh.gov.uk/. . ./PublicationsPolicyAndGuidance Article

Department of Health (2005) *Choosing Activity: A Physical Activity Action Plan*. London: Stationery Office.

Drever, F. and Whitehead, M. (1995) Mortality in regions and local authority districts in the 1990s: exploring the relationship with deprivation, *Population Trends*, 82, Winter, 19–25.

Drever, F., Whitehead, M. and Roden, M. (1996) Current patterns and trends in male mortality by social class (based on occupation), *Population Trends*, 86, Winter, 15–20.

Drever, F. and Bunting, J. (1997) Patterns and trends in male mortality in Denver, F. and Whitehead, M. (Eds.) *'Health Inequalities'*, decennial supplement. D.S. series no. 15. London: The Stationery Office.

Elster, J. (2000) *Cycling and Social Exclusion*. London: ESRC Research Centre for Analysis and Social Exclusion (CASE).

Exworthy, M. (2003) *Tackling Health Inequalities since the Acheson Inquiry*. Bristol, UK: Policy press.

GHS (General Household Survey) (1996) *Living in Britain*. ONS, London: The Stationery Office.

Graham, H. (1987) Women's Smoking and Family Health, *Social Science and Medicine*, 25: 47–56.

Graham, H. (2001) *Understanding Health Inequalities*. Milton Keynes: OUP.

Health Education Authority (1999) *Health Activity and Inequalities: A Briefing Paper.* London: Health Education Authority.

Kaplan, G. A., Panuk, E., Lynch, J. W., Cohen, R. D. and Balfour, J. L. (1996) Income inequality and mortality in the United States. *British Medical Journal,* 312, 999–1003.

Kawachi, I. and Kennedy, B. P. (1997) Health and social cohesion: why care about income inequality? *British Medical Journal,* 314, 1037–1040.

Kawachi, I., Kennedy, B. P., Lochner, K. and Prothrow-Stith, D. (1997) Social capital, income equality and mortality, *American Journal of Public Health,* 87, 1491–1498.

King, A. C., Taylor, C. B., Haskell, W. L. and De Busk, R. F. (1989) The Influence of regular aerobic exercise on psychological health, *Health Psychology,* 8, 305–324.

Kirby, M., Kidd, W., Koubel, F., Barter, J., Hope, T., Kirton, A., Madry, N., Manning, P. and Triggs, K. (1997) *Sociology in Perspective.* Oxford: Heinemann.

Kreiger, N., Williams, D. R. and Moss, N. E. (1997) Measuring social class in US public health research: concepts, methodologies, and guidelines. *Annual Review of Public Health,* 18, 341–378.

Lynch, J., Smith, G., Hillemeier, M., Shaw, M., Raghurathan, T. and Kaplan, G. (2001) Income inequality, the psychosocial environment and health: comparisons of wealthy nations, *Lancet,* 358, 9277, 194–200.

Loughlan, C. and Mutrie, N. (1997) An evaluation of the effectiveness of three interventions in promoting physical activity in a sedentary population, *Health Education Journal,* 56, 154–165.

McCulloch, A. (2001) Social environments and health: cross sectional national survey, *British Medical Journal,* 323, 208–209.

Mitchell, R., Dorling, D. and Shaw, M. (2000) *Inequalities in Life and Death: What if Britain were more equal?* A Joseph Rowntree Foundation report. Bristol: The Policy Press.

Muntaner, C., Lynch, J. and Davey-Smith, G. (2001) Social capital, disorganised communities, and the third way: understanding the retreat from structural inequalities – epidemiology and public health, *International Journal of Health Services,* 31(2), 213–237.

ONS (2000) *Standard Occupational Classification 2000 Volume 1: Structure and Descriptions of Unit Groups.* London: The Stationery Office.

Phillipson, C., Allan, G. and Morgan, D. (Eds.) (2004) *Social Networks and Social Exclusion.* Hants: Ashgate.

Roberts, K. and Brodie, D. A. (1992) *Inner-City Sports: Who Plays, and What are the Benefits?* Culembourg: Giordano Bruno.

Roberts, I. and Power, C. (1996) Does the decline in child injury mortality vary by social class?, *British Medical Journal,* 313, 484–786.

Rose, R. (2000) Uses of social capital in Russia: modern, pre-modern and anti-modern, *Post Soviet Affairs,* 16(1), 33–57.

Saplolsky, R. M. (1993) Endocrinology alfresco: psychoendocrine studies in wild baboons, *Recent Progress in Hormone Research,* 48: 437–468.

Shaw, M., Dorling, D., Gordon, D. and Davey Smith, G. (1999) *The Widening Gap: Heath Inequalities and Policy in Britain.* Bristol: The Policy Press.

Steptoe, A. (1992) Physical activity and well-being in Norgan, N. G. (Ed.) *Physical Activity and Health.* Cambridge: University Press.

Townsend, P., Davidson, N. and Whitehead, M. (1988*) Inequalities in Health: The Black Report and the Health Divide.* London: Penguin.

UNICEF, *Child Poverty in Perspective: An Overview of Child Well-being in Rich Countries*, Innocenti Report Card 7, 2007. UNICEF Innocenti Research Centre, Florence. The United Nations Children's Fund, 2007.

White, E., Jacobs, E. J., Daling, J. R. (1996) Physical activity in relation to colon cancer in middle-aged men and women, *American Journal of Epidemiology*, 144(1), 42–50.

Whitehead, M. and Drever, F. (1997) *Health Inequalities*, decennial supplement. London: The Stationery Office.

Whittemore, A. S., Wu-Williams, A. H., Lee, M., Shu, Z., Gallagher, R. P., Deng-ao, J., Lun, Z., Xianghui, W., Kun, C., Jung, D., The, C. Z., Changde, L., Hing Yao, X., Paffenburger, R. S. and Henderson, B. E. (1990) Diet, Physical Activity and Colorectal Cancer among Chinese in North America and China, *Journal of the National Cancer Institute*, 882(11), 915–926.

World Health Organization (1998) *Health Promotion Glossary*, Geneva. Copenhagen Regional Office for Europe: WHO.

World Health Organization Committee on Physical Activity for Health (2002) Move for health, *Bulletin of the World Health Organization*. Copenhagen Regional Office for Europe: WHO.

Wilkinson, R. (1996) *Unhealthy Societies: The Afflictions of Inequality*. London: Routledge.

Wilkinson, R. (1997) Health Inequalities: Relative or absolute material standards?, *British Medical Journal*, 314, 591–595.

Wimbush, E. (1994) A moderate approach to promoting physical activity: The evidence and implications, *Health Education Journal*, 53(3), 322–336.

CHAPTER 17

Getting Evidence about Physical Activity into Practice: Inequalities in Health and their Reduction

MICHAEL P. KELLY AND HUGO CROMBIE

Introduction

This chapter examines the evidence about effective interventions to promote physical activity, especially as it may relate to reducing inequalities in health. The evidence for the effectiveness of physical activity in disease prevention and health promotion is well established and is described briefly here. This chapter goes on to consider the implications of the evidence and then how to translate that knowledge into effective interventions at local level. From a public health point of view the issue is not whether physical activity is beneficial in health terms, but rather how to facilitate and encourage a more active population in order to get the benefits. The chapter also draws attention to the important health inequalities linked to physical activity and especially physical inactivity. The risk factors and the diseases for which physical activity is a significant ameliorative factor like heart disease, diabetes, obesity and depression, themselves show strong social class variation in mortality and morbidity, with the most disadvantaged being disproportionately at risk. The key policy problem is to ensure that those interventions which encourage and promote physical activity reach everybody and are appropriate to all sectors of the population, and do not further steepen the inequalities gradient.

Physical activity and health

The evidence linking physical activity to a wide range of health outcomes and diseases is extremely clear. The most up to date review of the evidence is to be found in the Chief Medical Officer for England's report published in April 2004 (Department of Health, 2004). The report provides a comprehensive summary of the issues. Overall, the estimated costs of physical *inactivity* in England are £8.2 billion annually, including costs to the NHS and costs related to the economy such as absence from work. This figure does not include the contribution of physical inactivity to obesity, the costs of which are estimated at £2.5 billion annually. Adults who are physically active have 20–30 per cent reduced risk of premature death, and substantial reductions in risk of developing major chronic health problems such as cardiovascular disease, diabetes, obesity, musculoskeletal problems and certain mental illnesses and cancers. Inactivity has a significant independent effect on coronary heart disease, stroke and other risk factors such as lipid profile and high blood pressure. Inactive people have roughly twice the risk of dying from coronary heart disease compared to active people, and there is a reduction of around 27 per cent in incidence and death from stroke in active compared to inactive people. Physical activity can also moderate other risk factors such as raised blood pressure and adverse lipid profiles. Reductions of around 3.8 mm Hg (systolic) and 2.6 mm Hg (diastolic) are reported, with the size of the impact being greater in those with raised blood pressure. The main benefits of physical activity on lipid profiles seem to be to raise the levels of HDL cholesterol (the 'protective' element) and to lower triglycerides.

Physical activity also has a substantial beneficial effect on type 2 diabetes, the most common form of the disease. Activity cuts the risk of developing type 2 diabetes by around 33–50 per cent, rising to around 64 per cent in those at high risk of developing the disease. With respect to obesity and overweight, physical activity alone can result in weight loss of around 0.5–1 kg a month, but most effective strategies involve a combination of increased activity and diet. It is likely that in the absence of a reduction in energy intake, around 60 minutes moderate activity a day will be required for weight loss and 60–90 minutes a day to maintain weight loss in those who were obese and have lost weight. Weight bearing physical activity is important in increasing bone mineral density in young people, maintaining it in adults and slowing its loss in older age. There are also substantial benefits from activities to promote strength, balance and power to reduce the risk of falls and consequent fractures. Physical activity can also help to reduce progression of osteoarthritis and recurrence of low back pain.

Physical activity has beneficial effects on mood, anxiety and self-perceptions, as well as improving sleep and some aspects of cognition in older people. Activity is effective as a treatment for mild, moderate and severe depression. Overall, there is a reduction of risk of cancer in people who are active. The most marked impact is on cancer of the colon, where the reduction is around 40–50 per cent. There is possibly a beneficial effect on breast cancer in postmenopausal women and on lung cancer. Obesity, and consequently physical activity, is thought to result in around 10 per cent of all-cause cancers in the US (Department of Health, 2004).

As can be seen, the impact of physical activity on the health of the individual is substantial, with the impact of inactivity and low fitness on coronary heart disease being at a similar level to smoking cigarettes. From a public health point of view, this importance is increased because of the prevalence of inactivity in the population. Overall, only 1 in 3 women and 1 in 4 men reach the guideline level of activity required to derive the health benefits (30 minutes a day five times a week). Estimates of the public health burden suggest that around 37 per cent of coronary heart disease is attributable to inactivity (McPherson et al., 2002). The World Health Organization (2002) has estimated the proportion of disability adjusted life years in developed countries from inactivity:

- 23 per cent of cardiovascular disease for men, 22 per cent for women.
- 16 per cent of colon cancer in men, 17 per cent in women.
- 15 cent of type 2 diabetes.
- 12 per cent of stroke for men, 13 per cent for women.
- 11 per cent of breast cancer.

Health inequalities and physical activity

The existence of inequalities in health across different causes of death, diseases and risk factors has been made clear over the years in reports such as the *Black Report* and the Acheson Inquiry (Townsend and Davidson, 1982; Acheson, 1998). Britain is now collectively healthier than it has ever been in its history. Life expectancy improves and some of the great killer diseases are in retreat as the benefits of a preventive approach to public health bears fruit (Unal et al., 2004; Capewell et al., 1999). However, at the same time, the problem of health inequalities remains stubbornly ubiquitous. While the health of the population as a whole is improving, the health of the least and less well off either improves more slowly than the rest of the population or, in some cases gets worse in absolute terms. In short there is a gradient from the most to the least advantaged, which shows variations in rates of mortality, with the poorest dying earlier. At each upward step in the hierarchy the health of the population gets better. Unequivocally, measured by occupation, there are marked differences in health from top to bottom of the social hierarchy.

The relationship between physical activity and measures of inequality is however complex. A number of publications have looked at the relationships (e.g. Coggins et al., 1999; Department of Health, 2000; Office for National Statistics and Health Education Authority, 1997; Sport England, 2000). It has been observed that people from professional groups were twice as likely to participate in any sport or physical activity, including walking for pleasure, as unskilled workers or those who were economically inactive (Office for National Statistics, 1998). Other surveys have shown small differences between socio-economic groups when all activity is examined, but larger differences when activity is restricted to leisure time, partly explained by the continuing but diminishing contribution of work based activity. Participation in moderate or vigorous physical activity is greater amongst people with educational or professional qualifications to GCSE level standard or equivalent. Twenty eight per cent of men and 23 per cent of women in rented council accommodation were defined as sedentary compared to 15 per cent of men and 14 per cent of women who were owner-occupiers. Levels of activity tend to be lower for people with disabilities. The 1999 Health Survey for England (Department of Health, 2000) examined participation in physical activity among the main minority ethnic groups in England. The survey found that compared with the general population, South Asian and Chinese men and women were much less likely to participate in physical activities, whether sport and exercise, walking, heavy housework or DIY. Bangladeshi men and women had the lowest level of physical activity: they were almost twice as likely than the general population to be classified as sedentary. Within black and minority ethnic groups, there are substantial differences for participation in sport and physical activity generally (see Figures 17.1 and 17.2).

There is a very large literature on health inequalities although a very much smaller literature on how to reduce health inequalities (Millward et al., 2003). The Health Development Agency has the task of developing the evidence base in public health in order to inform policy and practice to reduce inequalities. Between 2000 and 2005 the Agency has reviewed the evidence on health inequalities and on the effectiveness of interventions (after 2005 this task will

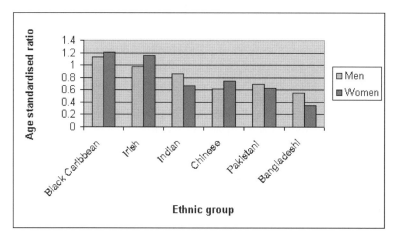

Figure 17.1 Participation in physical activity by ethnic group

Source: Health of minority ethnic groups, 1999 (Department of Health, 2000) Crown copyright material is reproduced with the permission of the controller of HMSO and the Queen's printer for Scotland

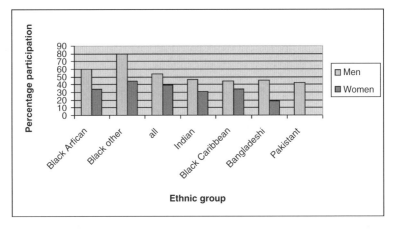

Figure 17.2   Participation in sport by ethnic group

Source: Sports participation and ethnicity in England (Department of Health, 2000) Crown copyright material is
reproduced with the permission of the controller of HMSO and the Queen's printer for Scotland

be continued by NICE). As well as reviewing evidence about physical activity
(Hillsdon et al., 2004), reviews have been undertaken of the evidence dealing
with the prevention of low birth weight (Bull et al., 2003), social support in
pregnancy (Bull et al., 2004), the prevention of drug misuse (Canning et al.,
2004), sexually transmitted infections and HIV (Ellis et al., 2003; Ellis and
Grey, 2004), accidental injury prevention (Millward et al., 2003), the management of obesity and overweight (Mulvihill and Quigley, 2003), the prevention
of alcohol misuse (Mulvihill et al., 2004) and smoking (Naidoo et al., 2004),
the promotion of breastfeeding (Prothero et al., 2003), and the prevention
of teenage pregnancy (Swann et al., 2003). The full results of these reviews
may be examined on <http://www.hda.nhs.uk/evidence> (see also Kelly,
2004). Without exception these reviews show the underlying problem of
health inequalities in all of these areas.

A number of overarching themes have emerged from the work that the
Agency has conducted in doing these reviews (Killoran and Kelly, 2004). First,
the conceptual apparatus to describe inequalities in health is surprisingly
limited. In general terms the conceptual basis for most of the data is a measure
of socio-economic status. The HDA reviews have found that the more discrete
dimensions of social difference like ethnicity, gender, disability, place, age and
geography, while never explicitly denied as important, are under developed
empirically and theoretically in the scientific literature. This is true with respect
to our understanding of physical activity and inequalities. The question
of social position, in other words, requires much more prominence in the
literature (and in policy making) than it has hitherto received. Second,
the relationships between the different dimensions of inequality which make

up social position (occupation, ethnicity, age, residence, etc), and the ways they interact with each other to produce health effects, is hardly to be found in the extant evidence at all. This is also true of the literature on physical activity. Third, the conceptual distinction between the determinants of health and the determinants of inequalities in health is frequently obscure (Graham, 2004). In the context of physical activity the determinants of health might be thought of as broad environmental ones which determine the availability of opportunities for leisure and work time physical activity, whereas the inequalities determinants would be those factors which differentially distribute the barriers to making use the available facilities which would be linked to the dimensions of social position, Fourth, different segments of the population as defined by social position respond very differently to identical interventions. So what is an appropriate intervention for one population group may be highly inappropriate for another. This means that it is very very important to tailor and target interventions to the needs of particular groups in a culturally sensitive way. In the case of physical activity what might appeal to a white professional woman in her late twenties and what might appeal to a male elder in the Afro Caribbean Community will likely be very different. An obvious point perhaps, and one which is borne out in the evidence, but one about which we know very little in enough detail, to use effectively. Fifth, the social variation in the population is considerable, and the existing measures of socio-economic status do not adequately capture these variegations in the population. This is linked to the previous point in that on the whole neither epidemiology nor sociology has mapped the social contours of the population in sufficient detail to link it to interventions in a systematic way. Sixth, there is a dearth of studies at topic level where inequalities and measures of inequality are key parts of the research questions, which have been investigated. So evidence about inequalities remains strongest at aggregate population mortality level, and much more diffuse at the level of individual topics like physical activity. The epidemiological data clearly show the social class gradient in the topics that the HDA has analysed, but few studies address inequalities *per se*. All of this applies to studies of physical activity; hence our ability to be very exact with respect to effective interventions is somewhat limited. Nevertheless, for the reasons arising from the epidemiology of heart disease, diabetes, obesity and cancer, physical activity is an important policy priority.

In December 2002 a report was published by the Department of Culture, Media and Sport (Department of Culture, Media and Sport, 2002) and the Strategy Unit entitled *Game Plan: a strategy for delivering the Government's sport and physical activity objectives* identifies potential benefits in a range of areas – such as the national 'feel good factor' of major international sporting success, the link between social and educational goals and sport or physical activity and the links between health and physical activity. It is because in this realm that the evidence is most compelling, the report suggested two overarching objectives:

- A major increase in participation in sport and physical activity, primarily because of the significant health benefits and to reduce the growing costs of inactivity.
- A sustainable improvement in success in international competition, particularly in the sports, which matter most to the public, primarily because of the 'feel good factor', associated with winning.

The targets associated with the first objective are:

- By 2020, 70 per cent of individuals to be undertaking 30 minutes of physical activity 5 days a week.
- An interim target of 50 per cent participation (at 5 episodes of 30 minutes activity a week) by 2011.

This represents a substantial increase in activity over the current level. The best current evidence suggests that around 37 per cent of men and 25 per cent of women are active at that level (Department of Health, 2000). To develop and coordinate efforts to achieve this target the Government set up ACT (Activity Coordinating Team). Much of the work of ACT will be in supporting the development of activities that have been shown to work in promoting physical activity.

In parallel with the realization of the importance of physical activity for health there is a concerted effort to identify and develop actions that will help produce these changes.

Part of the drive to address ill health and to reduce health inequalities included the setting up of the Health Development Agency. Within the work of the agency was a stream directed towards addressing physical activity. One of the first products in this process was the production of an *evidence briefing* on the effectiveness of interventions to promote physical activity in adults (Hillsdon et al., 2004). This document consisted of a review of evidence gathered from selected good-quality systematic reviews and meta-analyses on the effectiveness of public health interventions. The document identified a number of interventions in different settings and with different audiences that have been shown to be effective. The key points were:

- Brief advice from a health professional, supported by written materials, is likely to be effective in producing a modest, short-term (6–12 weeks) effect on physical activity.
- Referral to an exercise specialist, based in the community, can lead to longer term (>8 months) changes in physical activity.
- Short-term effectiveness of primary prevention interventions is associated with single factor interventions (physical activity only), which focus on the promotion of moderate intensity physical activity (typically walking) in a sedentary population.

- Interventions targeting individuals in community settings are effective in producing short-term changes in physical activity, and are likely to be effective in producing mid to long-term changes in physical activity.
- Interventions based on theories of behaviour change, which teach behavioural skills, and that are tailored to individual needs, are associated with longer-term changes in behaviour than interventions without a theoretical base.
- Interventions that promote moderate intensity physical activity, particularly walking, and are not facility dependent, are also associated with longer-term changes in behaviour.
- Studies that incorporate regular contact with an exercise specialist tend to report sustained changes in physical activity.
- Findings from studies examining the effectiveness of workplace interventions are inconsistent in promoting changes in physical activity.
- Interventions restricted to adults aged 50 years and older are effective in producing short-term changes in physical activity and there is limited evidence that they can be effective in producing mid- to long-term changes in physical activity.
- A range of intervention strategies is associated with increases in physical activity with no one approach consistently and significantly superior.
- Interventions that used individual-based or group-based behavioural or cognitive approaches with a combination of group- and home-based exercise sessions are equally effective in producing changes in physical activity.
- Interventions that promote moderate intensity and non-endurance physical activities (for example, flexibility exercises) are associated with changes in physical activity.
- Interventions that provide support and follow-up are also associated with changes in physical activity.

A number of attributes seem to be shared by effective interventions. These are:

- Individualised advice for behaviour change delivered verbally with written support.
- Setting goals for behaviour change.
- Self-monitoring.
- Exploring the cognitive and behavioural factors associated with behaviour change including beliefs about the costs and benefits of physical activity, reinforcement of changes in physical activity, perception of the health risks of physical inactivity, confidence to engage in physical activity.
- Ongoing verbal support.
- Intervention follow up.
- Promoting moderate intensity activity such as walking.
- Not dependent on attendance at a facility.

The HDA's approach in gathering the evidence was based on reviewing existing systematic reviews. As with all work of this sort this raises a number of issues. First, absence of evidence of effectiveness at review level is not the same as evidence of no effect. There are several hurdles to be crossed before studies are included in a review of this sort. These include the need for a project to have been evaluated adequately, for the evaluation to have been written up and successfully submitted to a journal and for it then to have been selected by one of the systematic reviews eventually extracted by the evidence briefing process. This not only excludes some interventions but also obviously has implications in terms of timescale. The second issue is related. The nature of the process gives weight to interventions coming from a particular methodological and scientific background – that is, ones based in a biomedical view which has a tradition of production of evaluation evidence, publication and review and the dominance of the randomised controlled trial as the method of preference. Interventions based on other traditions, such as those involving environmental changes are less likely to be evaluated in the same way, less likely to be published in reviewed journals and less likely to be suitable for collation into review articles. This is emphasised by the almost complete lack of interventions identified in the HDA's review, which looked at environmental changes to promote physical activity. However, gathering the evidence together in this way is a very useful first step in developing the evidence base (Kelly et al., 2002) the process is a key first stage in developing informed decision-making.

It is important to note that evidence, any kind of evidence in the field of public health, *only in very exceptional circumstances* prescribes precisely which policies or practices should be implemented. The reasons for this are that those interventions, which are reported in the scientific literature and reviewed in systematic reviews, are usually implemented under controlled scientific and well-resourced experimental conditions. They may be considerably less effective when applied under non-experimental routine service delivery circumstances. An evaluation of the likelihood of success of interventions has to be made and the policy and practice implications of this drawn out.

This chapter therefore identifies interventions where not only is the evidence strong, but also the likelihood of success is high. This judgement is made on the basis of the work the HDA has done when producing guidance for practice in the past, and ongoing work on getting evidence into practice (Kelly et al., 2004), and on the basis of accumulated other experience. On the basis of this evidence a number of broad implications for bringing about changes in levels of physical activity may therefore be identified.

National

- Incentives to employers to encourage walking and cycling to work should be introduced and the provision of existing locally based travel plans enhanced and encouraged through local authority grants.

- The development of a cadre of physical activity facilitators attached to primary care delivery agents should be established.

Regional

- Incentives must be introduced for local authorities to preserve playing fields and other open spaces and to address quality and safety issues and concerns among users, and to introduce safe play environments within open spaces, including ranger and park keeping schemes and safe walking environments. This can be coordinated with local schemes to promote walking for health by signed routes, maps, local publicity and advice from health professionals.

Local NHS

- Brief interventions to promote physical activity should be routine part of primary care using referral to properly trained and resourced physical activity and lifestyle coaches.
- Interventions that encourage walking and do not require attendance at a facility are the most likely to lead to sustainable increases in overall physical activity should be encouraged.
- There is strong evidence that individually adapted health behaviour change programmes are effective in increasing physical activity levels. These should therefore be used in primary care.
- Social support interventions in community settings are effective in increasing physical activity and therefore should be encouraged.

School

- School based physical education should be maintained and enhanced.

However, turning these implications into activities on the ground requires another set of considerations. This process has been described by the Health Development Agency (HDA) in the document *Getting evidence into practice in public health* (Kelly et al., 2004, see Figure 17.3).

As well as gathering the evidence and building the evidence base, the HDA is therefore involved a in a process of producing guidance in an integrated, systematic and empirical way, and in a way that involves practitioners (Kelly et al., 2003). This process involves testing the strength of research messages, examining how far the messages can be transferred and generalised and to the means of turning findings into action. It involves examining the evidence produced from published sources with the experience and expertise of

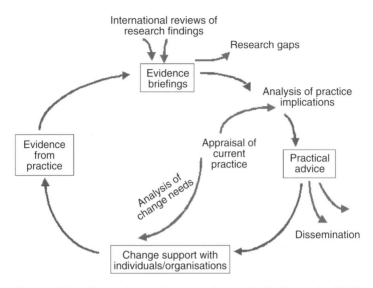

Figure 17.3 The 'evidence into practice cycle' (Kelly et al., 2004)

practitioners familiar with the issues in their day-to-day practice. From this, a systematic account of local issues and problems, together with case studies, can be built up. This gives the opportunity to consider the role of practical issues (such as staff time and engagement, knowledge of the benefits of physical activity, skills in delivering effective lifestyle advice, belief in their own efficacy in changing clients' behaviours, etc), reinforcing and enabling factors (such as the degree to which appropriate locations are used to deliver advise, the degree to which facilities such as primary care centres, leisure centers, etc, support lifestyle physical activity, e.g. walking, etc) and barriers to effective, long-term change in behaviour.

As far as physical activity is concerned the issues that have been identified are:

- The importance of developing individual-based lifestyle advice approaches within the context of a broad based strategic approach which takes account of local activities, needs and potential resources.
- The necessity of taking a strategic approach in order to utilise key local champions who can ensure that the issue is given suitable priority and action is followed through.
- The need to address barriers in the environment and policy arenas as part of the strategic approach to promoting physical activity as a part of daily life.

- The importance of getting an understanding of environmental and policy barriers, locally and nationally, in setting a context in which lifestyle advice can take root and flourish.
- The advantages of using staff and locations with whom and where the target group are comfortable, and involving the target groups in the development of activities.
- The importance of noting that key client groups are likely to be involved with a range of professionals/support groups with whom they have to develop relationships and whom they trust. Involving these groups in delivering messages appropriately and in locations which the individuals use as part of their normal lives can help the transition to activity as part of daily life.
- The significance of appropriate training for professionals who might be involved. Although they are likely to have an important role it should not be assumed that purely current 'exercise promotion' staff would carry out the delivery role.
- The provision of a broad range of activities suitable to the target groups.
- The acknowledgement that different groups will be attracted to different activities, and this is particularly true when the group has a wide range of functional ability (as is likely the case in, for instance, older age groups). Identifying and providing a range of activities which are attractive to the groups is important, and can best be developed with involvement of the target group.
- The recognition that current primary care staff is unlikely to be in a position to provide an effective physical activity advice service. Knowledge, skills, interest and time (particularly for GPs) mean that other individuals are more likely to be effective in providing these services.
- The acknowledgement that that this is likely to be compounded in areas of deprivation where pressures on staff and lack of available facilities are likely to be greater.
- The significance of accepting that where services are developed using other professionals; it is important that primary care staff are involved and able to direct patients appropriately.
- The imperative that lifestyle advice services need to be linked to information about opportunities and services locally available.
- The importance of the production, maintenance and co-ordination of information about local opportunities across health, local authority, private and voluntary/community services is a substantial undertaking but is important in encouraging the level of lifestyle shift required.
- The recognition that local media can support the dissemination of local examples.
- The importance of recognising that local organisations should promote physical activity through their design, attitude, policies and staff as well as through services and advice (HDA, 2004).

Conclusion

Changing and developing practice is a complex process that involves more than communication of 'best practice' and more than publishing evidence. It requires the integration of the best scientific information to hand, with the knowledge base in the field. It also requires sensitivity to the nuances of social variation in the population if inequalities in health are not to remain as blight on the population.

References

Acheson, D. (1998) *Independent Inquiry into Inequalities in Health: Report.* London: The Stationery Office.

Bull, J., Mulvihill, C. and Quigley, R. (2003) *Prevention of Low Birth Weight: Assessing Effectiveness of Smoking Cessation and Nutritional Intervention: Evidence Briefing.* London: Health Development Agency. <http://www.hda-online.org.uk/evidence>

Bull, J., McCormick, G. Swann, C. and Mulvihill, C. (2004) *Ante and Post Natal Home Visiting Programmes: A review of reviews.* London: Health Development Agency. <http://www.hda-online.org.uk/evidence>

Canning, U., Millward, L. M., Raj, T. and Warm, D. (2004) *Drug Use Prevention: A Review of Reviews.* London: Health Development Agency. <http://www.hda-online.org.uk/evidence>

Capewell, S., Morrison, C. E. and McMurray, J. J. (1999) Contribution of modern cardiovascular treatment and risk factor changes to the decline in coronary heart disease mortality in Scotland between 1975 and 1994, *Heart,* 81, 380–386.

Coggins, A., Swanston, D. and Crombie H. (1999) *Physical Activity and Inequality: a briefing paper.* London: Health Education Authority.

Department of Culture, Media and Sport (2002) *Game Plan: A Strategy for Delivering the Government's Sport and Physical Activity Objectives {DCMS 2002 821 /id}*

Department of Health (2000) *Health Survey for England 1999.* London: The Stationery Office.

Department of Health (2004) *At Least Five a Week: Evidence on the Impact of Physical Activity and its Relationship to Health. A Report from the Chief Medical Officer.* London: Department of Health.

Ellis, S., Barnett-Page, E., Morgan, A., Taylor, L., Walters, R. and Goodrich, J. (2003) *HIV Prevention: A Review of Reviews Assessing the Effectiveness of Interventions to Reduce the Risk of Sexual Transmission: Evidence Briefing.* London: Health Development Agency. <http://www.hda-online.org.uk/evidence>

Ellis, S. and Grey, A. (2004) *Prevention of Sexually Transmitted Infections (STIs): A Review of Reviews into the Effectiveness of Non-clinical Intervention. Evidence Briefing.* London: Health Development Agency. <http://www.hda-online.org.uk/evidence>

Graham, H. (2004) Social determinants and their unequal distribution: Clarifying policy understanding, *Millbank Quarterly,* 82, 101–124.

HDA (2004) *Effective Action Briefing: Promoting Physical Activity in Adults (pilot).* London: HDA.

Hillsdon, M., Foster, C., Cavill, N., Crombie, H. and Naidoo, B. (2004) *The Effectiveness of Public Health Interventions for Increasing Physical Activity among Adults: A Review of Reviews* (updated). London: Health Development Agency.

Kelly, M. P. (2004) *The Evidence of Effectiveness of Public Health Interventions – and the Implications.* London: Health Development Agency. <http://www.hda-online.org.uk/documents/evidence_effective_briefing_paper.pdf>

Kelly, M. P., Swann, C., Morgan, A., Killoran, A., Naidoo, B. and Barnett-Paige, E. (2002) *Methodological Problems in Constructing the Evidence base in Public Health.* London: Health Development Agency. <http://www.hda-online.org.uk/evidence>

Kelly, M. P., Chambers, J., Huntley, J. and Millward, L. (2003) *Method 1 for the Production of Effective Action Briefings and Related Materials.* London: HDA. <http://www.hda.nhs.uk/evidence/EIP_Protocol_july03.pdf>

Kelly, M. P., Speller, V., Meyrick, J. (2004) *Getting Evidence into Practice in Public Health.* London: Health Development Agency. <http://www.hda-online.org.uk/Documents/getting_eip_pubhealth.pdf>

Killoran, A. and Kelly, M. P. (2004) Towards an evidence-based approach to tackling health inequalities: the English experience, *Health Education Journal*, 63, 7–14.

McPherson K., Britton A. and Causer, L. (2002) *Coronary Heart Disease: Estimating the Impact of Changes in Risk Factors.* London: TSO.

Millward, L. M., Kelly, M. P. and Nutbeam, D. (2003) *Public Health Interventions Research: The evidence.* London: Health Development Agency. <http://www.hda-online.org.uk/evidence>

Mulvihill, C. and Quigley, R. (2003) *The Management of Obesity and Overweight: An Analysis of Reviews of Diet, Physical Activity and Behavioural Approaches.* Evidence briefing. London: Health Development Agency. <http://www.hda-online.org.uk/evidence>

Mulvihill, C., Taylor, L. and Waller, S. (2004) *Prevention and Reduction of Alcohol Misuse.* Evidence briefing, second edition. London: Health Development Agency. <http://www.hda-online.org.uk/evidence>

Naidoo, B., Quigley, R., Taylor, L. and Warm, D. (2004) *Public Health Interventions to Reduce Smoking Initiation and /or further uptake of Smoking, and to Increase Smoking Cessation: a review of reviews.* Evidence briefing. London: Health Development Agency. <http://www.hda-online.org.uk/evidence>

Office for National Statistics (1998) *Living in Britain: Results from the 1996 General Household Survey.* London: The Stationery Office.

Office for National Statistics and Health Education Authority (1997) *What People Know, What People Think, What People Do.* London: The Stationery Office.

Protheroe, L., Dyson, L., Renfrew, M. J., Bull, J. and Mulvihill, C. (2003) *The Effectiveness of Public Health Interventions to Promote the Initiation of Breast-Feeding.* London: Health Development Agency. <http://www.hda-online.org.uk/evidence>

Sport England (2000) *Sports Participation and Ethnicity in England. National Survey 1999/2000.* London: Sport England.

Swann, C., Bowe, K., McCormick, G. and Kosmin, M. (2003) *Teenage Pregnancy and Parenthood: A review of reviews: evidence briefing.* London: Health Development Agency. <http://www.hda-online.org.uk/evidence>

Townsend, P. and Davidson, N. (1982) *Inequalities in Health: The Black Report.* London: Pelican.

Unal, B., Critchley, J. A. and Capewell, S. (2004) Explaining the decline in coronary heart disease mortality in England and Wales between 1981 and 2000, *Circulation*, 109, 1101–1107.

World Health Organization. (2002) *World Health Report.* Geneva: World Health Organization.

CHAPTER 18

Global Health Promotion: Issues, Principles and Practice

CHRIS LLEWELLYN

Introduction

Other contributors to this volume evaluate examples of innovative policy interventions, and provide examples of good health promotion practice in the United Kingdom, and elsewhere, in the developed world. Others express due concern over persistent health inequalities and worsening problems (such as levels of obesity in the UK), despite the fact that the nation as a whole is healthier than at any time in its history. The aim of this chapter, however, is to look further afield, and to examine the contribution of the agencies and programmes of the United Nations system, particularly the World Health Organization (WHO), to the ongoing development of the theory and practice of health promotion throughout the world. These endeavours are motivated by the vision that health is *a fundamental human right* and that *Health for All* is an achievable target, notwithstanding the persistence of many infectious diseases, the emergence of new diseases, and the re-emergence of others previously considered under control. Problems have been exacerbated over recent years by the dramatic spread of chronic non-communicable disease to low and middle-income countries as a result of economic, political and social developmental processes such as globalisation, industrialisation and urbanisation. The 1997 World Health Report graphically described the emerging situation:

> The outlook for most individuals in the developing world is that if they do manage to survive the killer infections of infancy, childhood and maturity, they will become exposed in later life to non-communicable disease. This situation is known as the epidemiological transition – the changing pattern of health in which the poor countries inherit the problems of the rich, including not merely illness but also the harmful effects of tobacco, alcohol and drug abuse, and of accidents, suicide and violence. It is also referred to as the double burden because of the continuing weight of endemic infectious diseases.
> (WHO, 1997a: 2)

The United Nations system

International co-operation, in response to the threat of the spread of disease, has a long history. The first recorded efforts to create an international health organisation to fight epidemics of infectious diseases followed a particularly severe outbreak of cholera in Europe in 1830. The first International Sanitary Conference was held in Paris in 1851, to discuss the importation of plague into Europe. In 1892, the International Sanitary Convention was endorsed by several states as a measure to combat common threats, such as yellow fever, cholera, smallpox and typhus. The Pan American Sanitary Bureau – later to become the Pan American Health Organisation (PAHO), and the Regional Office of the WHO – was established in 1902, the Office of International Public Hygiene (OIHP) in 1907, and the Health Organisation of the League of Nations in 1919.

The creation of the United Nations, like its predecessor, the League of Nations, was the result of a determination to 'save succeeding generations from the scourge of war'. The Preamble of its Charter establishes the parameters and values that have guided the gradual development of the principles of Global Health Promotion. It expresses a determination, for example:

- To reaffirm faith in fundamental human rights, in the dignity and worth of the human person, in the equal rights of men and women and of nations large and small.
- To promote social progress and better standards of life in larger freedom.
- To employ international machinery for the promotion of the economic and social advancement of all peoples.
  (United Nations, 1945)

The system has evolved gradually and now encompasses an intricate network and extended community of principal organs, subsidiary bodies, programmes and funds, research and training institutes, functional commissions, regional commissions, related organisations, specialised agencies, and departments and offices. Many of these have the potential to make contributions to health promotion and the amelioration of wealth and health inequalities. These include: the Conference on Trade and Development (UNCTAD), the Environment Programme (UNEP), the Children's Fund (UNICEF), the Development Programme (UNDP), the Population Fund (UNFPA), the World Food Programme (WFP), the Human Settlements Programme (UNHSP or UN-Habitat).

An important milestone in the recent development of the UN system was the adoption of the *Millennium Declaration* by the General Assembly in September 2000. The largest ever gathering of Heads of State reaffirmed their commitment to the UN and its Charter as 'indispensable foundations of a more peaceful, prosperous and just world' (United Nations, 2000: 55/2).

The Assembly acknowledged that 'the central challenge . . . is to ensure that globalization becomes a positive force for all the world's people' and set out 'certain fundamental values to be essential to international relations in the twenty-first century'. These values were identified as freedom, equality, solidarity, tolerance, respect for nature and shared responsibility. A number of Millennium Development Goals were agreed that, it is hoped, will be achieved by 2015:

- Eradicate extreme poverty and hunger.
- Achieve universal primary education.
- Promote gender equality and empower women.
- Remove child mortality.
- Improve maternal health.
- Combat HIV/AIDS, malaria and other diseases.
- Ensure environmental sustainability.
- Develop a global partnership for development.

Another important development associated with the achievement of the Millennium Development Goals is a renewed focus on the role of sport in economic and social development. The right to participate in sport has long been acknowledged. In 1978, for example, the General Conference of the UN Educational, Scientific and Cultural Organization (UNESCO) had adopted the *International Charter of Physical Education and Sport*, many of the its articles echoing values implicit in the original UN Charter:

- Every human being has a fundamental right to access to physical education and sport.
- Physical education and sport programmes must be designed to suit the requirements and personal characteristics of those practising them, as well as the institutional, cultural, socio-economic and climatic changes of each country.
- They must give priority to the requirements of disadvantaged groups in society.
- International co-operation is a prerequisite for the universal and well-balanced promotion of physical education and sport.

Since the adoption of the Charter, many international development agencies have incorporated physical education and sporting activities in their programmes. In an attempt to maximise this effort, a United Nations Task Force was established in 2002 to review the role of sport within the UN system, its members representing those agencies, programmes and funds with experience of using sport in their development work. These included the WHO, the International Labour Office, the Development Programme, the Educational, Scientific and Cultural Organisation, the Environment Programme, the Children's Fund. The aim of the Task Force was:

> To promote the more systematic and coherent use of sport in development and peace activities, particularly at the community level, and to generate greater support for such activities among governments and sport-related organizations.
> (Kluka, 2004)

The Task Force was also asked to establish 'an inventory of existing sport for development programmes', and to 'identify instructive examples' and its final report (United Nations, 2003a), contains many examples in diverse areas: health, education, economic development, social development, the environment, volunteerism, both international and community-based peace initiatives, advocacy, social mobilization and HIV/AIDS. Its conclusions were:

> That sport – from play and physical activity to organized and competitive sport – is a powerful and cost effective way to support development and peace objectives. The many benefits . . . are not only enjoyed by the individual but felt throughout society (provided programmes are) implemented in a way that (are) equity-driven and culturally relevant. Sports programmes must be based upon the 'sport for all' model, ensuring that all groups are given the opportunity to participate, particularly those who gain additional benefits such as women, persons with disabilities and young people.
> (United Nations, 2003a)

Following the publication of the report, the General Assembly decided that 2005 should be proclaimed the International Year of Sport and Physical Education and adopted a further resolution (United Nations, 2003b) *Building a peaceful and better world through sport and the Olympic ideal*. It also adopted a resolution (United Nations, 2003a) *Sport as a means to promote education, health, development and peace*. This invited UN funds and programmes, national governments and sport-related institutions to:

- Promote the role of sport and physical education for all when furthering their development programmes, to advance health awareness, the spirit of achievement and cultural bridging and to entrench collective values.
- Include sport and physical education as a tool to contribute towards achieving agreed development goals, including the United Nations Millennium Declaration.
- Work collectively so that sport and physical education can present opportunities for solidarity and cooperation.
- Recognise the contribution of sport and physical education towards economic and social development and to encourage the building and restoration of sports infrastructure.
- Further promote sport and physical education, on the basis of locally assessed needs, as a tool for health education, social and cultural development.
- Strengthen cooperation and partnership between all actors . . . to ensure complementarities and to make sport and physical education available to everyone.

Whilst the Task Force was deliberating, the first International Conference on Sport and Development, attended by 380 representatives from various United Nations agencies and national and international sports organisations, was held at Magglingen in Switzerland. There are two useful developments from the Conference:

- The Magglingen Declaration which people are still invited to sign to indicate their commitment 'to create a better world through sport' which is 'sustainable, addiction-free, fair and ethical'.
- An international database of Sport & Development projects to facilitate 'the creation of a conscious, active online community to promote sport and development' (http://www.sportanddev.org).

The World Health Organization

In 1945, the United Nations Conference on International Organizations in San Francisco unanimously approved a proposal by Brazil and China to establish an autonomous international health organisation and, on 7th April 1948, the Constitution of the World Health Organization was signed and ratified by its 61 founding Member Sates. There are now 192 members. The WHO Constitution, adopted by its founding member states and accepted by all others joining subsequently, sets out a number of radical propositions or principles, sometimes considered as idealistic and even utopian, that 'are basic to the happiness, harmonious relations and security of all people'. The most noteworthy of these propositions being that 'the enjoyment of the highest attainable standard of health is one of the fundamental rights of every human being without distinction of race, religion, political belief, economic or social condition'. Moreover, the Constitution affirms that health is more than the absence of disease: it is 'a state of complete physical, mental and social well-being.' This definition was further refined in 1999: 'Health is a dynamic state of complete physical, mental, spiritual and social well-being, and not merely the absence of disease or infirmity' (WHO, 1948).

Agreement to the terms of the Constitution commits governments of member states to accepting that they have 'a responsibility for the health of their peoples which can be fulfilled only by the provision of adequate health and social measures', not least because 'the achievement of any State in the promotion and protection of health is of value to all'. The Constitution also affirms an acknowledgement of interdependence and the need for international co-operation:

- Unequal development in different countries in the promotion of health and control of disease, especially communicable disease, is a common danger.
- The health of all peoples is fundamental to the attainment of peace and security and is dependent upon the fullest co-operation of individuals and States.

Like the United Nations, the WHO is an intricate network. It is governed by its Member States meeting at the World Health Assembly (WHA). The main tasks of the Assembly are to approve the WHO programme, and the budget, for the following biennium and to decide major policy questions. An Executive Board, composed of 32 technically qualified health experts designated by member states and elected for three years, advises and facilitates the work of the WHA. The Secretariat is staffed by health professionals, other experts and support staff, working at headquarters in Geneva, and in six regional offices in Africa (Brazzaville), Europe (Copenhagen), South-East Asia (New Delhi), the Americas (Washington), the Eastern Mediterranean (Cairo) the Western Pacific (Manila). The structure at Geneva, and reflected in the regions, is divided into a number of lead units such as Communicable Diseases, Noncommunicable Diseases and Mental Health, Sustainable Development and Healthy Environments, Health, Technology and Pharmaceuticals, Family and Community Health and Evidence, Information and Policy.

The functions of the WHO are far reaching, consisting, in the main, of normative and technical dimensions. The former involves setting, validating and monitoring standards; the latter, includes managing information systems and testing new technologies. The most important responsibilities are to:

- Assist governments, upon request, in strengthening health services.
- Act as the directing and co-ordinating authority on international health work.

To 'assist governments' means that the WHO provides guidance to member states to help them improve their existing health and health care systems. It acknowledges that there are massive differences between systems resulting from past history, demographic trends, levels of social and economic development, availability of natural and human resources, threats from natural and man-made disasters, and much more. It offers examples of best practice, but accepts that local conditions will dictate what actually happens.

To act as 'the directing authority' on international health work' requires the WHO to, for example:

- Establish and maintain administrative and technical services such as epidemiological and statistical services.
- Promote and conduct research in the field of health.
- Promote improved standards of teaching and training in the health, medical and related professions.
- Study and report on administrative and social techniques affecting public health and medical care from preventive and curative points of view, including hospital services and social security.
- Assist in developing an informed public opinion among all peoples on matters of health.

- Establish, and revise as necessary, the international nomenclatures of diseases, of causes of death and of public health practices.
- Develop, establish and promote international standards with respect to food, biological, pharmaceutical and similar products.

To act as 'the co-ordinating authority' on international health work requires the WHO to:

- Establish and maintain effective collaboration with the United Nations, specialised agencies, governmental health administrations, professional groups and such other organisations as may be deemed appropriate.
- Promote, in co-operation with other specialised agencies where necessary, the improvement of nutrition, housing, sanitation, recreation, economic or working conditions and other aspects of environmental hygiene.

Much of the work of the WHO is carried out in partnership with Collaborating Centres, national institutions designated by the Director. There are over 60 of these centres in the UK alone working on programmes such as:

- Health Promoting Schools.
- Health Promotion and Public Health Development.
- Investment for Health and Health Promotion.
- Occupational Health & Safety Research.
- Patients' Rights and Users Views, Citizens' Participation.
- Policy and Practice Development in Women's Health and Gender Mainstreaming.
- Promoting Health in Prisons.
- Training and Research in Communications and Information Technology in Health Promotion and Disease Prevention.
- Training, Evaluation & Research in Diabetes.

The WHO also coordinates the activities of initiatives such as the Global Outbreak Alert and Response Network (GOARN). This is a collaborative effort of organisations and networks such as other UN bodies, technical and scientific institutions of member states, the Red Cross and Red Crescent Societies and international humanitarian nongovernmental organisations (NGOs) to pool human and technical resources to identify and respond to outbreaks of epidemic-prone and emerging disease, and, more recently, responding to the potential intentional release of biological agents.

The principles of Primary Health Care and Health Promotion

The complexity and diversity of the WHO network can be demonstrated by an examination of the processes whereby *Health Promotion* has become a defining feature of much of its work. More than 25 years ago, and almost 20 years after the creation of the WHO, and despite the aspirations of its founders and dramatic advances in disease prevention, eradication and elimination, over a billion people were still living in poverty and half the world's population did not have access to adequate health care. Consequently, the Thirtieth World Health Assembly decided that the main social target of governments and the WHO should be 'the attainment by all citizens of the world by the year 2000 of a level of health that would permit them to lead social and economically productive lives' (30th World Health Assembly. Resolution (1977), 30: 43).

The Thirtieth WHA was followed by a series of national, regional and international meetings on ways to attain the objective of Health for All, culminating in the International Conference organised by the WHO and the United Nations Children's Fund (UNICEF) on Primary Health Care in Alma-Ata, USSR, in 1978. The Conference, attended by representatives from 134 states, formulated a Declaration affirming that:

> The existing gross inequality in the health status of the people, particularly between developed and developing countries as well as within countries is politically, socially and economically unacceptable and is, therefore of common concern to all countries.
> (Declaration of Alma-Ata International Conference, 1978, WHO and UNICEF joint conference)

The solution was to be found in the creation of 'a New International Economic Order' in which Primary Health Care is 'the key' to attaining the target of Health for All. Primary Health Care (PHC) was defined as:

> Essential health care based on practical, scientifically sound and socially acceptable methods and technology made universally accessible to individuals and families in the community through their full participation and at a cost that the community and country can afford to maintain at every stage of their development in the spirit of self-reliance and self-determination.
> (Declaration of Alma-Ata International Conference, 1978)

Moreover, Primary Health Care is regarded as 'the central function and main focus' of a country's health system and as an 'integral part of . . . the social and economic development of the community'. The Declaration affirmed that PHC combines promotive, preventative, curative and rehabilitative elements and includes at least:

- Education concerning prevailing health problems and the methods of preventing and controlling them.
- Promotion of food supply and proper nutrition.
- An adequate safe water, basic sanitation.
- Maternal and child health care, including family planning.
- Immunisation programmes against the major infectious diseases.

- Prevention and control of locally endemic diseases.
- Appropriate treatment of common ailments and injuries.
- Provision of essential drugs.

A fundamental assertion is that health is not simply an issue for the health sector but for 'all related sectors, and aspects of national and community development, in particular agriculture, animal husbandry, food, industry, education, housing, public works, communications and other sectors: and demands the coordinated efforts of all these sectors'.

To summarise, the core principles of PHC health care worked at Alma-Ata are:

- Universal access and coverage on the basis of need.
- Health equity as part of development oriented to social justice.
- Community participation in defining and implementing the health agenda.
- An intersectoral approach to health.
  (World Health Organization, 2003: 104)

The Alma-Ata conference was followed by a series of WHO organised International Conferences on Health Promotion. The first was held in Ottawa, Canada, in 1986; the second in Adelaide, Australia, in 1988; the third in Sundsvall, Sweden, in 1991; the fourth in Jakarta, Indonesia, in July 1997 and the fifth in Mexico City in 2000. A Sixth Conference, the most recent – *Policy and Partnership for Action: Addressing the Determinants of Health* – was held in Bangkok, Thailand, in August 2005.

The *Ottawa Charter* is still widely acknowledged as the seminal health promotion document. It defined health promotion as 'the process of enabling people to increase control over, and to improve their health'. Building on established WHO principles, it re-affirmed that:

> To reach a state of complete physical mental and social well-being, an individual or group must be able to identify and to realise aspirations, to satisfy needs, and to change or cope with the environment. Health is, therefore, seen as a resource to everyday life, not the objective of living. Health is a positive concept emphasizing social and personal resources, as well as physical capacities.
> (WHO, 1948)

Significantly, the Declaration claimed that 'health promotion is not just the responsibility of the health sector, but goes beyond healthy lifestyles to well-being'. An indication of this holistic approach is provided by the identification of the basic 'prerequisites for health' as 'peace, shelter, education, food, income, a stable ecosystem, sustainable resources, social justice and equity'.

The Charter identifies three basic strategies for health promotion: advocacy, enablement and mediation:

- *Advocacy* is required to ensure that political, economic, social, cultural, environmental, behavioural and biological factors are favourable to health by putting health on the agenda of all policy makers in all sectors.
- *Enablement* is the process whereby people and communities are equipped to achieve their fullest health potential and, thereby, reduce health differences and move towards equity in health.
- *Mediation* is required between many interests because health promotion demands coordinated action by many actors: governments, health and other social sectors, nongovernmental and voluntary organisations, local authorities, industry and the media.

The participants at the Conference identified a challenging range of problems and obstacles: harmful products, resource depletion, unhealthy living conditions and environments, bad nutrition, occupational hazards, housing and settlements, and the health gap within and between societies. They argued, however, that Health for All could be achieved through action in five priority areas: building healthy public policy, creating supportive environments for health, strengthening community action for health, developing personal skills and re-orienting health services:

- Building health public policy entails the recognition that standards of health can be affected and influenced by policy formulation and implementation in areas other than health care. It is essential, therefore, that health issues must feature on the agendas of policy makers at all levels and in all sectors. Moreover, policies should combine diverse but complementary approaches and obstacles to health promotion must be identified and removed.
- Creating supportive environments is essential because health is influenced by environmental conditions. Health promotion programmes must seek, therefore, to contribute to the creation of safe and pleasant living and working environments.
- Strengthening community action is essential because health promotion can only be successful if communities are empowered and have ultimate control over their own initiatives and activities. Health professionals must learn to work with the communities they serve, to facilitate the effective utilisation of local human and material resources.
- Developing personal skills through the provision of health information and education will enable people to make healthy choices, to prepare them for the different stages of life and for meeting the demands placed upon them by possible disease and injury. Education needs to be learner-centred and experiential and should take place in the home, at school and at work and in other community settings.
- Reorienting health services is essential because the responsibility for health promotion has to be shared by individuals, health professionals, community groups, health service institutions as well as government departments.

The health sector must move beyond the provision of clinical and curative services, to a health promotion approach that is sensitive to cultural differences. Health workers at all levels must work within an ethical and caring framework to accommodate all patients. The reorientation of services should recognise the importance of integrated service provision based on inter-sectoral collaboration.

The 1988 Adelaide Conference identified a number of key policy priorities: health equity, governmental accountability, women's health, nutrition, the environment and the consequences of alcohol and tobacco usage and consequences. The 1991 Sundsvall Conference focused on the creation of supportive environments to promote and sustain health and its final report made an important contribution to the emerging debate on sustainable development.

The 1997 Jakarta Conference was the first to be held in a developing country and it is perhaps significant that a majority of participants came from the South. It was also the first Conference to engage the private sector in an active way. The conference reviewed the impact of the Ottawa Charter and its final report claimed that 'research and case studies from around the world provide convincing evidence that health promotion is effective' and concluded that:

- Comprehensive approaches to health development are the most effective. Those who use combinations of the five strategies are more effective than single-track approaches.
- Particular settings offer practical opportunities for the implementation of comprehensive strategies. These include mega-cities, islands, cities, municipalities, local communities, markets, schools, the workplace, and health care facilities.
- Participation is essential to sustain efforts. People have to be at the centre of health promotion action and decision-making processes for them to be effective.
- Health learning fosters participation. Access to education and information is essential to achieving effective participation and the empowerment of people and communities.
(WHO, Jakarta Report, 1997: 32)

The Declaration, however, warned of 'emerging threats to health' and asserted that:

New forms of action are needed. The challenge for the coming years will be to unlock the potential for health promotion inherent in many sectors of society, among local communities, and within families. There is a clear need to break through traditional boundaries within government sectors, between governmental and nongovernmental organisations, and between the public and private sectors . . . this requires the creation of new partnerships for health . . .
(WHO, Jakarta Report, 1997: 32)

Five priorities were identified and these were confirmed a year later in the *Resolution on Health Promotion* adopted by the World Health Assembly in May 1998:

- Promoting Social Responsibility for Health.
- Increasing Community Capacity and Empowering the Individual.
- Expanding and Consolidating Partnerships for Health.
- Increasing Investment for Health Development.
- Securing an Infrastructure for Health Promotion.

The next conference – *Health Promotion: Bridging the Equity Gap* – held in Mexico City in June 2000, was designated the Fifth Global Conference. The Conference noted that:

> At the start of the new century, two challenges remain: to better demonstrate and communicate that health promotion polices and practices can make a difference to health and quality of life the health promotion concept and a thread that runs through the previous conferences and their declarations. Our understanding of the root determinants of inequities in health has improved significantly. Yet inequalities in social and economic circumstances continue to increase and erode the conditions for health.
> (WHO, Jakarta Report 4, 1997)

A *Ministerial Statement for the Promotion of Health: From Ideas to Action* signed by Ministers of Health from 87 countries set out a set of required actions:

- To position the promotion of health as a fundamental priority in local, regional, national and international policies and programmes.
- To take the leading role in ensuring the active participation of all sectors and civil society in the implementation of health promoting actions which strengthen and expand partnerships for health.
- To support the preparation of country-wide plans of action for promoting health.
- To establish or strengthen national and international networks which promote health.
- To advocate that UN agencies be accountable for the health impact of their development agenda.

A sixth and most recent conference – *Policy and Partnership for Action: Addressing the Determinants of Health* – was held in Bangkok, Thailand, in August 2005. Its purpose was stated as:

> Almost 20 years (after Ottawa), many things have changed in the world, including the impact of globalization, the internet, greater moves towards private sector involvement in public health, emphasis on a sound evidence-based approach and

cost-effectiveness. The 6th Global Conference has been convened to meet these challenges and to better exploit the opportunities presented for health promotion in the 21st Century.

Consolidation: a Global Strategy for diet, physical activity and health

The Global Strategy (World Health Assembly, 2004: 17–20) adopted by the World Health Assembly on 22 May 2004 represents a synthesis of the principles worked out over the past 25 years and described above. The overall goal of the Strategy is:

> To promote and protect health by guiding the development of an enabling environment for sustainable actions at individual, community, national and global levels that, when taken together, will lead to reduced disease and death rates.
> (WHO, 2004a)

It is argued that any appropriate and effective strategy developed by member states or any other organisation must recognise the complex interactions of personal choices, social norms and economic and environment factors and must be:

- Based on the 'best available scientific research and evidence'.
- Comprehensive in terms of policy and action and should address 'all major causes of non-communicable diseases together'.
- Multi-disciplinary, multi-sectoral and participatory.
- Long-term, based on established principles of health promotion and take 'a life-course perspective'.
- 'Part of broader comprehensive and coordinated public health efforts'.

It is emphasised that 'priority should be given to activities that have a positive impact on the poorest population groups and communities', and that this approach 'will generally require community-based action with strong intervention and oversight'. In addition, it is stressed that due attention must be given to 'local and regional traditions', and be 'culturally appropriate' whilst being 'able to challenge cultural influences and respond to changes over time'.

The strategy recognises that 'bringing about changes in dietary habits and physical activity will require the combined activities of many stakeholders, public and private, over several decades' and argues that 'action is needed at global, regional, national and local levels, with close monitoring and evaluation of their impact'.

Whilst the strategy identifies roles for the WHO and regional bodies in implementing and developing it, it also emphasises that it is national governments that have 'a primary steering and stewardship role in initiating and developing the strategy, ensuring that it is implemented and monitoring its impact in the long term'. Important roles are also identified for international partners, civil society and non-governmental organisations and the private sector.

National governments are exhorted to:

- Build on existing structures and processes that already address aspects of diet, nutrition and physical activity.
- Ensure that national strategies, policies and action plans have broad support [which can only be assured] by effective legislation, appropriate infrastructure, implementation programmes, adequate funding, monitoring and evaluation, and continuing research.
- Invest in surveillance, research and evaluation.
- Build institutional capacity and finance national programmes.
- Consult with stakeholders on policy an provide accurate and balanced information.

Health ministries are acknowledged as having an essential responsibility for coordinating and facilitating the contributions of other ministries and government agencies, especially in ensuring that:

- Food and agricultural policies are consistent with the protection and promotion of public health.
- School policies and programmes should support the adoption of healthy diets and physical activity.

International partners are identified as being of paramount importance and possible actions are suggested:

- Contributing to intersectoral strategies . . . for instance, the promotion of healthy diets in poverty-alleviation programmes.
- Drawing up guidelines for prevention of nutritional deficiencies in order to harmonise future dietary and policy recommendations designed to prevent and control noncommunicable diseases.
- Facilitating the drafting of national guidelines on diet and physical activity, in collaboration with national agencies.
- Cooperating in the development, testing and dissemination of models for community involvement, including local food production, nutrition and physical activity education, and raising of consumer awareness.
- Promoting the inclusion of non-communicable disease prevention and health promotion policies relating to diet and physical activity in development policies and programmes.
- Promoting incentive-based approaches to encourage prevention and control of chronic diseases.

It is suggested that 'public health efforts may be strengthened by the use of international norms and standards' such as those drawn up by the Codex Alimentarius Commission. Areas for further development are identified as:

- Labelling to allow customers to be better informed about the benefits and content of foods.
- Measures to minimise the impact of marketing on unhealthy dietary patterns.
- Fuller information about healthy consumption patterns, including steps to increase the consumption of fruit and vegetables.
- Production and processing standards regarding the nutritional quality and safety of products.

Civil society and nongovernmental organisations are identified as having an important role to play in influencing individual behaviour and the organisations and institutions that are involved in healthy diet and physical activity and they are exhorted to 'play an active role in fostering implementation of the global strategy'. In particular, organisations are urged to:

- Ensure that consumers ask governments to provide support for healthy lifestyles, and the food industry to provide healthy products.
- Lead grass-roots mobilisation and advocate that healthy diets and physical activity should be placed on the public agenda.
- Support the wide dissemination of information on prevention of non-communicable diseases.
- Form networks and action groups.
- Organise campaigns and events that will stimulate action.
- Emphasise the role of governments in promoting public health.
- Monitor progress in achieving objectives.
- Contribute to putting knowledge and evidence into practice.

The private sector is identified as 'a significant player' with the food industry, retailers, catering companies, sporting-goods manufacturers, advertising and recreation businesses, insurance and banking groups, pharmaceutical companies and the media having important roles as 'responsible employers and advocates for healthy lifestyles'. Specific recommendations for the food industry and sports-goods manufacturers include:

- Promote healthy diets and physical activity in accordance with national guidelines and international standards and the overall aims of the global strategy.
- Limit the levels of saturated fats, trans-fatty acids, free sugars in existing products.
- Continue introducing new products with better nutritional value.
- Provide customers with adequate and understandable product and nutritional information.
- Practice responsible marketing that supports the strategy, particularly with regard to the promotion and marketing of foods in saturated fats, trans-fatty acids, free sugars, or salt, especially for children.

- Issue simple, clear and consistent food labels and evidence-based health claims that will help consumers to make informed and healthy choices with respect to the nutritional value of foods.
- Provide information on food composition to national authorities.
- Assist in developing and implementing physical activity programmes.

Global Health Promotion in practice

It is difficult to do justice to the range of health promotion activities inspired by the work of the World Health Organization, the regional organisations and the collaborative centres in what is, perhaps, best described as *A Very Short Introduction to Global Health Promotion*. However, two particular dimensions are useful: time (the global health calendar) and space (settings of health promotion).

The calendars of health promotion programmes throughout the world are largely determined by World Health Days. These have been held on the anniversary of the founding of WHO since 1950, the objective of each being to raise global awareness of a specific health issue and to launch a longer-term action programme or give a further boost to an existing programme. Most of these have had a specific health promotion theme and some have become annual events. One of the best examples is World No Tobacco Day. This was first held in 1987 and, subsequently, the WHA resolved to hold a similar event on May 31st every year (World Health Assembly 40). Chosen themes have been: tobacco free film, tobacco free fashion; tobacco free sports; second-hand smoke kills; tobacco kills, don't be duped; leave the pack behind; growing up without tobacco; united for a tobacco free world; sport and art without tobacco, play it tobacco free; tobacco costs more than you think; media and tobacco, get the message across; health services: our windows to a tobacco free world; tobacco free workplaces, safer and healthier; public places and transport, better be tobacco free, childhood and youth without tobacco: growing up without tobacco. In 2004 events focused on *Tobacco and Poverty*. Two important global initiatives have been developed during this time. The first, the Tobacco Free Initiative (TFI) established in 1998 'to coordinate an improved global strategic response to tobacco as an important public health issue' by monitoring developments in member states. The second, the Framework Convention on Tobacco Control adopted by the WHA in 2003.

Other good examples that demonstrate the collaborative nature of Global Health Promotion are Diabetes Day and Heart Day and Move for Health Day. World Diabetes Day has been held since 1991 and is co-ordinated by the International Diabetes Federation (IDF). Since 2001, it has focused on specific diabetes complications: cardiovascular disease, diabetes-related eye complications, diabetes and kidney disease. The theme for 2004 was *Fight Obesity* – Prevent Diabetes. World Heart Day is sponsored by the WHO and UNESCO and co-ordinated by the World Heart Foundation. This has been held on 24th September since 2000 and each year focuses on a specific theme. In 2004, this was *Children, Adolescents and Heart Disease* and the planned theme for 2005 is *Obesity*. Move for Health Day was the theme for WHD 2002 and subsequently the World Health Assembly (World Health Assembly 57: 16) not only urged Member States to celebrate a 'Move for Health Day' each year but to encourage and facilitate the development of a larger 'Move for Health Initiative'.

'Setting' is another fundamental concept health promotion theory and practice. The Jakarta Declaration had concluded that particular 'settings' offer practical opportunities for the implementation of comprehensive health promotion strategies. These range from mega-cities to local communities. Starting as a health promotion demonstration project in the European Region of WHO in 1986, Healthy Cities has developed into a global movement alongside Healthy Villages, Healthy Municipalities and Healthy Islands and Health Promoting Schools, Health Promoting Hospitals, Healthy Marketplaces and Health Promoting Workplaces. The general approach has been described as combining the 'art' and 'science' dimensions of public health.

> Linking ideas, visions, political commitment and social entrepreneurship to the management of resources, methods for infrastructure development, and the establishment procedures to respond to community needs. Intersectoral work is an integral part of the movement.
> (WHO, Jakarta Report 4, 1997)

Importantly, many of these initiatives have spawned global, regional and national networks such as the Healthy Cities network. Another significant spatial perspective is provided the Mega-Country Health Promotion Network that has the goal of mobilising the world's most populated countries to promote health in a concerted and collaborative way. Its members, representing rich and poor economies, are those countries with over 100 million people – Bangladesh, Brazil, China, India, Indonesia, Japan, Nigeria, Pakistan, Russian Federation, and United States of America – that make up approximately 60 per cent of the world's population.

Reflections

The WHO rightly claims that the Global Strategy, based as it is on the cumulative efforts of countless people in hospitals, clinics, laboratories, in field stations and at innumerable gatherings around the world, drafting and re-drafting thousands of resolutions, research reports, predictions, declarations and calls for action, provides a powerful tool for future action. It is hoped that this chapter has provided a flavour of what the process has entailed. Perhaps, the process started in smoked-filled rooms but culminated in smoke-free conference halls!

It is important to realise that the strategy cannot be imposed upon sovereign states but can only be taken as a model for action. There are as many national health systems as there are signatories to the resolution and each is at a different stage of development. Problems vary, as do resources available. A recent survey concluded that 'public health stakeholders show varying degrees of awareness concerning the rising burden of chronic disease' with:

- International public health agencies still largely preoccupied by infectious diseases and maternal-child health issues.
- International donors and development banks directing most of their funding towards infectious diseases and maternal-child health.
- Health ministries, although recognising the problem, having limited capacity.
- Governments generally failing to recognise the impact of chronic disease on economic development.
  (WHO, 2004b: 7)

It is also interesting to reflect that participation in the process has had a differential impact on the evolution of health policies and systems in developed countries. Canada, the host country of the first International Conference, can, in many ways, be considered an early leader in the field. In 1974, the *Lalonde Report* (Lalonde, 1974) argued for a shift in emphasis from the treatment of illness to the prevention of illness through the promotion of health, especially by focusing on issues such as diet and exercise. On the other hand, despite the findings of the *Black Report* of 1984 (Townsend and Davison, 1982) which pointed to social deprivation as a major determinant of poor health status, it was not until 1992 that the UK government published its *Health of the Nation* White Paper (Department of Health, 1992) setting out targets for reductions in death rates from non-communicable disease. It was not until six years later that the deliberations of the Acheson Inquiry (Department of Health, 1992) finally placed the aim of a reduction in health inequalities on the policy agenda.

Conclusion

Unfortunately, it has not been possible to consider all the twists and turns of development theory and practice over the period reviewed, or to examine debates about the ethics and morality of health politics. No direct reference has been made to other influential players such as the World Bank Group or the International Monetary Fund who have a massive influence on the direction of development throughout the world or to the increasing impact of non-government organisations (NGOs). There are many actors, often with conflicting interests, involved in the processes of negotiation and bargaining in the formulation, development and implementation of any policy, and health is no exception. Decisions about what goes on the agenda and who is invited to the meeting are, more often than not, contested. Power is differentiated and there are often conflicts in the interplay of global, regional, national and local politics and clashes between the aims and policy functions of international actors. Often, rhetoric does not reflect reality.

It must also be remembered that the WHO is, essentially, a bureaucracy – indeed, a mega-bureaucracy – and all bureaucracies are prone to problems associated with empire-building, parochialism and paternalism and, of course, being strangled by red tape. For all its faults, however, it is a necessary, even essential, component of the international system, particularly – bearing in mind the Ottawa message – for its role as advocate, enabler and mediator. It is obvious that the immediate problems are enormous: a global health workforce crisis, inadequate information, lack of financial resources, and much more. The potential problems are even more staggering: the effects of global warming, international terrorism, emerging diseases, and much, much more. Hopefully, the WHO as an integral part of the UN system will continue to provide an effective forum to focus attention on pressing international concerns and that new initiatives such as the *Commission on Social Determinants of Health* launched in 2005 will prove adequate to the task ahead.

References

Declaration of Alma-Ata International Conference on Primary Health Care (1978) Alma-Ata, USSR, 6–12 September.

Department of Health (1992) *The Health of the Nation*. London: Stationery Office.

Kluka, D. A. (2004) International year for sport and physical exercise: what's it all about? *JOPERD The Journal of Physical Exercise, Recreation and Dance*, 75.

Lalonde, M. (1974) *A New Perspective on the Health of Canadians*. Ottawa, Ontario, Canada: Minister of Supply and Services.

Townsend, P. and Davidson, N. (1982) *Inequalities in Health: The Black Report*. London: Pelican.

United Nations (1945) *The United Nations charter*. (http://www.un.org/aboutun/charter/)

United Nations (2000) *Millenium Declaration*. New York: UN, Dept. of Public Information.

United Nations (2002) *Resolution adopted by the General Assembly (55/2) United Nations Millennium Declaration*. (http://www.un.org/millennium/declaration/ares552e.htm)

United Nations (2003a) *Resolution adopted by the General Assembly (58/6) Building a Peaceful and Better World through Sport and the Olympic Ideal*. United Nations General Assembly. (http://multimedia.olympic.org/pdf/en_seport_759.pdf)

United Nations (2003b) Resolution adopted by the General Assembly (58/5) *Sport as a Means to Promote Education, Health, Development and Peace*. (http://www.who.int/hpr/physactiv/docs/pa_un_resolution_en.pdf)

World Health Assembly (1977) *Resolution adopted by the General Assembly* (30/43). WHO: Geneva.

World Health Assembly (1987) (40/43) Geneva.

World Health Assembly (2005) *Move For Health: Supportive Environments.* Geneva 25 May.

World Health Organization (WHO) (1948) *WHO Constitution.* (http://www.who.int/rarebooks/official_records/constitution.pdf)

WHO (1997) *The Jakarta Declaration on Health Promotion into the 21st Century.* Geneva: WHO.

WHO (1997a) *World health report 1997, Conquering Suffering, Enriching Humanity.* (http://www.who.int/whr/1997/en/)

WHO (2003) *The World Health Report 2003 – Shaping the Future.* Geneva: World Health Organization. Available: http://www.who.int/whr/2003/en/index.html.

WHO (2004a) *A Global Strategy for Diet, Physical Activity and Health* (http://www.who.int/gb/ebwha/pdf_files/WHA57/A57_R17-en.pdf)

WHO (2004b) NCD regional Advisers Meeting on Chronic Diseases: Meeting Report, Mexico City, 5–9 June 2000 (http://www.who.int/hpr/NPH/docs/mxconf_report_en.pdf)

CHAPTER 19

Australian Government Policy on Sport and Health Promotion: A Look at '*Active Australia*'

Trent D. Brown

Introduction

Sport is an often-used term, which has been used interchangeably with terms such as physical activity, fitness, exercise, recreation and rehabilitation. As previously discussed by Pawlaczek (see Chapter 2). The relationship between sport and health promotion/education has not been empirically demonstrated. However, governments including those in Australia, Canada and Great Britain have often promoted the virtue of sports participation to the public (Commonwealth Department of Health and Family Services (DHFS), 1998; Department of Canadian Heritage, 2002; Department of Communications Information Technology and the Arts (DCITA), 2001; Department of Culture Media and Sport and Strategy Unit (DCMS), 2002). Such contributions include the development of health, fitness and wellbeing, the development of personal and social responsibility, economic development and prosperity, entertainment and education. Several authors however, have questioned the use of sport as the sole vehicle for the promotion of health and lifelong physical activity participation, in a wide variety of programmes, for example, school physical education and extra-curricular activities to name a few (Bass and Cale, 1999; Cale, 2000; Fairclough et al., 2002; Green, 2002, 2004; Pawlaczek and Brown, 2004).

While the primary audiences of this text are students of sports science, the term 'sport' to many non-participants is an exclusive term. Martin Lee (2004) in his Fellows' Lecture to the Physical Education Association United Kingdom Conference, highlighted this point and proposed 5 functions of sport: 1) sport promotes elitism and pursuit of excellence, 2) sport fosters nationalism, 3) sport is entertainment, 4) sport is used as talent identification, 5) sport is an educational forum. While he suggests that sport has a place within the broader educational curricula, it is important to highlight how sport is defined within the educational context, and whether sport is helping or hindering efforts to make people active. In the state of Victoria, a government senate committee investigated physical and sport education within government schools. Sport was defined as 'vigorous physical activity which involves forms of competition either against oneself or another person/team' (The Directorate of School Education, 1993). This definition demonstrates that sport may be considered an exclusive activity, as participation in sport requires some initial degree of fitness level, and for some, this precludes many people from participating. Furthermore, epidemiological evidence has demonstrated that adults prefer physical activity within light to moderate physical activity intensities (United States Department of Health and Human Services (USDHHS), 1996). It is important therefore, that texts such as this educate our future health/sport/physical activity professionals about the differences and similarities which exist between terms such as sport, physical activity and health, to provide meaningful programmes that encourage, not discourage people from taking part in physical activity.

Over the past decade, the Australian government has published several policy documents, all under the auspices of the Active Australia campaign, which initially began as a national 'sports' policy, before the inclusion of the health sector developed it into a national public health document. Given the nature of the working relationships between Great Britain and Australia, it is timely that students of sports science/health promotion examine the Australian government's 'health' and 'sports' policies as there is great synonymy between our cultures in this area.

The following section will highlight government policy in relation to sport, with special reference to the *Active Australian* policy and the use of sport as a vehicle for promotion of lifelong physical activity, within an Active School concept. Which brings us back to the question 'why do governments continue to promote the virtues of sport as a method for increasing the physical activity levels of their people?'

Government policy

Government policy on health promotion and sport has only been a recent phenomenon. The publication in 1996 of the Surgeon General's Report (USDHHS, 1996) was the first meaningful government report promoting the virtues of physical activity and sport participation and its relationship morbidity, mortality and health. More recently, both the Australian and United Kingdom governments have published similar documents highlighting the current poor activity status of their citizens, however they have a slightly different theme associated with them. Both countries appear to have a strong focus on excellence in athletes, as opposed to mass participation in physical activity for all.

The British government's position is very clear: 'To be the most active and the most successful sporting nation in the world' (Sport England, 2004: 3). The rhetoric is very similar in Australia. *Backing Australia's Sporting Ability – A More Active Australia*, outlines a twofold policy objective – to assist our best athletes to reach new peaks of excellence, and to increase the pool of talent from which our future world champions will emerge (DCITA, 2004). However, the published document *Backing Australia's Sporting Ability – A More Active Australia* states clearly that the aim of the policy is at achieving four key goals, including: continued achievement in high performance sport and greater grass roots participation in sport for all ages, excellence in sport management and fighting drugs in sport. The disparity between what is published in hardcopy, and that promoted by the government, is important to note as distinct differences exist between the primary goals of the same document.

Sports policy and Active Australia

It could be argued that Australia's first true 'sports' policy was due in part to poor Olympic performances at the 1976 Summer Olympics in Montreal, Canada. The Australian Olympic team managed to bring home no gold medals, 1 silver medal and 4 bronze. While this has commonly been believed to be the catalyst for the formation of The Australian Sports Institute (now known as the Australian Institute of Sport (AIS)), the process of the setting up of this began three years prior to these poor performances (Australian Sports Commission (ASC), 2002).

The government's sport policy and its mission for the AIS was clear, to halt our ailing sporting reputation via the development of elite sport in Australia, by providing facilities and funding to sporting organisations and potential elite athletes (ASC, 2002). While this appears to be the mission of Australia's initial sports policy, the study group responsible for the formation of the AIS recommended the establishment of the institute 'as a step towards meeting the needs of sport in Australia, with respect to both mass participation and excellence' (Australian Department of Tourism and Recreation, 1975: 14).

Thirty recommendations were put forward by the study group examining the formation of the Institute only two wholly focused on the needs of the public and their participation in activity or more formally, sport. Recommendations 23 and 26 suggested that the Institute promoted participation in leisure sports, and to promote community fitness testing, exercise prescription and advice on health improvement both in associations with government departments and concerned organisations. Furthermore, the study group defined quite clearly that among one of the functions of the institute was to promote community fitness to the public. However, even in the early stage of development of the AIS, it is apparent that mass sport/physical activity participation, involvement of the community in participation was not really considered as most of the these documents were wholly aimed at 'elite' sport.

It is apparent that while the government acknowledges that mass participation of its population in physical activity has many benefits, it does not appear to be as important as athlete excellence at World Championships, Commonwealth or Olympic Games. Two apparent factors appear to conspire to this: organisational structure and budget. The current organisational structure of the ASC as set up by the Australian government is responsible for two key strategic areas:

- The AIS, responsible for the development of elite sporting excellence.
- The Sport Development Group (SDG). The aim of this initiative is to increase the number of Australians involved in sport and physical activity in the long term, primarily through the *Active Australia* initiative.

The structure of the ASC is responsible for both elite and non-elite sport participation. While the reliance on sport as the primary vehicle for increased physical activity participation among its non-elite majority may be the ASC's goal, it also appears that both the goals of the AIS and the SDG are of equal importance.

The government required outcomes for the ASC are: 1) an effective national sports system that offers improved participation in sports activities by Australians and 2) to secure excellence in sports performance by Australians. Total appropriations for the commission in the 2003–2004 budget is $122.472 million. While this budget appears to be more than adequate for two such stated goals, further investigation reveals that the budget is inadequate for the majority of the population. Improved participation in sports activities by all Australians receives 22 per cent of the total budget or $27.265 million, elite sport receives 78 per cent or $95.207 million. In other words, on a per capita basis, the government spends $1.36 per person (approximate population = 20 million) on physical activity promotion through sport, whereas the government spends $136010 per athlete (currently 700 athletes on scholarship) at the Australian Institute of Sport. The topic of funding and budget has received publicity in Australian scientific literature. Mitton et al. (2004) questioned the Australian government's spending on elite sport. On a per capita basis Australia spends 7 times as much on its Sydney Olympic Games team than did Canada. The author's suggest that neither country is correct or incorrect about their funding choices, but simply highlight the need for more discussion about such an issue. The debate is continuing with several letters to the editor (Orchard and Finch, 2004) or editorial comment (Orchard, 2004) discussing such issues.

What is *Active Australia?*

The *Active Australia* concept was devised by the ASC during 1996, and was developed to enable promotion of physical activity via collaborative efforts with outside organisations (Bauman et al., 2002). The *Active Australia* vision aims to:

1. Increase and enhance lifelong participation.
2. Realise the social, health and economic benefits of participation.
3. Develop infrastructure, products and services to ensure quality participation. (Australian Government Department of Health and Family Services, 1998)

Active Australia was developed after a submission was made by the ASC to the then Standing Committee on Recreation and Sport. The *Developing an Active Australia – A Framework for Action for Physical Activity and Health* (Australian Government Department of Health and Family Services, 1998) was launched in 1996 by the then Minister for Health and Family Services, Dr Michael Wooldridge MP and the then Minister for Sport, Territories and Local Government, the Hon. Warwick Smith MP. The framework for the *Active Australia* policy was initially broadened from its narrow focus on sport to include community recreation, outdoor recreation and fitness. With the later inclusion of the health sector within this framework from the then DHFS, *Active Australia* was extended to include all forms of physical activity, both organised and unorganised.

Four key strategies underpin the *Active Australia* policy. These key strategies include:

1. Education.
2. Environment.
3. Infrastructure.
4. Monitoring/evidence.[1]

Briefly, education was considered as the first key strategy in the government's *Active Australia* policy. It was to increase people's awareness and understanding of the benefits of regular physical activity participation. One of the first processes was to develop the National Physical Activity Guidelines for All Australians, see Figure 19.1 (Department of Health and Aged Care (DHAC), 1999).

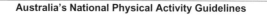

> **Australia's National Physical Activity Guidelines**
>
> 1. Think of movement as an opportunity, not an inconvenience.
>
> 2. Be active every day in as many ways as you can.
>
> 3. Put together at least 30 minutes of moderate intensity physical activity on most, if not all days of the week.
>
> 4. If you can, also enjoy some regular vigorous exercise for extra health and fitness benefits (DHAC, 1999).

Figure 19.1 Australia's National Physical Activity Guidelines

Other educational campaigns have included the *Active Australia* Day and the national Walk to Work Day. The second factor, environment, was to create opportunities for increasing both structured and incidental physical activity through appropriate planning of the physical environment. Infrastructure encompasses links with relevant sectors such as transport and the environment, to ensure a coordinated approach is used by all sectors, professional development of health professionals and development of complementary strategies. Finally, monitoring was included as a key strategy to monitor physical activity prevalence, monitor environmental and policy approaches and to coordinate data collected. The approaches developed in this first *Active Australia* policy were world leading, and such approaches are continuing to receive great attention in the scientific literature. For further reviews on a socio-ecological approach to physical activity promotion, the reader is advised to refer to the following articles (Jago and Baranowski, 2004; King et al., 2002; Sallis et al., 1998; Wattchow and O'Connor, 2003; Wechsler et al., 2000).

However the Australian government decided that this was not the best avenue to follow for the future, despite all the evidence to the contrary and decided that funding physical activity participation, as it relates to health, was unimportant. The new funding arrangements changed the direction of the *Active Australia* campaign to focus on sport only, therefore limiting the future opportunities with the health sector.

A change of direction

In 2001, the Australian government published the document *Backing Australia's sporting ability – A More Active Australia*, which moved the focus from physical activity participation to that of sports participation. Within the foreword of this 'new' policy it clearly states that the objective is to 1) assist our best athletes to continue to reach new peaks of excellence, and 2) to increase the pool of talent from which world champions will emerge. Yet the government department website from which the report was released, DCITA states that the new policy is 'one for all Australians, one to back our athletes and to encourage greater participation in sport, especially young people' (DCITA, 2004). Even within the government material there is great ambiguity about what are the true objectives of the policy, elite sport or mass participation in sport?

The four premises of the *Backing Australia's sporting ability – A More Active Australia* are:

1. Continued achievement in high performance sport.
2. Greater grass roots participation in sport for all ages.
3. Excellence in sports management.
4. Continuing to step up the fight against drugs in sport.

On closer inspection of the documentation, three of the four goals relate to excellence in elite sport participation. One could argue that the shift towards greater grass roots participation for all ages is an approach akin to specific talent identification programmes. In the report in the preamble to the more *Active Australia* approach it is quite clear that by increasing grass roots participation, it will enable Australia to continue its sporting prowess in the future. However, this position is a rather narrow minded view. There is little evidence that international success will develop into long-term participation levels for the majority of the population. For example, Finland is clearly the world leader in terms of mass participation in physical activity and recreation, approximately 70 per cent of the population report partaking in activity at least once a week, however, on the UK sporting index scale Finland ranks 20 in the world. Yet countries such as the United States, the United Kingdom and Australia to a degree, are ranked 1, 3 and 2 (UK sporting index scale[2]), yet have participation levels below 50 per cent of the population. Clearly this demonstrates that by increasing grass roots participation does not guarantee sporting success (DCMS, 2002).

One part of the action plan for greater grass roots participation in sport was to ensure that people regardless of where they live (rural/regional and metropolitan), culture, gender, race, capability, or age have the opportunity to participate in sport and physical activity (DCITA, 2001). One document which does provide some forward thinking of how to improve sport and physical activity is the UK document *Game Plan* (DCMS, 2002). It states that sport and physical activity is delivered through four distinct sectors, each of which the government liaises to facilitate physical activity participation. These four sectors include: local government, voluntary organisations, the private sector and finally the education sector (DCMS, 2002). Perhaps the Australian government realised it was being left behind by some future thinking strategies of other governments. There were no examples or intervention strategies with any of the abovementioned groups provided within the original *Backing Australia's Sporting Ability* document when it was originally published. In response to other governments' policies with relation to sport and physical activity during 2004 they announced a new government policy known as the *Building a Healthy Active Australia* aimed in part to tackling the obesity and physical inactivity problem of our children and youth through sports participation, thus linking to the previous Australian government policy on sport.

Building a Healthy, Active Australia – the role of sport within school and physical education

On 29 June 2004 the Australian government announced its latest government policy relating to sport. The document, *Building a Healthy Active Australia* has as its focus the promotion of lifelong participation in sport using the school as a centre point. While this initiative appears to be a promising step forward, the use of the school and physical education as a means of promoting physical activity is not new. At the Commonwealth International Sport Conference prior to the Manchester Games, 2002, Professor Neil Armstrong from the Children's Health and Exercise Research Centre, Exeter University presented a paper on the Active school model and physical education. He cited much of Dr. Lorraine Cale's (1997; 2000) work, who has published extensively on the concept of the broader health-promoting schools concept, which developed into a framework known as an Active school. The Active School (Cale, 1997) has policy, ethos, the environment, the curriculum, the informal curriculum, community links and care and support as variables within the Active School framework. The *Building a Healthy Active Australia* policy statement builds on similar sentiment to that constructed by Cale. The following paragraph will further elucidate this most recent Australian government policy.

Building a Healthy, Active Australia is a $116 million package over four years designed to overcome the low levels of physical activity and poor diets of Australian children. The package will provide a new national framework underpinned by four primary areas:

1. Active After-School communities (physical activity).
2. Active school curriculum (physical activity).
3. Healthy school communities (nutrition).
4. Information for Australian families (physical activity and nutrition).

While the current details of the policy are unknown at this moment, a cautious approach should be used so as not to replicate research/programmes that have failed to increase physical activity or to fully engage students in physical activity participation.

Active After-School communities

The Active-After School communities programme will be supported by $90 million over four years. Its goal is simply to provide Australian families with a convenient and practical opportunity to support healthy development of children aged 5 through to 12 years. The programme will employ over 170 physical activity coordinators who will be responsible for the liaison between the school and local community sporting organisations facilitated through national sporting organisations (Department of Health and Ageing, 2004).

One concern for the provision of active after school programmes is that those children who are less likely to be active for example, girls and the low-skilled are likely to be further alienated from participation due to the dominant nature of competitive team games within this type of programme. Yet the current Australian government policy is focused on sport and team games.

Cale's (2000) research has demonstrated that a lack of opportunities exist for students to participate in popular lifetime activities after school, for example circuit training, aerobics or weight training. With the current government provision on highlighting the benefits of participation in sport and liaison with national sporting bodies including Cricket Australia, Netball Australia and the Australian Football League, the government may in fact exacerbate the physical inactivity problem by denying those students, who most need it, the opportunity to develop lifelong recreation skills.

During an investigation of the contribution of physical education curriculum to lifelong physical activity participation, Fairclough et al. (2002) found that more lifetime activities were offered outside of the school curriculum compared with those inside. At first glance this seems to be appropriate; however the authors concluded that opportunities do not always translate into participation. While opportunities are offered and are available, these are more likely to be chosen and taken up by the gifted minority of students who are already skilled, physically active and physically fit (Office of Her Majesty's Chief Inspector of Schools in Wales, 1995).

McManus and Armstrong (1996) have also questioned whether programmes, policies and curriculums that have sport and competitive team games have been designed in an androcentric manner. While they were referring to the National Curriculum Physical Education document, such thoughts need to taken into consideration, especially when the Australian government policy is aimed at promoting sporting prowess. The recent Middle School Physical Activity and Nutrition (M-SPAN) Trial conducted by researchers at San Diego State University found that while boys physical activity increases during the intervention, girls' activity levels did not rise significantly. The researchers concluded this may have been due to the curriculum used in the intervention having a focus on team games and that in the future additional intervention strategies should include more activities preferred by girls, single-sex activities and different motivational and instructional strategies for girls (McKenzie et al., 2004). Harris and Penney (2000) has reaffirmed findings from previous studies about the distinct differences which exist between the content and delivery of programmes for boys and girls, and this would be appear to be no different here in Australia. For further information on gender and physical education, refer to the textbook by Penney (2002).

Active school curriculum

The government policy of setting two hours of physical activity per week within primary and junior high schools may seem to be a positive move forward, however it points to a question about how will this time be effectively used? Research has shown (Brown, 2003) that inactivity levels during physical education classes may be as high as 70 per cent and that time spent teaching about health and physical activity concepts during practical PE are non-existent. This phenomenon is not unique to Australia. Studies conducted in the UK have found similar results (Babiarz et al., 1998; Curtner-Smith et al., 1995a; Curtner-Smith et al., 1996; Curtner-Smith et al., 1995b). For example, if we were to extrapolate from the Brown study using the 120 minutes the government is proposing, only 36 minutes of activity will occur per week, much less than the recommended levels of physical activity for children and youth across the whole week (Cavill et al., 2001). While some have argued that moderate to vigorous physical activity (MVPA) during physical education should not be the primary consideration (Armstrong, 2002) it is nonetheless considered to be a primary goal and outcome of school physical education (Centers for Disease Control and Prevention, 1997; USDHHS, 2000).

The above problem may also be confounded by what is taught during school physical education. Sport and competitive team games continue to dominate the secondary school physical education curriculum (Fairclough and Stratton, 1997; Fairclough et al., 2002). While many children and adolescents enjoy team sport, sport within PE tends to focus on the 'able minority' (Penney and Harris, 1997) contrary to the goals of promotion of lifelong physical activity participation. Research has demonstrated that the competitive ethos is unacceptable to low-exercising boys, and both low- and high-exercising girls suggests that sport within PE is not meeting the needs of the majority of participants. In the future physical education teachers must expose youngsters to a balanced curriculum which integrates a range of cooperative, competitive, individual, partner and team activities.

While many physical education teachers may agree with Armstrong's (2002) statement that physical education curricula is the fulcrum of physical activity promotion within the school the truth is that teachers view sport and team games as the primary focus of school physical education (Green, 2000; Penney and Evans, 1999). This may be further exaggerated by the fact that Harris (1994) found that a majority of physical education teachers had not attended any professional development which related to physical activity promotion. More recent studies have demonstrated that physical education teachers do not possess the requisite content knowledge related to physical activity and fitness knowledge concepts (Brown, 2003). These results have important implications for the current government policy. Should the current programme employ ex-physical education teachers or other fitness professionals, adequate professional training would be a necessity that highlights all these issues discussed.

Healthy school communities

The healthy school communities part of the *Building a Healthy Active Australia* has been provided with $15 million to help schools to put into practice messages about healthy eating. This part of the package will not implement any direct intervention; rather ask schools to apply for a maximum of $1500 per school to fund activities to develop healthy eating patterns. The may include: developing healthy school canteens, cooking classes, healthy lunch-boxes, breakfast classes or awards for students.

Information for Australian families

The government has said that it will provide $11 million to raise issues related to physical inactivity and healthy eating, to provide practical pointers for parents and give children information on how to make the correct choices to be active.

Providing information (knowledge) to children about their physical activity behaviour is an equivocal research strategy. Determinant or correlate research provides conflicting results for both children 5–12 years and for youth aged 13–18 years of age (Sallis et al., 2000). Children require concrete reasons about why they should participate in physical activity, and are not able to conceptualise the notion of activity as it relates to health (Fox, 1991). Therefore this type of policy may be inappropriate if it is primarily targeted at children. However some studies have found that implementing a cognitive intervention with a focus on lifestyle fitness and wellness during middle school physical education may increase health knowledge and physical activity behaviour of participants (Dale and Corbin, 2000; Dale et al., 1998).

While simply providing information to children or adolescents has not been proven one way or the other in changing physical activity behaviour, research in the area of parental support of children's physical activity is evident. In a review of social and cultural factors (parental influences) on children's physical activity levels, the most commonly studied variable was parental physical activity level and this was found to have an indeterminate relationship with children's physical activity level. However, for adolescents measures of parent support, direct help from parents and support from 'significant' others were all consistently related to adolescent physical activity level (Sallis et al., 2000).

Conclusion

This chapter has presented an in depth analysis of the current Australian government sport policy, *Active Australia*. The government has continued to move its policy focus from the original physical activity and recreation for all the population to a sporting and elite focus. More recently an approach which involves schools using a socio-ecological concept has been developed to tackle problems associated with children's overweightness/obesity and physical inactivity. The chapter has meant to be critically reflective piece aimed at encouraging debate at all levels, especially to students of 'sports science'.

There are many positives that I can see in the future. While I do not believe the government was correct in moving away from their original socio-ecological position to that of a sporting focus, it is my belief that the government will move back towards this broader approach, if successful outcomes are achieved with the *Building a Healthy, Active Australia* approach. I believe the framework the government has chosen using an approach with schools is exciting and should be recognised as such. My concern lies with the way in which sport has continued to be place on the agenda, therefore promoting those already skilled at the expense at those who are less likely to benefit from the development of such a programme.

I am truly excited about the future in physical activity promotion, for children, adolescents and adults. Professionals need to understand that for quality promotion of physical activity to occur, we need to reflect critically on where we have been, recognise our mistakes and understand that this is a continual process that professionals must undertake to be truly effective.

Notes

1 Monitoring was changed to evidence in the *Developing an Active Australia: A work plan for 2000 to 2003*.
2 The UK sporting index is calculated on medal success or top 3 placings (male and female) in 60 sports – page 29 of Game Plan document (DCMS, 2002).

References

Armstrong, N. (2002) *Promoting Physical Activity and Health in Youth: the Active School and Physical Education*. Paper presented at the 12th Commonwealth International Sport Conference, Manchester, UK.

Australian Department of Tourism and Recreation (1975) *Report of the Australian Sports Institute Study Group*. Canberra: Australian Government Publishing Service.

Australian Government Department of Health and Family Services (1998) *Developing an Active Australia: A framework for action for physical activity and health*, Australian Government Publishing Service, Canberra, 1–18.

Australian Sports Commission (2002) *Excellence: the Australian Institute of Sport*. Canberra: Australian Sports Commission.

Babiarz, M., Curtner-Smith, M. D. and Lacon, S. A. (1998) Influence of National Curriculum Physical Education on the Teaching of Health-Related Exercise: A Case study in an Urban setting, *Journal of Sport Pedagogy*, 4(1), 1–18.

Bass, D. and Cale, L. (1999) Promoting Physical Activity Through the Extra-Curricular Programme, *European Journal of Physical Education*, 4, 45–64.

Bauman, A., Bellew, B., Vita, P., Brown, W. and Owen, N. (2002) *Getting Australia Active: towards better practice for the promotion of physical activity*. Melbourne, VIC: National Public Health Partnership.

Brown, T. D. (2003) *The Development, Validation and Evaluation of the Physical Activity and Fitness Teacher Questionnaire (PAFTQ)*. Unpublished Doctoral Dissertation, RMIT University, Melbourne.

Cale, L. (1997) Promoting Physical Activity through the Active School, *British Journal of Physical Education*, 28(1), 19–21.

Cale, L. (2000) Physical Activity Promotion in Secondary Schools, *European Physical Education Review*, 6(1), 71–90.

Cavill, N., Biddle, S. and Sallis, J. F. (2001) Health Enhancing Physical Activity for Young People: Statement of the United Kingdom Expert Consensus Conference, *Pediatric Exercise Science*, 13(1), 12–25.

Centers for Disease Control and Prevention (1997) Guidelines for School and Community Programs to Promote Lifelong Physical Activity Among Young People, *Morbidity and Mortality Weekly Report*, 46(RR-6), 1–35.

Commonwealth Department of Health and Family Services (1998) *Developing an Active Australia: A Framework for Action for Physical Activity and Health*. Canberra: ACT.

Curtner-Smith, M. D., Chen, W. and Kerr, I. G. (1995a) Health-Related Fitness in Secondary School Physical Education: a descriptive-analytic study, *Educational Studies*, 21(1), 55–66.

Curtner-Smith, M. D., Kerr, I. G., Kuesel, K. and Curtner-Smith, M. E. (1995b) Pupil Behaviours in British Physical Education Classes: A Descriptive-Analytic Study, *International Journal of Physical Education*, 32(1), 16–23.

Curtner-Smith, M. D., Kerr, I. G. and Clapp, A. J. (1996) The Impact of National Curriculum Physical Education on the Teaching of Health-Related Fitness: A Case Study in One English Town, *European Journal of Physical Education*, 1(1), 66–83.

Dale, D. and Corbin, C. B. (2000) Physically Active Participation of High School Graduates Following Exposure to Conceptual or Traditional Physical Education, *Research Quarterly for Exercise and Sport*, 71(1), 61–68.

Dale, D., Corbin, C. B. and Cuddihy, T. F. (1998) Can Conceptual Physical Education Promote Physically Active Lifestyles?, *Pediatric Exercise Science*, 10, 97–109.

Department of Canadian Heritage (2002) *The Canadian Sport Policy*. Ottawa: Canadian Government.

Department of Communications Information Technology and the Arts (2004) *Sport Policy*. Retrieved 6 August, 2004, from http://www.dcita.gov.au/Subject_Entry_Page/0,,0_1-2_14,00.html

Department of Communications Information Technology and the Arts (2001) *Backing Australia's Sporting Ability – A More Active Australia* Canberra.

Department of Culture Media and Sport and Strategy Unit (2002) *Game Plan: A Strategy for delivering Government's Sport and Physical Activity Objectives*. London: Cabinet Office.

Department of Health and Aged Care (1999) *National Physical Activity Guidelines for Australians*. Australian Government Publishing Service. Reprinted 2005. Canberra.

Department of Health and Ageing (2004) *Building a Healthy, Active Australia*. Retrieved 2 July 2004, from www.healthyactive.gov.au

The Directorate of School Education (1993) *Physical and Sport Education: Report of the Committee for the Review of Physical and Sport Education in Victorian Schools*. Melbourne, VIC: Directorate of School Education.

Fairclough, S. and Stratton, G. (1997) Physical Education Curriculum and Extra-Curriculum Time: A Survey of Secondary Schools in the North-West of England, *British Journal of Physical Education*, 28, 21–24.

Fairclough, S., Stratton, G. and Baldwin, G. (2002) The Contribution of Secondary School Physical Education to Lifetime Physical Activity, *European Physical Education Review*, 8(1), 69–84.

Fox, K. (1991) Motivating Children for Physical Activity: Towards a Healthier Future, *Journal of Physical Education, Recreation and Dance*, 62(7), 34–38.

Green, K. (2000) Exploring the everyday 'philosophies' of physical education teachers from a sociological perspective, *Sport, Education and Society*, 5(2), 109–129.

Green, K. (2002) Physical Education and 'the Couch Potato Society' – Part One, *European Journal of Physical Education*, 7, 95–107.

Green, K. (2004) Physical education, lifelong participation and 'the couch potato society, *Physical Education and Sport Pedagogy*, 9(1), 73–86.

Harris, J. (1994) Health Related Exercise in the National Curriculum: Results of a Pilot Study in Secondary Schools, *British Journal of Physical Education*, 14(Supplement), 6–11.

Harris, J. and Penney, D. (2000) Gender issues in health-related exercise, *European Physical Education Review*, 6(3), 249–273.

Jago, R. and Baranowski, T. (2004) Non-curricular approaches for increasing physical activity in youth: a review, *Preventive Medicine*, 39(1), 157–163.

King, A. C., Stokols, D., Talen, E., Brassington, G. S. and Killingsworth, R. (2002) Theoretical approaches to the promotion of physical activity: Forging a transdisciplinary paradigm, *American Journal of Preventive Medicine*, 23(2, Supplement 1), 15–25.

Lee, M. (2004) Values in Physical Education and Sport: a conflict of interests?, *British Journal of Teaching Physical Education*, 35(1), 6–10.

McKenzie, T. L., Sallis, J. F., Prochaska, J. J., Conway, T. L., Marshall, S. J. and Rosengard, P. (2004) Evaluation of a Two-Year Middle-School Physical Education Intervnetion: M-SPAN, *Medicine and Science in Sports and Exercise*, 36(8), 1382–1388.

McManus, A. and Armstrong, N. (1996) The Physical Inactivity of Girls – A School Issue? *British Journal of Physical Education*, 27, 34–35.

Mitton, C. R., Davies, H. D. and Donaldson, C. R. (2004) Olympic Medals or long life: what's the bottom line, *Medical Journal of Australia*, 180, 71–73.

Office of Her Majesty's Chief Inspector of Schools in Wales (1995) *Report by HM Inspectors: Survey of Physical Education in Key Stages 1, 2 and 3.* Cardiff: OHMCI.

Orchard, J. (2004) Editorial – Sport is more important to health than most realise, *Journal of Science and Medicine in Sport*, 7(2), iv–v.

Orchard, J. and Finch, C. (2004) Olympic medals or long life: what's the bottom line – reply, *Medical Journal of Australia*, 180, 655.

Pawlaczek, Z. and Brown, T. D. (2004) *Sport and Physical Activity: Antonyms and Synonyms; A Marriage or Divorce?* Paper presented at the Monash University – Sport and Physical Activity Research Workshop, Melbourne.

Penney, D. (2002) *Gender and physical education: contemporary issues and future directions.* London: Routledge.

Penney, D. and Evans, J. (1999) *Politics, Policy and Practice in Physical Education.* London: E. and F.N. Spon.

Penney, D. and Harris, J. (1997) Extra-Curricular Physical Education: More of the Same for the More Able?, *Sport, Education and Society*, 2(1), 41–54.

Sallis, J. F., Bauman, A. and Pratt, M. (1998) Environmental and Policy Interventions to Promote Physical Activity, *American Journal of Preventive Medicine*, 15(4), 379–397.

Sallis, J. F., Prochaska, J. J. and Taylor, W. C. (2000) A review of correlates of physical activity of children and adolescents, *Medicine and Science in Sports and Exercise*, 32(5), 963–975.

Sport England (2004) *The Framework for Sport in England – Making England an Active and Successful Sporting Nation: A Vision for 2020.* London: Sport England.

United States Department of Health and Human Services (1996) *Physical Activity and Health: A Report of the Surgeon General*. Atlanta, GA: Department of Health and Human Services, Centers for Disease Control and Prevention, National Center for Chronic Disease Prevention and Health Promotion.

United States Department of Health and Human Services (2000) *Healthy People 2010 – With Understanding and Improving Health Objectives for Improving Health*. Washington, DC: US Government Printing Office.

Wattchow, B. and O'Connor, J. P. (2003) *Re(Forming) the 'Physical' in a Curriculum / Pedagogy for Health: A Socioecological Perspective*. Paper presented at the Joint AARE/NZARE conference, Auckland.

Wechsler, H., Devereaux, R. S., Davis, M. and Collins, J. (2000) Using the School Environment to Promote Physical Activity and Healthy Eating, *Preventive Medicine*, 31(2), S121–S137.

Index

'Active for Life' programme   114
accident prevention   103, 133–7, 143, 176, 252
Acheson Report   223, 229–30, 243–5, 250, 279
action learning   35–44, 57
Active Australia   282–94
Active England   42, 45, 51, 57
adolescence   50, 63, 69, 73–80, 180–6, 197
adulthood   18, 63–79, 125, 187, 197–8, 211, 226, 236, 240
advocacy   208–11, 265, 270–1
ageing   35, 63–79, 104, 133–8, 143, 289, 294
Ajzen, I. and Fishbein, M.   105, 110, 115, 121, 126
Alma Ata   269
anabolic steroids   83–4, 88–9, 91, 94
anti-doping   84–5

Bandura, A.   54, 57, 120–7
BASE activity programme   114
Beattie, A.   143
behaviour   11–15, 36–9, 42, 46–8, 54–5, 58, 77, 80, 86, 90–3, 97, 101–17, 255, 257–8, 261, 271, 276, 292, 294
Bercovitz, K. L.   19–20, 50–1, 57
Biddle, S.   77–8, 104, 110–12, 115–17, 188, 294
Black Report   225–30, 237, 242, 279–80
Blaxter, M.   143
blood born virus   83
blood composition   68, 74, 76
blood pressure   12, 67, 75, 79, 81, 112, 118–29, 136, 161, 165, 249
bodies   25, 29, 49, 85, 95–102, 196
body fat levels   166
bone mineral density   69, 74, 78, 81, 135, 188, 249

cardiovascular system   20, 46, 64–8, 71–5, 77, 80, 112, 119, 127, 176, 181–3, 187, 235, 240, 249–50, 277

Cashmore, E.   98, 102
childhood   78, 97, 226, 277
childhood obesity   78
children   13, 29–32, 40–1, 48–50, 59, 63–4, 69, 73–80, 95–6, 113–14, 116, 135, 138–44, 147–53, 176, 183, 186–98, 215–16, 225–8, 230, 235, 262–9, 288–93
choosing health   1, 244
coaching   30, 33, 197, 209–15, 257
cognitive function   126, 255, 292
community   15, 19, 23, 25, 29, 37, 40–3, 81, 83, 133–50, 158–73, 177–82, 210–13, 230–9, 253–7, 263–78, 284–9, 294
community development   19, 97, 110, 150, 242
community development theory   154
consumption   66–7, 88, 97–100, 102, 276
Cooke's house of sport   27–8
coronary heart disease   11, 13, 18, 20, 129, 134–6, 157–72, 181, 227, 231, 249–50, 260–1
cross-culture   104, 183
culture   14, 21–5, 31–2, 42, 48, 50, 95–6, 100–2, 116, 119, 193–4, 198, 204, 223, 229, 253, 264–5, 271–4
cycling   38, 46–8, 58, 72, 76, 115, 152, 195, 231, 256

definitions   12, 21, 23
Delphi study   46
depression   112, 231, 235, 241, 248–9
deprivation   35–6, 44, 182, 229–34, 238–9, 243, 259, 279
diabetes   13, 64, 66, 71–2, 74, 112, 136, 176–84, 249–50, 268, 277
disability   30, 112, 114, 135, 146, 155, 203–19, 235, 237, 250, 265
disadvantage   116, 123, 176, 189, 192, 197, 240, 248, 264
DISCUS   3, 83, 86–8, 90–3
disengagement theory   143

doping 83–6, 93–4

drug use 3, 72, 83–95, 115, 151, 177–8, 234, 284, 287

Drugscope 86, 94

education 11, 16, 19, 20, 23, 36–9, 42–3, 49–50, 52, 103–16, 122–7, 136, 148–52, 160, 176–84, 186–201, 204, 206, 207–18, 224–43, 250–3, 257, 260, 264–5, 269–71, 275, 289–92

effectance motivation theory 105

employment 1, 11, 19, 36, 41–2, 135, 151, 171, 206, 230

ethnic minorities 14, 51, 98, 114, 146, 149, 151, 174–84, 187, 204, 237, 239, 251–3, 261

ethnicity 108

European Health Promotion Award 152

European Heart Network 11, 13–14, 20, 48

evaluation 37–39, 43, 45–56, 111, 154–5, 230, 256, 268, 274–5, 293, 295

exercise 12–13, 16, 18–19, 21–2, 24–5, 29, 31, 40, 42–3, 46, 56–8, 72–81, 94, 96, 98–100, 102–17, 136–7, 140, 146, 150, 157–73, 176, 181, 203, 223–44, 251–9, 279–86

exercise behaviour model 108

exercise prescription 118–29

Featherstone, M. 97, 102

'Fit for life' programme 114

football 147, 149–51, 153–4, 181–4, 191, 194, 210, 290

Foucault, M. 101

gender 29–30, 33, 47–8, 59, 95–6, 102, 140, 178, 186–201, 204, 237, 242, 252, 264, 268, 288, 290

Green, L. W. and Kreuter, M. 36, 43, 107, 116, 136

harm minimisation 83, 86–7, 90–1, 93

health action zones 57

Health Canada 52, 58

health development 123, 238, 251, 254, 257, 260, 268, 271–3

health promotion (models) 11, 28, 36–7, 39, 41, 81, 83, 86

health psychology 109, 127–8

Health Survey for England 33, 187, 236, 251, 260

'HELP' 157–73

'HEPA' network 113

hepatitis 83, 88–9

HIV 83, 86, 252, 264–5

house of sport 27–8

hypertension 67–68, 74–5, 79, 92, 113, 170, 227–8, 235

identity 14, 23, 50, 95–7, 124, 151, 178, 190, 195, 199, 210–11, 217, 232

index of multiple deprivation 35

international

competition 27, 254

conference on health promotion 270

games 213

monetary fund 279

Olympic committee 83–4, 94, 96

Paralympics 214

Sport Conference 289

swimming 15

Kelly, M. 35, 252–61

Kolb, D. A. 53, 58

learned helplessness 105

leisure 11, 20–1, 23, 27, 30–4, 42, 50–1, 66, 81, 95–7, 99, 102, 113, 115–16, 142, 158–71, 179, 236, 239–40, 284

lifespan 63, 105, 133

lifestyle 1, 11–13, 19–20, 25, 28–9, 32, 36, 42–3, 66, 71–4, 95–7, 99–101, 136, 158–71, 176–82, 187, 198, 228–43, 257–9, 292

Likert scale 47

Liver Function Test (LFT) 88–9, 93

locus of control 105–6, 109, 111, 126

longevity 64–5, 72, 78, 80, 135

Lupton, D. 98–100, 102

medical model 1, 12, 19, 53, 55, 161, 171, 205

medicalisation 85, 101

memory 71, 77

mental health 16, 18, 74, 77–8, 81, 103, 116, 134, 151, 158, 169, 238, 242, 267

Ministry of Culture, Sport and Media 14, 20

misuse of drugs 86, 91, 93–4, 252, 261

models 11, 28, 36–7, 39, 41, 56, 103, 107, 116, 120–1, 123, 126, 128, 133, 144, 159, 171, 275

morbidity 46, 71, 77, 80, 104, 112, 134, 137, 223–4, 236, 248, 283

mortality 42, 46, 66–7, 71, 77, 80, 104,
    112, 134, 176–7, 223–45, 248–53,
    260–4
motivation 36, 38, 49, 57, 103–7, 111,
    114, 116–29, 138, 163–73, 188, 194,
    203, 290
motivational systems theory 106
Mulvihill, C. 14, 20, 48, 252, 260–1

National Curriculum 190, 290
National Physical Activity Guidelines for
    Australia 286
National Service Framework 18, 143,
    169, 172, 238, 289
National Statistics 30, 33, 250, 261
needle exchange 86–7

obesity 33, 42, 64, 69, 74, 112, 170,
    176, 186–8, 198, 228, 238,
    248–9, 252–3, 261–2, 277–8,
    288, 292
older people 133–44, 147, 152, 169,
    173, 237–8, 244, 249, 255, 259
Olympic Games 22, 83–4, 84, 96, 203,
    214, 265, 280, 284–5
optimal experience theory 106

Peckham Pulse 25, 32
performance 22–3, 26–7, 33, 77, 84,
    89, 94, 106, 116, 153, 193, 203,
    213–17, 121, 126, 284–5, 287
performance enhancing drugs 83–6
physical education 21, 23, 26, 31–4,
    49–50, 114, 144, 160, 172, 186–98,
    207, 209, 211, 216, 264–5, 257,
    282, 288–92
Pikora, T. 38, 46–8, 58
planning 19, 26, 30, 32, 35, 43, 50, 52,
    56, 86, 107, 109–10, 120–1, 124,
    126, 133–4, 136, 138, 140, 143–4,
    148, 153, 155, 161, 213
policy 11, 24, 27, 33, 36–8, 42–3, 48,
    52, 84, 86–7, 94, 189, 196, 203–8,
    218, 248–80
preceed-proceed 37, 107
Prochaska, J. O. and DiClemente, C.
    C. 109–10, 116
project management 19, 35, 155
psychosocial 71, 86, 115, 128,
    231, 234
public health 20, 23, 44, 57–58, 86,
    102–103, 112, 133, 136, 144–5, 181,
    187, 229, 230, 244, 248, 250–7,
    260–1, 267–8, 273–9

Raphael, D. 15, 20, 45, 47, 53
rehabilitation 14, 18, 25, 119, 122–3,
    125, 127, 129, 206, 269, 282
risk 11, 13–14, 18, 30–1, 66–7, 69–81,
    85, 86, 90–1, 100, 108, 112, 114,
    119, 122–3, 136–8, 143, 151, 159–71,
    177, 182, 186–7, 192, 224–8, 231–5,
    242–3, 248–50, 255, 260

Sedgefield 35, 42, 51
Seedhouse, D. 11, 15, 20
self-determination theory 116
self-worth theory 105
skeleto-muscular system 69, 74, 76
smoking 19, 66, 110, 113, 116–17,
    159, 170, 250–3, 260–1
social
    capital 233
    change 14
    class 14, 53, 98–9, 175, 223–48, 253
    cohesion 23, 151, 232
    construction 33, 48, 50, 95–8, 135,
        174, 193, 203
    deprivation 51, 279
    exclusion 15, 33, 74, 101, 161, 223–47
    groups 30, 102, 232
    health 16
    inclusion 23, 223, 230–1, 238, 242
    inequalities 223–47
    integration 210
    issues 15, 28–9, 42, 46, 66, 90, 108,
        134, 181, 292
    marketing 114
    model 203–6
    problems 14, 37, 39, 83, 182
    support 124–5, 139, 252, 257
social-cognitive theory 114, 118, 120,
    126–7
socialisation 74, 97, 179, 210
social-psychological commitment model
    111
socio-economic 98, 107, 146, 179, 183,
    187, 204, 238, 267, 269, 273
sociology 33, 58, 94, 102, 179
socio-political 30, 141
sport
    action zones 239
    commitment model 211
    continuum 26
    development 25–8, 155, 207, 211, 285
    injury 119, 122
    models 21
    policy 283, 292
    psychology 117

sport – *continued*
  Sport England   23, 27–9, 57, 207–15, 284
  students   36, 57
stages of change model   109
standardised mortality ratio   42
stroke   67–8, 72, 74, 80, 249–50
Sunderland   78

Tannahill, A.   36, 44, 116
theory   35, 53–4, 57, 64, 105–6, 110–11,
    114–16, 123, 143, 154, 157, 173,
    262, 278–9
theory of planned behaviour   110, 123
theory of reasoned action   105
transport   46–7, 49, 67–8, 138, 140, 212,
    244, 277, 287
transtheoretical model   110, 114, 128
Turner, B.   101–2

unemployment   13, 150–1, 161, 176, 206,
    224–5, 240
UNICEF   232, 263, 269

values   11–23, 28, 33, 37, 45, 52, 72,
    75, 84, 88–9, 97–101, 107–9, 116,
    120, 123, 126, 138, 141, 155,
    178–9, 190

walking   11, 22–3, 29, 38, 44, 46–8,
    51, 58, 72–3, 81, 113, 115, 151–2,
    167, 170, 188, 236–7, 243, 250–8,
    287
walking bus   32, 34
weight control   12, 16, 18–19, 49, 66,
    68–9, 74, 81, 97, 113–14, 117,
    166, 170, 187, 249,
    252, 261
weight loss   70, 75, 85, 101, 196, 249
welfare dependency   51, 134
well-being   16, 49, 63, 66, 70, 72, 74,
    77, 114, 127, 133–44, 162, 169, 182,
    266, 270
Werner's Syndrome   64
Wilkinson, R.   20, 232–4, 243–4
World Anti-Doping Agency   84–5
world class   28
World Cup   14
World Health Organization   16, 20, 29,
    34, 44, 59, 103, 113, 117, 129, 150,
    186, 202, 233, 235, 250, 261, 270,
    277, 281

youth   30, 47, 49, 50, 58, 74, 80–1,
    114–17, 150, 154, 188–98, 208, 210,
    277, 288, 291–2